"A TOUR DE FORCE OF MARIAN THEOLOGY
AND HISTORICAL INTERPRETATION . . .
It gives new ground to Marian devotion in a world where feminism brings into question whatever constricts women in the name of religion. It breaks the plaster mold of the Marian model and makes Mary a real woman for the women of our own time."
—SISTER JOAN CHITTISTER, OSB
Author of *There Is a Season*

"*In Search of Mary* combines crisp scholarship and poignant anecdotes."
—*St. Anthony Messenger*

"Cunneen is at her best in her treatment of versions of Mary common in the 19th century, describing the discovery of Mary as a liberating figure by Protestant women writers such as Christina Rossetti and Margaret Fuller, and in her descriptions of the work of some modern artists fascinated by the figure of Mary."
—*Kirkus Reviews*

"By revisiting history and researching across cultural boundaries, Cunneen compels us to approach Mary through serious study. Within the diverse beliefs about Mary, the author discovers a woman who can speak to and guide us, regardless of our background, in our spiritual and intellectual growth—a woman who is a profound reminder of the presence of the holy in everyday life."
—*The Family Friend Magazine*

IN SEARCH OF

MARY

THE WOMAN
AND
THE SYMBOL

SALLY CUNNEEN

BALLANTINE BOOKS
NEW YORK

Permission acknowledgments can be found on pages 401–403

http://www.randomhouse.com

Library of Congress Catalog Card Number: 96-96361

ISBN: 0-345-38246-3

Cover design by Barbara Leff
Cover painting © Giraudon/Art Resource, NY. *Mater Misericordia*, by Jean Miralhet, central panel, c. 1422. Musée Massena, Nice, France
Text design by Debby Jay

Manufactured in the United States of America
First Edition: August 1996
10   9   8   7   6

To Joe, always

CONTENTS

ILLUSTRATIONS

PLATES

1. Study of the Virgin and Child, Matisse, from the Rosary Chapel at Vence, France. (Photo: Hélène Adant)
2. Sculpture of the Visitation, Church of St. Gabriel, Provence, France. (Photo: Zodiaque)
3. Madonna and Child, fourth-century Catacomb of the Cimitero Maggiore, Rome, Italy. (Alinari/Art Resource, NY)
4. Sculptured capital, The Just in the Bosom of Abraham, 1149, Musée d'Unterlinden, Colmar, Alsace, France. (Photo: Octave Zimmermann)
5. Mater Misericordia, central panel, c. 1442, Jean Miralhet. Musée Massena, Nice, France. (Giraudon/Art Resource, NY)
6. Silver Chalice, Northern Syria, sixth–early seventh century. The Metropolitan Museum of Art (1986.3.2), Purchase, Rogers Funds, and Henry J. and Drue E. Heinz Foundation, Norbert Schimmel and Lila Achesen Wallace Gifts, 1986.
7. Detail of the Mother and Child from the nave capital of the Flight into Egypt, Gislebertus c. 1120, Autun, France. (Giraudon/Art Resource)

ix

ACKNOWLEDGMENTS

I could never have written this book, presuming to cover two millennia of human history and multiple fields of learning in numerous languages, without depending heavily on the work and generosity of others. I am fortunate to have had access to the resources of the Weston-Episcopal Divinity School Library in Cambridge, Massachusetts, Union Seminary Library in New York City, and the help of librarian Dorothy Forman of Rockland Community College (SUNY), who obtained a number of books for me from faraway sources.

Besides the large number of authors and artists on whose work I lean, I am grateful to many people who offered personal support and help at every stage of my research and writing. First, I thank those who encouraged me in this project, some of them sharing personal observations as well as introducing me to relevant ideas, art, or people I might not otherwise have known: Rosemary Bannan, Ann Byrne, Sidney Callahan, Monique and Noel Copin, Edith Delos, Frank and Jean Getlein, Julia Gargiulo, Joanna and William Herman, Elizabeth Johnson, Pamela Kirk, Alice Laffey, Janet Larson, Maureen Lester, Gary MacEoin, Jane Damien McAuliffe, Giles Milhaven, Robert Minichiello, John Olin, Rosemary Ruether, Martica Sawin, Brita and Krister Stendahl, Raimon Panikkar, Helen Vendler, and Joanna Ziegler.

I am also grateful to those who read the manuscript in early stages and made suggestions that improved it: Ann Byrne, Martha Faulhaber, Josepha Clark, Gary MacEoin, and Madeleine Oswald. For critical suggestions on the entire manuscript, I am indebted to Maria Goldberg, to my husband, Joseph Cunneen, and to my unbelievably painstaking and cooperative editor at Ballantine, Joanne Wyckoff.

Next, I thank those who read with critical eyes the sections of the book related to their own fields of expertise: Janet Larson, John Lounibus, Gary MacEoin, Ann Plogsterth, Barbara E. Reid, O.P., and Eloise Rosenblatt, O.S.M. They are in no way responsible for the use to which I put their contributions, which were often humbling but always appreciated.

I am grateful to Robert Lentz for granting me permission to reproduce his icon, Mother of the Disappeared. I deeply appreciate the time and thought as well as the work contributed by the other contemporary artists interviewed in this book: Meinrad Craighead, Frederick Franck, John Giuliani, and Yaroslava Mills.

Finally, I want to thank the many women and men who responded in person and by mail to my questions about Marian imagery and to Mary's place in their lives. When they were not public figures or printed authors, I did not use their names, but I have used their trenchant observations and personal revelations throughout the book.

REDISCOVERING MARY

I F THIS BOOK HAD APPEARED FORTY YEARS AGO, YOU MIGHT well have assumed it was a pious work intended only for Catholics. Today no such assumption is warranted; Mary has entered mainstream discussion at the same time that Catholics themselves, particularly women, are divided in their attitudes to the mother of Jesus.

In fact, people have so many ideas of what a book about Mary should be that I feel I ought to give readers an early warning about what they will find here. This book represents the results of a personal search to piece together the images of Mary that have been important to me but whose meaning has changed considerably over the course of my life. I did not start out with a thesis, but with questions. Nor did I confine my research and thinking to my own experience, for Mary is a communal symbol that has been shaped over the centuries.

In my search for Mary, I looked for connections between the heavenly mother I turned to as a child and the woman in the New Testament I have been discovering with the eagerness of a Bible-deprived Catholic. But I also came to see that it is not possible to understand Mary adequately without seeing how her image has been shaped by all kinds of people in different eras. She has been a powerful and changing presence for millions of men and women for two thousand years. Simple and unchangeable as the image of mother and child may seem, Mary is far more complex than either those who pray to her or those who think of her as outdated might suspect.

When Marian devotions waned after the considerable reforms introduced by the church at the Second Vatican Council (Vatican II) in 1962–1965, I more or less forgot about Mary except at Christmas and in times of panic. I put my rosary away in the back of a drawer with other mementos of childhood. But as I dealt with the complications of raising children and later of teaching college students about styles of parental communication, unexpected memories of Gospel stories gave me an adult appreciation of Mary's parenting of Jesus. I took my rosary out again and placed it next to my bed. Tentatively I felt the beads, trying to see if I could relate my new questions to the Joyful, Sorrowful, and Glorious mysteries on which I used to meditate.

Why, I asked myself, does devotion to the Virgin Mother persist in this era of science and technology? Why do I still want to pray to her? Is it possible to find continuity between the strong, simple Jewish girl of two thousand years ago and the woman saluted as the mother of the Messiah? Do the theological affirmations that have been made about her in Christian tradition, including the papal definitions of her Immaculate Conception and Assumption, help or hinder those seeking a connection with the feminine divine? Can Mary still be the sign of hope and mercy she has been for so many centuries, a meaningful symbol even for non-European cultures? Can we see her whole, this heroine of a thousand faces, by revisiting earlier cultures with the eyes of the present? The mystery of Mary's continuing power calls out to our minds as well as our hearts; trying to see if the pieces fit together can be an education in understanding ourselves.

It has been just such an education for me. As the image of Mary slowly moved from the edges of my consciousness to its center, it became obvious that I had to understand her better if I wanted to integrate myself. Facing the difficult questions she raised helped me relate the strands of belief and critical thinking that formed my own upbringing. Our situation today is quite different from that of European Christians in the Middle Ages. Then, kings and peasants, clerics and housewives looked to this merciful mother as Queen of Heaven, and their belief was reinforced by the art that surrounded them in their churches. Our world, in contrast, is more attuned to jet planes and satellites than to angelic visitations, though angels have made a comeback in recent years. A world that accepts the scientific story of evolution and development does not quite know what to think about traditional descriptions of Mary, however. And neither did I.

To see how Mary's role developed over the last two thousand years, I had to look at how she functioned as a symbol in earlier cultures. It has been a daunting task, but one not completely unfamiliar to me. As a teacher of literature I was accustomed to dealing with symbols, keeping in mind that their many potential meanings depend on who is viewing and interpreting them. In Mary's appearances in legends and works of art over two millennia, as well as in her apparitions, she has been almost infinitely malleable. Sometimes the roles ascribed to her, like virgin and mother, model of goodness and refuge of sinners, seem so contradictory that it is hard to believe they coexist in one figure. But they do: Mary remains a living presence for enormously varied individuals and even for nations that have long been enemies.

Conflicting images, however, are neither alarming nor surprising. For example, many people's imaginations are captured by Marian apparitions, which hold little appeal for me. Nevertheless, in studying the details of their origins, I have come to see both that the church shares my caution and that these appearances often function as the creative theology of those who feel marginalized. It has also been rewarding to discover that many of my reflective contemporaries are beginning to take a fresh look at

Mary. In addition to reading many books in the endless library that has accumulated about her, I interviewed a considerable range of people and reviewed over two hundred responses to a questionnaire I devised about Mary's place in their lives.

The image of Mary as mother holding the child on her lap is probably the most palpable expression of Christian theology's insistence on God's incarnation in our world; it also serves as a compact symbolic description of humanity itself. At the same time, the image today leads many to reflect on other considerations—the still widespread cultural mandate that women be defined by motherhood, the possible coexistence of femaleness and discipleship. Despite entrenched opinion to the contrary, bringing such issues to the surface has always been one of Mary's functions. I have found that she stimulates thinking about what it means to be human, as well as about the real meaning of the good news that she helped bring into our world.

When I began this project I went first to the New Testament as understood by contemporary scholarship in order to discover Mary's place in the early church. To get a better sense of what she became in history, I not only reviewed church doctrine and liturgy but also looked at the art, prayer, poetry, and stories of those who have found her significant throughout the ages. Fortunately, the right climate and the resources necessary to explore the meaning of Mary with greater objectivity are widely available today. History, anthropology, and science are all on better terms with religion than they were in my childhood. Catholicism and Protestantism are no longer locked in acrimonious debate, and both are making important strides in overcoming centuries-old negative teachings about Judaism. Not only is there a healthier interreligious atmosphere, but in the last hundred years, many of the pieces needed for a study of Mary have become widely available for the first time, including apocryphal texts, many Eastern icons, and some little-known medieval art. In the last three or four decades the ability to decipher ancient texts, the growing body of archaeological evidence, and the wider knowledge of literary forms have also made it possible for interreligious teams of scholars to produce new and more reliable translations of the entire Bible.

Whether we are believers or nonbelievers, it is worthwhile to think about Mary today if only to clarify our attitude to religion in general. Surely I am not alone in the haphazard way I formed my beliefs, relying too much on unexamined sources, leaving some questions not only unanswered but unasked. Growing up, I accepted certain things too quickly from defensive Catholic sources; I was neither able nor willing to distinguish between fundamental beliefs and polemical additions. It has surprised me to discover, for instance, that neither Luther nor Calvin challenged Mary's perpetual virginity, and that Islam greatly honors Mary.

Bringing our thinking about religion into contact with our lives and with the rest of what we know is a challenge we all should accept. Mary is a good place to start. Since the beginning of Christianity, she has been a central figure in attempts to define a religion which claims that God became human. She has taken on an exalted role in history, devotion, and theology, but this should never prevent us from seeing her as a Jewish woman of her era, someone whose experience relates her to men and women everywhere. Following the thread she represents in the tapestry of Western culture, I have learned a great deal about how people create and respond to symbols that represent their deepest needs and beliefs. I have come to see her as the representative figure she is in the Gospels—a living presence incorporating not only the hopes but also the differences and fragmentation inherent in humanity itself.

To share the different and sometimes opposing views of her I have woven together a long tapestry from relevant threads of Scripture, history, art, and human experience. In the first chapter I present further reasons why a search for Mary is necessary to-

day, and indicate some guidelines and critical questions I have
tried to keep in mind. Chapter two examines Mary in the New
Testament, our chief source of information about her, and then
adds personal interpretations of the stories that deepen our
understanding of her as a woman. Chapter three looks at the role
of Mary in the struggling church of the early centuries and finds
theological reticence and ambivalence about her, along with
strong popular devotion. Chapter four describes how the post-
Constantinian church, despite the dualism and misogyny of the
wider culture, hailed the emergence of the feminine symbol of
Mary, declaring her *Theotokos*, or God-Bearer. Chapter five
evokes the effects of Marian devotion on the art, architecture,
history, and spirituality of twelfth-century Europe. Chapter six
deals with the split between Catholicism and Protestantism, in
which opposed attitudes to Mary among Reformation and
Counter-Reformation leaders reflected broader differences of belief at the dawn of European nationalism. My discussion then follows Mary overseas on Spanish military banners to Mexico,
where she is transformed into Our Lady of Guadalupe, a dark
madonna who cares about the conquered as well as the conquista-
dors. Chapter seven outlines the nineteenth-century explosion of
Marian apparitions and devotions in an anxiously defensive
Catholic Europe, at the same time that convert John Henry Newman used historical scholarship to reveal Mary as the representative of a developing faith. That chapter also discusses some
Protestant women writers who began to appropriate Mary as a
useful feminine symbol to dignify women's spirituality and to
elevate their public position. In chapter eight, which brings us to
the present, men and women who have wrestled with traditional
interpretations of Mary share fresh discoveries that have implications for their own lives and thoughts. The final chapter affirms
and extends this revisionary thinking in the work and words of
contemporary artists who see Mary in a surprisingly current, cosmological context.

There is far more diversity even in our supposedly "traditional" understanding of Mary than I suspected at the outset. Yet I have also found patterns that repeat themselves: Mary has almost always and everywhere been both a comforter of the oppressed and a challenge to thought. As the most flexible of symbols, she has been able to escape constraint. At each turn in human history, Mary has taken on a different appearance and significance. It is a tribute to her remarkable power that she transcends cultural and religious bounds and speaks to perennial human need.

One final way to speak about what I am doing in this book might be to say that I am attempting a kind of midrash on Mary. In the Jewish tradition, midrash means a sustained searching of the biblical texts to bring out their hidden meaning in new words. My model is Rabbi Ben 'Azzai, who sat and expounded upon the words of the Torah and the prophets until fire flashed all around him. When Rabbi Akiba asked him the cause of this fire, he explained that the words were rejoicing as they met one another.[1]

I have brought together into my midrash on Mary not only theological insights and art from earlier eras, but also interpretations and creations by contemporary viewers. My hope is that this encounter of old and new will make it possible for others to rediscover the woman who has so long served to connect the human and the natural with the divine. For me, this search has been a journey to new perception. I hope it is one on which you can accompany me for a time as part of your own journey.

IN SEARCH OF MARY

CHAPTER ONE

WHY SEARCH FOR MARY?

What have you done to me? What have you made of me?
I cannot find myself in the woman you want me to be . . .
Haloed, alone . . . marble and stone:
Safe, Gentle, Holy Mary.
—from "Marysong" at 1987 Asian Women's
Theological Consultation[1]

. . . the mystery of Mary brings a new word about the world, about this world where men and women are born, grow, love, suffer, live, clash, rejoice and die.
—IVONE GEBARA and MARIA CLARA BINGEMER[2]

W HY DO WE HAVE TO SEARCH FOR MARY? AREN'T WE constantly running into her as it is, not just in churches and on Christmas cards, but in museums, and even in some backyards— to say nothing of her shrines at Lourdes, Guadalupe, Fatima, and now Medjugorje? For the 1995 Christmas season, the U.S. Postal Service issued seven hundred million stamps bearing the image of the Madonna and Child created by the fourteenth-century Florentine painter Giotto di Bondone. An angel had been slated to replace Mary, but popular demand brought back her image. Even the last desperate pass by the quarterback of a losing football team is known as a "Hail Mary" play.

But awareness of Mary's presence or even devotion to her doesn't mean we really know who she is. The typical reminders we get of her role as mother of Jesus can be misleading—pictures in museums and on Christmas cards can leave us with the impression that she was a woman of the Italian Renaissance. Our memories may be full of vague details that attach themselves to what we think we know about Mary, but that are simply not true. I grew up believing that much of this lore must be somewhere in the New Testament—for instance, the identity of Mary's mother and father, Anne and Joachim—when in fact they were added to her story over the centuries. Not that I'm suggesting we should eliminate these additions, but I do think it's important to find out where they came from, and to get a sense of their relative importance.

In the village of Provence where I wrote much of this book, for instance, the figures around the Christmas crib in church

5

included several representative citizens from more recent times; one even carried a tiny bottle of the famous local muscat. I love the instinct behind this practice, which makes the Christmas story one that keeps on happening in each localized space. But the story of the Nativity must also be understood against a longer, more complicated background.

What did Mary mean to the first Christians? What does she, can she, mean to us today? Difficult questions about Mary arose within the early Christian community, and church councils tried to formulate her role in language that drew on the most sophisticated thinking of the time. The creedal formulas of the church fathers are still normative for believers, but that doesn't mean that their words were unaffected by the political and cultural context of their period. Such formulas are meant to guide our thinking, not stifle it. If we're seriously looking for Mary, we can profit from earlier statements about her, but we may need to rethink the meaning of her virginity and her motherhood today.

Past interpretations do not explain why this Jewish woman who lived two thousand years ago is still an important presence in our supposedly post-Christian world. And unless we review some of that history, we will not understand why even Christians, all of whom honor Mary, can disagree so much about her, offering different interpretations of her role and significance. We must not be surprised to see her invoked on behalf of the whole spectrum of political and social positions from extreme right to extreme left. *Time* magazine summarized its own search for Mary in a 1991 cover story with the topical question: "Was the most revered woman in history God's handmaid or the first feminist?"

Though Mary has much wider name recognition today than in the first few centuries of Christianity, she is not easily understood; many people are ambivalent about her, some even hostile. At the same time, the persistent and global interest in Mary, two thousand years after she responded to the angel Gabriel's announcement, is not easily explained away. Each year millions of pilgrims visit the site of her apparitions at Lourdes and leave psychologically restored, even if they are not physically healed. Just as many flock to Mexico City to invoke Our Lady of Guadalupe, who played such a central role in restoring dignity to the indigenous people of Mexico, and continues to energize the faith of Hispanic people in North and South America. Mary has also become part of twentieth-century cultural lore: she is invoked in the Beatles ballad "Let It Be" as well as in Paul Claudel's play *The Tidings Brought to Mary*; in a cycle of poems by Lucille Clifton and another by Rainer Maria Rilke; in Margaret Atwood's novel *Cat's Eye*, Muriel Spark's comic short story "The Black Madonna," and Jean-Luc Godard's movie *Je vous salue, Marie*. In the United States she even lives in Garrison Keillor's mythical-real Lake Wobegon under the amusingly appropriate name, Our Lady of Perpetual Responsibility.

In my childhood Mary inhabited separate worlds that did not communicate with one another: Catholic and Protestant, sophisticated and popular, devotional and secular. Today, despite widespread criticism of earlier preaching about Mary, a reviving interest in her cuts across old boundaries. She is no longer imprisoned within denominational or ethnic barriers; she has entered our general consciousness, become part of our common vocabulary. As we struggle for greater unity in a divided world, suddenly these separate views are beginning to interact and cross over, sometimes bridging different groups and divided aspects of individuals like myself. No single image of Mary has yet emerged; each group is finding something different to say about the real woman of the New Testament who has also been such a powerful feminine symbol in Western civilization for the last fifteen hundred years. The first reason we need to search for Mary, therefore, is that her presence is not self-explanatory.

Catholics weren't aware of this complexity when I was growing up. Mary was simply part of the heavenly scenery I shared as an American of Irish descent with several other varieties of ethnic Americans in Providence, Rhode Island. She was a kind of Catholic fairy godmother, more understanding than my own mother, who sometimes chastised or disappointed me. I could talk to her intimately whenever I needed help, which was frequently, for I was an emotional, imaginative child. No one was more sympathetic than the Blessed Mother—or had better connections.

It was comforting to have a direct line to heaven, but that didn't mean Mary was a role model. I associated her with the May altars and stained-glass windows I loved, but I was uncomfortable wearing a white veil during the May processions before her statue at St. Sebastian's. In retrospect, I realize that my devotions were naïve and self-centered. At novenas to Our Lady of Perpetual Help, I raised the constant question before her icon: What should I do with my life? In keeping with her traditional humility, Mary did not answer me herself. I did get an answer, however, one day after school, when I was about eleven. I dropped into the dark, empty church to consult God about my vocation: "When I am grown up, can I be a cowgirl?" I asked. In the only such experience of my life, I heard a deep but kindly male voice respond: "If you want to be a cowgirl when you grow up, you will be one."

The message I received that day was deeply reassuring; now I realize how tactful it was. It came from a force that sympathized with the hopes and difficulties of someone growing up female. Even though the voice was male, I was grateful to Mary, whom I believed had carried my question to the proper authority. Of course, my idea of God may have been unconsciously formed in response to my supportive father, who missed no occasion to tell me about the accomplishments of such women as Amelia Earhart, Margaret Bourke-White, Babe Didrikson, and Clare Boothe Luce. Despite what I felt was God's belief in my power to make mature decisions, it was Mary to whom I turned later that year when I thought I was dying of appendicitis. She was a profound comfort to me, as she has been to all those over the centuries who have repeated the concluding words of the Hail Mary: "Pray for us sinners, now and at the hour of our death. Amen."

By the time I went to college, however, I had relegated this comforting mother to the sidelines of my life. Even after graduation, when I worked as a writer-researcher and later as a wife and mother, I didn't think much about my mother in heaven. The sermons I heard about the Holy Family seemed quaintly irrelevant as I was bringing up my four sons. Nor did a holy card that was popular in the fifties answer my emotional needs: it took Mary off her pedestal, all right, but only to put a broom in her hands. There was an annoyingly satisfied smile on her face as she swept. Even in those days when opportunities for women were more restricted, this image of Mary the Housekeeper was not my model of female behavior.

Vatican II was probably the major religious event of the twentieth century. Whatever its wider impact, it created a sea change in the lives and behavior of Catholics, including their attitude to Mary. During this unexpected renewal, when priests were asked to face the people and mass was finally celebrated in the vernacular instead of Latin, Pope John XXIII insisted that "The Madonna is not happy when she is placed before her son." He had no intention, of course, of downgrading Catholic devotion to Mary; he was simply warning against theological excess in explaining her role in God's plan of salvation. John wanted to "update" the church, to open its windows to the modern world, to learn from that world's discoveries and listen to its questions. He hoped to heal the wounds caused by "Christian" anti-Semitism and to encourage constructive talk between Catholics, Protestants, and Eastern Orthodox. Because excessive Marian devotion had been a sore point among Christians since the Reformation, placing Marian theology within the overall tradition of the church and its relationship to Christ was a positive approach to

Christian unity. The formal declaration on Mary at the Council (in *Lumen Gentium*) had a restraining effect on Marian extremists. While it affirmed Mary's role as that of "cooperating in the work of human salvation through free faith and obedience," it insisted that Christ's mediation was unique and that the Blessed Mother's "saving influences . . . on men" derived only from divine pleasure. It exhorted "theologians and preachers of the divine word that in treating of the unique dignity of the Mother of God, they carefully and equally avoid the falsity of exaggeration on the one hand, and the excess of narrow-mindedness on the other."[3]

One unintended result of this declaration was a temporary near-cessation of Catholic preaching on Mary and fewer devotions in her honor. Though popular devotion has increased in recent years, and Pope John Paul II has visited a number of Marian shrines, a generation of younger American Catholics has grown up with little understanding of what some of them must consider the quaint habits of their parents involving rosaries, litanies, and May processions.

The Catholic world today contains a great variety of attitudes to Mary, from unintended neglect to excessive adulation, but the old sense of cozy familiarity is largely gone. This book is to a great extent an effort to see if it can or should be recaptured, and if so, how. What struck me most as I began to ask Catholic women about their attitudes to Mary was that so many spoke about their mothers' devotion, not their own. One woman, a dean in a public college, described her mother's behavior with the skill of a sociologist:

> My mother, whose inner thoughts came out of her mouth without noticeable delay, used to piteously beseech God to "let the car start," and before longer voyages "to keep us safe on this trip." However, during childbirth, in hospitals, and during family troubles, she addressed her audible remarks to Mary. For most of

her life, my mother had rosary beads in her purse, ready for any emergency.

Similarly, I remember Latin American specialist Gary MacEoin telling me that his Irish mother said the rosary constantly when visiting him in New York. Once, after they had negotiated an endless traffic jam in the Holland Tunnel, she commented matter-of-factly, "That was a three-decade tunnel." More recently, such familiarity with Mary is rare; the last incident I remember was in Dublin two summers ago when a woman, who was on her way to visit her sick mother and had rushed to the train, told me with great relief: "Our Lady gave me four green lights and I made it."

For many Catholics, including the woman who told me about her mother's devotion to Mary when I had asked about her own, maturity meant placing such devotion at arm's length:

I certainly prayed the prayers and processed the processions. I knew very quickly that the loveliest and simplest prayers were the Hail Mary, the Memorare, and the Magnificat. I liked the May crowning of Mary in my grammar schools. When I hit college, Mary had become like the scrim on a stage—there, but invisible. In my Young Christian Student period the spiritual focus shot straight to the Mystical (universal) Body of the (male) Christ, God within each person, particularly the underdog, and the Brotherhood of Man. No room for Mary.

By the time I was forty, the Virgin Birth began to seem too ridiculous to bear thinking about. Accustomed by then to being asked by my best friends how I could possibly believe this or that (and, quite comfortably, responding that it was a mystery, that all things were possible to God), it began to dawn on me that I was indulging in denial, that while attempting to be good was insanely difficult, attempting to actively believe in this particular detailed theology (or any other) was beyond me.

So who is Mary for me now? Invisible, endlessly supportive of her son, a householder, kind probably, but represented almost exclusively and excludingly as a mother, something which is only one part of me.

This woman's ambivalent attitude raises some of the central questions addressed in this search. The first is whether Mary can be with and *for* other women. Overemphasis on her virginity has often meant that young people find her ideal of purity unattainable, while praise of her utter selflessness as a mother has created unhealthy guilt feelings and needless alienation among many married women.

As long ago as the early sixties I discovered that quite a few Catholic women found Mary not only irrelevant to their lives, but sometimes a positive barrier to their attempts to become responsible adults.[4] What is striking today is the growing number of Catholic women who agree with them. A therapist in her fifties states it well:

> For the first twenty-five years of my life Mary was very significant for me. At its worst, this influence, with its emphasis on the Virgin Birth, produced a kind of desexualization; at its best, it held up to me a symbol of loving, caring femaleness. I see most of what was presented to me as gentleness as really passivity, and her virginity as a distortion of humanness. I can't separate her from the church's treatment of women as second-class citizens, good for cleaning churches, and taking care of priests and husbands, but not really equal.

Half the women interviewed in Jane Redmont's *Generous Lives: American Catholic Women Today* feel much the same about Mary as a possible role model. "Virgin Mother! What kind of an example is that?" exclaims one, while another mocks Mary's unreality: "Never did she misslice a tomato or drop a bean on the floor instead of in the soup." The other half, however, still find strength and support in Mary for a variety of reasons. A Latina woman responds to Mary's multicultural availability: "She's *morena* [dark] like I am." Many others see her as a compassionate mother; they associate Mary with the feminine dimension of God: "None of this plaster sweetness, because a plaster sweet mom wouldn't have lasted. . . . It makes me real angry when people talk about Mary as a sort of sweet wimp who can get around Jesus and get him to do things for you. . . . She's sort of the God that can mother."

In the midst of such divisions, new attitudes to Mary are emerging. Clarissa Pinkola Estés, author of *Women Who Run with the Wolves*, emphasizes Mary's strength. If she were alive today, Estés insists, perhaps with a gleam in her eye, "Mary would be a teenage girl gang-leader." An Italian-American friend who has little contact with the church is nevertheless grateful to the Madonna whom she knew as a young woman; she encountered her primarily through art, and found her a force for passion, an education in sensory development, and an affirmation of life in all its forms. A Protestant friend tells me that secretly she's always been strengthened by the idea of "a powerful woman up there in heaven with the men." For centuries, ordinary people, as well as theologians and artists, have projected their own needs onto Mary. In different times and cultures, they have interpreted the symbol of the Virgin Mother to suit those many needs, and amazingly, she has met them. One crucial question I ask in this book is whether there is any limit to her adaptability, or if there are some causes she instinctively resists and others she constantly advocates.

Despite my distance from her as I grew up, I found that Mary kept turning up unexpectedly in my life, suggesting things about herself and our relationship that I needed to reconsider. I could hardly claim to have tried to imitate her, even at St. Sebastian's. I was forming my identity at the time with the help of Anne of Green Gables, and later through the movies, rooting for Ginger Rogers to keep up with Fred Astaire, learning from Katharine Hepburn as she sparred with Spencer Tracy. But on a trip to France before I got married, I saw images of a Mary—

particularly Notre Dame de la Belle Verrière, in a stained-glass window at Chartres cathedral—who was a woman of undeniable power, beauty, and compassion (Plate 15). It was the very window that in 1900 had stunned historian Henry Adams, who saw in it, for the first time, the force of the feminine, and understood why it had shaped so much of earlier history.[5] I took home a poster of that image, and I hung it up over the fireplace each Christmas for my growing family to share. Never quite sure why Mary's presence felt so reassuring, I often wished the picture could talk.

In a way it did, slowly and indirectly, through my own reflections. When my oldest son died, one of my few comforting insights during the disruption and long sorrow this event caused our whole family was that Mary, too, had been through such a tragedy. I no longer saw Pietàs, in which the mother holds the body of her son across her knees, as simply pious images; they became representations of a completely human woman who shared the pain of all mothers—all parents—who have lost their children. At times this grieving Mary seemed to blend with my own dead mother, who had lost her only son to scarlet fever just before the drugs that might have cured him were discovered. I began to feel a deeper connection with both these mothers, and to consider the thought of looking for Mary in a way that was impossible in my self-centered childhood.

When I taught writing and literature at our local community college, Mary surprised me by showing up there as well. Team-teaching courses on family life with a wonderful psychologist who was also a grandmother, I learned a great deal from her and from our adult students about the strength, imagination, and skill it takes to be a good mother. As I began to hear parents define the job of parenting in their own terms, I gained a very different impression of mothering from the one I had picked up from popular culture, church pamphlets, or child care manuals. I discovered it to be a difficult, central human occupation, not simply a natural job for women. It was some comfort to me—since my children were now grown—to realize that probably no other work is as difficult as parenting. You have to provide nurture and support, then let go, but still remain available even when older children think they don't need or want you, always hoping for friendly relations on an equal basis.

As I made these discoveries, remembered bits of Mary's story recurred to me, and I went back to the Gospel of Luke as if for the first time. What struck me with special force was the effectiveness of Mary's mothering in terms of contemporary guidelines for human development. Take, for example, the time when the family went to Jerusalem and the twelve-year-old Jesus became separated from Mary and Joseph for three days (Luke 2:41–52). They were frantic, of course, and after they found him in the temple, Mary spoke right up, indicating the strain she had undergone. "Son, why have you done this to us? Your father and I have been looking for you with great anxiety." But when the boy asked her why she had been worried—"Did you not know that I must be in my Father's house?"—she did not chastise him for impertinence. She realized his tone was not disrespectful, even though she did not quite understand what he meant. Wisely, she decided to think it over. As Luke puts it, she "kept all these things in her heart."[6]

Was the supermother who was the object of my childhood devotion the same person as this increasingly credible woman I was meeting in Scripture? What was she really like—this Mary who brought up her child quietly in Galilee and taught him religion? Why had her image developed in ways that seemed contradictory?

Perhaps an experience in church about four years ago explains as much as anything how my understanding of Mary was changing. It was December 8, the feast of the Immaculate Conception, which does not, as many think, refer to Mary's virginal conception of Jesus, but to her own exemption from sin at the moment she was conceived. At mass I found myself near the front of the church facing a statue I hadn't seen in a while. Probably it had been stored in the basement after the reforms of Vatican II. I looked at the lady in blue—pretty, like a young woman in a magazine illustration but more innocent, her eyes lifted to heaven, her bare feet resting on a green snake—and recognized a sister of the statue used in the May processions of my youth. At that time I knelt before it without reflection; now I studied it with open eyes.

This statue had absolutely no connection with the Mary I was getting to know. Its unreality made it hard for me to pray but greatly stimulated my thinking. If the purpose of church art is to make doctrine come alive or foster devotion, this mass-produced work was a failure. Later I learned that it was inspired, along with many statues and medals of similar design, by the intense nineteenth-century devotion to Mary as the Immaculate Conception—a devotion that emphasized her purity and her ability to triumph over evil. Statues like this one in my parish church appeared everywhere then; in our age they no longer seem beautiful or powerful. It was probably one much like it that prompted one bishop answering my questionnaire to confess, "The terrible nineteenth-century saccharine, mass-produced statues common in my childhood were the worst images of Mary I have experienced."

The Mary I saw in this statue certainly did not represent the strong mother I respected. But the snake beneath her feet captured my attention: it was large and green, with an uplifted wing revealing it to be the devil. Growing up, I had often heard reference to the story in Genesis declaring that the woman would crush the serpent; we were told that the woman prophesied in that text (Genesis 3:15) was Mary. Since then, however, I had learned that the snake was a symbol of eternal life in Eastern imagery, and that snakes represented the wisdom and power of the Goddess in many Near Eastern and Mediterranean images. The clash of interpretations made me read the biblical passage again, and I discovered that the text said something different than I thought. Instead of having Yahweh tell the snake that "she," the woman, meaning Mary, "shall strike at your head," my copy of the Bible read: "I will put enmity between you and the woman, and between your offspring and hers; He will strike at your head, while you shall strike at their heel." In other words, the woman is Eve. In some versions the pronoun is translated "they," meaning all her offspring. When, as here, it is translated "he," it refers to Jesus. It connects him—and Mary—with the long chain of humanity that follows Eve, the rest of us. This discovery exhilarated me while making it even clearer that the statue in church did not communicate authentic biblical teaching. It failed to relate Eve and Mary to all of us humans, united in an effort to overcome the snake, which at least in the Genesis story is not a positive symbol but the agent of temptation.

I began to suspect that Eve would show up frequently in my search for Mary, and she did. Definitions of their relationship have been crucial to our understanding of women—and, consequently, of men—down to our own time. From Ambrose and Augustine to Luther and Kierkegaard, male interpreters have separated Mary and Eve, seeing Eve as disobedient, wanton, and undisciplined. In contrast, the great twelfth-century abbess Hildegard of Bingen saw Eve as a representative of mutuality in relationships between men and women. The nineteenth-century novelist Charlotte Brontë went even further, seeing Eve as the Mother God visible in all creation. Only today is it possible to see how the widespread anti-woman bias in the early church has continued to affect the way Mary, Eve, and women have been understood. It is remarkable, too, to note the rehabilitation of Eve that accompanies the emergence of a more human Mary.

Whatever my confusion regarding different interpretations of Eve and the snake, kneeling in church before the statue that day I was at least sure that this sugar-sweet image of Mary could never crush anything. The notion of goodness it represented had nothing to do with the harsh realities of the Gospel. Ironically, on the feast of the Immaculate Conception, I found myself getting angry at one of its typical representations, unable to pray before an image that distorted Mary, biblical meaning, and women in general.

Instead, I thought of a photograph of Dorothy Day, founder of the Catholic Worker movement, that gave me a more credible idea of the inner strength Mary must have had. Dorothy is almost seventy in the picture, sitting down because she is tired after a long day's march with Cesar Chavez, the founder of the United Farm Workers. As she looks up at a circle of policemen standing around her, hands on their holsters, her calm face shows no fear. Despite the threat of violence, she will not abandon her witness on behalf of the poor. Here is a wise woman, strong despite her vulnerability because of her attachment to others similarly vulnerable. A woman such as Mary must have been equally strong and vulnerable after her son's death.

But why do we seldom see such images of Mary? There are, I believe, two central reasons. First of all, adequate symbols of Mary are not easy to create. Anthropologist Victor Turner has pointed out that any specific image of Mary is "a signifier meant to represent not only the historical woman who once lived in Galilee but the sacred person who resides in heaven, appears at times to living persons, and intercedes with God for the salvation of mankind."[7] The Mary at Chartres carries all these meanings, as do many of the great Byzantine icons in the Eastern Orthodox tradition. Not accidentally, these images speak powerfully to contemporary viewers and, like Mary herself, do not belong exclusively to Christians. The portrait by Matisse in the Chapel of the Rosary at Vence is another example of Mary's ability to inform an image that transcends religions and cultures. Scores of tourists seek this out-of-the-way chapel, the majority drawn by the fame of the artist. Once there, however, they become deeply reflective as they stand before Matisse's portrait of Mary, her features blank yet somehow wonderfully evocative. Surrounded by clouds, this Everywoman-Mary holds her child (Plate 1).

The second reason for the prevalence of distorted images of Mary is that, until very recently, both church and society have had distorted notions of women in general. We seldom used to hear women describe their lives in their own voices, or knew what it cost them to speak up in public. Reading Dorothy Day's autobiography, *The Long Loneliness*, I sensed the isolation of a woman who was widely admired but not really understood by many in either the church or the country she loved and served. I remember her telling me once how hard it was to make her need for spiritual growth meaningful to male confessors. Invariably they tried to label and quantify everything into "sins" and "numbers of times," a process quite foreign to her way of thinking. Only since the 1960s have we finally been able to read about the inner lives and histories of women as they experienced them. Now we can listen not just to European aristocrats and intellectuals, but to women of every continent and color, including the poor and the abused. With the awareness of what has been suppressed or left out of the history that has been handed down to us, it becomes possible to think more accurately about how Mary's story was shaped in the New Testament, recorded by male evangelists in terms of the cultural assumptions of their day. The recognition that "human" is not the same as "man" has finally arrived in all fields of study, including religion. With contemporary women poring over biblical and theological texts and finding things that have been overlooked or distorted—and, inevitably, disagreeing among themselves as well—we are in a better position than ever to go back in time and recapture a fuller sense of the human Mary. After all, the fundamental problem underlying poor Marian art, like the statue I knelt before on the feast of the Immaculate Conception, is often the inadequate thinking behind it. The clichés used to represent Mary have a great deal to do with long-dominant but mistaken images of mothers, idealistically conceived but ultimately demeaning.

Not surprisingly, many women are angry as they strain to recover their own history; some of them feel they must reject Mary because they see that her image has so often been manipulated to subordinate women. Pioneering feminist theologian Mary Daly charges that the Immaculate Conception presents Mary as a model rape victim, and that the Virgin Birth reduces her to a "hollow eggshell." Abandoning Christian conceptions, Daly has come to see Mary's most accurate image as that of a goddess, since Daly believes that only the feminine divine can empower living women. Marina Warner's *Alone of All Her Sex: The Myth and Cult of the Virgin Mary* reveals the pain of a more nostalgic disillusion. The beautiful symbol of her convent school years was lost, Warner says, because "the church" used it to denigrate both humanity and women. Her thesis is that an impossibly pure image of Mary kept both men and women immature. "The reality her myth describes is over," Warner concludes; "the moral code she affirms has been exhausted." In Warner's opinion, the Virgin, like goddesses before her, most probably "will recede into legend."[8]

But other women, equally aware of misogynist and puritanical interpretations of Mary, do not see them as central to her meaning or influence. Biblical scholar Elisabeth Schüssler Fiorenza claims that the veneration of Mary in the Catholic tradition allowed her as a child to imagine and feel God in the figure of a woman, offering feminine language and imagery to speak of the divine. "The other liberating experience which the Catholic tradition provided for me as a woman is the assertion that everyone is called to *sainthood*."[9] Mary's presence was not a limiting sexual or social model to Schüssler Fiorenza but a reminder that women could be great saints. In the same spirit, novelist Mary Gordon has cautioned against hasty rejections of Mary:

We must not forget the history of woman has been a history of degradation, oppression, the idealization whose other side is tyranny. But we must resist as well the temptation to reject the lovely, the exalted, the resonant life built up for centuries by living men and women. I have wanted to create for myself a devotion to Mary that honors her as woman, as mother, that rejects the wickedness of sexual hatred and sexual fear. I wanted this particularly as I grew older; I longed for it with a special poignance as I experienced motherhood for the first time. It has come to me, then, that one must sift through the nonsense and hostility that has characterized thought and writing about Mary, to find some images, shards, and fragments, glittering in the rubble. One must find isolated words, isolated images; one must travel the road of metaphor, of icon, to come back to that figure who, throughout a corrupt history, has moved the hearts of men and women, has triumphed over the hatred of woman and the fear of her, and abides shining, worthy of our love, compelling it.[10]

In my search for Mary, I have to a large extent traveled the road Gordon advised. I have looked back at the history of art and writing about the mother of Jesus, believing it was necessary to revisit tradition with fresh eyes in order to recover those "shards and fragments." Reexamining them in successive cultures against the portrait of Mary in the New Testament, I have discovered a woman more significant to me now than she was in my childhood.

This personal journey has repaid my curiosity by liberating Mary from mistaken assumptions about her; she is neither changeless nor a mere puppet, but rather a living communal presence who often reflects existing divisions within the community. In coming to see her more clearly, I have also gained a better view of the wider church in which she has been a central figure since the fifth century. Hierarchical authority has by no means been the major factor in shaping the meaning of Marian symbols. Though powerful, it is only part of a wider movement of ordinary believers, baptized men and women, who played their roles in a church that was always struggling to be a sign of reconciliation to humanity. As the Council of Ephesus demonstrates dramatically in the fifth century, every time the official church tried to contain the divine mystery in clear but inevitably restricted theological formulas, as if to compensate, a spontaneous dynamism produced a new burst of Marian piety. Devotion to Mary has emerged again and again from the lived experience of ordinary people— peasants and mystics, housekeepers and poets, midwives and artists.

Our conception of Mary greatly influences our understanding of the nature of the church and our sense of the relationship of Scripture to tradition. The present pope, for example, accepts popular devotions to Mary but limits her to the role of mother, not prophet. Citing Scripture to support his position, John Paul II uses this image of Mary as one "who received neither the mission proper to the Apostles nor the ministerial priesthood" in order to close off discussion on the possibility of women priests. Cardinal Newman, on the other hand, saw Mary as representing the whole church's ability to understand doctrine differently over the centuries. One traditional reading of Scripture has viewed Mary as a prophet, and many groups of believers as well as theologians today support and find strength in this view of her.

Consultation among all Christians with regard to Mary's role and meaning is especially relevant now. Many Protestants as well as Catholics recognize that a faith that continues to renew itself inevitably bursts the limits of the language and thought-world of the New Testament. We need to distinguish between what is culture-bound and what is timeless if church teaching is to be meaningful today. Jaroslav Pelikan, Lutheran theologian and author of a comprehensive modern history of Christian thought, has pointed out that Mary is "in many ways the most striking among all the examples of doctrinal development."[11] If we want to see how traditional doctrine can be faithful to its origins and continually reformulate itself, we need to look more closely at Mary.

I brought to my examination of the past the questions, theories, needs, and even the anger of contemporary women and men. As Brazilian liberation theologians Ivone Gebara and Maria Clara Bingemer affirm: "It is life today that gives life to Mary's life yesterday."[12] In each time frame, I tried to keep in mind the pointed questions that biblical scholar Alice Laffey raised in a personal letter:

> How do we know whether or not Mary was wise? beautiful? humble? merciful? devoted to the poor? How can we know (even if we could know how women behaved at that time in Palestine) if she was consistent with the norm or an exception? To me the key question is, can we (women, feminists) depict her so that she can be a model (function as empowering) for women and girls today? Is there anything in the tradition that permits or encourages such depiction?

These and other questions provided me with guidelines for critical reappraisal of a long and frequently misunderstood tradition. At the same time, I considered it imperative to be sensitive to people in earlier ages, and not assume that they ought to have seen everything as we do. As Gebara and Bingemer observe, "We cannot make her into an eternal model, or way of being; this historical figure of Mary must always enter into dialogue with the time, space, culture, problems and actual people who relate to her."[13]

As I progressed in my research, it became clear that Mary was not simply a protean symbol. Both the Gospels and human experience revealed definite continuities in the messages she mediates. Chief among these is her ability to make women and men, despite conflicting religious needs and opinions, feel they are part of a community. Other patterns, too, began to emerge, crossing individual cultures and repeating themselves in different eras. Mary has become for me both a human woman and a feminine symbol of the divine dwelling in the human; she wears whatever face can be recognized by particular people at particular moments. When that face is true to the woman of the New Testament, it demands a whole response, both inner humility and outer justice, similar to the one Mary expressed in her Magnificat: "He has thrown down the rulers from their thrones/but lifted up the lowly."

I have come to believe that these words about a compassionate God reveal an emerging human consciousness in the face of an ever smaller world. In the memory and imagination of many people today, Mary represents the unity of humanity beneath every kind of diversity. Without losing the wonder I felt as a child, I have begun to discover that such a Mary closes the gap between the ordinary and the holy.

But it is still necessary to search for Mary because Christianity is a religion that mediates not merely the word of God but the image of God as well. Genesis teaches that human beings were made in that image that unites all of us, as Eve's descendants, in the task of living in harmony with creation. The New Testament proclaims that Mary bore a human infant who was God's Son; in time she was acknowledged to be *Theotokos*. Whatever our beliefs or difficulties with belief, Mary can still be a God-Bearer in her contacts with us today. She is not exclusively Catholic or Jewish, Western or Eastern, but a sign of what men and women can be when they participate in the ongoing mystery that links the divine to all that is. For that reason, the meaning of Mary as it emerges in history and human consciousness can help us understand better who we are and what we can be together. In looking for her, we are looking for ourselves.

CHAPTER TWO

MIRIAM OF NAZARETH, MARY OF THE NEW TESTAMENT

There is more pathos and beauty in those few words of the Scripture, "Now there stood by the cross of Jesus his mother," than in all these galleries put together. The soul that has learned to know her from the Bible, loving without idolizing, hoping for the blest communion with her beyond the veil, seeking to imitate only the devotion which stood by the cross in the deepest hour of desertion, cannot be satisfied with these insipidities.

—HARRIET BEECHER STOWE[1]

"For a sermon on the Blessed Virgin to please me . . . I must see her *real* life. . . . They show her to us as unapproachable, but they should present her as imitable, bringing out her virtues, saying that she lived by faith just like ourselves, giving proofs of this from the Gospel."

—ST. THÉRÈSE OF LISIEUX[2]

In the center of the Christian story stands not the lovely "white lady" of artistic and popular imagination, kneeling in adoration before her son. Rather it is the young pregnant woman, living in occupied territory and struggling against victimization and for survival and dignity.

—ELISABETH SCHÜSSLER FIORENZA[3]

Where and how can we find the real Mary? Is it even possible? New Testament scholars tend to say no. History says precious little about her except that she was Jewish and the mother of a son, born in 7–4 B.C.E., who was put to death in his thirties by the Romans in Jerusalem.

If Jesus caused little reaction in the Jewish and pagan literature of the time, Mary caused even less. History treated her like any woman who was not a queen, rendering her largely invisible. In the eyes of the sophisticates in Jerusalem, she and her family might have seemed like country hicks. The fact that she was the mother of a man executed by the Roman authorities as a criminal would hardly make her a heroine. The first-century Jewish historian Josephus refers to Jesus as one of some twenty men called Joshua or Jesus (the name is the same in Greek) who lived in this period. Other men were put to death as well, but Jesus alone was said to be "of Nazareth" and called "Christos," the Greek translation of the Hebrew "Messiah," meaning "anointed" or "chosen one."

That information is not all we have to go on, however. Mary is presented as a faithful observer of Jewish customs, including the yearly pilgrimage to the temple at Jerusalem. The life and message of her son, whom the New Testament suggests she raised, also give us clues to her own life. And when the Jewish Nazarenes—as the early followers of Jesus were called—began to spread his message among the Gentiles, legends as well as apocryphal scriptures developed about Mary's life, reflecting popular

27

and often non-Jewish views. There are, too, some hostile references that belittle both the Nazarene and his mother.

Let's begin with what we know from history and geography.
Miriam, as she would have been known in her world, lived in the
town of Nazareth. Although it was a small village on the southern
slopes of the Galilean hills, it was only a few miles from Seppho-
ris, and Mary's family would have had dealings with this major
city constructed during Jesus' boyhood. Joseph and Jesus were
woodworkers, but most of the Nazarenes made their living
through agriculture; historians would call them peasants rather
than farmers. The soil was not rich; the climate was Mediterranean. The hills were probably carpeted with wildflowers in the
spring, dotted with the cypresses and olive trees that still grow in
this region. At night, the stars would have appeared close and
bright; it is no wonder they were seen as significant omens in the
Christian story, as in the wider world of the time.

Though Mary's family was Jewish, Nazareth was part of the
larger Greco-Roman world. Just before and after the beginning
of the Common Era—the dating changed eventually because of
her son's birth—the Roman Empire held dominion over the entire Mediterranean area. Augustus Caesar was emperor when
Jesus was born, and Herod the Great, whom Augustus had
appointed, was nearly at the end of his rule over the Jews. Although Mary's lifetime was one of relative peace under one of
Herod's sons, the tetrarch of Galilee, Herod Antipas, her country
was occupied by Roman soldiers, as earlier it had been ruled by
other monarchs who suppressed traditional Jewish religious and
ethnic customs. The revolt in 175–c.163 B.C.E. by the Maccabees
against their hellenizing rulers had renewed strong traditional
Jewish feelings in the area. The names of ancient patriarchs
abound in the extended family of Jesus and in his genealogies,
and suggest that the people in Mary's family shared this religious
fervor.

For more insights we must look at the New Testament, which

provides the oldest and most reliable source of information about Mary's existence in the drama of Christian salvation. It is worth remembering that no one recorded the lives and words of Jesus or Mary in our modern sense. No one took notes. There were no cameras or tape recorders. Moreover, with the possible exception of John, none of the four evangelists was one of the twelve apostles who formed the original company of Jesus during his public ministry. In accordance with the writing practices of the period, the community of Christians that followed a particular apostle's tradition authenticated the version of the Gospel that bore his name. The evangelists took upon themselves the awesome task of narrating the meaning of Jesus' ministry, death, and resurrection for these communities, all of which believed in him but carried on his tradition with slightly different emphases. As Raymond Brown, the foremost interpreter of the narratives concerning the birth, childhood, and death of Jesus, puts it: "The Gospels . . . are not simply factual reporting of what happened in Jesus' ministry, but are documents of faith written to show the significance of those events as seen with hindsight."[4] The Gospels were composed some thirty to sixty years after the events they record. Mark was probably written in the sixth decade of the Common Era, Matthew and Luke in the seventh and eighth, John in the ninth. The differences in time as well as in church communities reveal different understandings of Jesus and of Mary in these Gospels, though their primary focus, of course, is on Jesus, not Mary.

The first mention of Mary is by St. Paul in his epistle to the Galatians (4:4), and states merely that Jesus was "born of a woman." Each of her small number of appearances in the Gospels (and in the Acts of the Apostles) is important, but needs analysis. What is said of her can only be understood against the background of the Jewish Christianity of the primitive church of which she became a part. Yet since she most probably died before the destruction of Jerusalem and the temple in the rebellion against Rome in 70 C.E., that church no longer existed when Matthew, Luke, and John wrote their Gospels. They wrote for church communities scattered throughout the Greco-Roman world, for cultural centers like Alexandria and Antioch as well as Rome. All of their communities contained not only Jewish-Christians, but Gentiles who ranged from those familiar with Judaism to those who knew nothing about it. Paul originally came from Tarsus in Asia Minor; he was part of the large Jewish population dispersed throughout the region. Luke's origins are uncertain. He wrote largely for Gentiles, yet his work emphasizes Jewish tradition and Judaism; he may have had a Greek father and a Jewish mother. At best, in the writings of the four evangelists, we catch brief but unforgettable glimpses of the woman Mary and hear her speak words that highlight her place in her son's story. Because of my focus on Mary, I may blur somewhat the quite separate purposes of the different evangelists. But I hope not to distort them or suggest that they all agree about Mary, for their very differences helped me to see her in a new light.

Like Paul, the evangelists often mention Mary without naming her. Though John includes her in two crucial scenes that no other evangelist reports, in both she is called "the mother of Jesus." In this respect she is treated like most women of her time, whose names were not handed down and whose definition hinged on their relationship to a male. Mark calls her by name once (6:3). Matthew and Luke confirm that she was called Mary (Miriam in Hebrew). It was a popular Jewish name for girls, since it was the name of the sister of Aaron and Moses, a prophet herself, who helped lead her people to freedom from the bondage of Egypt.

Though the Gospel stories are not meant as biography and it is impossible to establish an exact time frame, I follow a trail that seeks out Mary's appearances in all of the Gospels in rough chronological order. Such an approach helps me imagine her better as a real person. I also report on what biblical scholars say are the different intentions of the evangelists in those stories. At the end of the chapter, I look again at the woman who lived the simple yet extraordinary life hinted at in the Gospels' incomplete portrait.

THE INFANCY NARRATIVES

What is striking in the Gospel stories is how seldom Mary is mentioned. Many of the scenes and characters I assumed were there are not; they were added by legend, art, and devotion in later centuries. No St. Anne, for example—a figure that is part of my own family myth, since my mother had prayed to her for my birth in the church of St. Jean Baptiste in New York City, then visited St. Anne de Beaupré in Quebec to thank her after I arrived. The New Testament tells us nothing of Mary's parentage. Nor does it have Jesus appear to his mother after the Resurrection, something later believers found hard to accept. The rosary seemed to include her in this and other glorious mysteries, but that popular Catholic devotion, which focuses almost more on Mary than on Jesus, was not fully developed or widely used until the late Middle Ages. What we know from Scripture is that because Mary's son existed, so did she. References to her in the Gospels range from laudatory (Luke) to critical (Mark). Most of her scenes relate to the birth or childhood of Jesus, which are reported only by Matthew and Luke in the Infancy Narratives with which they begin their Gospels. These sections were in fact written last, after the rest of their Gospels, and already reflect a development of thought by both evangelists about the identity and meaning of Jesus.

It is essential to try to understand what Matthew and Luke actually said about Mary and why, for their narratives are the closest accounts we have reflecting earlier oral traditions. To work our way back to the real Mary, we need to brush away for a time the imagery and interpretation with which the Gospels have been overlaid. I will try to distinguish between the unfinished and conflicting portrait the evangelists present and the later images we cannot—and probably do not wish to—forget.

Take, for example, the first image of Mary in Luke's Infancy Narrative, when the angel tells her that she is to become the mother of the Lord. For most of us, a familiar scene springs to mind. In an interior setting of columns and paneled walls, a respectful, long-haired angel addresses a lovely young woman who is dressed in colorful robes. "Hail Mary, full of grace," says the messenger of God. Interrupted in her studies, the listening maid still has her finger in the book on her lap.

But such a conception of the scene shows the influence of Renaissance painters like Fra Angelico or Piero della Francesca. The young Jewish woman in the narratives of Matthew and Luke would probably have been only twelve or thirteen. She would most likely have worked hard, made her own clothes, and gone to the well to fetch scarce water for her family. There would have been no pillars or satin robes, and certainly no book.

What is the Annunciation like in these two Gospels? Matthew has the angel come to Joseph, who is troubled about Mary's pregnancy:

> Now this is how the birth of Jesus Christ came about. When his mother Mary was betrothed to Joseph, but before they lived together, she was found with child through the holy Spirit. Joseph her husband, since he was a righteous man, yet unwilling to expose her to shame, decided to divorce her quietly. Such was his intention when, behold, the angel of the Lord appeared to him in a dream and said, "Joseph, son of David, do not be afraid to take Mary your wife into your home. For it is through the holy Spirit that the child has been conceived in her. She will bear a son and you are to name him Jesus, because he will save his people from their sins." (Matthew 1:18–21)

In this passage Matthew touches all the important points he hopes to communicate to the mixed community of Jewish and Gentile Christians that make up his audience. He wants to confirm and instruct both groups in their faith. Above all, Matthew's Jesus is the Messiah of Davidic origin. But this much was also known to Mark, who never mentions his birth or childhood. Matthew, like Luke, reflects a further awareness of the nature of Jesus that developed later. Jesus' followers came to realize that if he was the son of God at his death and resurrection, he must also have been so earlier, from his very conception and birth. It is this new awareness that is conveyed in the infancy story.

Familiar with the Hebrew Bible, Matthew seized upon a text from Isaiah referring to the birth of a child of the Davidic line some seven hundred years earlier which he felt could further support the claim that Jesus was God's son: "Behold, the virgin shall be with child and bear a son, and they shall name him Emmanuel" (Isaiah 7:14; cf. Matthew 1:23). He had read the biblical text in Greek, which translated the Hebrew *almah*, meaning young unmarried girl, as *parthenos*, or virgin. Though this interpretation laid the groundwork for later exegetes to stress Mary's physical intactness as a model of the "higher" celibate life Christians were urged to adopt in the later Greco-Roman world, the distinction was not central to Matthew, whose emphasis was on God's intervention in the birth.

Since Matthew presented Mary as the only biological parent of Jesus, today's reader finds it illogical that the genealogy Matthew provides is Joseph's and not hers (Matthew 1:1–17). But in patriarchal society legal parentage was what counted, and this came through the male. However, neither Matthew's nor Luke's genealogy was strictly factual; the necessary information was simply not available. Both were composed to make the more significant point that Jesus was descended from David through Joseph.[5]

Matthew included four women in Joseph's ancestral tree,

however, an unusual feature. The women themselves were also surprising: Tamar, Ruth, Rahab, and "the wife of Uriah" (Bath-sheba), most likely selected because they all performed exemplary acts in an irregular way. There was a hint of slander attached to all of these women, yet they were honored for their devotion to God and Israel. The childless widow Tamar dressed as a prostitute to trick her own father-in-law into sleeping with her so she could continue her dead husband's line in keeping with her rights as a widow. The Moabite Ruth depended upon her Jewish mother-in-law Naomi's loyalty and know-how to promote her marriage with Naomi's rich relative Boas in order to continue Naomi's line. Rahab was a prostitute, but her initiative made it possible for the Israelites to enter the promised land. Bathsheba, the woman for whom King David lusted, and whom he married after he had her husband, Uriah, killed, later gave birth to Solomon, a great and wise king.

New Testament scholar Krister Stendahl speaks for many other exegetes when he calls the inclusion of these women in the Davidic pedigree a deliberate preparation for Mary's virginal conception of Jesus, an even greater holy irregularity.[6] The presence of the four women in Matthew's genealogy both substantiates the Davidic line for Jesus and suggests the divine intervention that makes the irregularities these women represent acceptable. After placing suspicions of her infidelity in Joseph's mind, Matthew overcomes them by means of this genealogy as well as through the angel's revelation to Joseph that the child has been conceived "through the holy Spirit."

Matthew and Luke both record a virginal conception of Jesus in their narratives, expressing a conviction that probably rests on earlier oral traditions. They did not see each other's manuscripts, yet both merged a virginal conception demonstrating God's action in the birth with a legal genealogy that made Jesus a descendant of King David.

This so-called Virgin Birth, which is really a virginal concep-

tion, bore no antisexual message; it had nothing to do with reproductive physiology. The question of whether the brothers and
sisters of Jesus mentioned in the Gospels are Mary's children is
left unclear. It was not of great interest to the evangelists. It
would become of interest to church Fathers in later centuries
when they would claim not only a virginal conception but also a
life of perpetual virginity for Mary. By the fourth century,
church scholars maintained uniformly that Jesus had no real sib-
lings, merely cousins, and most Roman Catholics still believe
this. However, Protestant biblical scholars today generally believe that Mary had four other sons: James, Joses, Simon, and
Jude, and two or three daughters, none identified by name. Although Catholic teaching has consistently held otherwise,
Catholic New Testament scholar John Meier finds no reason not
to believe that Jesus had sisters and brothers.[7] Nothing in Scripture supports the idea that Mary remained physically intact while
giving birth, or that she had no sexual relations with her husband
after Jesus was born, though both of these claims become important in later Marian theology and devotion. What is important to
Matthew and Luke is that the child, the anointed one of Davidic
ancestry, is the result of the intervention of the Holy Spirit, and
that Mary is his mother.

There is evidence that some earlier oral sources suggested an
irregularity in the birth of Jesus that lay behind Matthew's account. Community gossip at the time of his birth could have led
later enemies of Jesus to call him illegitimate, and his supporters
to defend him by calling the birth miraculous. Apparently both
Matthew and Luke saw the Christological implications in these
stories circulating about Jesus' birth and were prompted to use
them to express their conviction that he was the son of God from
his very conception. Though the issue is obviously impossible to
settle factually, the Roman Catholic and Orthodox traditions
have always accepted the virginal conception because it is attested
both in the Bible and in long-standing church tradition. Yet

other interpretations of the evangelists' account are possible. An ecumenical group of contemporary Lutheran and Catholic New Testament scholars offers an alternative hypothesis: that Jesus may have been born prematurely.[8]

The only written suggestion of the possible illegitimacy of Jesus comes late, long after the Gospels were written. Celsus, a second-century pagan author, wrote an angry polemic against Christianity in which he repeated a story he had heard from a Jew that Jesus was really the son of a Roman soldier, Panthera (Ben Pantere in Jewish sources). Celsus's text is lost, but we know of the charge because of Origen's angry counterattack in the third century. The story had circulated in the mid–second century among Jews in the diaspora around the Mediterranean, not in Palestine. Meier believes it to be a "mocking, polemical reaction to the claims of the Infancy Narratives, perhaps filtered through popular debates."[9] On the other hand, a Catholic feminist scholar, Jane Schaberg, recently suggested that Mary might have been raped, a scandal which would have been hushed up in this patriarchal society.[10]

The tendency to discount the miraculous in our scientific era makes these alternate theories, with their picture of a more vulnerable and possibly frightened Mary, attractive to many people today. But the question of the specific nature of divine intervention in the conception of Jesus was never spelled out in the Gospels. None of the other possibilities—including that of rape—diminish or undercut the central message the evangelists convey: God's action in Jesus' birth and Mary's wholehearted response brought new hope and joy to humanity.

Luke's Infancy Narrative includes no hint, as Matthew's does, of anything inappropriate. Mary dominates Luke's story; he treats her with greater honor than do any of the other evangelists. For this reason he is often said to have known Mary; his vivid portrait is probably at the root of the later tradition that believed Luke was an artist, and attributed many paintings of Mary to his hand. But there is scant evidence that the evangelist ever met Mary. He carefully composes a moving story, using complex allusions to the Hebrew Bible, to depict the mother of Jesus as a bridge between Jewish and Gentile Christian communities. His narrative has a wider context than that of the other Gospels, not merely Palestine but the whole known world: "In those days a decree went out from Caesar Augustus that the whole world should be enrolled" (Luke 2:1).

Luke's narrative is the source of many familiar and moving artistic scenes, for instance that of the Annunciation, which takes place in Mary's native Nazareth (Luke 1:26–38). "Hail, favored one!" Gabriel says (in contemporary translation). "The Lord is with you." Mary is understandably troubled at this greeting. After telling her not to be afraid, Gabriel announces that she will bear a son who will be king over Israel forever. Mary may be disturbed but she is quite rational. "How can this be, since I have no relations with a man?" she asks. The angel explains to her that the power of the Most High will "overshadow" her, and for that reason "the holy child to be born will be called holy, the Son of God." The term "overshadow" has no sexual connotation here; it recalls instead the Spirit of God that hovered over the waters before the Creation in Genesis 1:2, suggesting a new creation. Luke's story conveys its meaning powerfully. Mary says she knows not man. That is the point. This is God's action, not man's. Her question answered, it remains only for her to say yes or no, and she replies promptly: "Behold, I am the handmaid of the Lord. May it be done to me according to your word."

Feminist biblical scholar Alice Laffey observes that this passage includes intentional verbal parallels to descriptions of the great prophets of Judaism. The evangelists do not say explicitly that Mary is a prophet, but that idea is embedded in the language they chose. In the Bible, prophets are those chosen to deliver God's message to their contemporaries; they live by it themselves whether or not they are heeded. When asked by God, Abraham leaves his father's house, his country, and his kindred (Genesis 12:1–4). He obeys the Lord's will; so does Mary.

Later, in a vision, Abraham asks the Lord: what good will your gifts be when I am childless? The Lord says to Abraham, "Fear not," and tells him he will have as many descendants as there are stars in the sky. When the angel who appears to Mary speaks the words "Fear not" and says that she has "found favor" with the Lord, he is combining phrases, Laffey insists, that have been spoken elsewhere in the Bible only to Abraham and Gideon. With both Abraham and Mary, God's favor results in a child: for Abraham, the heir of the covenant; for Mary, the offspring who will renew God's covenant. "With both Gideon and Mary," Laffey concludes, "the favor results in deliverance and salvation; for Gideon, an Israelite victory over the Midianites; for Mary her son's victory over sin and death."[11]

Like Noah, Joseph, Abraham, Jacob, and Esther, Mary is told that she has "found favor" with God. She is thus placed in a whole line of Israel's heroes and heroines, whose life stories reveal a common destiny of God's unbroken care and support. Laffey believes that Luke's Annunciation also underlines Mary's likeness to Moses. When Moses first encountered Yahweh in the burning bush, he questioned Yahweh, asking why Pharaoh would listen to him, a poor speaker. When Mary encounters the angel, she, too, raises a question. Not until the reply satisfies her does she, like Moses, agree to carry out the task to which God has called her. Both stories reveal a God who wants human participation and is eager to help Moses and Mary overcome self-doubt. This God does not order people around. Pointing to the parallels between Mary's response and those of Abraham and Moses, Laffey asks, "Is not the literary structure of God's call of Mary to become the mother of Jesus similar?" Yet exegetes have played down the importance of Mary's prophetic response, she adds, and focused instead on the angel's announcement.

Immediately after the encounter with Gabriel, which implies a conception, Mary sets out for a village (Ain Kerim) in the up-lands of Judah to visit her much older cousin, Elizabeth, who, the angel has told her, is also pregnant. In Luke's story, Elizabeth's child is John the Baptist, and the infant stirs in her womb when Mary enters the house. Elizabeth herself cries out in one of a number of memorable canticles or songs in the Lucan narrative (Luke 1:41–45). "Most blessed are you among women, and blessed is the fruit of your womb."

We recognize in this passage, as in the earlier words of Gabriel to Mary, phrases from the familiar Hail Mary. That prayer was pieced together over the centuries with the same sense of faith-fulness to the New Testament that Luke shows here to the He-brew Bible. My attempt to follow Mary through her life cycle is just one more telling of a story that has been powerfully conveyed in visual terms for centuries. There are innumerable representa-tions of this encounter between Mary and Elizabeth in later art, each translating the scene in terms of the artist's culture. Luke is not presenting a naturalistic image of their meeting in his text but creating a pattern of references that reveal Mary as the represen-tative of Israel even as she becomes the mother of Jesus. There is no other evidence that John the Baptist was related to Jesus by blood except this gracious story. It is Luke's symbolic way of showing the relationship that existed between the disciples of the John the Baptist movement and the Jesus movement in his own time, and it makes the point that John was the forerunner of Je-sus. Story is thus used as theology at the very outset of Christian tradition.

Elizabeth's greeting to Mary echoes the biblical Deborah's greeting to Jael, "Blessed among women be Jael" (Judges 5:24), and Uzziah's proclamation to Judith: "Blessed are you, daughter . . . above all the women on earth" (Judith 13:18). The prayer Luke gives Mary in response is perhaps the most familiar can-ticle in his narrative, one known in the Western church as the Magnificat:

My soul proclaims the greatness of the Lord;
  my spirit rejoices in God my savior.
For he has looked upon his handmaid's lowliness;
  behold, from now on will all ages call me blessed.
The Mighty One has done great things for me,
  and holy is his name.
His mercy is from age to age
  to those who fear him.
He has shown might with his arm,
  dispersed the arrogant of mind and heart.
He has thrown down the rulers from their thrones
  but lifted up the lowly.
The hungry he has filled with good things;
  the rich he has sent away empty.
He has helped Israel his servant,
  remembering his mercy,
according to his promise to our fathers,
  to Abraham and to his descendants forever.

                                              (Luke 1:46–55)

Obviously, Mary did not compose this prayer in a spontaneous
burst of inspiration, as I used to assume. Luke pieced together a
mosaic of phrases from the Hebrew Scriptures that are appropriate for Mary, words the real mother of Jesus might have prayed.
In his story, Luke particularly stresses the antecedent of Hannah,
the mother of Samuel, who sang a similar hymn of thanksgiving
when she went to the temple at Shiloh to praise the Lord for
sending her a long-desired son: "My heart exults in the Lord, my
horn is exalted in my God. I have swallowed up my enemies; I rejoice in my victory" (1 Samuel 2:1). Luke adds echoes of another
biblical heroine, Judith, who like Mary identified herself with the
poor and oppressed. Having had to cut off the head of Nebu-
chadnezzer's general Holofernes to save her people, she sounded
a more militant note (Judith 13:17–18), similarly echoed in
Mary's words. The Magnificat also recalls Psalm 149:4: "For

the Lord takes delight in his people,/honors the poor with victory."

The "great things" done by the Mighty One in Mary's prayer echo the language of Exodus and the Sinai covenant as well, making her the equivalent of Israel, now entering a new covenant with the Lord. Mary did what the prophet Miriam did, sang a victory song in praise of God's awesome accomplishments. Like the prophet Deborah, she praised the Lord for helping Israel, for bringing down the powerful and lifting up the lowly. In her own time, Mary may be thought of as speaking not only for the poor and for Israel, but for all those under the heel of Roman military rule. It is intriguing that, like Hannah, she sounds this note of God's power in connection with having a child.

Alice Laffey believes that Mary's motherhood, like Hannah's, has blinded the majority of commentators to the prophetic roles of both. While Miriam's and Deborah's songs were about specifically military victory, Mary's and Hannah's were about childbearing, though both Mary and Hannah used metaphors that spoke of shattering the Lord's enemies. Their language seemed to extend their personal victories, represented by childbirth, into a corporate victory of the oppressed over their oppressors.[12] Luke, as we know, was speaking to believers throughout the Roman empire. There was already an expectation of such renewal there; Virgil had written of it a century before in his Fourth Eclogue. He spoke of a golden era symbolized by the birth of a child who would "receive divine life" and "rule over a world made peaceful by the virtues of his father." "Behold," he wrote, "how all things rejoice at this age to come."[13]

Misinterpretation of Mary's humility has constantly presented another stumbling block to understanding her prophetic role. When she mentions her "lowliness" in the Magnificat, however, she is speaking about her social condition, not her personal attitude. Luke seems to attribute to her an awareness of post-Resurrection church experience, a tradition to which he was trying to be faithful. There was real poverty and lack of worldly power among the Jerusalem Christians who were the nucleus of that community, in which he placed Mary (Acts 1:14). Her words in the Magnificat—spoken at the time of her son's conception— suggest a link with aspects of Jesus' later ministry. Since Luke composed the Magnificat later than the account of that ministry, he again gives Mary lines he considers appropriate for the mother of the adult Jesus.

After the Annunciation and Visitation, Luke leads us swiftly to the birth of Jesus in Bethlehem. He contrives a census to get Joseph and Mary there from Nazareth, while Matthew has them living there and devises reasons for moving them later. It cannot be determined for certain whether Bethlehem was the actual birthplace, but an earlier tradition placed the birth of Jesus there in the city of David, and this location affirmed the important point that Jesus was David's heir. It might be nice to have some hard facts about this birth; we know only roughly when and where it occurred. What was significant to Luke and Matthew was their truthful record of a real birth. We have no idea of the actual date of Jesus' birth, but symbolically it is fitting that it is celebrated when the winter darkness has reached its peak in the northern hemisphere and the light of the sun is about to increase.

Luke makes the claim that Jesus' birth is an entry of divinity into full humanity; he believes it should totally change our understanding of who we are and how we treat each other. He tells us almost nothing about Mary during the Nativity except that she wrapped the infant in swaddling clothes and laid him in a manger (Luke 2:7). His emphasis is on the angel's message to the frightened shepherds: "I proclaim to you good news of great joy that will be for all the people. For today in the city of David a savior has been born for you who is Messiah and Lord" (Luke 2:10–11). Here he echoes the words from Isaiah that all lovers of Handel's *Messiah* know: "For unto us a child is born." After the shepherds leave, however, Luke adds: "And Mary kept all these things, reflecting on them in her heart" (2:19); thus he returns the focus to the mother and recalls her earlier thoughtful response to Gabriel's proclamation.

Luke's story contains no visit from Magi following a star, and no flight into Egypt to escape Herod's call for the slaughter of all male children in Bethlehem and its vicinity who were two years old or younger. These elements occur only in Matthew and may not have been meant to be read as actual historical events. They recapitulate in the infancy of Jesus the history of the Jewish people, similarly exiled for years in Egypt and then liberated. Matthew has arranged the texts so as to bring out associations between Jesus and the patriarch Joseph, who lived in Egypt, as well as to draw parallels between the births of Jesus and Moses, who also needed to be hidden. These scenes add greatly to our ability to feel the danger as well as the beauty in the circumstances of this birth.

Throughout the whole history of Christianity, believers have taken bits of Matthew and added them to Luke to make one Nativity story. Never mind that the pieces cannot be reconciled factually; they have entered the human imagination together. Some of the finest Christian art and legends were inspired by the visit of the Magi and the flight into Egypt, as told in Matthew. Among the most charming examples are the small stone sculptures carved by Gislebertus in the twelfth century on the capitals of pillars in the cathedral of St. Lazarus at Autun, in France. The sculptor pokes sly fun at Joseph, who is nodding off during the birth, but later shows him bravely leading Mary and Jesus to Egypt on a donkey (Plate 7).

Luke rounds out his Infancy Narrative in two memorable scenes. The first is the Presentation of Jesus and the Purification of Mary according to Jewish law in the temple at Jerusalem. Leviticus 12:1 ff. required the consecration of all firstborn males to the Lord. Luke moves Mary and Joseph to the temple at Jerusalem so that Jesus can be acknowledged as the Messiah by

Simeon and Anna, two aged holy people who represent the Jewish tradition. Jewish scholar David Flusser praises Luke's loving portrayal of the atmosphere in this scene. Simeon and Anna meet the Holy Family in the temple and cry out with joy. The widow Anna recalls the biblical Judith in her fasting, prayer, and concern for the poor. She may well be like some of the widows Luke knew in the early church, where they were significant figures. Like the Magnificat, Simeon's canticle is pieced together from the Hebrew Scriptures:

> Now, Master, you may let your servant go
> in peace, according to your word,
> for my eyes have seen your salvation,
> which you prepared in sight of all the peoples,
> a light for revelation to the Gentiles,
> and glory for your people Israel.
>
> (Luke 2:29–32)

Simeon is willing to die now, for he has seen his hopes realized. His words may have been part of an earlier Jewish prayer at death. Since the fifth century, this canticle has been included in Compline, the prayer in the Divine Office to be chanted (and later read) by all priests and religious before going to bed. Its stately cadences seem equally suited to express readiness for sleep, death, or the mysterious fulfillment of messianic promise.

Simeon goes on to prophesy soberly that the child will be "a sign that will be contradicted." To Mary he says that a sword will pass through her. Raymond Brown suggests that this phrase indicates the sword Jesus mentions when he says he came not to bring peace but a sword. It can be understood as the sword of discrimination Jesus used to distinguish the physical family from the family of disciples who hear and keep the word of God. It can also be understood as the sword that separates those who hear and believe him from those who do not. In either case, the sword would pierce his own mother's heart.

This theme of the sword heralds the life that lies ahead for Mary. The last scene of Luke's Infancy Narrative has the twelve-year-old Jesus remaining behind in Jerusalem, where his family has taken him for the feast of Passover. Joseph and Mary start back to Nazareth with a caravan of friends and relatives, noticing his absence only after a full day's journey. They rush back and find him at last, on the third day, listening to the teachers of the law in the temple court and asking them questions (Luke 2:43–49). In this scene, which I mentioned in chapter one, Mary and her son exchange impulsive words. When the boy rejoins them and goes home, Luke tells us again that Mary "kept all these things in her heart" (Luke 2:51). The sword Simeon prophesied has already begun to cut. In the first two chapters of his Gospel, Luke has presented Mary as a faithful human disciple, one who hears and keeps the word of God even when she does not—as he shows us here—quite understand it.

The importance of Mary in bringing up her son is shown by implication. Keep in mind that in Christian doctrine Jesus is fully human; he had to struggle to understand his mission. He would have been able to get some education in the local synagogue, but, Meier says, "it is reasonable to suppose that Jesus' religious formation in his family was intense and profound, and included instruction in reading biblical Hebrew."[14] The adult Jesus was a master storyteller and could argue brilliantly with his political and religious enemies. Joseph taught him carpentry and probably the religious texts of Judaism, but Mary would have passed on its stories and practices. Luke's inclusion of Mary's Magnificat helps us to see Jesus as Mary's son in his dedication to a Jewish tradition of justice and prophecy. In his advocacy of the poor, which angered both Roman rulers and high priests, he mirrored his mother's faithfulness.

FROM CANA TO THE CROSS

If we follow Mary's life, her next appearance in Scripture after the Infancy Narratives is at the wedding in Cana, mentioned only by John. Although his Gospel was written later than the others, John's story of Cana shows the same combination of mutual trust and misunderstanding between son and mother with which Luke's infancy story ends. About thirty, Jesus is on the brink of his public ministry as he and Mary both attend the wedding of a friend at Cana. When his mother sees that their hosts at the feast have run out of wine, she points it out to Jesus. He replies: "Woman, how does your concern affect me? My hour has not yet come." It would appear to be a rebuke, yet Mary turns confidently to the servants and says: "Do whatever he tells you." And Jesus proceeds to turn six enormous jars of water into wine that the headwaiter pronounces better than any they have drunk before (John 2:1–11).

The marriage at Cana has long been presented as a cozy scene showing the power of the mother over her divine son, but the evangelist may have had something else in mind when he told the story as he did. Even though Jesus responds to his mother's request, he seems to be trying to separate his mission from her expectation. Whatever John's intentions in telling this story, the event marked the beginning of the public life of Jesus. Elisabeth Schüssler Fiorenza interprets the language of Jesus to Mary neither as a rebuke nor as the response of a son who can't deny his mother, but as the proper way to address her as a disciple. Mary's ability to proceed confidently would mean that she accepted this role.[15]

In Mark 3:20–35, Jesus distinguishes sharply between his biological family and his chosen family of disciples on two separate occasions. These scenes of confrontation and growing alienation occur early in his public life, after the first healing and preaching at Capernaum and the Sea of Galilee. He has just appointed the twelve apostles and come home to Nazareth. Mark reports that "his relatives set out to seize him, for they said, 'He is out of his mind.' " Jesus continues teaching in parables until his mother and his brothers arrive. The crowd tells Jesus, "Your mother and your brothers [and your sisters] are outside asking for you." He replies, "Who are my mother and [my] brothers?" Looking around at those seated in the circle, he answers his own question: "Here are my mother and my brothers. [For] whoever does the will of God is my brother and sister and mother." Although Jesus is stressing the positive point that relatedness to him does not depend on blood ties, Mark raises the distinct possibility that at this time Mary may have been scandalized by Jesus' activities. At the very least, he must have been a source of real tension within the extended family and with sarcastic neighbors. Mark 6:1–6 records another such confrontation when Jesus returns to Nazareth later and preaches in the synagogue. The skepticism of the townsfolk becomes the occasion for his recognition that "A prophet is not without honor except in his native place and among his own kin and in his own house."

Luke interprets more kindly what might seem to be a harsh judgment on the lack of belief of Jesus' immediate family, including Mary. In a related episode (Luke 11:27–28), a woman cries out from the crowd: " 'Blessed is the womb that carried you and the breasts at which you nursed.' " Jesus responds, " 'Rather, blessed are those who hear the word of God and observe it.' " Since Luke has always made Mary first among those who hear, this familiar distinction between disciple and mother again includes Mary in the family of disciples, more important than that of kin.

John is the only evangelist who actually places Mary at the foot of the cross; the scene is significant. Sympathetic observers were not present to count the crowd and describe the scene; that would have been too dangerous. But the Gospel of John tells us that

Mary and three other women remained with the disciple (John himself) as Jesus endured his agony on the cross: his mother's sister, Mary the wife of Clopas, and Mary of Magdala. Since their relationship in some later art and cultural history would become one that contrasted them, it is worth noting that John portrays Mary and Mary of Magdala as companions in discipleship under duress at the Crucifixion. Later, after encountering the empty tomb, Mary Magdalene is the first follower to whom the risen Christ appears (Mark 16:9).

John begins and ends his account of Jesus' ministry with his mother Mary. He tells us that Jesus, just before his death, said to Mary, "Woman, behold, your son," and to the disciple, "Behold, your mother" (John 19:26–27). Jesus addressed Mary not as "mother," but as "woman," the same term he used at Cana. Schüssler Fiorenza says that Jesus' choice of words in this passage clearly shows Mary to be one of the apostolic women disciples.[16] In her view, Mary and John are here designated as the models of an egalitarian, inclusive discipleship that is meant to mark the church community to come. True to his message in life, in this last act Jesus honors his mother's struggle to place the word of God above her biological motherhood.

As we have seen, the Gospels are not concerned with Mary's feelings, nor with what we think of as psychology; their intent is theological. Mary is presented largely in tableaux: a young woman is told she will bring forth a son contrary to all human understanding. Luke's Gospel has her respond to this challenge in memorable words. She is silent throughout the apparently painless birth; she is even silent as she stands under the cross where her son gives up his life, mocked by political and religious authorities. After that, there is just one reference to her presence—in Acts, where she is noted among the disciples. There is no mention of her death, no reference to a tomb. Mary lives out a unique destiny, largely private yet consistent with the thirst for social justice that Luke portrayed in her prayer when she visited Elizabeth.

REFLECTIONS ON MARY'S EXPERIENCE

When I review Mary's life in these small pieces of the New Testament, I am struck by the way in which her flexible mind and spirit turned the events into faithful witness. Each fragment reveals neglected dimensions of her character, while traditional interpretations often capture only one aspect. For example, commentaries on the Annunciation by church Fathers who have seen her response as perfect obedience and by theologians who have called it a total renunciation of self miss much of the human reality. These male authorities do not seem to understand that the more difficult thing for women is not the giving of self, to which they have been largely conditioned, but the necessary prior task of becoming a self able to give. Luke's Gospel surprised me by showing constant growth in Mary as she shaped an identity strong enough to be faithful to her Jewish tradition, yet ultimately able to respond to unexpected turns in her son's mission. Just as Jesus had to grow into his vocation, so did Mary. While her son distinguished between Mary as disciple and Mary as mother, she had to make a unified personal response to his challenge, one in which motherhood was instructed and stretched by discipleship.

Think of how young Mary was when she accepted God's invitation, probably between twelve and thirteen. In her studies of adolescent female development in the present day, educational psychologist Carol Gilligan has observed that many twelve-year-old girls are passionately and outspokenly concerned for justice. At puberty, however, most are conditioned to public silence. In Luke's Gospel, Mary starts out like those outspoken young girls:

it took courage to question an angel. Even more remarkably, in
later life she seems to have transcended the fears that accompany
social pressures for conformity and gave witness to her beliefs before hostile authorities.

Reexamining Mary's life, I was also struck by the realization
that she really chose to have a child. I was taught that her "yes"
was necessary, but I don't think that I ever understood the real-
life courage her answer entailed. A man in his forties recently
confessed to me that pictures of the Annunciation have taken on
an indescribable attraction for him since he became a parent. His
wife and he had worked with pad and pencil listing all the pros
and cons about having children, without coming to a decision; finally, still scared, they simply reached out their hands to one another. He is impressed with the clarity and bravery of Mary's
response to the same challenge. Another first-time father wrote
me that he could not understand why childbirth was not regarded
as the ultimate model of heroism. Perhaps it is only in our time
that men as well as women can understand why Hannah and
Mary could speak of God's victory in childbearing in the heroic
terms usually reserved for warfare.

Parenting can be—for both men and women—a task opening
to religious faith. As Nancy Mairs explained to a new father who
had confessed the "protectiveness and fear" he felt for his newborn son:

> Parenthood teaches—forces?—prayer. Please God don't let him
> stop breathing in his crib, you say now, and in no time at all he'll
> be off in Zimbabwe and you'll be saying, Don't let him get cere-
> bral malaria or fall off his moto and need a transfusion of AIDS-
> contaminated blood or fail to see in time the next cobra that shows
> up in his kitchen.[17]

As surely as being in a foxhole motivates the religious impulse,
so does a parent's concern for the good of a child. It is concern of
a high order, since it is on behalf of someone else. Family rela-

tionships are an aspect of religious tradition and a school for moral growth in traditional societies. Today, however, they are an area of endless difficulty on which we receive almost no guidance from religious institutions. We must thread our way among popular psychological guides to self-esteem, ways to overcome abuse, paths not chosen, and tough love. Mary is a parent who seems to have managed both to choose her child and to form him, to have survived differences of opinion between them, and to have remained open to what she could ultimately accept in his unexpected new witness.

The parallel between Abraham and Mary as progenitors is extremely suggestive. Abraham's daring to argue with God in Genesis (18:22–32) in order to spare Sodom and Gomorrah for the sake of ten innocent people is matched by the persistence of Mary's attempts to wrest repentant sinners from God's justice in later Christian tradition. I have always loved the twelfth-century sculpture that I saw in a museum in Colmar, France: a bearded Abraham is carrying his children in a sort of cradle close to his bosom. If we place this image beside the late medieval pictures of the Mother of Mercy holding her cloak over people of every class and kind, we should realize that both of these prophets are defined by their advocacy for others in the spiritual battles of everyday existence (Plates 4 and 5).

Recalling the Annunciation scene, I became convinced that from a psychological perspective Mary's response to Gabriel involved more than the courage to become a mother; it modeled the human attitude of attention that is essential for seeing the sacred possibilities of ordinary life. Annunciations are happening all the time, according to Thomas Moore, author of *Care of the Soul*: "The angel and the Virgin are always engaging in dialogue: the angel announcing some impossibility, the Virgin taken aback, questioning, agreeing."[18] Mary's attitude tells us to pay attention to unexpected inspiration from our unconscious, the realm of such angelic messages. We are often afraid, unprepared to believe that some possibilities could become real. Psychotherapist Gary Pearle suggests that Mary's virginal attitude, her willingness to overcome her assumptions, her openness to mystery, is precisely the one we need if we are to be responsive to life.[19] "Virginal" here does not mean "unspoiled" or "undamaged," but rather "open." It suggests fertile ground for something truly new, as well as patience to wait and persistence to work for a hitherto unimagined fulfillment. Such an understanding of virginity calls for the strict spiritual discipline of humility, by no means a passive virtue. Moore redefines it as an attitude that allows "a world to exist beyond the one we know and understand." This contemporary psychological interpretation of Mary's response to the Annunciation is quite in keeping with the sketch Luke left us.

The Visitation, too, reveals new meaning today. Mary first told her good news to her cousin Elizabeth, taking a short but difficult trip to visit her in the village of Ain Kerim. A mosaic in the Visitation church there portrays Mary seated on a donkey, attended only by angels, though in life she may have come in a caravan. As women often do, Mary and Elizabeth shared feelings with one another about their pregnancies. The poet Rainer Maria Rilke imagined this scene of feminine solidarity:

> She had to lay her hand upon the other
> woman's body, still more ripe than hers . . .
> Each one, a sanctuary, sought refuge with her
> closest woman kin.[20]

The emotional and spiritual power of this encounter is vividly conveyed in a stone bas-relief above the front door of St. Gabriel, an old country church I visited just northeast of Arles. The angel to whom the church is dedicated has been damaged by time's vicissitudes, but the amazement at God's action in the eyes of Mary and Elizabeth—which are like those in Coptic icons—has survived the centuries (Plate 2).

In Luke's account, Elizabeth's welcome elicited the Magnificat. As Mary pours forth her faith to her cousin, heralding the meaning of the birth to come, she reveals a surprising sureness that God cares for her personally. But she speaks as a representative figure, not only of Israel but of all believers struggling against conventional power and the domination of wealth. As her prayer shows, the God who "has done great things" for her is not the God of the rich and mighty, but of the poor and lowly. Centuries of rote recitation of her prayer have often obscured the boldness of these affirmations and their social implications.

Reflecting again on the Magnificat helped me imagine the passion and dedication with which Mary must have taught Jesus. As a young mother she would have told her son the stories of their people: of Abraham and Sarah, Isaac and Rebecca, of Moses, her namesake Miriam, the Maccabees, Deborah, and Ruth. Is it any wonder that Jesus had women friends and disciples?

But almost from the beginning, Mary's motherhood was marred by sorrow. A frequent medieval version of the Nativity shows the baby Jesus laid out on a miniature altar to suggest his future sacrifice. And Mary became a refugee when the Holy Family fled to Egypt. The sword Simeon said would pierce Mary's heart soon pierced other mothers as well when soldiers slaughtered the innocents. In telling the story of Herod and the three Wise Men, Matthew deliberately associated Mary with Rachel (Jeremiah 31:15), the suffering Jewish mother of the First Covenant:

Then was fulfilled what had been said through Jeremiah the prophet:

"A voice was heard in Ramah,
     sobbing and loud lamentation;
Rachel weeping for her children,
     and she would not be consoled,
     since they were no more."

(Matthew 2:18)

In his novel *Mary*, Scholem Asch depicts Mary praying to Rachel as the patron of all mothers, animal as well as human. In one powerful scene Rachel appears and tells her: "You and I were elected to taste every mother's sorrow. . . . Your heart shall be the sponge of your son's agony." Together this fictional Rachel and Mary envision the future agonies of Israel's children. Then Rachel tells Mary, "You shall be mother to the nations of the world."[21] It is only with the memory of the combined suffering of Rachel and Mary on behalf of all who suffer that the constant liturgical prayers urging Mary to rejoice—especially the great Exsultet of Easter Saturday—can be fully appreciated.

There were other, more subtle kinds of suffering for this mother as her son became a man. The minimal record from Luke indicates that Mary did not understand him during most of his public life. At Cana they may well have disagreed about what he should do. Jesus' question in response to her pointing out the shortage of wine—"How does your concern affect me? My hour is not yet come"—indicates in Hebrew either hostility or denial of common interest. Even if she felt Jesus' words were a rebuke, Mary ignored the hostility or divergence of interest. She did not argue, but moved with trust in her son's right action as well as in her own judgment.

Frances Queré, the late French Protestant theologian, gives even greater significance to the Cana incident. She says that, after having given birth to Jesus in Bethlehem, Mary gave birth to Christ again at Cana, forcing him to overcome his fear of committing himself to the ministry that would lead him to the cross.[22] Aware of tensions between them, Mary nevertheless was to some extent responsible for the beginning of his public life, just as she had been for the beginning of his physical life. Her words and actions suggest a later version of the young woman Luke had depicted, who showed such ability to tolerate uncertainty and ambivalence when confronted by the angelic messen-

ger. At Cana, Mary neither yielded her own opinion nor judged
her son's; she did not impose a decision, but rather helped him
make one.

The disagreements between mother and son become clearer
during his visits to Nazareth. Mark suggests that Mary was not
only divided within herself but torn by critical views of Jesus
from her numerous, older relatives. And though she taught Jesus
to respect women, she must have worried about the way he traveled freely with women and men alike. Was he not going too far?
Was he still observing the law that was so important to her? Was
he taking unnecessary risks in standing up to the priests in the
temple? David Flusser believes we honor the memory of Mary
when we see her as a worried and suffering Jewish mother. He
says a Jew can well understand her pain when Jesus left to take on
his dangerous way of life. His mission made this familiar son a
mystery to his mother. But are not all growing, changing children
mysteries to their parents? The inevitability of different perspectives, no matter how great the love, brings Mary close to every
uncertain parent. Rilke imagines the depths of Mary's suffering
as she argues with Jesus before the Passion:

> Oh, if you wished this, you ought not have dared
> to issue forth from any woman's loins . . .
> why didn't you fiercely burst from me and leave?
> If you need only tigers to break and tear you,
> why was I reared in the women's house, to weave
>
> and make for you a soft clean swaddling-gown
> in which was not the smallest seam to chafe
> your body? Even so was my whole life—
> now suddenly you twist nature upside down.[23]

The poet's words remind us that, though the church insists on
Mary's sinlessness, her goodness could coexist with much doubt
and confusion. And if Mary had other children, biological or not,

why were they not under the cross with her? If it was because
they did not believe in their older brother's cause, that would
have brought their mother unbearable anguish. All we can say for
sure is that, although Jesus was abandoned on the cross except by
a few women and the beloved disciple, his brother James later led
the group of Jewish Christians in Jerusalem.

But it was not only as a mother that Mary was present at this
Roman execution; she was also a witness. In her book *Longing for
Darkness: Tara and the Black Madonna*, China Galland tells us
how she came to understand the enormous courage such witness
takes when she read about the mothers and grandmothers of the
Disappeared in Argentina. They defied the ban on demonstra-
tions even after the military government arranged to have some of
them "disappear" as well. Galland began to see Mary at Calvary as
witness to a new community, born in the face of public scorn and
violence that the apostles were still unready to confront:

> The witness is one who looks, who does not turn away, who does
> not despair or give up, who is willing to be called upon, who
> will speak up and testify in public, who will take an oath, who will
> bind themselves to the truth, "so help me God," to the commu-
> nity, for the community, for without the witness there can be no
> community.

Galland appreciated the strength it took for Mary to stand and
witness in the face of official force, even though "It appears that
one is doing nothing."[24]

Mary's presence at the cross in John's Gospel also makes her a
witness to all those struggling to understand and be faithful to
what they believe despite unanswered questions and doubts. For
in the Gospels she has been portrayed not simply as a follower of
Christ but as one who listened and pondered, trying to think
things through. In Luke's eyes, that made her a disciple, and
John placed her at the foot of the cross, a representative of all

those to come later who would also ponder and reflect as a necessary part of their faithfulness to tradition.

After the Crucifixion there is no further mention of Mary in
the New Testament except Luke's statement in Acts that she
was present in the upper room, praying with the disciples
(Acts 1:13–24). Her presence there suggests what is reiterated in
legends, stories, and art, that after her son's death she came to
understand him better, and that she faithfully continued to teach
and pray within his community until her unmarked, unrecorded
death. To speak in contemporary psychological terms, it is clear
that Mary dealt successfully with the life stages the late
Erik Erikson and his wife, Joan, have said we must all negotiate—
especially the last and most difficult one of wisdom, in which we
reach out to future generations despite our own approaching
death. Between the cross and the upper room, Mary mastered her
grief in order to transfer her dedication to the wider community
of her son's followers. She is a true figure of human wisdom.

Despite the lack of information about her in history books and
the gaps in the New Testament accounts, Mary has become
an increasingly real woman to me. Of course her portrait in
Scripture is not complete; her life, like that of Jesus, is told in
stories that both indicate what the evangelists believed and sum-
mon readers to integrate what they find there into their own
experience.

THE REST OF OUR SEARCH FOR MARY WILL FOLLOW THE
complex stream of what later generations of men and women
have made of these Gospel stories. Some of their interpretations
make it hard to remember the human Mary of Scripture, but any
adequate understanding of her must keep in mind the woman
who bore witness to the mystery recorded there. In review-
ing these later understandings, it will be helpful to remember the

question Jaroslav Pelikan raised about the transformation of Mary's image from New Testament times to our own:

> Would there have been such anti-Semitism, would there have been so many pogroms, would there have been an Auschwitz, if every Christian church and every Christian home had focused its devotion on icons of Mary not only as the Mother of God and Queen of Heaven, but as the Jewish maiden and the new Miriam?[25]

In fact, we should apply Pelikan's questioning attitude to other developments as well. For in the centuries we are about to visit, when Christianity began to grow away from its roots, distorted notions of women, of social organization, and of physical reality itself became inextricably entwined with the good news of the Gospels.

CHAPTER THREE

STORIES AND STRUGGLES:
Mary's Transformation in the Greco-Roman Church

As the human race fell into bondage to death through a virgin, so it is rescued by a virgin.

— IRENAEUS, *Against the Heresies*

And he [Joachim] placed her on the third step of the altar, and the Lord God put grace upon the child, and she danced for joy with her feet, and *the whole house of Israel loved her*. And her parents went down wondering, praising and glorifying the almighty God because the child did not turn back. And Mary was in the Temple nurtured like a dove and received food from the hand of an angel.

— *The Protevangelium of James*[1]

I FOUND THE CHRISTIANITY OF THE FIRST THREE CENTURIES much harder to understand than that of the New Testament, where the scenes and stories were familiar. The Greco-Roman church presents an ambiguous picture of Mary, including much that alienates the contemporary sensibility. This lack of coherence can be understood only in the context of the church's struggle to become established in the powerful yet declining Roman Empire. Christianity was becoming de-Judaized under the constant threat of Roman persecution, which in turn fostered intense competition to solidify church authority.

When I began exploring this early Christianity I couldn't find Mary where I had assumed she would be. There are no records of feast days devoted to her in the liturgical services carried on in the house-churches of the time. The Christian art of the period suggests that believers focused on the life-giving message of the adult Jesus. There were only a few scattered paintings of Mary as a Roman mother, in comparison to the many examples of catacomb art that showed her son healing and saving. Paintings of Moses, Daniel, and Jonah were also plentiful, because the actions of these biblical figures were seen to foreshadow those of Jesus.

Some early manuscripts referring to Mary surprised me, like this description of the Nativity:

> She brought forth like a strong man with desire,
> And she bore according to the manifestation
> And acquired with great power.[2]

These arresting lines occur in the Odes of Solomon, which their editor and translator from the Syriac, James Hamilton Charlesworth, calls "the earliest Christian hymnbook." He tells us that these prayers, similar to psalms, were probably composed in the late first century, at roughly the same time as some New Testament texts, and were used in public worship services during the second century. The odes, which come from a vital Syrian Christian tradition that had been unknown to Western Christianity until very recently, were my introduction to the diversity that marked the church of this time. They also provided the first hint that I would never quite be able to fit together all of the pieces in what is still a mysteriously puzzling period in church history.

It is difficult to realize today, but in the church of the first two centuries there was no single ruling body, nor even a clear canon establishing which books were to be accepted as Scripture. The gospels and epistles were shared within communities that reflected their founders' differing emphases, such as Peter's stress on church organization or John's emphasis on the Spirit. Additional stories about Jesus, Mary, and the apostles also circulated widely in texts we call Apocrypha. This term covers a number of different kinds of writing, both learned and popular, that dealt with material related to events in the New Testament. Many apocryphal texts were from Christian sources, but a number were inspired by the complex and pervasive phenomenon of Gnosticism, a religious movement that sought to gain spiritual knowledge or enlightenment (gnosis) through ascetic discipline. The young Christian church tried to supplant paganism and define itself in the great cities of Alexandria, Antioch, and Rome where religions and ideas from the East were as prevalent as the traders who mingled there. Gnostic and Christian themes are often impossible to disentangle in a time when philosophy as well as religion seemed to denigrate the physical and separate it from the spiritual. The church that spread throughout the Roman empire had many voices, often in heated debate with one another. It is fortunate that a number of written documents (some only recently discovered or translated) have survived to give us a sense of this diversity. They were the testimonies to which I turned as I tried to understand why Mary's image developed so slowly and in such piecemeal fashion.

Eventually, two significant but very different portraits of Mary emerged. One was a careful theological parallel between Eve and Mary by the earliest Fathers of the church, those teachers and theologians who were the first to write under their own names after the Apostolic Era. The other image of Mary arose in popular stories first told in the East. Both portraits have been highly influential in Christian tradition; the art, stories, and theology they have inspired continue to form attitudes to Mary today. These two dominant images differ in certain key respects, however, even though each was shaped by the assumptions of the larger Greco-Roman world. What is crucial to note is that, in different ways, both detach the mother of Jesus from her historical and religious roots.

EVE–MARY THEOLOGY

The Eve-Mary theology that began in this period has been foundational for later thinking about Mary. Almost all theological discussions about her before the Second Vatican Council refer back to the parallels and contrasts between Eve and Mary. Like the artists of the catacombs, the early church Fathers drew on figures, or "types," from the Hebrew Scriptures, while pointing to the fuller meaning they believed Christ brought to them. Just as Paul had called Christ the New Adam (Romans 5:12 ff.), second-century theologians Justin Martyr, Irenaeus, and Tertullian began to call Mary the New Eve.

Justin Martyr (d. c.165) appears to have been the first to state this Eve-Mary relationship. Born of pagan parents in Palestine, he first searched for truth in the philosophies of Aristotle, Pythagoras, Plato, and the Stoics. After he converted to Christianity in 130, he became one of its chief apologists, probably the first who tried to reconcile faith with reason, in deference to the truth he had already encountered in philosophy. He developed the Eve–Mary relationship in his *Dialogue with Trypho*, a disputation with a Jewish thinker in which he tried to answer charges against Christianity:

> For Eve, being a virgin and undefiled, having conceived the word from the serpent, brought forth disobedience and death. The Virgin Mary, however, having received faith and joy, when the angel Gabriel announced to her the good tidings . . . answered: Be it done to me according to thy word.[3]

In Justin's view, Christianity is to replace Judaism; Mary, consequently, becomes a purely Christian figure. She is praised for her obedience, which seems to separate her from Eve and other women. Justin blames Eve forcefully for the introduction of sin into the world. Employing a powerful physical metaphor which suggests that Eve gave birth to death through the agency of God's enemy, the serpent, he introduces sexual undertones to her disobedience.

Like the Pandora of Greek myth, Justin's Eve is responsible for the world's troubles, and becomes a constant threat to Christian male virtue as well. This position is by no means uniquely Justin's, but reflects contemporary assumptions both in Greek tradition and in Jewish thought. According to Carol Meyers, a religious scholar who has done archaeological research in the Middle East, after the second century B.C.E. "The misogynist expansions of the Eden story in early Christian and Jewish literature began to emerge. A new concept of Eve associated with sin, death and suffering is superimposed so indelibly on the assertive and productive figure of the Eden narrative that we can hardly see the original woman of Genesis 2–3."[4]

Knowledge of this tendency to blame Eve and all women for the introduction of evil into the world helps us to understand the later development of an unreal Mary. During this period, Jewish writers showed great interest in a myth, referred to in Genesis 6:1–9, in which earth women were raped by fallen angels, called the Watchers, and produced a race of evil giants. The Apocrypha of Moses suggests that Satan sexually seduced Eve, and this theme was taken up in other apocryphal Jewish works that said that the resulting evil, for which the women were held partly responsible, continued to exist.[5] These works tended to idealize Adam. Allusions to the Watcher myth also occur in the New Testament (2 Peter 2:4 and Revelation 12). Women's concern for adornment was blamed for luring the angels, and fear of women's weakness and their nature as temptresses influenced the early Fathers.[6] All this helped me understand why the usually balanced Clement of Alexandria (d. c.215), who encouraged women to attend his lectures, was so passionate in his denunciation of women who wore bracelets and brooches in the form of snakes:

> these women do not blush when they wear such conspicuous symbols of wickedness. Just as the serpent deceived Eve, so, too, the enticing golden ornament in the shape of a serpent enkindles a mad frenzy in the hearts of the rest of womankind.[7]

Even Irenaeus (d. c.202), the first great theologian, tried to exonerate Adam, saying that "Eve was made the cause of death."[8] In taking up the Eve-Mary parallel, however, he extended it with an emphasis quite different from that of Justin. Born in Asia Minor, Irenaeus brought some of the early Marian devotion we find in Eastern tradition (like that reflected in the lines from the Odes of Solomon) into the West when he became bishop of Lyons. In *Against Heresies* (3.21.10) he emphasizes the central Christian theme that the Resurrection of Christ is a turning point in history, and that all earlier revelation prefigures this new stage of creation. But Irenaeus seems to see the beginning of the new era as part of a process, not a break. In his view, Mary's obedience dissolves Eve's disobedience, "so that the virgin Mary might become the advocate of the virgin Eve."[9] Irenaeus calls Mary an intercessor, one who can appeal to the divine on behalf of humans, yet he feels free to criticize what he interprets as her hasty behavior at Cana, which did not serve her son's mission. "When Mary hurries to the admirable sign of the wine and before the time desires to participate of the mixed cup . . . the Lord repels her untimely haste."[10]

Both the positive connection with Eve and the chiding of Mary are possible for Irenaeus because he sees Mary as a human being, someone perhaps like his own mother. Neither devotion nor dogma separates her from other women. Irenaeus associates Mary closely with humanity and the church. His reverent tendency is to place her, through her motherhood, at the center of the process of redemption, "the pure womb which regenerates men unto God."

On the other hand, Tertullian (d. c.220), the first theologian writing in Latin, steers clear of any mention of intercession or of mystical associations with Mary's motherhood in his Eve-Mary parallelism. As bishop of Carthage, he feared that such references might suggest dangerous connections between her and the Egyptian goddess Isis. The worship of Demeter, Cybele, and Isis, still lively in Egypt and Rome, was considered idolatrous by Christians. But a close look at the Isis cult by the second-century poet Lucius Apuleius offers a positive reading. His fictional tale *The Golden Ass* is a serious appraisal of the Mother Goddess, whose priest he became. At first the book seems to be a ribald series of adventures, spiced with local lore and myths, in which the foolish young narrator is literally transformed into an ass. Forced to suffer great indignities, however, he receives a moral education and arrives at religious commitment. Late in the story, just as Lucius—still an ass—is about to be forced to have sex with a female murderer in the arena at Corinth for the entertainment of the public, he escapes to the seashore, prays to Isis for rescue, and falls asleep.

When he wakes, an apparition of an extraordinarily lovely woman rises from the middle of the sea and stands poised upon its surface. He tries to describe this transcendent vision, a woman with "long thick hair in tapering ringlets on a lovely neck" and a disc round as the moon above her brow. Like the vipers and the ears of corn rising from her hair, her mantle embroidered with glittering stars and a bright and fiery moon reveals her identity even before she speaks:

> I am Nature, the universal Mother, mistress of all the elements, primordial child of time, sovereign of all things spiritual, queen of the dead, queen also of the immortals, the single manifestation of all gods and goddesses that are. My nod governs the shining heights of Heaven, the wholesome sea-breezes, the lamentable silences of the world below. Though I am worshiped in many aspects, known by countless names, and propitiated with all manner of different rites, yet the whole round earth venerates me. . . . Call me by my true name, Queen Isis. I have come in pity of your plight, I have come to favor and aid you.[11]

The goddess helps Lucius become a man again, and he becomes her priest. His initiation reveals the asceticism, not license, that marked her service. In reading this tale I was struck by the cosmic dimensions and merciful attributes of this beautiful figure, which I found strangely familiar. She resembled pictures and medals of a much later Mary, standing on the crescent moon with stars circling her head. The bishop of Carthage must have feared such associations in the third century, and consequently he took great care to discuss Mary's motherhood in simple, factual terms.

Tertullian had another reason to focus narrowly on Mary's human motherhood; he had to counter the Gnostic groups in his diocese who placed their emphasis on Christ's spiritual nature,

and discounted his humanity. The Incarnation, the doctrine that
the Word became flesh, was the most fundamental assertion of
the church. Obviously, the authenticity of Mary's motherhood
was central to this belief. For Ignatius, bishop of Antioch, the fact
that Jesus was "carried in the womb" by Mary was proof that his
was a real human birth. Although Tertullian continued this
teaching, his assessment of Mary seems exceptionally harsh.
He did not believe she was among her son's followers. Expanding a connection he saw between Mary and the "unbelieving"
synagogue, he wrote that Christ rejected her and "transferred
the blessedness from the womb and breasts of his mother to his
disciples."[12]

Ambivalent about both Eve and Mary, Tertullian praises the
latter primarily in terms of her obedience. He is speaking, of
course, about obedience to God, but in talking about Eve and
Mary, he seems equally concerned to keep real women in line. He
lashes out at them, explicitly mentioning that they must wear
veils because of the shame of having lured angels. Introducing
sexual innuendoes into his interpretation of Eve, he writes that
"in fact she gave birth to a devil" (*De Cultu Feminarum* 1.1) and
suggests that all women should walk in mourning and repentance
like Eve, so that they might expiate the ignominy of the first sin:

> Do you not know that you are (each) an Eve? . . . You are the
> devil's gateway; you are the unsealer of that (forbidden) tree: you
> are the first deserter of the divine law: you are she who persuaded
> him whom the devil was not valiant enough to attack. You de-
> stroyed so easily God's image, man. On account of your desert—
> that is, death—even the Son of God had to die.[13]

Whatever the positive intentions of Tertullian and other Fathers in developing a coherent explanation of Christian salvation
through this separation of an obedient, virginal Mary from other,
inherently guilty women, I cannot help but hear in this invective
a tendency to place the blame for sin on women alone. Tertullian

sounds like a father with too much authority and too little feedback in this developing church-family; he shuts out the views of others whose experience might have led him to a different interpretation of their common existence in a sinful world. Certainly his style of talking with church members is strikingly different from that which Luke presents as Mary's style of communication. His Mary seems as distorted as his Eve.

Despite its clear limitations, however, there is something powerful in the Fathers' Eve-Mary parallel, since it presents two women as essential to the salvation of humanity. This parallel, at least as Irenaeus developed it, often transcends cultural distortions when it appears in later ages. At this point in our discussion, however, it is useful to look at the other major portrait of Mary composed in these early centuries—the Mary of popular legend.

THE MARY OF POPULAR LEGEND

It is striking to see how, in this male-dominated world, ordinary believers made an unusually well educated and comparatively independent heroine of the mother of Jesus. They imagined her life to be almost angelic, but at the same time they made her humanly accessible and provided her with an extended family not mentioned in the New Testament. Mary and Joseph became leading characters in legends composed by Christians in Syria, by Egyptian farmers, and by sailors of the Nile who carried them as far as Arabia. These fictional inventions supplied imaginative details and dialogue for what the Gospels left out.

By far the most influential and artistic of these apocryphal presentations of Mary is the Protevangelium or Book of James,[14] which has come down to us in Greek, Slavonic, Syriac, Irish, and Latin texts. The book was probably written around 150 by a single author, who shows great skill in reading back into Mary's life much of the material Matthew and Luke used in their Infancy

Narratives of Jesus. The Protevangelium ends with a fictional statement purported to be by James, the brother of the Lord, claiming authorship—a well-known literary device intended to give a text special authority. One of the many pseudoepigraphical books in these centuries that claims the names of apostles and saints for such a purpose, the Protevangelium contains characters, plot, and dialogue from other, more legendary sources, all focusing on Mary's birth, childhood, and motherhood.

The Book of James opens with the story of a charitable and prosperous older couple, Joachim and Anna, who are childless after twenty years of marriage. On "the great day of the Lord" Joachim is told that it is not fitting for him to offer his gifts because he has "begotten no offspring in Israel." Sadly he withdraws to the desert to do penance, while his wife, Anna, laments her childlessness: "O God of our Fathers, bless me and hear my prayer, as thou didst bless the womb of Sarah . . . and gavest her a son, Isaac" (p. 426). The biblical comparison invoked between Mary's aged parents and Abraham and Sarah is reinforced in this prayer which, like her name, Anna (Hannah), and her childless condition, reminds the reader of the mother of Samuel and echoes Hannah's prayer.

Before long, twin angels appear to Joachim and Anna separately, heralding the birth of a child who will be a gift of the Lord, in words anticipating the Annunciation to Mary. Anna joyfully promises that she will dedicate this child to the Lord "all the days of its life" (p. 427). Joachim offers lambs, calves, and kids, then rushes to embrace Anna at the gate of Jerusalem. From their kiss, Mary is conceived. It is a tribute to the power of good fiction that in the ninth century Pope Leo III consented to have this nonbiblical scene portrayed in the church of St. Paul in Rome.

The mother can hardly let this miraculous child walk on her own feet; after Mary takes seven steps, Anna picks her up: "As the Lord my God lives, you shall walk no more upon this ground until I take you into the temple of the Lord" (p. 428). At age three, Mary is taken there, to live as a dedicated virgin. The priest welcomes her with a preview of her own words in the Magnificat:

> "The Lord has magnified your name among all generations; because of you the Lord at the end of the days will manifest his redemption to the children of Israel."

In the sixteenth century, Titian painted the child Mary courageously mounting the steps alone toward the great portals of the temple and its somewhat forbidding priest. And early in the twentieth century, the poet Rilke portrayed the scene in the same way:

> the threatening one on whose breast jewels burned
> seemed to receive her; but she passed through it all,
> small as she was, forth from every hand,
> into her destiny prepared, more ample
> than the hall and heavier than the temple.[15]

The Book of James continues with a description of Mary's life in the temple, where she is fed by angels as she pursues her studies. When she is twelve, however, the high priest Zacharias insists she must leave and be married; otherwise, as an adult female, she will pollute the sanctuary. Confident that the Lord will guide him, he gathers together an assembly of widowers. When a dove leaves the staff of Joseph and flies onto his head, Zacharias insists that Joseph is the man who should be Mary's husband.

Joseph refuses, however: "I already have sons and am old, but she is a girl" (p. 430). He does not want to be "a laughing-stock to the children of Israel." He will be just that, of course, to medieval and later peasants, but he will also be beloved. The priest reassures him, and the betrothal to the daughter of the tribe of David is completed. Joseph takes Mary to his family's home and leaves immediately; the author wants no question to arise about Mary's virginity.

The priests soon ask Mary back to the temple to help weave the sacred veil for the tabernacle; she is honored by being given the valuable scarlet and purple threads for her part of the work. Back home, when Mary goes to the well to draw water, she hears a voice say: *"Hail, thou that art highly favored, the Lord is with thee, blessed art thou among women"* (p. 430). She is inside her house again, weaving, when the angel appears, and the Annunciation unfolds almost exactly as in Luke.

The Book of James, like the Gospel of Luke, has Mary visit Elizabeth, but the plot changes when Joseph discovers that she is with child. Wrestling with himself—as in Matthew—he accuses her of deceiving him, of behaving like Eve to Adam. "For I received her as a virgin out of the Temple of the Lord my God. . . . Who has deceived me? . . . Has the story [of Adam] been repeated in me?" (p. 431). Here is a new note: Joseph assumes that Eve led Adam astray, and that this act of disobedience was related to sexual transgression. This is one of the first indications we have that Eve's role was already recast in the popular Christian imagination of the time.

Mary cries bitterly and defends her purity in the Book of James, convincing Joseph of her innocence. (He is not told about it by an angel as in Matthew.) But the community is not convinced. The couple is assumed to have sinned and must submit to the public test of innocence, detailed in Numbers, for a wife suspected of infidelity: they must drink the water of the conviction of the Lord. When they survive the bitter brew, they are declared innocent.

Notice how the author has integrated the story of Joseph, as presented in Matthew, with that of Mary, as told in Luke, making their human and social responses more credible. He picks up again from Luke's text as the couple follows the decree of Caesar Augustus and travels to Bethlehem. Bits of touching dialogue occur here and in the later flight to Egypt: "Joseph, take me down from the ass," Mary requests, "for the child within me presses me, to come forth." The Nativity as retold here includes an additional theological motif. Worried about her condition, Joseph turns around to look at Mary as she rides, seeing her first sad, then laughing. How can this be? he asks her. "Joseph, I see with my eyes two peoples," she explains, "one weeping and lamenting and one rejoicing and exulting" (p. 433). This is a reference to Genesis 25:23, in which the Lord tells Rebecca that two nations are in her womb, quarreling, but that the older shall serve the younger. The words Rebecca spoke when she was pregnant with the twins Jacob and Esau, who contended for their father's birthright, are here placed in Mary's mouth, now referring to Judaism and Christianity. The popularity of the Book of James again shows the instinctive tendency of early Christians to see the birth of Jesus as the turning point of religious history; it also reveals how they read Scripture backwards, searching the Hebrew Bible for prefigurations of Christian meaning.

The Protevangelium tends to look back at the Gospel story, too, through the assumptions of the day, one of these being a complete assurance that Mary was always a virgin. Describing the Nativity, the Book of James has the sons of Joseph sit by Mary in the cave while Joseph searches for a midwife:

> And he found one who was just coming down from the hill-country, and he took her with him, and said to the midwife: "Mary is betrothed to me, but she conceived of the Holy Spirit after she had been brought up in the Temple of the Lord" (p. 433).

The midwife enters the cave, sees the mother and child, and cries out (echoing the prophetess Anna in the Presentation scene in Luke): "How great is this day for me, that I have seen this new sight" (p. 434). Later the midwife tells the story to another midwife, Salome, who scoffs at her account of a virginal birth. Like doubting Thomas who, after Jesus' Resurrection, puts his hand on the Lord's side to be sure it is he, Salome insists on examining Mary. When she tries, her hand is badly burned, and it does not heal until she touches the baby. The story thus claims that Mary remained physically intact during and after the birth of Jesus.

The narrative in the Book of James obviously represents an attempt to meet the desires of a wide public that craved more details about the lives of Mary and Joseph. At the same time, many incidents are intended to rebut second-century slurs against them. For instance, in case the genealogical line through Joseph was not enough to guarantee the ancestry of Jesus, the story provided Mary with a Davidic ancestry as well. The addition of a doubting midwife whose hand is burned when she tries to test Mary's virginity is offered as powerful testimony against the charge, still circulating, that Jesus was the illegitimate son of a Roman soldier. Joseph is presented as a fatherly guardian rather than a normal husband; in the logic of the narrative, Joseph's advanced age and his grown children become further "proof" that Mary's physical virginity was permanent.

The Book of James reflects the popular belief, an addition to the Gospel accounts, that Mary remained a virgin throughout her life. Its image of an elderly Joseph, whose children are the half-brothers of Jesus, was to become accepted in Greek and other Eastern (later Byzantine and Orthodox) churches. The Latin church felt that the New Testament did not justify this interpretation. In the fourth century the testy biblical scholar Jerome would denounce the Protevangelium as "delirious nonsense." Jerome came up with a more acceptable theory of the "brothers" of Jesus as "cousins" in order to explain Mary's now necessary perpetual virginity. This was the view that would win out in the Western church as it became less and less conceivable that the mother of Jesus ever had sexual relations with her husband. In this way, two somewhat different portraits of Mary were able to coexist in many Christian minds: the obedient Virgin Mary of theology and the pure, sympathetic heroine of popular legend.

Legends about Mary continued to proliferate wherever Christianity spread. Among the more charming tales are those clustered around the Flight into Egypt. One tells of Joseph and "the lady Mary" being captured by two robbers in the desert. One of the robbers, Titus, pleads for their freedom; when the other refuses, he puts up his own forty drachmas for their release. Touched by his kindness, Mary tells Titus that God will uphold him and grant him forgiveness of his sins. Jesus then says to Mary, "In thirty years, mother, the Jews will crucify me in Jerusalem, and those two robbers will be fastened to the cross with me . . . and . . . Titus will go before me into paradise." "God preserve you from that, my son," replies his mother.[16]

The wide dissemination of the Book of James in many translations and other apocryphal stories like these would influence art to the end of the Middle Ages and after, filling the minds of ordinary Christians with gracious images of the mother of Jesus.

PRIVATE DEVOTION, BIBLICAL EXEGESIS, AND THE IDEAL OF VIRGINITY

In addition to the chief portraits of Mary developed in Eve-Mary theology and popular legend, there are fragmentary elements of other images of Mary that were not only significant at the time but reappeared in later centuries as well.

First is the Mary of private devotion. An inscription in Greek on a papyrus fragment from the third or early fourth century, later incorporated into the Byzantine liturgy, is said to be the earliest known prayer to Mary: "We flee to your protection, O holy Mother of God. In our needs do not disdain our prayer, but save us at all times from all dangers." Its language is familiar, for it is much like the popular medieval prayer, the Memorare, still in use today.

In other circles a few voices hint at emerging Marian devotion.

The Alexandrian biblical scholar Origen (d. c.254), a pupil of Clement's, shows his reverence for Mary in the prologue to his commentary on John: "No one can seize its meaning who has not leaned on Jesus' bosom, and has not received from Jesus—Mary, who has become his mother also." Origen may well have been the first theologian to use the term *Theotokos*, or God-Bearer, for Mary.

It seems appropriate that a pupil of his, Gregory the Wonder-worker, so called because of his remarkable success as a bishop, should have had the first recorded vision of Mary.[17] Before he was called to the priesthood, the young Gregory lay in bed one night in some confusion pondering theological doctrine. Suddenly a saintly form appeared who calmed the startled young man, saying that he had been sent by divine command to reveal the truth and help him overcome his doubts. He then pointed to a shadowy feminine figure in the room. Gregory dared not look at either figure directly, but heard the two discussing the very subject of his doubts. The woman referred to the first figure as John the Evangelist, whom she asked to disclose to Gregory the mystery of godliness. John, in turn, said he wished only to comply with "the mother of the Lord." When he arose in the morning, Gregory wrote down all that he had heard, drawing on this vision in all his later preaching.[18]

Biblical commentators were also searching the Scriptures and finding further "evidence" of Mary's importance. When Origen and his fellow scholars at Alexandria combed the Hebrew Bible for types of the divine plan that pointed to the emergence of Christ, they also looked for other types of Mary besides Eve. Origen saw one in Exodus, in the burning bush in which Moses encountered Yahweh; just as the bush burned without being consumed, so did Mary remain unharmed by the fire of the Spirit. I remember my surprise when I came across a magnificent representation of this conception in the Cathedral in Aix-en-Provence. I assumed at first that the fifteenth-century painting by

Nicholas Froment was the artist's original idea. There sat Mary in elegant robes holding Jesus on her lap on top of the burning bush—actually it was a circle of trees whose leaves were tipped with flame—while Moses reverently knelt below her. The artist had conflated two events into a single scene in which Jesus became the fruition of Yahweh's appearance in Exodus. Only later did I realize that the subject was as old as the typological thinking begun by these Alexandrian biblicists.

Origen drew on the Eve-Mary motif, too, but within a biblical context and with an emphasis on Mary's representative humanity. He did not believe Mary was without sin, since she needed the ordinary purification of Jewish women after childbirth. Further, he thought she had doubts at the Crucifixion; but, he hastened to add, so did the apostles: "Why should we believe that, when the Apostles were scandalized, the Mother of the Lord remained immune from scandal? If she had not suffered scandal in the passion of the Lord, Jesus would not have died for her sins."[19] He saw her as human, one of us, very much as she was in the New Testament.

With one important exception: to Origen, Mary remained a physical virgin throughout her life. In this respect he reflected a concern shared by the faithful and the Fathers of the second- and third-century church. In presenting sexual renunciation as an ideal, Christianity had made a significant break with Judaism as well as with the pagan world. This new attitude toward sexuality had emerged in Christian circles as early as the mid–first century; later, along with a willingness to be martyred for their beliefs, it almost defined Christians to the wider society. By the second century the physician Galen said of Christians, "Their contempt for death is patent to us every day, and likewise their restraint from intercourse."[20] Mary was not a martyr, but given the assumption that a life consecrated to virginity was the holiest one, she *must* have been a perpetual virgin.

Origen stresses the positive ideal behind sexual renunciation:

It is the way to union with God. Only through the holy body of a virginal woman was God able to join humanity.[21] Mary's virginity after the birth of Jesus is equally important; Origen sees the "brothers of Jesus" as the half-brothers the Book of James claims they were. For Origen, virginity was mystical and liberating; he is said to have had himself castrated at twenty. He was a pioneering spokesperson for the increasing numbers of Christians who would take to the desert, the mountains, and even the cities in the name of a historic mutation in which men and women were to be transformed spiritually by overcoming their bodily sexuality. Admirable as such asceticism can be, it is a choice that denies the more ordinary but equal heroism of living in loving relationship with others, of giving birth to actual children and raising them. Whether through the Eve-Mary theology, popular legend, or a common assumption of her lifelong virginity, the biblical image of Mary as representative human being was being reshaped to fit the spiritual assumptions of a different cultural era.

GNOSTICISM

As we have seen, the Western Fathers hesitated to praise Mary too much. At the same time, they felt compelled to give her a positive role in the history of salvation. A brief consideration of Gnosticism may help explain these contradictory tendencies. Fear of associations with the Goddess kept the Fathers almost silent about Mary's real motherhood, but the inclination of many Christians to think of Christ exclusively as pure spirit was a danger that forced them to emphasize it. The Fathers met this challenge by defending the human nature of Christ, leaving later times to deal with what appears to be a legacy of dualism.

In the early church, Docetism, from the Greek verb "to seem," was the name given to the tendency to consider the humanity and sufferings of the earthly Christ as apparent rather than real. It reached its peak among the Gnostics, whose attitudes permeate texts of this period. During the second century most Gnostics were Christians, but by its conclusion, the majority had established their own sects. The absence of a New Testament canon made it much easier for ideas later judged unorthodox to be widely disseminated during these years. For this reason it is often hard to distinguish a Gnostic work from a Christian one that sounds quite similar. The exotic language of the Odes of Solomon, quoted early in this chapter, was part of the public prayer of the Syrian Christian community. The odes seem grounded in Jewish Christianity in their insistence that the Lord became human, yet they share with Gnostic writings and some apocryphal gospels the belief that the Holy Spirit is feminine. In the ode I cited on page 61, the poet suggests a parallel between the power of the Spirit overshadowing Mary's womb and that of the Spirit that stirred the waters of Genesis at the original Creation. An extraordinary passage in the same ode calls the Holy Spirit "she" who milked the breasts of the Father— "milk" was often a metaphor for the Word, the text's editor tells us—and directed the milk at the womb of the Virgin. This early prayer goes on to express the same belief in a painless birth that we find in popular legend:

> . . . she did not require a midwife,
> Because He caused her to give life.

The Ascension of Isaiah, a first-century apocryphal text, describes the Nativity in similar terms:

> And it came to pass, while they were alone, that Mary straightaway beheld with her eyes and saw a small child, and she was amazed. And when her amazement wore off, her womb was found as it was before she was with child.[22]

This latter birth, however, stresses Mary's vision of a divine appearance, an emphasis more related to the Gnostic theme of illumination than to ordinary human birth. But there is just not enough information about the origins and uses of this text for us to be certain it is Gnostic. Its story of painless childbearing may well have arisen in a second-century Jewish-Christian community applying rabbinic legends about the birth of Moses to the birth of Jesus. The story is not very different from the Nativity of popular legend. Note that it, too, extends Mary's virginity (in the sense of physical intactness) during and after birth. And it may well have been transmitted and used by Gnostic sects later. Accurate information about reproductive physiology was of no concern to any of the story's hearers or tellers; their interest lay in the divine nature of Mary's son.

Some popular apocryphal works, on the other hand, seem distinctly Gnostic. The second-century Infancy Story of Thomas is one of these. It borrows legendary motifs from Indian, Egyptian, and Persian tales to describe the somewhat arbitrary actions of a divine child residing in a human body. Often added to the Book of James, it, too, was an influential source of later Christian art.

One scene in this story shows the boy Jesus amusing himself by bringing clay pigeons to life. Another describes him losing his temper when a boy with a willow branch scatters the water Jesus has gathered. "You insolent, godless dunderhead," Jesus cries. "What harm did the pools and the water do to you?" Immediately, the offending boy dies.[23] After several similar incidents, the parents in the neighborhood complain, but Mary and Joseph have little control over this young man. Even his teacher begs Joseph to take him away: "This child is not earth-born; he can tame even fire. Perhaps he was begotten even before the creation of the world. What belly bore him, what womb nurtured him I do not know."[24] Sometimes, however, there is a tender scene, which may help account for the tale's popularity:

When he was six years old, his mother gave him a pitcher and sent him to draw water and bring it into the house. But in the crowd he stumbled, and the pitcher was broken. But Jesus spread out the garment he was wearing, filled it with water and brought it to his mother. And when his mother saw the miracle, she kissed him, and kept within herself the mysteries which she had seen him do.[25]

Thomas's Infancy Story ends with the twelve-year-old Jesus sitting comfortably among the teachers in the temple. You can hear the echo of Luke in the statement about Mary above, but Thomas's account focuses on the spiritual nature of Jesus from birth. It is a fitting boyhood for the adult Jesus of the Gnostic Gospel of Thomas, probably composed in the second century in Syria, which presents him as a spiritual teacher and a revealer of secrets, but not the Jewish Messiah. Followers of the apostle Thomas are believed to have gone to India, and some have suggested Buddhist influence on the text.

How do we know so much about Gnostic beliefs? We know more about them than earlier generations did because the Gospel of Thomas and many other works were discovered among ancient Coptic manuscripts at Nag Hammadi in 1945. An Egyptian peasant found them buried in a large jar, where they had been hidden in the desert for sixteen hundred years.[26] The fact that these manuscripts were buried strongly suggests that those in authority in the fourth century were extremely suspicious of the dualistic split between matter and spirit they revealed and would have destroyed them as heretical. Elaine Pagels, however, who worked on the original Nag Hammadi manuscripts, points out that those who wrote them did not think of themselves as heretics. Probably influenced by Eastern thought, such Christians sought personal enlightenment through extreme asceticism.

Nevertheless, certain elements in these texts posed a clear threat to orthodox belief. They translated the pessimism and dualism of the Hellenistic world into a doctrine of redemption that sought to escape the physical world altogether. For Irenaeus,

however, the Incarnation of the historical Jesus meant the renewal of divine power behind all creation: in his view, this power
so permeated bodily nature that the bodily became the sacramental bearer of the divine. His five-volume *Against Heresies*—in
which his Eve-Mary theology was just a small section—was
clearly a polemical work, but some passages that reflect the life-
affirmation of earlier Judaism and a cosmic sacramentality are of
crucial importance. If the flesh is not capable of salvation, "then
neither did the Lord redeem us with His blood, nor is the cup of
Eucharist the communion of His blood, nor is the bread which
we break the communion of His body."[27]

But true doctrine was not the only concern of the Fathers in
the struggle against Gnosticism. Endeavoring to establish the
grounds on which believers would know what was true, they affirmed that the authority of Jesus was transmitted only through
the twelve apostles, Peter foremost among them. Gnostics rejected that formula, claiming that spiritual vision was a substitute
for such transmission; in their emphasis on the inner experience
of the Lord's presence, they tended to minimize the importance
of authority. As Pagels indicates, many elements of Gnosticism
were distasteful to local bishops not simply on grounds of belief
but because they diminished the power and influence of their
office.

In their emphasis on the primacy of spirit, Gnostics did not
turn to the mother of Jesus to represent their differences with the
official church. Instead they developed texts choosing the figure
of Mary Magdalene, the first witness to whom the risen Jesus had
appeared, to stand for those who acted on the authority of spiritual vision rather than that of apostolic tradition. In the second-
century Gnostic Gospel of Mary, Mary Magdalene comforts the
apostles by sharing the special revelation given her by the Lord.
Most of the text describing this communication is unfortunately
missing; only the beginning and end remain. At the end, Mary
Magdalene describes how the enlightened soul breaks free of all

material elements, rising through her own gnosis (the soul is always feminine in these discussions) to achieve eternal rest. In response, Andrew challenges her:

> "I at least do not believe that the Savior said this. For certainly these teachings are strange ideas," Peter answered. . . . "Did he really speak with a woman without our knowledge (and) not openly? Are we to turn about and all listen to her? Did he prefer her to us?"[28]

Mary Magdalene begins to weep and asks Peter if he thinks she made up her story, or is lying. Levi ends the argument by admonishing Peter:

> "Peter, you have always been hot-tempered. . . . If the Savior made her worthy, who are you indeed to reject her? Surely the Savior knows her very well. That is why he loved her more than us."

Finally at peace, they all leave together to proclaim and preach.[29] Peter and Andrew here represent a stiff-necked insistence on authority; they deny both the truth of visions and the right of women to teach. Since this was the attitude real women were facing from church leaders in the second century, we can understand why these texts might be attractive to women of that time—and to others today who have no interest in reviving Gnosticism.[30]

The fact that Mary Magdalene was Peter's opponent in such dialogues would have been doubly threatening to orthodox officeholders, for they knew that women were considered equal to men in the Gnostic sects of this period. Church leaders like Tertullian, in contrast, severely restricted women's activities: "It is not permitted for a woman to speak in the church; but neither is it permitted her to teach, nor to baptize, nor to offer, nor to claim for herself a lot in any manly function, nor a say in any sacerdotal office."[31] In Gnostic groups women were allowed to prophesy, baptize, and be elected to the priesthood, a revolving rather than a permanent office. At a time when this split was widening in orthodox circles, Gnostics did not divide their adherents strictly into clergy and laity. Furthermore, Gnostics used feminine imagery for each person of the Trinity, addressing God as Our Mother as well as Our Father.[32]

WOMEN'S RELIGIOUS OPTIONS: GNOSTICISM, MARTYRDOM, AND COMMITTED VIRGINITY

The limited options for women in these centuries made it difficult for them to draw directly on the two main portraits of Mary presented in this chapter as models for their own lives. Nevertheless, hints of devotion to Mary are found in their involvement in Gnosticism, their embrace of martyrdom, and their commitment to a dedicated life of celibacy, all of which would be incorporated in images of Jesus' mother that appear later.

We have seen why Gnosticism might have considerable appeal; the fact that church authorities were hostile toward it would only confirm its value for some women. Choosing to be a member of a Gnostic sect, however, could hardly have been easy. For one thing, Gnostics accepted only celibates. They drew on an elite constituency, getting most of their followers from the intense study circles that arose in Christian groups toward the end of the second century. Gnostic teachers tried to help individual believers pass through a healing transformation to achieve wholeness. In the Gospel of Thomas, Jesus says, "When you make the male and female one and the same, so that the male not be male and the female female . . . then will you enter [the Kingdom]."[33]

Although it is difficult to interpret such highly metaphorical language with any finality, this quotation seems to suggest the pursuit of psychological wholeness. But the words also meant that people had to overcome their sexuality in order to become pure souls. The Gnostic Gospel of Philip describes sexual differentiation itself as the result of the Fall. Though it is impossible to be sure if "male" and "female" in the text refer to actual people or to archetypes, we should recognize that in the Gnostic lexicon the female is secondary to the male in this world and in heaven. The Gospel of Thomas explains that baptism begins the process of remaking the female into a male and restoring the lost unity of the original human being. Notice how Jesus defends Mary Magdalene at the end of this Gospel:

> Simon Peter said to them, "let Mary leave us, for women are not worthy of life." Jesus said, "I myself shall lead her in order to make her male, so that she too may become a living spirit resembling you males. For every woman who will make herself male will enter the kingdom of heaven."[34]

The difficulties of such a transformation—metaphorical or not—must have kept down the number of women in Gnostic sects, though we have little solid information in this area. On the other hand, it was certainly not easy for women to have a sense of complete acceptance in the Greco-Roman church. The orthodox position reflected the situation of the vast majority who would marry and bear children. Clement of Alexandria expressed official teaching when he warned against the "dangerous mystique of continence" and upheld the value of orderly married life. Yet he, too, considered women inferior by nature. In his influential work *The Instructor*, he describes his disgust at seeing a woman wearing cosmetics and reveling in drink. Then he adds, "For nothing disgraceful is proper for man, who is endowed with reason; much less for woman, to whom it brings shame even to reflect of what nature she is."[35]

It was suitable, then, for bishops (like Clement and Tertullian) to observe a spartan diet and abstain from sex in order to maintain control over themselves as well as over the "weaker" members of their own dioceses. Attempts to regulate the behavior of women, now associated with a tainted bodiliness, became a primary concern. A tendency in this direction was already present in some New Testament texts, but it was balanced by Paul's willingness to work with women and by the emphasis on spiritual equality in John's Gospel. Unfortunately, the first-century freedom of Christian women in house churches and even as missionaries decreased as local churches came under the control of bishops. Most of those responsible for organization and management were men who sought order, an institutional emphasis already reflected in the New Testament Letters to Timothy:

> men should pray, lifting up holy hands, without anger or argument. Similarly, [too,] women should adorn themselves with proper conduct, with modesty and self-control, not with braided hairstyles and gold ornaments, or pearls, or expensive clothes, but rather, as befits women who profess reverence for God, with good deeds. A woman must receive instruction silently and under complete control. I do not permit a woman to teach or to have authority over a man. She must be quiet. For Adam was formed first, then Eve. Further, Adam was not deceived, but the woman was deceived and transgressed. But she will be saved through motherhood, provided women persevere in faith and love and holiness, with self-control. (1 Timothy 2:8–15)

These attitudes reflect the influence of pagan Rome, in which men—as natural rulers—were to control their anger, while women were to control their minds, bodies, and behavior. The Letter to Titus, who was responsible for the development of the church in Crete, also endorsed the limited, private sphere as the only proper one for women's activities:

> older women should be reverent in their behavior, not slanderers, not addicted to drink, teaching what is good, so that they may train younger women to love their husbands and children, to be self-controlled, chaste, good homemakers, under the control of

their husbands, so that the word of God may not be discredited. (1 Titus 2:3–5)

One of the reasons why church leaders insisted on controlling women was to deflect the anger of powerful pagans who saw their wives and daughters escaping their control under the influence of Christianity. Understandably, bishops did not want the church to be discredited just as it was gaining greater acceptance in the wider world of paganism. The fact that many women, despite the restrictions on them, saw Christianity as an attractive alternative to the official religion dramatizes the degree of misogyny in the empire. Paul's declaration in Galatians remained a stirring ideal: "There is neither Jew nor Greek, there is neither slave nor free person, there is not male and female; for you are all one in Christ Jesus" (Galatians 3:28). Women and slaves readily embraced the new faith, while male heads of household, holding positions of power and authority in a society in which the family was part of the state, were often the last to be converted. Religious conversion in a poor family usually caused little trouble, but when—as happened often—a middle- or upper-class woman converted, her husband might be angry enough to appeal to the authorities against her.

The second-century pagan Celsus intended to insult Christianity when he called it a religion of women, children, and slaves. Church leaders sought to modify the scorn of such writers and the anger of pagan rulers by advising obedience in all things—men to the state, women to their husbands. Elisabeth Schüssler Fiorenza points out that this strategy of the official church transformed its original message of good news to the poor into one of private asceticism accompanied by social behavior acceptable to the pagan world. To distinguish itself from the wider pagan culture, the church emphasized other forms of liberation; readiness for martyrdom and acceptance of sexual continence now became the hallmarks of Christianity.

Because martyrdom was the outstanding sign of faithfulness in the first centuries of the church, Mary could not be its most visible symbol. Women willing to become martyrs were considered to have "become male"; martyrdom was a sacrifice in which they could distinguish themselves as readily as men. Only after persecution ceased could ordinary Christians appreciate Mary's sufferings as another kind of martyrdom; for the present, their model would be someone like Polycarp, the second-century bishop of Smyrna, who was put to death in the amphitheater before a cheering crowd.

The centrality of martyrdom as the model of Christian holiness also widened the split with Gnosticism, because many Gnostics did not accept martyrdom as a valid form of witness. In their emphasis on a purely spiritual Jesus, some questioned whether he suffered at all during the Crucifixion; they argued that what he asked of his followers was not martyrdom but enlightenment. Nevertheless, the example of the martyrs powerfully impressed the Roman world and contributed to the growth of the church. Tertullian and Justin, for example, were both pagans who became converts after they witnessed the heroism of Christians being burned, beaten, and devoured by wild animals. They saw the attitude of Gnostics as an insult to those who gave up their lives so bravely. Irenaeus, a disciple of Polycarp's who was himself later martyred, was infuriated at the Gnostics, since many of his flock at Lyons had been brutally put to death.

A twenty-two-year-old Carthaginian Christian mother, Perpetua, has left us a journal that she wrote in prison while she awaited martyrdom along with several others in 203. (An anonymous editor, perhaps Tertullian, provided an introduction and conclusion to the text.) In the first of several visions she had there, she saw herself facing a ladder; a dragon lay underneath, trying to prevent the Christian prisoners from going up. "I trod on his head," she tells us. She was then able to climb to the garden above, where an old shepherd gave her sweet milk from his sheep that she could still taste when she awoke. She knew then that she must suffer, and "began to have no hope in this world."[36]

Her pagan father begged Perpetua not to destroy her life as well as her family by rashly bearing public witness to Christianity. Although she grieved for him and realized that he spoke out of love, her answer was that God must decide. The procurator Hilarion urged her: "Offer a sacrifice for the safety of the Emperors." When she refused, she tells us in her journal, "he passed sentence on the whole of us, and condemned us to the beasts; and in great joy we went down into the prison."[37] Miraculously, her breasts were no longer engorged, the baby she had brought with her to prison no longer needed her milk, and Perpetua commended him to her mother's and brother's care.

The night before she was to be killed, she had a final dream-vision in which the deadly games were about to begin in the amphitheater. Evil men came forward to fight, but attendants came to help her, oiling her down for the combat. The male-centeredness of the age comes through poignantly in her simple statement: "And I was stripped and was changed into a man." In her dream, she overcame her adversaries in battle, and a mysterious stranger handed her a green bough with golden apples. Awakening, she realized that her struggle was not "with beasts but with the Devil"; but, she wrote, "I knew the victory to be mine."[38]

The editor of Perpetua's journal added details of her actual martyrdom along with that of the slave Felicitas, who had just given birth to a baby. Both Perpetua and Felicitas refused to put on the garment of the goddess Ceres and were led into the arena. After the male martyrs were killed by bears and leopards, a mad heifer was chosen to kill the women. Although Perpetua was in such ecstasy that she seemed hardly aware of her pain, she remained, the editor notes, "mindful of her modesty," covering her thighs with her torn tunic and asking for a pin to fasten her disordered hair. Such concerns seem totally foreign to the woman who had recorded her conflicts and dreams so vividly. Her editor tells us that when the beasts did not succeed in killing her, she guided the uncertain sword of the gladiator to her own throat. "Perhaps so great a woman," he comments, "who was feared by the unclean spirit, could not otherwise be slain except she willed."[39] Within the bounds of orthodox control, a woman might be praised for a strong will and even for her visions, but she should still pay attention to the modesty of her appearance.

As we have seen in the Odes of Solomon, a virginal Mary was said to "have brought forth [Jesus] like a strong man with desire." Both Perpetua and Mary could be considered heroic by Greco-Roman Christians because their strong wills had made them like men. And despite the absence of records of women's devotion to Mary, she may well have been a source of strength to them, even to Perpetua. Her example, however, would more likely have encouraged the other path Christian women could take to gain self-determination: the life of a committed virgin. It, too, would permit women to elude the household control of husbands and "become male."

Illustrations of this life were prevalent in the popular Christian fiction that began to develop in the second century, featuring adventurous women leading heroic lives of celibacy. Seven such apocryphal Acts of the Apostles emerged among the Hellenistic communities of the Eastern Mediterranean. Some scholars suggest that these stories not only indicate that real women chose chastity as a way to control their own lives as religious beings, but that the hearers and quite possibly the authors of these stories were women.[40]

Evidence exists that groups of women vowed to virginity lived in community before Antony of Egypt devoted himself to a life of ascetic denial in 270. Widows who did not remarry already held an honored place in Christian circles, carrying out ministries of prayer and service to other women in the church. Women married to pagans, however, were in a difficult position if they felt called to the chaste lives Christian leaders urged upon them. Mygdonia in the apocryphal Acts of Thomas turns away from her husband, but the apostle urges her to return to him. Like the other women in these stories, however, she puts her religious ideal first. These popular romances celebrate celibacy, not marriage. Their heroines refuse to marry or, if married, to have relations with their husbands; they travel, dress in male clothes, and ultimately succeed in their mission to become preachers and teachers on their own terms. It seems most likely that they, like real women of the time, were not trying to "become male," but rather to lead lives free of the patriarchalism of the surrounding culture. Orthodox teaching told them that they were equal in spirit, but society gave them no way to be so.

One of the most popular of these heroines of continence was Thecla. The Acts of Paul and Thecla, a section of the longer Acts of Paul, tells the story of this virgin of Iconium, who sat by her window to hear the apostle Paul preach outside. She "listened night and day to the word of the virgin life as it was spoken by Paul" until her worried mother begged her fiancé Thamyris to come and speak to her. Thamyris's approach, however, lacked appeal: "Turn to thy Thamyris and be ashamed."[41] Self-abnegation was no match for the religious heroism Paul demanded. Thinking her bewitched, Thamyris plotted to have Paul brought before the governor and put in prison.

Late at night, however, Thecla bribed the gatekeeper with her bracelets, and the jailor with a silver mirror, so that she could listen to Paul in prison. "And her faith was also increased, as she kissed his fetters." Both she and Paul had to suffer for their convictions. Paul was scourged, while Thecla was sentenced to be burned in public for not marrying Thamyris "according to the law of the Iconians." Even her own mother cried out, "Burn the lawless one. Burn her who is no bride in the midst of the theatre, that all women who have been taught by this man [Paul] may be afraid!"

As Thecla was brought naked into public view, the governor wept and marveled at the power in her. She climbed on the pyre, making the sign of the cross, but the flames did not touch her. Released, Thecla begged Paul to baptize her, but he refused, counseling patience. Nevertheless she followed him to Antioch, where her trials continued. A Syrian tried to buy her and even force her to have sex with him—any female wandering about freely was assumed to be a loose woman. When she defied him, she was again brought before a governor.

At this point, Thecla began to acquire female support—a development that probably represents the sentiment not only of the wealthy women characters in the tale, but also of its tellers and hearers. Tryphaena, a queen who had lost her own daughter, embraced Thecla. When the governor condemned Thecla to the beasts, "the women were panic-stricken and cried out before the judgment-seat: 'An evil judgment, a godless judgment.' " Even the lioness gave up her life fighting other beasts to save her.

Somehow the indomitable Thecla managed to baptize herself in the stadium. Flinging herself into a great pit of water filled with what the text calls carnivorous seals, she exclaimed: "In the name of Jesus Christ I baptize myself on the last day!" The seals died immediately and a cloud of fire covered her nakedness. More ferocious animals were let loose—to no avail. When the governor asked Thecla why the beasts would not destroy her, she replied in Marian paraphrase, "I am a handmaid of the living God." Impressed, he had her clothed and released. At this point "all the women cried out in a loud voice and as with one mouth gave praise to God, saying, 'One is God, who has delivered Thecla!,' so that all the city was shaken by the sound." Much amazed, Paul finally acknowledged her call: "Go and teach the word of God!"

Although this story and its heroine are generally considered fictitious, Thecla has long been honored as a saint. When the European (probably Spanish) nun Etheria made a pilgrimage to

Constantinople and the Holy Land in the fourth century, she wrote in her diary that she visited the beautiful church of St. Thecla outside Seleucia, and that "the whole of the acts of St. Thecla" were read at the monastery there.[42] Perpetua also became famous in the West—Augustine's sister was named after her—but it is Thecla, not Perpetua, who caught the popular imagination and became a model of future holiness. Methodius, a third-century Christian teacher on the southwest coast of Turkey, even composed a dialogue based on Plato's *Symposium* in which Thecla replaced Socrates at the banquet; the guests were ten virgins who came together to celebrate the only "fecund union," that of Christ and the church. The supporting chorus of women in Thecla's story suggests that her bravery appealed to many women who now saw celibacy as the only path to a religious life of their own in the Greco-Roman Christian church.

Is it possible to determine what women who became martyrs or who committed themselves to lives of celibacy thought of Mary? Did they invoke her name in prayer as they fought their battles and endured their trials? Thecla's reply to the governor that she was the "handmaid of the living God"—a repetition of Mary's words at the Annunciation—suggests that some of these women did derive strength from Mary's example. The Odes of Solomon called Mary a woman of power; Irenaeus and Origen saw her as an intercessor and mediator on behalf of all believers. True, neither the uniquely obedient Mary of the early Fathers' Eve-Mary theology nor the popular Virgin Mother of legend was a model that most women could follow in life. But her obedience to divine, not human, rule undoubtedly made her a source of comfort and strength to many women who had to resist human law and church pressure in order to respond to their own religious calling.

THE QUESTIONS OF BARTHOLOMEW

The apocryphal Questions of Bartholomew, in which Mary figures prominently, sums up the mysterious gaps and contradictions that accompany the evidence of Mary's presence in the church of the first three centuries. This work is related to a missing Gospel of Bartholomew, known to be a third-century popular narrative reflecting Gnostic as well as ancient Egyptian thinking.[43] I find the Questions of Bartholomew inspiring, mysterious, and at times oddly if unintentionally comic.

The story it tells takes place after the Resurrection. The apostles want to ask Mary "how she conceived the incomprehensible . . . or how she bore so much greatness." But they are not sure who should speak first. Bartholomew says it ought to be Peter, because he is their chief. Peter says John should ask the question because he is chaste. Bartholomew abruptly speaks up on his own and questions the "highly favored tabernacle of the Most High."

Mary replies: "Do not ask me concerning this mystery. If I begin to tell you, fire will come out of my mouth and consume the whole earth" (p. 543). Since the apostles insist, however, she has them all rise and pray. Again they argue politely about who should go first: Mary says Peter should because the Lord said that the head of the man is Christ, but the head of the woman is the man. Peter replies, "In you the Lord set his tabernacle and was pleased to be contained by you." The document continues in this vein, with deferential biblical and poetic compliments at each step of the way revealing contemporary tensions and differences of opinion among believers.

Mary finally agrees to pray before them, and starts by recalling the greatness of Creation—how God brought order from chaos, separated light from dark, caused the waters to flow, and nourished the creatures of the earth and air: "Who didst give to the earth its place and didst not wish it to perish, bestowing upon it abundant rain and caring for the nourishment of all things." Her powerful affirmation of creation is followed by a kind of third-century Magnificat: "The seven heavens could scarcely contain thee, but thou wast pleased to be contained in me, without causing me pain, thou who art the perfect Word (Logos) of the Father, through whom everything was created" (p. 544).

Then Mary relates, as if from her own experience, James's apocryphal account of her early life in the temple and the visit of the angel. But in her version the angel strikes the right side of his garment and produces a large loaf, which he places on the altar of the temple. The angel eats first; then, she says, "gave to me also." This pattern is repeated with a cup of wine: "And I looked and saw that the bread did not diminish and the cup was full as before." This reminder of the loaves and fishes that did not diminish as the earthly Jesus fed the hungry crowd is overlaid with the suggestion that the Eucharist has similar, continuing power to feed the spirit. Mary is here both prophet and symbol of the church, one who preaches the life-giving power of Jesus and its continuation in the chief sacrament of the church.[44]

As she speaks to the apostles, fire does come from her mouth, and it seems as if the world is about to be consumed. Jesus arrives quickly and tells her to say no more. He takes the apostles and Mary to a mountain and sits among them, telling them to ask anything they want from him because in seven days he must ascend to the Father. Again Mary and the apostles go through their elaborate routine as to who should speak first, she stressing that Peter is the rock on which the church is built, Peter insisting that she is the tabernacle of God. Mary responds that Peter is the image of Adam, who was created before Eve, who sinned: "In me the Lord took up his abode, that I might restore the dignity of women" (p. 545–6). But Peter insists: "You made good the transgression of Eve, changing her shame to joy. So you ought to ask."

At the end, Bartholomew breaks out into a paean of praise to Mary:

> "O womb more spacious than a city! O womb wider than the
>   span of heaven!
> O womb that contained him whom the seven heavens do not
>   contain. You
> contained him without pain and held in your bosom him who
>   changed his
> being into the smallest of things."
> (p. 547)

This prayer reveals deep reverence for Mary, with none of the fear that Latin-speaking church Fathers exhibited regarding the significance of her motherhood. The courteous exchanges between Mary and Peter show Mary not only undoing the traditional disobedience assigned to Eve, but also restoring Eve's and all women's dignity.

The strange drama contained in the Questions of Bartholomew seems to sum up the contradiction in the attitude of the early church to Mary: divided between its awe at her role in the Incarnation and its own need to regulate women and to guard against goddess worship. But as Raymond Brown has observed, "The great anomaly of Christianity is that only through institution can the message of a non-institutional Jesus be preserved."[45] An inevitably imperfect church should never be confused with the kingdom of God; in this period, while laying the foundation for an enduring institution, it also accepted many of the ideas and attitudes of Greco-Roman culture. Such enculturation is reflected in the image of Mary it presented. Jesus and his mother were being de-Judaized in a Gentile world while popular religion added miraculous events and powers to the simple Gospel story.

As understanding of Mary grew in this church, her presence remained complex and impossible to control. The mysterious Questions of Bartholomew, like the earlier Odes of Solomon and the popular legends about Mary, show that some, possibly many, believers prayed to a Mary intimately related to their inner lives. While some Christian thinkers kept her role to a minimum, others already found it central to the revelation of Jesus in body, spirit, and in the public worship of the Eucharist. These seemingly contradictory attitudes would come together into a single symbol only in the late fourth century, after the church emerged from the era of persecution and entered into a new relationship with Roman society.

CHAPTER FOUR

TRIUMPH OF THE CHURCH, EMERGENCE OF THE GOD-BEARER

(313–431 C.E.)

Mary . . . was a pure Virgin, with a harmonious disposition. . . . She did not want to be seen by men. . . . She remained continually at home, living a retired life and imitating a honeybee. . . . She generously distributed to the poor what was left over from the work of her hands. . . . She prayed to God, alone to the alone, intent on two things: not to let a bad thought take root in her heart and to grow neither bold nor hard of heart. . . . Her speech was recollected and her voice low.

—ATHANASIUS, Letter to the Virgins[1]

"Come, all you who have discernment,
vocal advocates of the Spirit,
prophets who beheld hidden things
in your true visions;
you farmers who sowed seed, and slept in hope,
rise up and rejoice at the harvest: look, in my arms
I clasp the wheat-sheaf of life
that provides bread for the hungry,
that feeds the needy. Rejoice with me, for I carry
the sheaf full of joys."

—EPHREM OF SYRIA[2]

I<small>N THE LAST THIRD OF THE FOURTH CENTURY, A COHERENT</small>
figure of Mary began to emerge from the disparate strands of theology and devotion that marked earlier centuries of Christianity. No longer a Jewish mother or an obedient daughter of the Greco-Roman church, she became the God-Bearer, adorned with regal honor and biblical imagery, capable of evoking reassuring memories of an earlier feminine divinity in the vast popular unconscious. After a stormy period of religious and political infighting, a strong, unified church, now allied with imperial power, proclaimed Mary as *Theotokos* (God-Bearer) at the Council of Ephesus in 431.

How did the humble Mary of Nazareth break through the hesitation of Western church leaders and become this officially sanctioned Virgin Mother? To examine how dramatic this change was and why it occurred, it is necessary to trace the results of the new relationship between church, emperor, and people that the triumph of Constantine initiated. This relationship formed the background against which art, popular devotion, and ultimately ecclesiastical approval would at last converge in honoring Mary as mother of God. For no such image of Mary was apparent when Constantine proclaimed his Edict of Toleration in 313, allowing Christianity to emerge from the shadow of persecution and become a visible public religion on an equal footing with paganism.

101

THE CONSTANTINIAN CHURCH

According to its historian, Eusebius, the fourth-century church was full of openness, variety, and enthusiasm. Eusebius had personally witnessed the martyrdom of his fellow biblical scholar Pamphilus in 310. As bishop of Caesarea, he saw Constantine's accession to power as part of God's plan in history, the fulfillment of the promise to Abraham. To Eusebius, the Roman Empire was part of God's providence, coming to dominance as it did at roughly the same time that Christ was born. When Constantine ended the persecution of Christians, he also made possible the triumph and expansion of the church.

> for those of us who had fixed our hopes on the Christ of God there was unspeakable happiness, and a divine joy blossomed in all hearts as we saw that every place that a little while before had been reduced to dust by the tyrant's wickedness was now, as if from a prolonged and deadly stranglehold, coming back to life.[3]

Much of the energy and wealth of the newly empowered bishops was in fact spent on building and decorating churches to signify and promote greater participation in this new life. Rome at the time was still two-thirds pagan, so Christianity vigorously entered the competition to win over the public imagination. As Paul had earlier used the image of the body and its members to convey the unity and variety of the church, Eusebius now chose the image of the new cathedral, its light reflecting "the clear light of truth in everyone," its stones the "human souls" who were its true foundation.[4]

Many new and different types of church buildings sprang up in this brief era of comparative peace throughout the empire, replacing the house churches of earlier centuries where small groups had gathered in private. Unlike pagan temples, which only the priest entered, the new basilicas were designed so that crowds could become involved in the liturgy, or public worship, of the church. Although most of these churches are today only ruins, eyewitness accounts and inventories indicate that they contained rich wall paintings, mosaics, and lavish displays of gold and silver.[5] The splendor of these churches served to instruct the new converts, conveying the underlying message that the Christian interpretation of life was at home in *this* world.

Constantine's soldiers had victoriously carried the cross of Christ on their military banners; since the focus of art was on the power of the adult Jesus, converts saw little of Mary in the basilicas. She was usually presented in the background, a mother with a baby, a woman standing among the apostles. The new visual language of Christianity appropriated both biblical and pagan imagery, reorienting it to express the new life Christ brought to the baptized. When worshipers celebrated the Eucharist on the Lord's Day, biblical images of this new life greeted their eyes through other figures: Moses striking water from the rock, Daniel being saved from the lions, Jonah emerging from the whale. The beauty of creation in all its forms, both natural (vines, peacocks, wild animals) and fanciful (satyrs and cupids) was incorporated into this inclusive Christian vision. The shepherd carrying the sheep on his shoulders represented philanthropy in Roman art; he became the Good Shepherd, Jesus. The Orante, a praying figure with arms upraised, was a Roman symbol of piety; many figures in this conventional pose, including Mary, now appeared on the walls of Christian catacombs (Plate 3).

These images were hopeful, even those in the catacombs, which conveyed a firm belief in future life. There were no scenes of the Crucifixion, which, as Paul had predicted, was still a scandal to the Jews and foolishness to the Greeks. There were as yet few feast days—even Christmas was not established until the mid–fourth century, when it was strategically placed at what had been the pagan feast day of the Sun. The reported concerns of one bishop in the previous century give us some insight into the

way a wise pastor tried to adapt pagan customs in order to ease
converts into the new religion. Gregory the Wonderworker, the
same third-century bishop of Pontus who had received the first
reported vision of Mary, tried to lessen the strain on those who
accepted the yoke of the faith by turning the sober memorializa-
tion of the deaths of martyrs into social occasions like picnics,
with food and music. The point of the change was clear in the description by Gregory of Nyssa:

> as he saw that the raw and ignorant multitude adhered to idols on
> account of bodily pleasure, he permitted the people—so as to se-
> cure the most vital matters, i.e., the direction of their hearts to
> God instead of to a vain worship—he permitted them to enjoy
> themselves at the commemoration of the holy martyrs, to take
> their ease, and to amuse themselves.[6]

Later in the fourth century, when Bishop Ambrose of Milan
told the newly baptized that they were anointed as athletes of
Christ—"You contend in the world, but you are crowned by
Christ"[7]—he was metaphorically adapting a pagan custom reserved for gods, athletes, and the male dead, in order to emphasize the quality of spirit and hope of everlasting life open to
everyone who was baptized. It was part of a successful cultural
transformation that has endured to our own day, visible in our
springtime custom of crowning statues of Mary.

Such adaptation of pagan ways to Christian purposes was the
beginning of a long process that would see Ambrose—and later
other bishops—succeed in turning the saints into patrons and establishing church altars and cemeteries as the proper depositories
of their powerful relics.[8] These strategies, like the art of the basilicas, motivated converts to become part of an inclusive church
that turned the "foolishness" of Jesus into an appealing new
power they could share.[9]

More than any of the other artistic images, that of Jesus himself best conveyed the new life and freedom of the early fourth-

century church. Since no physical description or painted image of the historical Jesus existed, he could be imagined in countless ways, all emphasizing that the power he represented was real but different from that of the emperor or the old gods. Jesus emerged at this turning point in history as a light to the Gentiles, with little surviving hint of the earlier Rabbi.[10] He was the healer, the magician, and finally the Lord who replaced all the gods in the pantheon.[11] He was depicted in ordinary clothes, often carrying a scroll in one hand to show he was a philosopher (a respected role in this world). Frequently he carried a wand to indicate that his magic was stronger than that of eastern and pagan competitors, since magic was very important in the ancient world. Defending Jesus against the charges of Celsus that Christ's miracles were in fact magic, Origen in effect agreed that he was a superior magician, one who made permanent cures and conversions without spells and took no money for his work.[12] It is understandable, therefore, that the miracles of Jesus became a primary subject of fourth- and fifth-century art.[13] On sarcophagi, Moses, too, is shown as a magician, holding up his wand as he leads the Israelites through the Red Sea.

This emphasis on magic also led to the great popularity of the scene depicting the Adoration of the Magi, representatives of Gentile nations who had come to acknowledge the power of Jesus. This was the chief scene in which Mary appeared on fourth-century sarcophagi, seated on a wicker chair with the child on her knees, accepting their gifts. The gold, frankincense, and myrrh that the Magi brought were understood, by Origen and others, as materials associated with their role as magicians. In this way Mary became an integral part of a story which signified that this divine child had come for all people, not only the Jews.

But in most instances when Jesus was shown, he was not presented as a child. This Gentile Jesus was portrayed with characteristics like those of the God of Mary's Magnificat. He was a healing figure among the vulnerable for whom he cared. A beardless young man in a Roman toga, he was shown curing the woman with an issue of blood or raising Lazarus from the dead. In addition, the image of Christ as it appeared in different churches, and often within a single church, was truly polymorphous. He might be old or young, bearded or beardless; at times he looked surprisingly androgynous. In many sculptures depicting his triumphant entry into Jerusalem he rode sidesaddle, as no Roman man would—it was a woman's position. From the middle of the fourth century to the early years of the sixth, a number of examples of a feminine Christ appeared in Gaul, Rome, Ravenna, and Thessalonica.[14] His androgyny could be taken as a symbolic expression of Paul's point that the sexes were reconciled in Christ. It might also reflect the early Jesus tradition of belief in the Wisdom of God or Sophia, represented in feminine form. Jesus probably understood himself as Sophia's prophet, and the earliest Palestinian interpretations of his life and death were as Sophia's messenger and later as Sophia herself.[15] In any case, this immense diversity of representation made Christ accessible to women as well as to men, and would probably have pleased the real Mary. To ordinary believers, it was more richly suggestive of his person than the creedal definitions that would be hammered out throughout the century.

Mary herself was visible in art only where she complemented this reconstruction of meaning, as in her necessary presence in the scene with the Magi. But though she appeared rarely in the mosaics and paintings of fourth-century churches, she became increasingly important after 313 as a new model of Christian behavior. The Constantinian alliance of church and state brought secular responsibilities as well as privileges to ecclesiastical officeholders. There were obvious advantages for the church as an institution in the new relationship, for bishops and priests now gained tax and inheritance benefits earlier limited to pagan priests. Inevitably, some ecclesiastical officeholders took on the attributes of bureaucrats rather than of priests. Partly as a reaction, individuals anxious to exercise a more heroic religious life turned to asceticism and sexual renunciation, which were by now well established in the church. Eusebius, for instance, spoke of two ways of life pleasing to the Lord: dedicated virginity, which was "above nature," and marriage, which was "more humble." "More humble" was the highest praise marriage and childbearing received from the institutional church in this period. Even in his eulogy of the open church Eusebius stressed its "many-blossomed ornament of chastity and temperance." In this church, Mary would take on a role the real woman of Nazareth could hardly have imagined.

MARY: MODEL OF VIRGINITY

From the second century on, small groups of Christian men and women committed to sexual renunciation scattered throughout the eastern Mediterranean as missionaries of celibacy. Filled with a sense that the end of the world was near, they wanted to halt the cycle of procreation and live a more radical freedom by renouncing married life. In 285, Antony of Egypt, who had earlier given away all his possessions and committed himself to a life of prayerful celibacy, retired completely from "the world" into the desert to achieve a disciplined life of holiness. By 400 c.e., some five thousand monks had followed his example, entering the desert on both sides of the Nile, fleeing the worldliness that accompanied the church's collaboration with imperial power. Many women as well as men chose this path.

As the enthusiasm for permanent sexual renunciation grew, it won over bishops like Athanasius, Basil, and Augustine, who decided to give these monks some direction; the result was the development of the first rules for monastic communities. This official advocacy of celibacy as a way of life distinguished Christianity sharply from both paganism and Judaism. Lifelong commitment to virginity on a massive scale was scandalous to pagans. Vestal virgins had been sacred in Rome because they were exceptions. They did not choose to serve; they were elected, and their term was limited. It was something quite different for the church to present the virgin as the ideal Christian. And as the celibate life was increasingly praised by church leaders, it in turn shaped their understanding of Mary. Her lifelong virginity was claimed as fact by Ambrose. Augustine would add that Mary had made a vow of virginity in childhood; he was the first among Latin-speaking Fathers to do so.

Even the renowned biblical scholar Jerome let his assumptions about virginity extend beyond the Gospel testimony. His thinking about Mary was honed in controversy with Helvidius, a theologian who defended marriage and virginity as equally valuable ways to lead a Christian life. Helvidius declared Mary a perfect model of virginity before the birth of Christ, and of married love and motherhood after—a position acceptable in many Christian circles then and today. Jerome employed his formidable biblical learning and polemical talent to argue not only for Mary's perpetual virginity but for Joseph's as well. He scorned the suggestion in the Book of James that Joseph was a widower, insisting that "He who deserved to be called the father of the Lord remained a virgin together with Mary."[16] Contemporary exegete John McKenzie says that such thinking seems to make human judgment the final criterion of what it is proper for God to do. In the absence of historical evidence, Jerome and others substituted their own ideas of theological propriety. Since it was "fitting" for God to have such a virginal mother and father, therefore it was true. McKenzie finds a kind of Gnosticism in this attitude of the Fathers, which seems to identify sexuality with sin.[17]

Part of the reason why childbearing was not considered an admirable calling for women by fourth-century Western Fathers was that they shared the widespread apocalyptic expectation that the end of the world was near. Jerome insisted that there was no need for more children; Augustine pointed out that there were already enough pagans who needed to be converted to keep all Christians busy. Belief that the final days were at hand, however, somehow managed to coexist with efforts to solidify the church's earthly structures.

Increasingly, for fourth-century spiritual leaders, Mary became the perfect model for the behavior of cloistered virgins. The popular themes of her life in legend made it easy to present her as a heroine of the new asceticism. In the process, however, the Fathers read into Scripture their own androcentric assumptions about human nature and the body, greatly changing the meaning of Mary's virginity and minimizing the value of her humanity. The evangelists' emphasis on the intervention of God in the birth of Jesus was exaggerated in such a way as to make Mary's role passive, as woman's role in conception was understood to be in the gynecology of the period. A Coptic document included among the proverbs of the Council of Nicaea (325) shows the extent of male clerical fantasy in this process. "A wise virgin resembles Mary," it says, who preserved her virginity "like a precious treasure" despite giving birth:

> Mary never saw the face of a strange man, that was why she was confused when she heard the voice of the angel Gabriel. . . . She ate and slept only enough to keep alive and withdrew to her mother's house where she faced East and prayed continuously, refusing to see her brothers, living among angels. . . . When she put on a garment she used to shut her eyes. . . . For she did not know many things of this life, because she remained far from the company of men. . . . If, therefore, a girl wants to be called a virgin, she should resemble Mary.[18]

Confusing ignorance with innocence, such advice would leave a woman dangerously open to abuse, deceit, and violence in everyday life. It would also incapacitate her to carry out the work of mothering in the real world or educate a child to maturity.

Hilda Graef, the usually reserved historian of Marian doctrine, observes that "Mary is here portrayed not as she appears in Scripture, but as the ideal of the fourth-century consecrated virgin, who always stayed at home and prayed, meticulously guarded against any masculine society, whereas the Mary of the Gospels did not hesitate to visit her cousin Elizabeth, went up to the Temple for the feasts and generally behaved like a normal Jewish girl of her time."[19]

It is astonishing to hear Athanasius of Alexandria, the great champion of orthodoxy, describe Mary in his Letter to the Virgins as a perfect model because "she did not want to be seen by men. . . . She remained continually at home, living a retired life and imitating a honeybee." Such a portrait makes Mary an inhuman cipher with no concern in life except to bear and mourn her son. Much of what contemporary women resist in the symbol of Mary derives from this mistaken ideal, which robs her of subjectivity and removes her from the human context.

ADAM AND EVE AGAIN

In addition to reinterpreting Mary's virginity, influential Western Fathers amplified the differences between Mary and Eve in their new reading of the perennially significant story of Adam and Eve. Unfortunately, these interpretations tended to separate Mary further from ordinary women, most of whom did not choose a lifelong commitment to virginity and hence were seen as Eves. Ambrose, for example, in his treatise *On Paradise*, claimed that because Eve was created second, she was therefore inferior—made to be a helpmate for man, and important primarily for procreational purposes. He blamed Eve for the Fall: she sinned "with forethought, and knowingly made her husband a participant in her own wrongdoing." Adam "fell by his wife's fault, and not because of his own." Ambrose clearly equated Eve with all women, summed up as "woman," one in nature: "We can discern the sex which was liable first to do wrong. . . . The woman is responsible for the man's error and not vice versa." She is a sign of the senses, while "man" represents "our minds."[20]

Contemporary feminist biblical interpreters, with greater knowledge of the language, form, origin, and late editing of the Genesis text, read the same passages quite differently. To Phyllis Trible, for example, "helpmate" holds no connotation of inferiority, nor does Genesis 1–3 suggest that Eve is more responsible than Adam for eating the fruit of the tree of knowledge. The entire story is seen as a complex myth about God's relation to the world and human beings, one that does not pretend to account for "woman's nature" or focus on a particular human act in the past, but rather focuses on the need to be responsible for an inherently good creation. Nevertheless, the fourth-century understanding remains powerful: most of my college students, who represented a wide range of attitudes to religion, believed that the fourth-century interpretation represented the story itself.

Augustine drew even more frequently on the story of Adam and Eve, echoing some of the opinions of Ambrose. Even in Paradise, Eve existed to produce Adam's children. For "if it was company and good conversation that Adam needed, it would have been much better . . . to have two men together, as friends, not a man and a woman."[21]

In his *Confessions*, Augustine acknowledged his own struggle against sexual impulses throughout his early career and sought to explain the weakened state of the human will and its lusts as the effect of the Fall of our first parents. The Paradise he envisioned was one of calm and order, where rational joys reigned. If there had been sex in Paradise, Augustine speculated, it would have been a dispassionate sowing of seed without pleasure, desire, or the brutish willfulness of the sexual impulse.

In Augustine's eyes, Eve, and women in general, seem less than fully human. In common with most Christian male teachers of the time, he linked Eve's weakness, which led to her disobedience, with a dangerous tendency shared by all women, who thus became sources of temptation to sin. As he told a young man complaining of his mother's interference in his life, "Whether it is in a wife or a mother, it is still Eve [the temptress] that we must beware of in any woman."[22] Avoiding women seems to have been a powerful motivation for male spiritual development. After he became bishop of Hippo, Augustine lived a severe monastic life, never unchaperoned when he saw a woman, not allowing even his female relatives to visit him alone.

We gain insight into the roots of his reasoning in the *Confessions*, where his prayer of praise to the Lord for a good creation mirrors a separation between mind and matter, and the need for rational man to control woman, more liable to go astray because of her sex:

> we see man, made to Your image and likeness, that is by the power of reason and understanding; and just as in the human soul there is one element which takes thought and dominates, another which is subjected to obedience, so woman has been created corporeally for man: for though she has indeed a nature like that of man in her mind and rational intelligence, yet by her bodily sex she is subjected to the sex of her husband, much as appetite, which is the source or action, must be subjected to reason if it is to learn the rules of *right* action.[23]

In his world Augustine was not blamed for dismissing the concubine who had lived with him faithfully for fifteen years and who had borne him a son. His mother, Monica, represented the attitudes of both society and church in recommending such a move in order that he could make a more beneficial and "moral" first-class marriage with a Roman heiress. In book nine of his *Confessions*, Augustine tells us that the break made his heart bleed. He may well have loved this woman, but he does not express concern for her; we do not even learn her name.

When it came to the city of God, however, Augustine was able to set aside sexual distinctions. He did not hesitate to use the feminine image of Sophia for Jesus: "She is sent in one way that she may be with human beings; she has been sent in another way that she herself might be a human being" (*De Trinitate* 4.20.27). Were he living today, he would probably have realized earlier than most the parallel between equality and relationality in the Trinity and women's relational way of being in the world.[24] Like even the most brilliant among us, however, he was a person of his time; it is up to us to make the distinctions our culture makes possible without undervaluing earlier contributions.

Augustine's attitudes to human sex made the Virgin Birth supremely important, for it meant that Jesus was born without any of the taint of sin with which other human babies were afflicted. It also implied that Christians were potential members of a city of God, and hence could resist the pressures of social conformity that accompanied paganism in decline. Augustine's opinions on Mary, which were accepted despite their lack of clarity, represented the peak of Western Mariology.

A widening split between real women and the Fathers' views of an idealized Mary would also lie at the root of the representation of women in Western art, where Mary was almost never portrayed as a sexual being. She was always shown fully, often voluminously, clothed, except in the scenes in which she awkwardly but decorously nursed her child. Eve, on the other hand, was frequently portrayed as naked and voluptuous—and appropriately punished. Other influential images divided saintly women into two types as well: the virginal Mary and the repentant Magdalene. The latter is a remarkable transformation of the first witness of the Resurrection, the only woman all four evangelists mention by name. From close disciple in the group around Jesus, and visionary alternative to authority in the second and third centuries, Mary Magdalene was turned into a sexual sinner, her story conflated with that of several other women in the New

Testament.[25] Because she was seen as contrite, she could be used both to reinforce moral cautions to women and to express a range of emotions natural in one who repents. Historical theologian Margaret Miles says that Magdalene made "the perfect foil for the dignified restraint of the Virgin and a model with whom most people could readily identify."[26] The two became inseparable in medieval and Renaissance art depicting the Crucifixion, the Magdalene's flowing red hair and mobile gestures compensating for Mary's limited emotional and physical repertoire.

THE LIVES OF CHRISTIAN WOMEN

One cannot examine the changing attitudes to Mary at this time without also looking at the actual lives of women. The limitations placed on real women help us understand the implications of what was being taught about Mary. When we know that Athanasius praised Mary for "living a retired life and imitating a honeybee," we can readily anticipate what the possibilities for women might be in this period.

If you were a fourth-century woman and wanted to lead a dedicated Christian life, what could you do? Your best option was to be a consecrated virgin. Women willing to lead lives committed to celibacy no longer needed to struggle with their bishops, as Thecla had done, or go into the desert. They could stay at home, fully cloistered, like Ambrose's sister Marcellina. Bishops began to include women who did not want to marry in their official households. Such virgins brought honor and stability to the church and new wealth to the basilicas, to which they donated their possessions. In turn, they could live simple lives of prayer and service, largely to other women, without economic care. Equally important, choosing consecrated celibacy provided a sanctioned way to avoid total domination by a man. For Ambrose, these virgins were "like altars that touch their priests with holy awe."[27] Appealing to upper-class women to join their ranks, he and other church leaders painted lurid (but unfortunately true) pictures of the sorrows and pains women would undergo in marriage, submitting to the double curse of male domination and childbearing. As Ambrose put it, "She only that is married, not that is a virgin, is under the power of her husband. The virgin is free from all these things who has vowed her affection to the word of God."[28] Jerome was less restrained, referring to the sexual bondage of wives as "the vomit of marriage."[29]

Although fourth-century women who desired to live holy or even good lives had very restricted options, if they embraced celibacy and were also wealthy they had more opportunities. The young Spanish widow Melania, avoiding remarriage, supported a beleaguered monastery in Alexandria before settling in Jerusalem in 372, where she ruled a monastery of fifty virgins on the Mount of Olives. She helped bishops, monks, and pilgrims with the money her son sent from her estates, and chose two talented male ascetics as her friends and advisers. Another wealthy young widow from Constantinople, Olympias, managed to elude pressures to remarry but was forbidden even to talk to bishops or clergy in her palace until she was thirty. She then became a deaconess and her wealth was great enough to finance the projects of ambitious clerics as well as to permit bishops to aid the poor.[30]

If a woman were willing to accept voluntary celibacy and to hide her female attractiveness, she could even become a learned companion to a great clerical scholar. Take, for example, the studious Paula, whose friendship with Jerome is most instructive as to the rewards for women in such female-clerical alliances. Scholarly spiritual guides were supported largely by the patronage of women and were often looked on with great suspicion by jealous local bishops. Like many other patrician Roman women of the time, Paula thirsted for learning and found in Jerome the teacher she desired.

Despite his conventional antifeminine rhetoric, Jerome neither disliked nor avoided women, but spent a good deal of time with them, constantly exhorting them to virginity. If they were married, he urged them to chastity, comforting them with the thought that their children might yet be virgins, and that they themselves could look forward to the holy state of chaste widowhood when their husbands died.

Jerome maintained deep spiritual companionship with women who lived the ascetic, scholarly life he advocated. He counseled circles of aristocratic Roman women, offering to take over the complete education of their daughters if they would dedicate them to virginity and keep them completely secluded from an early age. He strongly advised that these young virgins not attend the public baths, where they might encounter the "revolting" spectacle of pregnant women.[31]

The women who followed his advice—like those who responded to the earlier call to martyrdom—gained their freedom. Virginity made them equal to men as souls if they could disguise and even disfigure their female bodies. Jerome's praise of Paula's beauty delineates this ideal:

> Of all the ladies in Rome, but one had power to subdue me and that one was Paula. She mourned and she fasted. She was squalid with dirt; her eyes were dim with weeping. . . . The Psalms were her only songs; the gospel her whole speech.[32]

Jerome saw nothing wrong in urging Paula to leave her family in Rome to join him in setting up a monastic community in Palestine, where he would remain for thirty-five years working on his Latin translation of the Bible—the Vulgate. "You must act against nature," the brilliant scholar urged her, and she sailed away from her home, her property, and her children, including an infant son. Paula's money paid for Jerome's library, his Hebrew lessons, and his stenographer, and she had enough left over to set up a convent in Bethlehem for other gentlewomen-exiles. These women copied and distributed biblical translations and commentaries, advised the male scholars, and often intervened in theological controversies. Jerome called Paula his superior in her knowledge of languages and Scripture. To his astonishment, she could read the Psalms out loud in Hebrew without an accent. Yet he advised her not to teach; that would have been immodest. And he was adamant that she and other women not write, convincing himself, if not us, that he was saving them from arduous polemics to serve a better cause: "Wasn't Mary, the Mother of God, able to write books in her own name? To avoid dishonoring her head by placing herself above men, she did not do so."[33]

Another option for a woman was to become a renowned spiritual guide like the older sister of Basil of Caesarea and Gregory of Nyssa. When their mother was in labor with this sister, Macrina, she had a vision of St. Thecla, and determined to let her daughter be what she herself had not been free to become, a consecrated virgin. Macrina was later visited in her convent at Annesi by men and women who valued her counsel. Gregory tells us that she represented the quiet, sacred center of life that he and the other great Cappadocian bishops—his brother Basil and Gregory of Nazianzus—were forced to neglect as they carried out their institutional duties and their active care of the poor.

Christian women like Paula seem to have accepted what they could not change, showing no trace of resentment, and living as fully as their money, strength, and imagination allowed. Retinues of great ladies visited the Holy Land, some to stay in convents. Seeking holiness, learning, friendship, and careers as counselors and administrators, they chose permanent sexual renunciation as the only way that allowed them to participate as equals in living and spreading the Christian faith.

Despite strong efforts to stop women from writing or speaking publicly, evidence suggests that they continued to maintain positions of influence in the church. Women must have been quite active or the fourth-century Apostolic Constitutions would not have bothered to insist that "We do not permit our women to teach in the church but only to pray and listen to those who teach." Of course, there is no way of knowing to what extent women actually followed the advice they received, since we cannot hear their voices; their writing has been lost or destroyed. Even the documentation of the great spiritual friendship between Jerome and Paula is one-sided; we have all his letters, but only one of hers.[34]

Yet groups of Christian widows and virgins multiplied, and the names and reputations of many have come down to us because of the respect in which they were held by men as well as women. The official church accepted their ministries to other women and to the poor. These women must have found in Christianity something better than society offered them. When marriages were so often loveless contracts offering wives almost no freedom and the near-certainty of continual childbearing, the regular company of intelligent, caring women would have had extra appeal. In addition, entering a community meant getting an education denied to other women. I suspect that the image of Mary that provided sustenance to them was not that of the honeybee, but rather the one that came from the apocryphal stories of Mary's childhood: the image of the young Mary studying in the temple.

The remarks of Epiphanius, a bishop of Salamis, reveal the underlying assumption of the time that regardless of what women did, they were lesser human beings. In his *Panarion* or Medicine Chest, a response to his fellow bishops' request for a complete list of heresies, Epiphanius mentions the Collyridians, a sect of women that flourished in Thracia and Upper Scythia. It is the only evidence of a Marian cult at the time.

Predictably, Epiphanius refers to their activities with contempt: "What happens is that certain women decorate a chair or square stool, spread out upon it a cloth, and on a certain day of the year put out bread and offer it in Mary's name. All partake of this bread." Epiphanius deplores the practice, not because it appears to echo the worship of the Great Goddess, but because no woman, not even Mary, should exercise priestly functions. Mary is "a chosen vessel, but a woman. Which of the prophets ever bade us worship a man, to say nothing of a woman? . . . let these women be silenced. Let them not say, we honor the Queen of Heaven."[35]

THE ARIAN HERESY AND MARIAN REVISIONING

The constant pressure of dissident groups within the church, however, exerted pressure that eventually pushed Mary's image in a more heavenly direction. A major element in this change was the necessity to respond to the challenge of Arius (250–336), a charismatic priest from Libya who claimed that Jesus was not fully divine—almost the opposite of earlier Gnostic beliefs. Constantine personally convened the first ecumenical council of bishops at Nicaea in 325 to settle the dispute, since he saw unity and order in the church as essential to order in the empire. Although some church Fathers were worried about the alliance with imperial power, they nevertheless drew on it to quell dissidents and preserve their authority. With the help of the persuasive young Alexandrian Athanasius, Nicaea condemned Arius's position, declaring that Christ was "of the same substance" as the Father.

Despite the agreement reached at the Council of Nicaea, Arian beliefs continued to divide the empire; it would take a century of maneuvering before they were finally defeated. The imperial presence was to continue at later councils such as Chalcedon (451), which promulgated the doctrine of the Incarnation, that God became enfleshed in Jesus. As the combat with the Arians continued, pressure on the Fathers to relate the humanity of Jesus more closely to his divinity made them stress his oneness with the Father in heaven from the beginning. All this made it logical to turn again to Mary, redefining her role to affirm that oneness. The Council of Constantinople (381) was the first to mention her in its creed. Against Arius, Athanasius, now bishop of Alexandria, insisted that Christ took his manhood from his "ever-virgin" mother and his Godhood from the Father.[36] Yet there was always the possibility that this distinction might seem to split him in two. The Greek Fathers who defended the single nature of Jesus preferred to speak of Mary as *Theotokos*, or God-Bearer, since that title implied the birth of the Word of God made flesh as a single, unified person. Although their emphasis was on the divine-human nature of the child, not on Mary's motherhood,[37] her role was thus seen as unique and central, as Irenaeus had pointed out some two hundred years before.

It took time for orthodox church factions to agree on the term *Theotokos* in the struggle against Arius. Ambrose developed a doctrine that yielded neither to the Arians nor to the followers of the Mother Goddess Cybele, whose worship still continued in Italian cities and was in fact encouraged during the short reign (361–363) of the pagan emperor Julian. Ambrose hardly ever used the term "God-Bearer" for fear Mary would be confused with Cybele, yet his Christmas hymn, composed to strengthen his people's faith against Arianism, proclaims: "Come, Redeemer of the nations, show forth the birth of the Virgin; let all the world marvel, such a birth befitted God."[38] Now that many noble women were attached to his basilica as virgins and patronesses, the influential bishop of Milan was beginning to use the power of tradition and office to develop a rich and positive view of Mary as symbol of the church. It is instructive to note that, unlike the earlier shapers of Eve-Mary thinking, none of the fourth-century Fathers criticized the Virgin. Like Ambrose, they did not wish to see failings in the Virgin Mother who symbolized the church.

Before Ambrose died, near the end of the century, Theodosius, the first emperor since Constantine who did not support Arianism, passed strict decrees against the practice of any pagan religion. In 380, he established Christianity as the official religion of the empire with a new edict: "And we require that those who follow this rule of faith should embrace the name of Catholic Christians, adjuring all others as madmen and ordering them to be designated as heretics." Such heretics would suffer "divine punishment" and "the vengeance of that power which we, by celestial authority, have assumed."[39]

Backed by imperial decree and no longer fearing competition from goddess worshipers, Ambrose began to apply biblical imagery to Mary in his sermons to an extent hitherto unknown in the Latin West. He envisaged her as patroness of the church, a model for male and female celibates. In his last years, he made her perpetual virginity the center of that representation, rejecting the view of the Milanese monk Jovinian, who claimed that Mary bore children after Jesus. Ambrose applied to her the words from Ezekiel 44:2, "This gate is to remain closed," the gate of the sanctuary. Like the church, Mary had become a virginal fortress.

To be fair to the Fathers, virginity is a many-sided concept. No doubt, it is an extreme commitment, not applicable to the wide mass of believers, and prone to unhealthy results when strongly and widely mandated. But it does not, as twentieth-century people tend to think, represent only sexual repression, or an attempt to counter "pagan" license, or the duality of body and spirit. In the fourth century it bore elements of nonviolent resistance to the social-familial control exercised by the Roman state, including its control of sexuality. The freedom that a conscientious choice of virginity provided was also a commitment to a wider, nonbiological family dedicated to Christ. Virginity can thus be understood as an attempt to live out Jesus' distinction between biological families and those "families" that heard the word of God and kept it.

Ambrose's understanding of Mary as a symbol of the church and Augustine's reiteration of this idea laid the foundation for Marian thinking in the Catholic West. "Whence, I ask you, is

Mary the mother of Christ, if not because she gave birth to the members of Christ?"[40] Augustine wanted to preserve the freedom and inclusiveness of the church suggested by its open architecture, its art, and its accessible Jesus. Despite his preference for virginity, he told his nuns not to scorn their married counterparts, for they, too, could be holy. Nevertheless he felt it necessary to call on the force of the state to put down heresy, and a note of control rather than freedom pervades his apostrophe to the church he loved so dearly:

> It is you who make wives subject to their husbands . . . by chaste and faithful obedience; you set husbands over their wives; you join sons to their parents by a freely granted slavery and set parents above their sons in pious domination. . . . And you it is who warn the peoples to be subservient to their kings.[41]

Augustine's emphasis on the need for domination in all relationships was rooted in his pessimism about nature and the human will, and it colored his otherwise trenchant observations about Mary and the church. "The truth of Christ is in the mind of Mary," he reminds us; "greater is what she bears in her mind than in her womb."[42] This is a distinction feminists have made their own today. In the overall context of Augustine's thought, however, it seems to separate the physical from the spiritual and to emphasize the need for hierarchy rather than cooperation between them. Control and rule are necessary because, in Augustine's view, every birth except that of Christ and Mary—the latter an exception "out of honor to the Lord"—is marked by the effects of sin, a clouded mind and a defective will, which only grace can overcome. Among these foundational Western Fathers, then, the "good news" to humanity took on tones of hierarchy and subservience quite different from the joyous noises heard by the shepherds at Bethlehem. But when Augustine distinguished between Mary's womb and her mind, he was also suggesting the complexity of this Virgin Mother as a symbol of a church that unites both flesh and spirit in the new dispensation of the city of God.

EPHREM AND THE EASTERN MARIAN TRADITION

Although her position in the Western church was ambivalent, Mary was always central to the good news celebrated in the art and devotion of Eastern Christianity. Very early popular traditions in the East had created enduring legends of Mary's life. She was venerated there in liturgical worship, which developed with the same exuberant freedom as early fourth-century art. Eusebius called her a prophetess inspired by the Holy Spirit; he did not hesitate to describe her as *panagia*, or "all-holy." A feast called the Commemoration of Mary existed in the East even before the Council of Ephesus; it was celebrated in many places on the Sunday before Christmas.

Among the great Cappadocian Fathers—Basil of Caesarea, Gregory of Nyssa, and Gregory of Nazianzus—it was natural to express creedal beliefs in imaginative forms that complemented and enriched doctrinal statements. To the Eastern mind, the most fundamental image of the Father was the Son. All other images reflected and participated in this basic image-making within the Trinity, Mary most of all. Basil, the founder and legislator of Eastern monastic life, was also a champion of visual art for the purpose of teaching. "Arise now before me, you iconographers of the saints' merits," he exhorted, believing that writing and painting both transmitted the word of God, one to the ear, the other to the eye.[43]

The Cappadocians thought of Mary's virginity more as a metaphor of human purity than as literal physical intactness. Although Basil revered virginity and taught that Mary was ever-virgin, in his homily on the birth of Christ he insisted that "virginity should be honored, but marriage not despised." His brother, Gregory of Nyssa, went further; he was married, and thought that only those weak of will should be celibate, since the highest rank in virtue belonged to the person who could combine lower and higher good in "right ordering."[44] He revered holy women, including his own mother and sister, as well as those of his friend, Gregory of Nazianzus, all of whom he called virgins. Building on the mystical, devotional traditions of Alexandria and Syria, these men expressed themselves in language which showed a deep devotion to Mary as central to the life of the church.

Some have attributed this language, which found its way into Byzantine liturgy, to their meeting with Ephrem of Syria (c.306–373), the first great poet and musician of Marian devotion and the father of liturgical music. Whether or not such a meeting took place, examining Ephrem's work is the best way to grasp the theological mind-set shared by Byzantine and Orthodox liturgy with their distinctive emphasis on Mary.[45] His work is not widely known, since much of the material has only recently been translated from the Syriac. Yet in the third and fourth centuries, Syriac was the third international language of Christianity—after Greek and Latin—and it was used in missionary work in Persia, Armenia, Georgia, India, and Ethiopia. The availability of Ephrem's work today gives us access to an influential stream of Marian tradition outside the influence of Greco-Roman thought.

Ephrem was a biblical exegete and poet-theologian who found definitions of the holy dangerous and even blasphemous, since they had a deadening effect on what he thought should be a continuing human search for God. He worked through symbol and paradox to stimulate the thinking necessary for such a search: "The Establisher of all entered in his richness but came forth poor; the Exalted one entered her, but came forth meek" (Nativity 11:7).[46] Although Ephrem saw the gap between Creator and created as a "chasm," he believed we could come to discern the divine through the types and symbols in which God has made revelations. Because the Incarnation was the chief place of such self-revelation, "whatever we say in praise of the Mother touches the Son, and when we honor the Son we detract nothing from the Mother's glory."[47] Ephrem's use of images was rooted in his belief in the Incarnation: Creation gave birth to Christ in symbols as Mary did in the flesh.[48] He encouraged us to follow the example of Mary, whose "luminous eye" saw all things clearly; we should all seek types and symbols to express our glimpses of the divine.

Ephrem's ideas, which he extended to words and music, lie behind the Orthodox creation and defense of icons as revelatory objects. He is the living example of Basil's teaching that an artist, visual or poetic, must participate in a religious tradition through devotion before he can portray it. His language is figurative, like that of biblical writers, because it rests on belief in the sacramental character of the created world. That world and the Bible are God's two witnesses, their hidden mystery visible only to the "eye of faith."

> In his book Moses described
>   the creation of the natural world,
> so that both Nature and Scripture
>   might bear witness to the Creator.
> Nature, through man's use of it,
>   Scripture, through his reading it;
> they are the witnesses
>   which reach everywhere,
> they are to be found at all times,
>   present at every hour,
> confuting the unbeliever
>   who defames the Creator.[49]

For Ephrem, everything in creation was able to point to the Creator. "Blessed is He who has appeared to our human race under so many metaphors."[50] In the Syrian tradition to which he belonged, celibacy had long been revered, but it was experienced as a positive way of wholeness for a man or a woman, not as denigration of the flesh. Mary was a model of this wholeness, and her physical virginity was taken for granted:

> In the pure womb of the river
> you should recognize Mary, the daughter of humanity,
> who conceived having known no man,
> who gave birth without intercourse.   (Church 36:3–6)[51]

This fourth-century Christian insistence on Mary's physical virginity, however, was the flashpoint of an acrimonious competition between Jews and Christians. Sadly, Ephrem made use of Mary in this anti-Jewish polemic. In his Hymn 7 on Mary, she asks the prophet Isaiah to "raise your voice and rebuke the harlot Sion who spurned you, and refused to believe that I gave birth in my virginity, as you yourself testify."[52]

Such disputation was never a major theme in Ephrem, however, though it was part of an ugly and continuing "teaching of contempt" for Judaism that persisted within Christianity until modern times. More typically, in his cycle of hymns on Paradise, Ephrem presents a loving Creator who "clothed Himself in language, so that He might clothe us in His mode of life."[53] This "Good One . . . toiled by every means/so that we might act pleasingly to Him of our own free will." For if He had forced us, "we would have resembled a portrait someone else had painted."[54] These reflections on Genesis 1–3 seem the very antithesis of St. Jerome's counsel that we must always act against nature.

Nor did Ephrem interpret the story of Adam and Eve as the beginning of human history, like the Western Fathers, but saw Paradise as a hint of things to come at the end—an idea that also occurs in the First Book of Enoch, a Jewish apocalyptic work of

the second century. Ephrem considered a completely literal interpretation of the Bible an abuse of God's condescension to us, a
lack of gratitude for that "Grace which stooped" to the level of
our childish language. In this view, unlike that of Gnosticism,
both word and body are valid, but they must both be understood
as metaphors for a different mode of reality. Like the author of
the Odes of Solomon, Ephrem used graphic feminine imagery for
God: the Creator is also a weaver and a housekeeper; Christ is a
mother whose "living breast" feeds all.

The ultimate aim of the Incarnation, Ephrem explained in his
Commentary on Genesis 2:23, is to raise humanity to the position of honor Adam and Eve would have occupied if they had
not disobeyed. God wanted them to acquire infallible knowledge
and to live forever. In Ephrem's theological vision, virginity is
based on metaphysical ideals embodied in biblical types: Christ
the bridegroom will come and the wise virgin will accompany
Him to the bridal chamber. This erotic imagery is applied to the
individual soul, male and female, and to the church as a whole,
seen as the bride of Christ, prefigured in Mary: "She was your
mother, she was your sister, she was your bride, too, along with
all chaste souls" (Nativity 11:2). Only Mary, however, was fully
married to Christ in historical time in the sacred bridal chamber
of her body.

In this perspective, further developed in Hymn 17 on the Nativity, the parallel with Eve is subtly shifted. If Eve clothed herself with "leaves of ignominy," Mary "has clothed herself in her
virginity with the garment of glory, which is sufficient for all. A
piece of clothing she has given to him who clothes all."[55] In Gregory of Nyssa's Paradise, the bodies of Adam and Eve are glorified—a contrast with their condition after they are expelled from
the garden and must wear garments of skin. In one of his hymns
on Paradise, Ephrem has Adam's wife, "the capable one," cleverly fashion the clothes which humanity wore until Mary,

through the body she gave her son, provided humanity with a new and glorious garment.[56]

Ephrem did connect Eve to the Fall, but he wove Mary even more intimately into the texture of redemption:

> With the body from the Virgin he entered Sheol . . . and came to Eve, the mother of all the living. She is the vine, whose wall the Evil One pierced with her own hands and by whose fruit he made men taste death. And Eve, the mother of all the living, became the source of death for all the living. But Mary caused a new branch to sprout forth from Eve, the ancient vine, and in this the new life made its abode.[57]

There is a kind of companionship between Mary and Eve in Ephrem, a development of Irenaeus's idea, mostly absent in the West, of Mary as Eve's advocate, emphasizing that men and women, by living holy lives, can regain the Paradise God intended for them. There is also a transcendence of sexual difference—or rather, a shifting use of sex as metaphor—that suggests human wholeness. Drawing on feminine imagery not only for Christ but for himself, Ephrem prayed like the barren Hannah that his mind might prove fertile. He was personally devoted to the legendary mother of Mary, St. Anne.

Ephrem's poetry is primarily liturgical, to be sung in public worship, and it bears the sense of double time that accompanies the ritual enactment of myth: it happened then and it is still happening now. God generates a son eternally; Mary, too, brings him forth in the recurring present. The timeless, Wisdom-oriented understanding of the Eastern concept of the *Theotokos* can be heard in Ephrem's address to God the Father: "Thou who gavest birth to thy mother" (Hymn 16, on the Nativity). Such links continue in the Eucharist: the bread is "from the praised sheaf" (Mary), the wine is "grape of Mary." Ephrem's hymns are also filled with Hebrew typology and imagery applied to Mary. Miriam, Rachel, Deborah, and Esther are her "types"; she is the enclosed garden, the sealed fountain, the palace where the King lives (Proverbs 9:1). Ark of the Covenant, gate of heaven, she "bore Christ in her virginal womb as the bush on Mount Horeb [Exodus 3:1 ff.] bore God in the flame."[58]

It is important to remember the theological framework into which Ephrem works such figures and yet limits their meaning. Mary is all-holy, but she is always human. "Mary has become a heaven for us, because she bears God," but she is also the "soil" on which Christ the sun could shine on the world and humanity.[59] She represents what all who do the will of God can be in the Paradise of the endtime. For the first time in Christian literature Mary is called "the bride of Christ." Taken in context, this image glorifies God's mercy and ennobles humanity as a whole. "She alone is Your mother/but she is Your sister, with everyone else." As we have seen, Ephrem calls her "the daughter of humanity," never to be confused with God. In the Eastern tradition, uninfluenced by Augustine's pessimistic view of human nature, men and women were considered to some extent able to avoid sin by their own efforts. Augustine saw Mary as sinless "out of honor to the Lord"; for Ephrem, her purity was part of God's plan for humanity, expressed in poetic paradox in his homily on the Nativity:

> This day Mary has become for us
> the heaven that bears God,
> for in her the exalted Godhead
> has descended and dwelt;
> in her It has grown small, to make us great.[60]

Ephrem and the Cappadocian Fathers thought alike; their sermons sounded the same themes and figures. Gregory of Nyssa, too, saw Mary prefigured in the burning bush of Moses, where earlier theologians (like Clement of Alexandria) had seen a sign of Christ. In Eastern theology, Mary's place was not so much intellectually formulated as experienced and performed in liturgy with emotionally charged, highly sensory biblical imagery. In this way, despite the Arian controversy, veneration of the mother of Christ developed in the East as an integral part of personal and communal belief.

THE ROAD TO EPHESUS

All the fourth-century theological debates were really about the nature of Christ, not about Mary. Even the decision of the whole church at Ephesus in 431 that she was *Theotokos*, or God-Bearer, defined Christ, not Mary; it guaranteed the unity of Christ's nature against those who would split divine and human in two. The term stressed Mary's biological role, since *tokos* was used in medicine and conjured up the experience of giving birth. Nevertheless, the decision expressed the conviction that a human Mary had given birth to a single person, both divine and human, and this was precisely the Fathers' intention. In the minds of the Cappadocian Fathers, the title *Theotokos* united the attributes of the Virgin. A statement by Gregory of Nazianzus in 379 sums up their position: "If anyone does not accept the holy Mary as *Theotokos*, he is without the Godhead." He delivered these words in a sermon in the Anastasia, a small church that had become an orthodox sanctuary in Constantinople under emperors who were still Arians.

The events of history seemed to support Gregory's words. An Arian mob tried to destroy the Anastasia but did not succeed. And when the new emperor, Theodosius, sided with orthodoxy in 380, Gregory was made patriarch. Mary was widely perceived to have helped Gregory triumph over heresy, and the large church built on the site of the old Anastasia was believed to manifest divine power. Petitioners there were cured of diseases and found relief from the difficult problems of life; according to the historian Somozen, writing in the 440s, "The power was attributed to Mary, the Mother of God, the holy Virgin, for she does manifest herself in this way."[61]

Most people were interested in Mary because of just such manifestations of power, which were a major factor behind her official acceptance as *Theotokos*. The emphasis on asceticism by church leaders offered little direction for the everyday life of workers and peasants, who were joining the church in large numbers now that it was the approved state religion. In these brutal and uncertain years, it is not surprising that people turned to a human mother of God, someone who had given birth to a child, endured his death, and was with him in heaven where she commiserated with their trials and sufferings. Mary was needed to fill what Cardinal Newman, in his nineteenth-century explanation of the development of doctrine, would describe as "that new sphere . . . in the realms of light, to which the church had not yet assigned its inhabitant . . . a throne . . . far above all created powers, mediatorial, intercessory."[62]

Christian art echoes this development. The earlier Jesus, diverse and somehow close at hand, had become one with the Father in heaven, both in visual and theological description. After the decision of the Nicene Council to stress the oneness of Father and Son, Alpha and Omega symbols were added to the left and right of mosaic and fresco images of Christ, affirming his existence with the Father from the beginning to the end. On the apse at St. Pudenziana in Rome (a mosaic of the 390s), a larger-than-life Christ wears a golden robe, a sign of divinity, and sits on a gem-encrusted throne like that used earlier only by gods. He is pictured with the full beard and long dark hair of Jupiter, and the apostles sit slightly below him on either side. The scene was reenacted in the church as well, where the bishop sat below the apse on his *cathedra* (a special seat facing the people), with his priests surrounding him. As art historian Thomas Mathews observes, "The church, in the imagination of late antiquity, was replacing eternal Rome and all her gods as the universal vehicle of hope."[63]

It would not be long before Mary's son would become the Cosmic Christ, the Pantocrator—in the words of Basil, the one who has "primacy over all created things."[64] Inevitably, when Christ was placed high on the dome of Byzantine churches among the fixed stars, he was no longer experienced as the available shepherd with whom believers could easily identify. Hence the exaltation of Christ created a deep need for a protector closer to earth; in the fifth-century church Mary would become a central symbol of the new life that her son had imaged early in the fourth century.

Across the length and breadth of the empire people were subject to constant invasion by Huns, Vandals, Goths, and Persians. In this context, Theodosius's ban on pagan worship and his destruction of statues and temples to gods and goddesses were keenly felt by the country people, now forced into the cities for safety. Historian Pamela Berger observes that "The exclusion of any female images from the Christian concept of deity was particularly hard on agricultural people whose experience with growth and life-producing forces had been connected with the female principle for millennia. At the same time, Christian doctrine was becoming devoid of all imagery incorporating a female aspect into the divine."[65] Augustine might make connections between Sophia-Wisdom and God, but Gnostic texts invoking God as Father and Mother had largely been suppressed.

A complex process of political infighting and intrigue was still necessary, however, before Mary was finally accepted as *Theotokos*. When Nestorius became patriarch of Constantinople in 428, a public clash over Mary's role took place in the cathedral itself. Proclus, a well-known orator, delivered a sermon in which he spoke of Mary with the poetic ardor of Ephrem. She was "the only bridge between God and man," "the gate closed to all but the Lord, the God of Israel": "Behold, an exact description of the holy *Theotokos* Mary!" Infuriated at what he considered inflated and heretical notions, the patriarch Nestorius marched to the pulpit and suggested that the eloquent speaker verged on pagan myth; Mary deserved all praise as the mother of Jesus, but she could not be the mother of God.

The ensuing conflict had enormous consequences. Cyril, bishop of Alexandria, came to the defense of Proclus. Eager to promote himself and his rival see, now considered less important than Constantinople, he sent a barrage of letters to the pope, the two emperors, and to Nestorius, challenging the latter's orthodoxy on the grounds of dividing Christ into two separate natures. Acrimony, outrage, and even prison terms for both Nestorius and Cyril marked the course of this controversy, but eventually church and state arrived at a joint decision.

After persuading Pope Celestine to condemn Nestorius, Cyril managed to take over the ecumenical council the emperors had called for Pentecost at the city of Ephesus in 431. (According to some legends, Ephesus was the last place Mary had lived.) Nestorius was deposed and excommunicated, and Mary was declared *Theotokos*. Cyril's apostrophe to Mary at the council was effusive:

> Hail Mary, Mother of God, majestic common-treasure of the whole world, the lamp unquenchable, the crown of virginity, the scepter of orthodoxy, the indissoluble temple, the dwelling of the Illimitable, Mother and Virgin . . . through whom Angels and Archangels rejoice, devils are put to flight . . . and the fallen creature is received up into the heavens.[66]

Declaring Mary *Theotokos* was apparently a very popular decision. The crowds who had been roaming the streets in Ephesus went wild with joy. They led Cyril and his followers to their lodging with torches, crying, "Praised be the *Theotokos*! Long live Cyril!" A number of commentators today attribute this enthusiasm to the city's having long been the seat of worship to Diana; a new church dedicated to Mary would soon rise over the old temple to the goddess which had been destroyed in 400.

Proclus was made patriarch of Constantinople, where Cyril

delivered a speech filled with the biblical images of Ephrem and
the Alexandrian school, again calling Mary the "scepter of orthodoxy." This image of imperial power as the force defending doctrinal truth sums up the reversal that the new relation between
church and state had brought about in Mary's status. From
humble peasant woman of Nazareth she had become noble
Mother of God, protector of the true faith. In all its complexity,
the symbol of Mary as God-Bearer became a vital part of the
church from this time on.

Since there was more preparation for this understanding of
Mary in the East, it is hardly surprising that the new doctrine affirmed at Ephesus led to the introduction of new feasts of Mary
into the church calendar there. About 600, the Emperor Maurice
ordered Mary's Assumption into heaven, which had already been
observed in some Eastern churches before Ephesus, to be celebrated on August 15. New churches proliferated in her name: the
year after Ephesus, Pope Sixtus III began work on the basilica of
Santa Maria Maggiore in Rome, celebrating the Virgin's victory
at that council by raising a church in her honor. In the mosaics of
the sanctuary arch she attained a grandeur new in Christian art,
wearing the costume of an Eastern empress, with diadem, ear-
rings, and a pearl necklace. The connection between the birth of
Jesus and the presence of Christ in the Eucharist found visual
confirmation in carvings of Mary in the Orans position opposite
Christ on sixth-century Syrian chalices (Plate 6). In the West, the
attributes of Holy Wisdom, or Sophia, would also slowly accrue
to Mary.

The decision at Ephesus greatly encouraged the artistic representation of the Virgin in Eastern iconography as well. Because
Mary was now officially recognized as a central part of God's plan
for humanity, Cyril and others speculated about her birthplace,
and a new icon depicting her birth as well as a feast day would
follow in the sixth century. These icons of Mary's birth paral-
leled those of the Nativity. In both cases the artists imitated pa-

gan pictures of the time that portrayed the births of important people in the rooms in which they took place; the birth of Jesus was presented in a cave, while Mary's was in well-appointed rooms, with St. Anne being assisted by serving women (Plate 9).

Just as Ephesus sparked interest in Mary's birth, so did it lead to a search for information about her death. Epiphanius had dropped the first hint of a popular belief that Mary had been taken up into heaven body and soul, suggesting that Scripture was silent about her death because of the "great marvel" he only dared think of. Again, it "seemed fitting" that such a woman might not have died like most mortals. When Constantine's mother, Helena (d. c.330), carried out excavations in Palestine to look for relics and to mark sites connected with the life of Jesus, she discovered what she believed to be the true cross but found nothing connected with Mary's death. Whether or not the absence of a tomb was significant, stories of Mary's "dormition," or falling asleep, indicating that she did not suffer physical death, circulated widely in the East. Belief that she was raised into heaven was closely related to an influential apocryphal legend called the *Transitus*, or Passing, which was accepted as John the Evangelist's account of Mary's death. The *Transitus* was rooted in the Johannine tradition, which held, even in the pre-Nicene church, that Mary was taken up into heaven body and soul. In differing Greek, Latin, Arabic, Syrian, and Coptic (Egyptian) versions, the story was widely distributed throughout Christendom from the fifth century on, reaching the West largely in the Latin version attributed to Melito of Sardis.[67]

In the legend, an angel with a palm visits Mary to announce her forthcoming death. Mary then summons all the apostles who gather around her deathbed. Jesus arrives just after his mother's death. Many later illustrations show Jesus carrying his mother's soul in his arms like a tiny baby—a visual reversal of the Nativity scene (Plate 8). Later, the last apostle, Thomas, arrives from India on a cloud. Knowing that he is the doubter who needed proof of Jesus' Resurrection, the others show him that Mary's grave is empty. He says he already knows this; he had seen angels lifting her up to heaven on his flight into Jerusalem. In some accounts he shows them her belt, which the angels have given him.

The versions of the *Transitus* vary in details, but in all of them, hostility to the Jews is part of the narrative. The legend maintains that when the Jews heard the apostles singing as they carried Mary on a bier, they tried to take her body and burn it. But when their high priest touched the bier, his hands dried up and stuck to it. Crying out, he was told by St. Peter that he could be cured only if he confessed his faith in Christ and the one who bore him. The high priest immediately called out that he believed; his hands became free, but his arms were still withered. St. Peter advised him to kiss the coffin and say, "I believe in Jesus Christ and in Mary who carried him in her womb and remained a virgin after bearing him." The priest did as he was told and was immediately healed.

Despite this evidence of the hardening of attitudes toward Judaism, which this influential legend reads back into apostolic times, the center of the narrative is the popular affirmation of Mary's holiness and her presence in heaven. It is astonishing that this story endured for over eight hundred years, and that the differences in details from one version to another—such as the precise time when Mary's soul and body were reunited—remained live questions well into the Middle Ages.

The change in Mary's status because of Ephesus can perhaps best be seen in the change in the way she was presented. The shift is visible in the Adoration of the Magi scene in a sixth-century mosaic in Ravenna's Basilica of St. Apollinare Nuovo. In earlier portrayals, Mary had been seen from the side, as part of the action. Now she and the son on her lap are turned to full frontal position, a sign of divinity. Seated on a throne of gold and ivory, she faces her risen son, who is similarly enthroned on the opposite wall. A procession of virgins holding the martyr's crown of palms approaches her, preceded by the Magi holding their gifts. Two archangels on either side now separate this Queen of Heaven from the smaller attendant figures.

These early icons were not "art" in our modern sense; their anonymous painters were trying to express the invisible, representing holy men and women not primarily by rendering their external features but by capturing their inner reality, illumined by divine light. The importance of these images in Byzantine churches—and in Orthodox churches even today—can be seen by their presence on the *iconstasis* or screen separating the sanctuary from the nave where people gather for worship. In this way icons, with those of Mary prominent among them, are both guardians of and guides to the holy of holies.

During the later war over images—the iconoclastic controversy (725–842)—most of the early icons from the period following Ephesus were destroyed. Those at the monastery of St. Catherine at Mt. Sinai take on added significance, therefore, because of their rarity. Reproductions of these restored icons have been widely published only in this century. One of the icons from St. Catherine's, inspired by the definition at Ephesus, portrays the Virgin sitting on a red cushion on a gem-studded throne of ocher flanked by two standing warrior saints, Theodore and George, who wear the ceremonial robes of the imperial guard. Art historian Kurt Weitzmann says that this icon represents the rich, complex art found only in Constantinople during this early period of Byzantine iconography. Mary's otherworldliness is suggested by the olive green of her face and eyes, as well as by the light streaming from the hand of God above her head. Her son's dual nature is visible in the free, childlike movement of his legs, combined with the mature head that reveals his other, divine nature.[68] Similar to the mosaic at Ravenna, but with Mary now wholly separated from the Magi, this image would eventually penetrate Christendom in many variations, particularly through the illuminated manuscripts and songbooks used in the common prayers of monks and nuns (Plate 10).

The enthusiastic acceptance of Mary as God-Bearer can perhaps best be understood as a decision of the whole church, humble believers as well as leaders of every degree, who found hope in a single symbol that allowed them to preserve their differences as well as their communal ties. Pure, spiritual virgin and real, comforting mother, Mary could stimulate both public and private prayer. Faith in her intercession became so strong that in the seventh century she was depicted with Mary Magdalene encountering the resurrected Christ. In no way based on biblical evidence, this icon reveals the widespread popular perception that Mary came to understand the truth about her son and must therefore have been a witness of the Easter event.[69]

The whole church rejoiced in this Mary who linked the human and the natural world. Religious historian Peter Brown claims that "the cult of the Virgin offered the luminous inversion of the dark myth of shared, fallen flesh." It was no accident that her ascent should take place at a time when Jesus was moving ever higher into heaven, the church was in league with earthly power, and enemies were invading the empire on all sides.

As God-Bearer, Mary began to take over some of her son's functions; she was invoked for healing and protection. She also became associated with new biblical symbols such as the woman in Revelation, "clothed with the sun, and the moon under her feet, and on her head a crown of twelve stars." This woman was threatened by a dragon as she was about to give birth, but was given "two wings of a great eagle, that she might fly into the desert." Long accepted as a figure of the church trying to survive as it brought forth new life, the symbol was seen by Epiphanius as the Virgin Mary, too. By the first half of the sixth century the Greek philosopher Oecumenius claimed that Revelation "describes the *Theotokos*" now in heaven, "wholly sublime . . . even though she shares our human nature and being."[70]

Ephesus fostered verbal as well as visual art. The sixth-century Syrian poet Jacob of Sarug wrote a long ode on the Blessed Virgin Mary in the emotional, exalted style of Ephrem, developing the new images of the Mother of Mercy and the Mother of Sorrows, both previously absent from Greek and Latin writing. And the most important Marian hymn of the Orthodox church, the Akathistos—whose name indicates that, out of reverence, it was to be sung while standing—was probably composed by the Syrian poet Romanus to celebrate the deliverance of Constantinople from the barbarians in 626. The populace believed that Mary's intercession was responsible for the sudden terrible storm in the Straits of Bosporus that scattered the ships of the Persians, Slavs, and Avars who were about to invade the almost unprotected city. Mary's role as Mother of God can be felt in the sense of awe that dominates this great prayer. The Akathistos is an emotional compendium of devotion; each of the twelve parts develops a theological theme, then closes with an invocation and the almost untranslatable and paradoxical refrain, "Rejoice, thou Bride unwedded." Joy is the central message of this great prayer-poem, and the centrality of the *Theotokos* to the mystery of the Incarnation is the source of that joy.

All the now customary images of the Mother of God drawn from nature and Scripture are in the Akathist hymn: Mary is called "Throne of the King," "She that causest the Sun to appear," "heavenly ladder," "Pillar of Fire," "Successor to manna." But there are new phrases that indicate her growing role in the church: "Silent voice of the Apostles," "courage of the Martyrs," "thou who quelchest the fiery furnace of error," "thou who didst cast down from power the inhuman tyrant." And there are others that describe the intercessory role she has now assumed for all believers: "Wood of leafy branches whereby many are sheltered,"

"Robe of confidence for the naked," "thou through whom transgression is annulled." Finally, there are praises for her role in pointing to the mystery of divine truth and showing how to seek it in community: "Thou who showest forth philosopher fools . . . who provest logicians illogical" and "thou who makest things that differ to agree."[71]

Rome had fallen and the great church Fathers were dead, but Mary's role as fulfillment of biblical prophecies, cosmic mediator, and representative of the church was now firmly established in the imagination of the Christian people.

MARY, HER SON, AND THEIR EXTENDED FAMILY:
Twelfth-Century Europe

Today a closed portal
has opened to us the door
the serpent slammed on a woman:
the flower of the maiden Mary
gleams on the dawn.

—HILDEGARD OF BINGEN[1]

. . . how can we fear,
when our salvation or damnation hangs on the will
of a good brother and
a devoted mother?

—ANSELM OF CANTERBURY[2]

FOR A THOUSAND YEARS AFTER THE COUNCIL OF EPHESUS, the implications of Mary's definition as God-Bearer would penetrate the Europe that replaced Rome and Constantinople as a world power. An emerging Europe whose peoples were not yet divided into powerful nation-states was unified principally by the church and its monasteries. The twelfth century marked the height of this Christendom and Mary's full incorporation within it. This century translated what it believed into art, and in so doing revealed how that belief developed and what it meant for all levels of society.

To find the Mary of the Middle Ages, I went to France, where her joyous presence is still visible almost everywhere. Shopping in any small village, if I raised my eyes I would see a statue of Mary in a niche on the corner or above someone's door. In Burgundy she held grapes. In Provence she looked up at her mother, Anne, who was, like any good French mother, always instructing her. I was not consciously looking for Mary when my husband and I first spent a year in the Vaucluse (the closed valley in northern Provence where Petrarch lamented his Laura); I wanted to see Romanesque churches and Van Gogh's olive trees, and to have friends come to visit.

But from the first day of our arrival in Beaumes de Venise, Mary refused to be ignored. Above our bed our tasteful landlords had placed a poster of the Coronation of Mary. Into a timeless heavenly event, the fifteenth-century painter Enguerrand Quarton had incorporated local towns and scenery still recognizable to us. In its center, Mary formed a bridge between heaven and earth, her blue robe blending into the blue sky, as Father, Son, and Holy Spirit together placed a crown on her head. Below her lay a richly peopled earth, and below that, an equally populated purgatory and hell. On both sides of the heavenly realm, angels and saints in glorious color celebrated this Queen of Heaven. This poster was our first sign that the art, architecture, and landscape of this region still bore memories of a time when Mary was its most beloved resident.

In May we journeyed with the rest of the parish from the seventeenth-century church in town to the Romanesque chapel just outside to celebrate mass. This pilgrimage was an annual event. The usual small group of shopkeepers, vineyard workers, and retirees, as well as the lady from the chateau that makes the highly prized local muscat, all took the narrow road winding between the vineyards to Notre Dame D'Aubune. The soft yellow-gray stone church, distinguished by its bell tower, lay just before a sheer rocky cliff.

Outside after mass, we were told that the chapel had been built by Charlemagne in thanksgiving to the Virgin for helping him drive back the Saracens on this very plain. One of our informants pointed out a large rock on top of the hill behind the church, explaining that when the chapel was built, the jealous devil had tried to destroy it by hurling that very rock. The Virgin, however, rose up brandishing her distaff and stopped the rock just where it sits today. Clearly the curé and parishioners who told these tales still treasured them. They had been handed down in Provençal verse, the word "distaff" signaling a connection with the tradition stemming from the apocryphal Book of James, which describes Mary weaving. The fact that Charlemagne lived in the eighth and ninth centuries and the church wasn't built until the twelfth didn't in itself invalidate the story. Such churches were always being rebuilt, just as this one had had to be later in the seventeenth and eighteenth centuries. And Charlemagne really did get around, raising Mary's image on his banners as he resisted attacks by the Arabs (then known as Saracens) in Italy and Spain. The legend helped to explain the powerful impetus that Arab conquest provided for the development of European Christendom. Thrown on their own resources, the people of France, England, Spain, and Germany began to develop pilgrimages and shrines in their own lands to compensate for their inability to visit the Holy Land.

EASTERN DEVOTIONS,
MEDIEVAL ART

Mary could be found, I was discovering, in legends kept alive in surviving architecture and art. Even before I arrived in Provence I had been powerfully affected by the medieval art I had seen in museums and cathedrals in northern France. On my first visit I was made aware of Mary's continuing presence. What struck me on my return nine years later, seeking the sources and meaning of that presence, was the positive interpretation the Middle Ages gave to the images, legends, and theology inherited from Byzantium and the ancient Roman world. The presence of the Mother of God seemed to unify and vitalize the Christian story in its passage to the medieval imagination, making it acceptable across the sharp economic boundaries of feudalism.

The idea of the "happy fault"—if Adam had not sinned, Christ would not have come—goes back to Paul and was frequently drawn on by the church Fathers. It recurs in an early English lyric, with Mary replacing Christ: if the "appil" had never "taken been," we would not have "heaven's queen."[3] The song helps us see how common themes crisscrossed Europe with the movement of monks and pilgrims, slowly bringing the art forms and legends of the East into the more sober, landlocked West. Most people could not read, write, or understand the Latin used in the mass. Visual art, therefore, was their main medium of instruction; the cathedrals were their schools. There, according to art historian Emile Mâle, they saw all that was useful for them to know, "the history of the world since its creation, religious dogma, the example of the saints, the hierarchy of virtue, the various sciences, arts and crafts."[4] A common vision cut across class and educational lines, and its chief heroine was Mary.

Even the intellectuals in Paris called schoolmen accepted her legends and wove them into their teaching of Scripture and their sermons. Anselm of Canterbury's pupil Honorius of Autun spread Marian devotions through a widely read book of model sermons for feast days throughout the year. In sermons for the Annunciation and the Nativity, for example, he used Old Testament figures to suggest Mary, such as the burning bush and Gideon's fleece damp with dew, as well as natural symbols of plants and animals. Honorius saw in the fabulous unicorn a symbol of Christ, the Incarnation, whom only a virgin could capture. His widely influential book, *Speculum Ecclesiae*, along with more sober sources of information, greatly encouraged belief in Mary's central place in Christian teaching.

Both in their art and in the liturgy, the cathedrals bore witness to the profound absorption of Scripture by the medieval mind. Ordinary people needed no guidebook to see Mary in Old Testament figures. The burning bush observed by Moses was understood to be an image of "her who without being consumed, had received the divine fire in her womb." This interpretation became part of the Office of the Virgin, included in the great cycle of prayers sung by monks, religious, and clerics throughout the year. Gideon and the fleece upon which fell dew from heaven in Judges was developed as an image of Mary by St. Bernard in one of his sermons, and along with the burning bush was translated into cathedral windows in Laon and Lyons.

Mary's power extended even to the depths of hell. One of the best known and most influential medieval legends was that of

Theophilus, which was the inspiration for the later story of Faust. In the eighth century, Paul the Deacon had translated this fifth-century Greek miracle story into Latin. In the tenth century, it was rendered into a verse drama by the learned Benedictine abbess Hrosvitha of Gandersheim. The legend recounts the story of Theophilus, deacon of the bishop of Cilicia, who at first is so humble he refuses the bishopric. But then the devil tempts him and he becomes ambitious. He signs an official contract in blood, giving over his soul to the devil at death; after that, he quickly achieves honor, power, and glory. But he also begins to feel guilty. Increasingly desperate, he prays before a statue of Mary until he falls asleep. In a dream he sees Mary tear up the contract; when he awakes, pieces of real parchment lie scattered around him. He thanks Mary, confesses to the bishop, and dies in peace a few days later.

Many churchmen used the Theophilus legend to instruct the faithful. The most important theologian of the early eleventh century, Fulbert of Chartres, the man under whom the building of the cathedral of Chartres began, used the story in his sermon on the feast of Mary's Nativity (September 8). It proved, he said, "that the Mother of the Lord rules everywhere in great magnificence, that she can easily send the holy angels to minister to us and cancel the pacts of hell according to her good pleasure."[5] The legend was known by everyone; it was retold in a window at Chartres, in two at Notre Dame in Paris, and in windows at Laon, Beauvais, Troyes, and Le Mans.

But chief among those developing and reinforcing Marian veneration were the ubiquitous monks, whose monasteries transcended national lines. In Anglo-Saxon times, they extended her feast days and chanted an Office of the Virgin. Bede (d. 735), the monk known as the "father of English history," composed the first known Western sermons in Mary's honor, but advised caution in regard to legends about her death. By the second half of the tenth century, however, the liturgical book of Ethelwold, bishop of Winchester, who had been a monk at Glastonbury, included an artistic rendering of the fifth-century apocryphal text describing Mary's dormition and her arrival in heaven. At Canterbury cathedral in the eleventh century, Mary is shown with a crown and a scepter, symbols of power that suggested her active participation in redemption.

On the continent, there were further developments in Marian piety. At the court of Charlemagne, the great humanist Alcuin (d. 804) dedicated the cathedral of Aix-la-Chapelle to Mary, instituted a Marian mass on Saturday—which became Mary's day—and applied to her Office the Wisdom text from Ecclesiasticus (24:9): "Before all ages, in the beginning, he created me, and through all ages I shall not cease to be." Later Alcuin added Proverbs 8:22–23: "The Lord begot me, the first-born of his ways; . . . From of old I was poured forth, at the first, before the earth." In the eleventh century, Peter Damian, close friend of the reformist Pope Gregory VII, went even further, connecting Mary's role not only with the birth of Christ in the flesh but with his appearance on the altar in every mass, a connection already known in Eastern Christianity. Damian, who also includes the Wisdom texts in his Office of Mary, asserts that both Christ and the church come forth from Mary. His hymns show complete confidence in her intercession; they ask the "queen of the world" and our "ladder to heaven" to "Pay what we owe, avert what we fear, obtain what we wish, and accomplish what we hope."[6]

In this way, devotional themes and enthusiasm that had been familiar in the East since the end of the fourth century slowly penetrated Western art and liturgy. The result can be experienced in the best-known Marian chants, for instance the Advent antiphon "*Alma Redemptoris mater*":

> O kindly mother of the redeemer,
> you who are still the open gate of heaven
> and the star of the sea: aid this

fallen people which strives to rise.
You who gave birth to your holy father,
while Nature looked on in wonder[7]

ANSELM AND BERNARD

St. Anselm of Canterbury and St. Bernard of Clairvaux are two
monastic figures who made important medieval contributions to
Marian thought. Continuity with ideas from the ancient church
and the new attitudes to Mary can be seen clearly in Anselm
(d. 1109), one of the first scholastic theologians. Much in his treatise on the virginal conception, for instance, could have come
from a fourth-century Father: it "was fitting" that "this Virgin
should shine with a degree of purity than which no greater can be
imagined apart from God," because "to her God determined to
give his only Son." Anselm's private prayers, however, indicate
a different context of belief and reveal intense personal devotion
to Mary:

> O most blessed,
> all that turns away from you, and that you oppose,
> must needs be lost,
> and equally it is not possible that whatever turns to you
> and you regard with favor, should perish.
> For just as, Lady, God begat him
> in whom all things live,
> so, O flower of virginity,
> you bore him by whom the dead are raised up. . . .
> you are mother of justifier and the justified,
> bearer of reconciliation and the reconciled,
> parent of salvation and of the saved.[8]

There are significant differences here from the attitude to
Mary in the ancient church. First, Anselm addresses her with the
courtly title of "Lady" (the feminine equivalent of Lord), letting

us understand that for monks Mary takes the place of the feudal
lady praised by troubadours and served by knights. Anselm also
takes it for granted that a tender human relationship exists between son and mother, in heaven as on earth, something that
would have been inconceivable to many fourth-century Fathers.
Further, he believes that Mary's role as mother of God gives her
partial responsibility for human salvation.

A second prayer reveals Anselm's confidence that he, too, is
part of the intimate concern of both mother and son:

> For he was born of a mother to take our nature,
> and to make us, by restoring our life, sons of his mother. . . .
> With what confidence then ought we to hope,
> and thus consoled how can we fear,
> when our salvation or damnation hangs on the will
> of a good brother and
> a devoted mother?[9]

Anselm's theology emphasizes the humanity of a Jesus who is
also God, active in the world not only in the past but now. Such a
view permeated the entire church in this monastic era, whose focus on common worship made such connections palpable. As
Anselm claimed, the fact that God became human through Mary
made people of every degree members of the same family, rooted
in a physical creation that reflected and was meant to imitate the
goodness of God. "As God is the Father of all created things,"
said Anselm, "so Mary is the Mother of all recreated things, not
only human but natural." This is an age when animals, places,
and even the cure of specific diseases all had their own saints,
when wildflowers were called Mary-buds, the sea's phosphores-
cence was St. Elmo's fire, and the Milky Way was known as the
way of St. James. Central to this two-way traffic between heaven
and earth, as Anselm observed, was Mary:

> O woman full and overflowing with grace, plenty
> flows from you to make all creatures green again.

> O virgin blessed and ever blessed, whose blessing
> is upon all nature, not only is the creature
> blessed by the Creator,
> but the Creator is blessed by the creature too. . . . [10]

The implications of Anselm's point that nature and grace are interconnected can be viewed in the windows and sculptures of twelfth- and thirteenth-century cathedrals, almost all dedicated to Our Lady. In them each form of nature—from flowers to seasons to animals—and every kind of human craft and worker, male and female—farmers, spinners, weavers, vintners, and furriers—are respectfully represented. The stage of Mary's activity was vast; it was she, rather than her adult son, who was the day-to-day link between humanity and God. Christ was more often seen on the tympana of the cathedrals separating the sheep from the goats at the Last Judgment, hardly an image that inspired poor human sinners.

THE CAREER OF BERNARD OF CLAIRVAUX (1090–1153), probably the most powerful figure in twelfth-century Europe, reveals the paradoxes that accompanied the growth of monastic tenderness in personal devotion to Mary. Her role, he said, was to be the "aqueduct" of God's grace, the channel all should use because God himself provided it.

Born into an aristocratic family in Burgundy whose mother trained her children "for the cloister rather than the court,"[11] Bernard brought his spartan tastes to the monastery. He joined the new Cistercian order, which was intent on reform and known for ascetic discipline, and later dedicated all its monasteries to the Mother of God. When Bernard visited his friend Peter the Venerable at the Benedictine monastery of Cluny, he was appalled by what he considered the uselessness of its carvings, which mingled fantastic beasts and foliage with religious figures in the new

Gothic style. "In the cloisters, before the very eyes of the brothers reading, what are those ridiculous monsters doing?" Bernard inquired with distaste. "If we are not ashamed of these absurdities, we should at least bemoan what they cost."[12] He did not object, however, to the manuscripts his monks were reading, even though their illuminations had inspired many of those carvings.

I gained some insight into Bernard's reasoning when I visited the twelfth-century Cistercian monastery of Senanque, in a low river valley near the hill town of Gordes in Provence. The gray stone church and cloister have an austere beauty that is enhanced by the rural setting, particularly in early summer when the fields of lavender are in full bloom. Inside, natural light and shadow are the only decoration in a church whose acoustics are ideal for plainchant. Bernard wanted nothing visual to distract his monks from their interior meditations and communal singing. Abbot Suger of St.-Denis in Paris might show his veneration for the Virgin in stained-glass medallions depicting her Triumph in heaven, but Bernard would use only rhetoric and song.

Bernard's rhetoric was, in fact, an immense influence in stimulating popular devotion to Mary. But Bernard was also the guardian of the church's orthodoxy, its greatest censor and power broker. When he felt that ecclesiastical authorities at Lyons had overstepped the bounds laid down by the Bible and the Fathers by celebrating the feast of Mary's Immaculate Conception, he chided them for believing in the superstitions of "simple people." He also criticized the hypocrisy, "regal pomp," and "whorish splendor" that motivated so many to seek high office in the church. Influential in establishing Innocent II in the papacy against bitter rival claimants, he later used his influence with that pope to have the teaching of the proud and ambitious Peter Abelard branded heretical in a council at Paris. Deeply suspicious of the new logic, he considered the critical thinking Abelard applied to the mysteries of faith an example of theological arrogance. Yet Abelard, too, was devoted to the church and to Mary, accepted her bodily assumption into heaven, and drew on her legends in his theological reasoning. It is hardly surprising that Héloïse, who appears to have loved Abelard more than either herself or the church—and perhaps for this reason remains a heroine in France—called Bernard a false apostle. Even Peter the Venerable, who provided a refuge for the aging Abelard, wrote to Bernard: "You fast, you watch, you suffer, but you will not endure the easy ones—you do not love."[13]

Nevertheless, love was what Bernard valued most and tried to encourage among his monks. He was famous for the tenderness of his praise for Mary; perhaps she helped him develop what he knew he needed. The Memorare—still a common prayer in the church—was often attributed to him; it is quite similar to the idea he expressed in his fourth sermon on the Assumption: "May he be silent about your mercy, Blessed Virgin, if there should exist one who has called on you in his necessities and remembers that you have failed him."[14] Legend provides a reason for his trust in Mary. When as a sickly child he prayed to the Virgin at the altar of Châtillon, he is said to have received three drops of milk from her breast as a sign of her nourishing favor. Several paintings depict the adult Bernard receiving this milk as he kneels in prayer. Bernard's associates testify to his emotional closeness to Mary, which seems to have strengthened him throughout his life. His first homilies about her were written when he was a frail young abbot of twenty-five. They were composed at night in the simple cabin, away from the new monastery, where the bishop had ordered him to take a rest from his duties. They were the products of deep meditation, not so much original as intense and beautifully expressed; Hilda Graef believes that Bernard's sermons did as much to confirm medieval Christians in their faith in Mary's all-powerful intercession as the legend of Theophilus.

In a later sermon on the Annunciation, Bernard developed the theme of the popular medieval hymn "Ave Maris Stella" (Hail, Star of the Sea), exhorting his listeners to accept Mary as the

compassionate mediatrix of God's grace. He uses repetitive
waves of rhetoric:

> If the storms of temptation arise, if you crash against the rocks of
> tribulation, look to the star, call upon Mary. If you are tossed
> about on the waves of pride, of ambition, of slander, of hostility,
> look to the star, call upon Mary . . . if you begin to be swallowed
> up by the abyss of depression and despair, think of Mary! In dan-
> gers, in anxiety, in doubt, think of Mary, call upon Mary. . . .
> When you are terrified by judgment or in despair, think of
> Mary," [for] "if she holds you, you will not fall, if she protects
> you, you need not fear.[15]

With similar elaboration and variation, Bernard applied every
metaphor in the Song of Songs to the Mother of God. She is the
dawn that in this world precedes the sun of justice. She is the intermediary between man and God. In every Marian sermon he
would bring that lesson back to his listeners, urging them to ask
for and to deserve Mary's help in terms that might seem applicable only to Christ.

If the imagery is inflated, the theology is always centrist. For
Bernard as for Anselm, Mary's place was accepted and encouraged by church tradition. Still, there is no question that his private devotion was intense, and that he deserves his reputation as
the first troubadour of Our Lady. In his commentary on the Ave
Maria—a prayer that at the time consisted of only the first part of
the prayer we now have—he rises to lyrical heights developing
the meaning of every word. He invokes Mary in every gracious
biblical image Ephrem had used in the fourth century, all now
embedded in liturgical prayer and chant: the burning bush, the
ark of the covenant, the flowering branch, the bridal chamber, the
gate open only to God, the enclosed garden, and Jacob's ladder.

Bernard's lyricism was imitated by many monks of the time;
the amount of courtly verse written out of devotion to Mary ex-
ceeded that of the secular love poetry written by the jongleurs.

One well-known legend suggests how the psychological as well as theological needs of celibate males might be served by an ideal virgin in heaven. Mary was said to visit the monk Hermann of Cologne in the guise of a beautiful young girl whom he called Rose. His colleagues nicknamed him Joseph because of his devotion, but this annoyed Hermann, who felt unworthy to bear that saint's name. In a vision, however, he underwent a mystical marriage with the Blessed Virgin, performed by an angel who gave him permission to be called Joseph because he, too, was now espoused to Mary.[16] Even the scholarly Anselm of Canterbury did not hesitate to pray to Mary in the erotic language of the Song of Songs, now part of the regular readings for her feast days:

> O beautiful to gaze upon, delightful to love,
> whither do you go to evade the breadth of my heart?[17]

Feminine images for God were frequently used by medieval monastics. Some abbots deliberately used feminine language to speak of Christ and themselves in order to stress their common humility. Like them, Bernard wanted to help the monks in his charge develop their affective lives within their commitment to celibacy, which would in turn create a more communal, supportive life in the monastery. And like Aelred of Rievaulx, who saw himself as a mother to his charges, Bernard was ambivalent about power. It seems paradoxical that despite his preference for service rather than power in the church, Bernard encouraged the aristocratic order of monks called the Templars to fight against the "infidels," using the pulpit at Vézelay to call for the Second Crusade in 1146. Pope Urban II had earlier launched the First Crusade in 1095 at the Marian shrine at Clermont-Ferrand, granting remission of sins not only to those who fought but also to those who took part in Saturday devotions to Mary to ask for her help in victory.

Of all the causes for which Mary's support has been claimed in history, the crusades seem least appropriate, for they placed her in a role she would never have chosen herself. Muhammad (d. 629), prophet and messenger of Allah to the "infidel" Arabs, regarded Mary with esteem and sympathy. The Qu'ran, most probably written during his lifetime, records stories about her similar to those in the apocryphal Book of James, though with some significant changes. It tells the story of Mary's birth to "a woman of Amran" who had vowed that the child in her womb would belong to Allah. It describes that girl-child's life under the tutelage of Zacharias, who discovers to his astonishment that Allah sends her food. At the Annunciation the angel tells Mary that it is the will of Allah that she bear a son, and she accepts. When, after giving birth, Mary is alone in the shelter of a palm tree, she bursts out, "Oh, would that I had died before this, and had been a thing quite forgotten."[18] Allah tells her instead to shake the tree, eat the dates that fall, and quench her thirst at a fountain he himself provides at her feet. When her relatives insult her, her newborn child speaks and defends her innocence.

In retrospect, the pope's and Bernard's choice of Mary to lead the crusades points out the tragic misunderstanding that lay behind those so-called Holy Wars. For Mary is deeply honored in the Qu'ran, in Islamic exegesis, and in Muslim piety. She is the only female identified by name in the Qu'ran; her name appears there (thirty-four times) far more often than in the whole New Testament. The Arabic name for Mary has a wonderful meaning: "the woman who loves human company and conversation." Sura 3:42 of the Qu'ran suggests that she prays a kind of universal prayer, and the writer asks her to do so for "us," an attitude quite similar to that of medieval European believers.[19]

SECULAR WOMEN OF POWER

Despite the monks' frequent use of feminine imagery in devotion and self-description, there is no evidence that such sensitivity carried over into attitudes toward real women. Although Bernard wrote with graciousness and tact to individual women, in particular to Hildegard of Bingen, whom he asked to pray for him, historian Caroline Bynum says that he feared contamination from actual encounters with women.[20] Nor did the language of loving service for the Lady that originated in feudal courts translate into reverence for women in everyday life. Nevertheless, this courtly ideal reflected the presence of powerful and highly talented women in this period. It is just possible that such women may have inspired a special scene found in some twelfth-century cathedral sculptures—on the tympanum at Senlis, for example— which presents Mary in Triumph sitting side by side with her son in heaven. In later Coronation scenes Mary generally kneels, bowing her head, hands folded, as she receives a crown from Christ, or from all three divine persons. But in the twelfth-century scenes of Triumph, as in earlier Byzantine liturgical texts, Mary is the bride of the Song of Songs, the Queen of Heaven with scepter and book in her hands.

French laws at this time allowed women to inherit property, and historian Henry Adams calls Eleanor of Aquitaine (d. 1204), the greatest heiress of the age, perhaps its most talented and successful political force. Stories of her romantic adventures in the Holy Land, linking her even with Saladin himself, leader of the Saracen forces, may be of the kind that accrue to a rich and independent woman. We know as fact, however, that Eleanor forced King Louis VI, to whom she had been married at fifteen, to give her a divorce in 1152, for which she gained Bernard's reluctant approval. She then married Henry Plantagenet, King of England. Eleanor, her daughter Marie, and her granddaughter Blanche were responsible for inspiring the Court of Love with its elaborate rules of courtesy, putting the Lady on a pedestal. Personal devotion to the Mother of God ran deep among these noble-women and their extended families. Their exquisite taste and wealth were largely responsible for the magnificent statues and stained-glass windows at Chartres, where the queenly Mary is never haughty, but welcoming and compassionate to all.

Eleanor survived both her husbands and her son, Richard the Lion-Hearted, and at the age of eighty she managed to arrange a marriage that would place her granddaughter Blanche of Castile on the French throne. Despite scandal that surrounded Blanche— as it had Queen Eleanor—she, too, played an important role in setting an idealistic cultural and social tone for her era, encouraging the growth of Gothic architecture in Paris and Chartres. She was regent for her son, St. Louis, often making decisions of moral force and clarity. When a group of Jewish petitioners came one day to plead their cause after Louis had permitted the Talmud to be burned, Blanche treated them with wisdom and understanding. The chroniclers remember her also as a protector of the poor.[21]

WOMEN MONASTICS: ELIZABETH OF SCHÖNAU AND HILDEGARD OF BINGEN

Women like Eleanor of Aquitaine were clearly exceptions in the power they exercised, however. Héloïse, Abelard's lover, had a keener understanding of the limits placed on most women of the time. Brilliant and well educated in classical thought, she pleaded with Abelard not to marry her, for it would ruin his career. He was not yet ordained, but she realized that marriage would greatly diminish his reputation. For love of him, she entered a monastery for the rest of her life.[22]

For a variety of reasons, there were so many women entering monasteries in the twelfth century that the heads of such orders as the Premonstratensians and the Cistercians became alarmed and curtailed the increase in their female associates. Not only was life in the convent the only real alternative for unmarried women in the Middle Ages, it could be a fulfilling one. Nuns could pray and chant together; they might also try their hand at crafts and musical composition; frequently they grew herbs in their gardens and served as healers for the local population. Hildegard of Bingen, for example, left detailed studies of diet, diseases, and cures, as well as instructions for the use of gems and herbs as remedies.[23] Only in the next century did suspicion of women in such roles develop, leading to the suppression of such activity and to the destruction of many healers in fifteenth-century witch-hunts.

The convent also provided a base of spiritual power. Visions, unlike ecclesiastical office or a good education, were not confined to male monastics. Though third- and fourth-century Fathers would have disapproved, such spiritual experiences led to prophetic careers for two extraordinary twelfth-century Benedictines, Elizabeth of Schönau and Hildegard of Bingen.

Elizabeth of Schönau (d. 1164) was the tenth child of a pious, well-established family in the Rhineland. At the age of twelve she was placed in a reformed Benedictine convent in the diocese of Trier, where she would spend the rest of her short life. At twenty-three she began to have visions, which tortured rather than comforted her. She called them arrows of the Lord, and was deeply depressed because, although she felt God was telling her to publicize what she saw, she was afraid of what people would think if she did. Her torments were finally ended when a regal Mary in priestly clothes appeared to her. Mary signed Elizabeth with the sign of the cross, and told her that the threats of devils would not harm her. The result was that Elizabeth's relationship with Mary has none of the sentimentality so often found in the Marian devotion of monks. Instead of the psychosexual integration Mary seemed to offer some male monks, the "devoted mother" supplied Elizabeth with the psychological strength needed to carry out a singular vocation.

Six months after these visionary appearances began, Elizabeth had an experience of rapture in which an angel lifted her up to heaven. The angel would be a continuing presence in her visions. From that time on, Elizabeth saw her role as that of an intermediary between heaven and earth, someone responsible for the conduct of the church on earth. The angel told her to act "manfully" and to preach repentance to others. One day during Matins, she burst into sharp criticism of the clergy in words she said the Lord put into her mouth.

Her new sense of herself as a preacher and prophet was no doubt strengthened by her awareness of the work of Hildegard, who lived not far away in the Rhineland. The angel had told Elizabeth that "the book of God's ways" would be "revealed to you, when you will have visited your sister Hildegard and heard her."[24] Hildegard encouraged the younger nun, suggesting they had a common vocation as prophets. In a letter to Elizabeth she shrewdly defined the role in humble terms that would make women acceptable in it: they simply sang the mysteries of God "like a trumpet," which "does not work unless someone breathes into it."[25]

Hildegard's advice comforted Elizabeth. Moreover, the *Scivias* (a shortened form of *Scito Vias Domini*, or *Know the Ways of the Lord*, the great work in which Hildegard's twenty-six visions ranging from creation to redemption were transcribed and illustrated) inspired Elizabeth to write down her own. Until she died at the age of thirty-six, Elizabeth continued to preach against both the exaggerated asceticism of the Cathars and the avarice of the clergy. But the center of her life and of the public's interest in her were the mystical visions that accompanied her daily experience of monastic life. During mass, Elizabeth would often see the host as flesh and blood pouring from Jesus' side to the chalice, while tongues of fire appeared over her sisters' heads as they received communion.

One remarkable vision suggests why her experience of the Eucharist had the power to heal and strengthen her. She saw a beautiful virgin with hair streaming down her shoulders, sitting in the middle of the sun and holding a golden cup. When a dark cloud obscured the sun, the virgin cried. Elizabeth's interpreting angel explained that this figure was "the sacred humanity of the Lord Jesus." When she was later questioned about this mixing of genders, she suggested that the figure might also represent Mary. Since she had seen the vision during mass on Christmas Eve, when Christ's humanity is so closely connected with his birth from Mary, such multiple meanings are understandable. It is nevertheless obvious that Elizabeth, like many later religious women, believed that Christ shared her own female nature. Accordingly, she found receiving Christ in the Eucharist an affirmation of her own life as a woman.

Priests, on the other hand, had a different view of the sacrament. They saw their consecration of the bread and wine at mass as parallel to Mary's act in giving birth to Jesus. A well-known twelfth-century text reads: "O revered dignity of priests, in whose hands the Son of God is incarnated as in the Virgin's womb."[26] The text reflects twelfth-century efforts to aggrandize the role of priests. Emphasizing their separation from the laity, priests distanced the Eucharist from daily life. By the thirteenth century, says Caroline Bynum, although women mystics might still experience the Eucharist as union with Christ, they would no longer criticize the clergy, as Elizabeth had, but rather would support their authority.

Elizabeth's best-known vision was recorded by her brother Ekbert, a learned monk, who suggested that in her ecstasy she might raise a question the schoolmen continued to debate: Was Mary really assumed into heaven?

"What you seek you cannot know," Mary told Elizabeth when she first asked. A year later, however, on the feast of the Assumption, Elizabeth was rewarded with a scene which she considered to be divinely revealed, but which harmonized with her own beliefs. She saw a woman emerging from a tomb, and then being lifted up to heaven to be greeted by the Lord. Elizabeth's angel told her that it was Mary, who had been assumed into heaven, body and soul. Ekbert, retaining the habits of his scholasticism, pressed his sister to find out how long a time had elapsed between Mary's death and her Assumption. When Elizabeth asked her angel about this, she was told that the time was forty days; it had not been revealed to the early Fathers, the angel confided, yet they had believed it.

Belief in the Assumption was indeed very old and had been celebrated as part of the liturgical year in the East at least by the fifth century. Anselm implied Mary's presence in heaven when he spoke of the Virgin Mother as Queen of the Angels. Bernard suggested it in his sermons, and the cathedrals portrayed other versions of the scene Elizabeth described. Questions remained, however, as to when and how Mary's body and soul had been joined in heaven, and whether she had died or merely gone to sleep. Widely circulated at the time, Elizabeth's vision confirmed the general belief that Mary now lived with her son in heaven, body and soul.

Visions also dominated the long career of Hildegard of Bingen (1098–1179), for whom Mary was central to an understanding of God's plan. "Ever since my infancy," she wrote, "I have always had the gift of vision in my soul."[27] Hildegard was frail and suffered from migraine headaches all her life. This disability, along with her special gifts, may have motivated her parents to send her at the age of eight to a hermitage connected with the male monastery of St. Disibod, where she received her education from the anchoress Jutta. There the Benedictine rule of work and communal prayer based on the liturgical year focused her visions and shaped her talents. Later she was elected abbess of the female community within the larger monastery.[28]

From an early age she composed music for her sisters; more than a way to praise God, for her it was a way of living in heaven here on earth. Mary is central in Hildegard's compositions. In the thirteenth vision of the *Scivias* Hildegard hears the citizens of heaven in the lucent sky calling to those on earth, telling them to persevere: "And their song, like the voice of a multitude, making music in harmony praising the ranks of heaven," is directed to Mary:

> O splendid jewel, serenely infused with the Sun!
> The Sun is in you as a fount from the heart of the Fathers;
> It is His sole Word, by Whom He created the world,
> The primary matter, which Eve threw into disorder.
> He formed the Word in you as a human being,
> And therefore you are the jewel that shines most brightly,
> Through whom the Word breathed out the whole of the virtues
> As once from primary matter He made all creatures.[29]

In Hildegard's cosmic understanding, informed by the Wisdom texts of Mary's feast days, the mother of Jesus is the centerpiece of God's plan, his beloved from before the beginning of time. The image of the gem in this song appears in some medieval paintings of the Annuciation; instead of destroying its beautiful color, light enhances it, just as God's power acts on Mary's virginity. For Hildegard, the Virgin Birth was as important as the cross.[30] The Incarnation would have happened even if humanity did not sin; it was the very purpose of creation. Whereas Bernard could not see how Mary could have been conceived in holiness because she was conceived sexually, Hildegard, like Ephrem, shifted the emphasis to the virginal Mary, necessary to produce Christ's purity in the flesh.

In arranging the order of the liturgical songs in her *Symphonia*, Hildegard placed those to the Mother of God between those to the first and third persons of the Trinity. As the necessary means of the Incarnation, Mary dwells always in the heart of God. With her son she is the revelation of a new creation, her virginity serving to unite heaven and earth. In her *Play of the Virtues (Ordo*

Virtutum), a morality play performed within the convent, Hildegard portrayed the triumph of the soul's struggle against evil by having the Virgin place her heel on the head of the Devil.[31]

Though Mary is Eve's opposite in this divine drama, in Hildegard's timeless vision she is also Eve's archetype—and hence the archetype of woman herself. Instead of blaming Eve, God made use of another woman to more than compensate for the fault that was committed; Mary was Eve's advocate, as Irenaeus had suggested earlier. Like Ephrem, Hildegard used multiple metaphors to convey Mary's lightness and purity: Mary is the dawn who disperses the clouds with which Eve overshadowed the world, the "form of woman," the "sister of Wisdom."[32] Hildegard identified Wisdom (Sapientia) as the consort of Solomon in the Song of Songs. Mary was Wisdom's sister because she was the mother and consort of the true Wisdom, Jesus. In all these figures, Hildegard centered her theology on the Creator's love of creation. Classic Christian interpreters saw the bride in the Song of Songs as the Church, the soul, or the Virgin Mary; Hildegard saw her as the world wedded to its maker. By means of the Incarnation, Mary and Eve were now unified. "Mary *is* Eve: there is only one Woman, she who was born of Adam in order to be, like Wisdom, the mirror of God's beauty and 'the embrace of his whole creation.' " Both Eve and Mary are cosmic theophanies of the feminine whose purpose is to manifest God in the world. In Hildegard's vision, creation itself is "Wisdom's vesture": "at every level the feminine is that in God which binds itself most intimately with the human race, and through it with the cosmos."[33] Woman has thus "graced the heavens more than she once disgraced the earth."[34]

Hildegard developed this conflation of Eve and Mary in several songs, most fully in *"O virga ac diadema,"* where she brings together all her Marian themes in a lovely lyric. The nuns in her order reported that their aging abbess used to chant this sequence to herself with a special radiance as she walked in the cloister. It sums up Hildegard's positive vision, unifying themes that were widely accepted in the twelfth century despite the dualism inherited from the Greco-Roman church.

In Hildegard's imagery, as in the theology of Ambrose and Augustine, Mary was also the archetype of Mother Church: "And as the Holy Spirit overshadowed the blessed Mother so that, without pain, she wonderfully conceived and bore the Son of God yet remained a virgin, so also the Holy Spirit illumines the Church, the happy mother of believers."[35]

In these words Mary is linked to baptism—an idea propounded by many Fathers since the fourth century. But Hildegard went further, stressing Mary's connection with every Eucharist: "that same power of the Most High which formed flesh in the Virgin's womb changes the oblation of bread and wine on the altar into the sacrament of flesh and blood, brooding over it with his power." Baptism and Eucharist are similar transformative events, both dependent on the power of the Holy Spirit, which in the Hebrew and Syriac traditions is feminine. Rather than dividing priests and laity, men and women, Hildegard's vision united them in response to the power of the Spirit.

Mary's timeless significance was underscored by Hildegard's use of the word "brooding" to connect the theme of the Spirit of God brooding over the waters in Genesis 1:2 with the twelfth-century idea of the Annunciation as a second genesis.[36] Mary renews life itself because the potency within her is that of the Spirit re-creating the world. And since the life of that world, the Christ she bore, is daily reborn in the church through the Eucharist, she is continually bringing him forth.

At the age of forty-three, Hildegard believed that she received a mandate from God to make her views known to the public. She had confided them previously only to Volmar, a monk of St. Disibod who was her lifelong friend and secretary. As frail as she was powerful, she suffered torments of indecision, calling herself a "wretched creature, more than wretched, being a woman" in a letter of 1147 to Bernard of Clairvaux, begging him to tell her whether she should reveal her visions openly or stay silent. As with Elizabeth, the conflict she underwent between what she knew was her "place" as a woman and what she felt God asked of her must have added greatly to her emotional and psychological pain.

At a council in nearby Trier in 1147–48, Pope Eugenius III heard of Hildegard's still unfinished *Scivias* and sent for a copy. He was so favorably impressed that he read sections to the assembly. Bernard chose this opportunity to speak on her behalf, and soon she received a greeting from the pope granting her apostolic license to continue writing. Her prophetic vocation confirmed, she proceeded to exercise it with skill and determination for the rest of her life. Out of love for the church, she never hesitated to criticize the clergy for their buying and selling of office and for their failure to teach the people. She even chastized Bernard for encouraging military activity among the clergy, complained about several popes for their failures in leadership, and challenged the Emperor Frederick Barbarossa for precipitating a power struggle with the papacy. Hildegard knew she needed male authority to operate in her world, but when she obtained it, she never looked back.

Hildegard was and understood herself to be a prophet, not only because of her personal gift, but because her thinking was formed by biblical Wisdom literature—Proverbs, the Wisdom of Solomon, and Ecclesiasticus—all very popular in the Middle Ages. Like many others, she was drawn to the passages about Sophia as God's feminine collaborator in the work of creation. She sought feminine manifestations of divine action, for they harmonized with her own belief—and that of Elizabeth—that God showed Himself in weakness. Since women were weak, the purpose of the feminine was to manifest God in the world—an amazingly positive reversal of social disparagement. In keeping with the medieval tendency to allegorize and personify ideal concepts in feminine form, Hildegard described Wisdom and Charity as powerful feminine figures who personified the eternal circulation of divine love.

In the *Scivias* her vision embraced the divine economy from Creation to the Last Judgment, when the bones of the dead would leap up whole and alive. Hildegard cared primarily about the place of the human person in this history, and she conveyed a dramatic sense of the cosmic dance in which all interact. In her view the fragile human soul made its precarious way in the world under the guidance of Church and Empire, free at every moment to rebel or to obey.

Hildegard's grasp of God's cosmic plan was first of all visual: in one of her illuminations a colorful watery frame displays the heads of assorted sea and land creatures breathing and roaring into the inner circle that contains at its center the fourfold globe of the earth, on whose circular rim trees are growing and men and women work and play. Red dots and blue lines move from outer to inner rim, suggesting the interconnectedness of all nature.

Nevertheless, there is a dualism in Hildegard's thinking that does not match the unity of her vision. Though she saw the feminine dimensions of the divine, she accepted the social inferiority of women prevalent in her time. She affirmed a joyful physical creation, but her belief in the sinfulness of sexual relations seemed to deny it. Mary is never envisioned as a human person. She is a state of existence, the garden where God dwells; she is joy, innocence, asexual love. Her virginity is that of Paradise. In this monastic era, both Mary and Mother Church are holy in Hildegard's visions because they are virginal. The nun, not the married woman, is the figure of the unique virgin bride who reminds us of Eve in the garden before the Fall. Hildegard's idea of virginity, however, is free and joyful, like Thecla's or Ephrem's. She designed special white costumes and headdresses for the members of her community. When questioned by another abbess about these "tiaras," she defended her sisters' right to have such special emblems: all the virgins she saw in heaven had them!

POPULAR PIETY

Although Hildegard was known as a prophet and a healer in her own day, her music was for the convent and her writing was in Latin; their influence, therefore, was confined to a small elite. What fed the piety of ordinary folk who lived and worked in cities, had children, and left us no texts? Since few written sources survive, I found it necessary to follow tentative clues and develop speculative answers. There are fabliaux from the towns, often bawdy and anticlerical, showing resistance to clerical dominance; Chaucer's *Canterbury Tales* offers a few examples. But such stories circulated principally in towns. Where did the majority, the rural people who worked on the vast feudal landholdings, get their knowledge of religion? Their contact with the clergy was probably limited to baptisms, weddings, and funerals. Their bishops were probably seen more as feudal lords than as pastors, and even Rome was not so much a place of spiritual authority as the home of St. Peter's tomb. Salvation seemed more available to such people if they made donations to the monasteries, or asked monks and nuns to pray for them and assure their right relationship with God. As for their more immediate needs, such as the success of their crops or the health of farm animals, they sought out local wisemen and -women—like Hildegard, who was known for her skill in healing—or prayed before the relics of saints or the Virgin.

A number of the clergy wrote of wanting to moderate "the dangerous excesses of folk piety"; some even felt that Bernard's Mariology encouraged the fertility cults of earlier ages to infiltrate Christian piety.[37]

And perhaps it did. Deeply embedded in the consciousness of the peasantry was the need for a feminine manifestation of the divine. Despite their conversion to Christianity, the Frankish peasants under Charlemagne clung to old beliefs well into the Middle Ages, as did similar peasants in Ireland, England, and throughout Europe. Historian Eileen Power observes that Christianity could not completely efface the heathen charms and prayers they used because "the tilling of the soil is the oldest and most unchanging of human occupations . . . and the old gods stalk up and down the brown furrows, when they have long vanished from houses and roads." Incantations to the earth mother during the sowing of seed were an intimate part of daily life:

> Earth, Earth, Earth! O Earth, our mother!
> May the All-Wielder, Ever-Lord grant thee
> Acres a-waxing, upwards a-growing,
> Pregnant with corn and plenteous in strength.[38]

Natural disasters and famine were regular possibilities, and there is evidence that twelfth-century peasants still carried out festivals recalling the old spring ritual in which a statue of the goddess was carried over the field in a cart to assure its fertility. Church authorities tried to destroy statues and shrines to such goddesses and considered some folk festivals demonic. But as art historian Pamela Berger points out, peasant folklore mingled the stories of Mary with those of the mother goddess who helped bring back to life the young god whose sacrifice was necessary for the growth of the crops. One example is the legend that added a grain miracle to the Virgin's activities during the Flight into Egypt. When Mary passed by a farmer's field, the story goes, she graciously offered to help him raise an instant crop. In that way he would not have to lie to the soldiers when they asked if Mary had passed by recently. "Just when I planted this field," he could say.

Such mingling of Mary and the mother goddess can also be

heard in the gypsy version of an enduring medieval folk ballad
whose symbols suggest its pre-Christian meaning:

> And carry home your ripened corn,
> That you've been sowing this day. . . .
> And keep Christ in your remembrance
> Till the time comes round again.[39]

When tempted to dismiss something as pagan, it is useful to remember that the word "pagan" is rooted in "pays" (land), and related to "paisano" (landsman). Awareness of this derivation may
help us approach the religious sensibility of people who spent
their whole lives working the soil in one locality, were dependent
on its seasons and its fruits, and felt the presence of spirit in all its
manifestations.[40] For medieval peasants, getting enough food was
always a serious problem. Disease was prevalent, infant mortality
high, and the life span limited. Just as the statues of ancient goddesses often show them as comforting maternal figures bearing food, so did responsibility for food and life gradually accrue
to Mary.

It should be easy to understand why peasant rituals in the
churchyard were disturbing to the local clergy. Bawdy dances
and songs that may have derived from the old Mayday festivals
persisted up to the time of the Reformation. As they had earlier,
church leaders tried to meet popular need; they introduced other
kinds of devotions and celebrations and sometimes employed
male saints like Blaise to take over functions earlier attributed to
the goddess.[41] Attempts to teach the country folk to pray to Our
Lord and his mother instead of to the Earth Mother and Father
Heaven were only partially successful. For example, the bee-
keeper was to call on Mary, adapting an old charm to her virtues:

> Sit down, sit down bee
> St. Mary commanded thee . . .
> Sit very still,
> Wait God's will.[42]

Emphasis on the Mother and her Son rather than the Father who was in heaven reflects a degree of continuity in iconography between Mary and earlier goddesses whose functions she now assumed. Just as a church in Mary's honor had been built over the temple of Diana at Ephesus not long after she was declared God-Bearer in 431, now churches dedicated to Mary rose in Europe over earlier shrines to Celtic and Roman goddesses. At Chartres, the cathedral guidebook informs the visitor that before the Christian era, the site had been consecrated to an ancient druidic cult. The ebony statue honored in this sanctuary was "la Virgo paritura," probably Belisima, the goddess of fecundity worshiped by the local Carnutes. Women went to her shrine for divine help in childbearing. When Bishop Fulbert of Chartres consecrated an altar with martyrs' relics to Mary in 1020 in the crypt of his church, he placed upon it a statue of Mary holding her son on her knees, and Belisima was dethroned.

By my third visit to the cathedral, I was able to appreciate the marvelous continuity with which the figure of Mary could represent the qualities of mercy embedded in earlier pagan cultures, an idea which once would have seemed un-Christian to me. Now I understood that this was the way in which popular belief had slowly softened the harsh separation between the divine and the natural in the ancient church. The little side chapel at Chartres with its small, dark statue to Our Lady of the Pillar is still sought out by those who come not as tourists or esthetes, but simply to pray. Every day people bring petitions and thanks there to the north side of the cathedral, where for centuries women have sought help in conception and childbirth. Even in today's largely post-Christian France, there is continuing response to such Christian symbols. When I met a young medieval historian whose book about black madonnas had been helpful in my research, I discovered that at the suggestion of her mother's friends, during her first pregnancy she had worn an ancient belt believed to be Mary's and preserved in their church. This sophisticated woman gratefully accepted a physical sign of the caring solidarity of women, a reminder that reached back imaginatively to identification with the real Mary of Nazareth. Her attitude made me realize how superficial our understanding may be of medieval believers and their seemingly credulous pursuit of relics.

THRONES OF WISDOM AND
BLACK MADONNAS

The original statues of Mary at Chartres and Le Puy, like those at Marseilles, Rocamadour, and Montserrat in Spain, were Thrones of Wisdom, examples of a uniquely Romanesque form that was the most popular icon of the period. These statues—also called Virgins in Majesty—were carved from a single block of wood, light in weight and less than life size. Most of the originals were painted in polychrome, some were overlaid with gold, and a considerable number—all those above, for example, which were linked with the greatest number of miracles—were black. They were carried in slow processions among the people—reminiscent of processions for the Great Goddess—so that people could touch Mary, hold up their sick children to her, or have her bless special objects.

There is a family resemblance and yet enormous artistic diversity among these statues, although all are small, around three feet high. These Virgins in Majesty range from primitive to sophisticated, and the expression on the mother's face varies from impassivity to tenderness. In all of them, however, Mary sits on a simple throne, the Christ child on her knees, both erect in a frontal position. She does not look at us but into the distance, perhaps seeing the eternal, perhaps the unending suffering of humanity. She is presenting her child, who resembles her exactly; he is flesh of her flesh, not a baby but a small man-child who often makes a sign of blessing with one hand and holds a book in the other. Ephrem had already provided a verbal portrait of the Throne of Wisdom: "The heaven is the throne for His glory, yet He sits on Mary's knees."[43] This is the mother who is literally God-Bearer, whose son has only her human features. The abstract Romanesque folds of Mary's drapery ripple with life; in many such statues she wears a crown. Her disproportionately large hands suggest her peasant origins; her queenly pose reminds us that she is the mother of God. Here is perfect tension between the human and the hieratic. Except for the hands, each Virgin in Majesty is like a Byzantine icon come to life, disengaged from architecture, meant to be mobile and accessible.

And in fact the sources for the pose appear to be Byzantine and Mediterranean; the statues are direct descendants of the large mosaic on the wall of the early sixth-century Basilica of St. Apollinare Nuovo in Ravenna, and of the sixth-century madonna enthroned between SS. George and Theodore in the monastery of St. Catherine at Mt. Sinai. The image penetrated Western art largely through manuscript illuminations of the antiphonaries and the Divine Office, which were central to the worship of every monastery. For example, an enthroned madonna appears in the eighth-century Irish illuminated manuscript of the Gospels known as the Book of Kells (Plate 11). There Mary is a queen, but her playful redheaded son is more a baby than a pantocrator. The decoration and lettering are Irish and Anglo-Saxon, but the pose probably was taken from the illuminated Byzantine and Mediterranean books Pope Gregory I sent to Ireland with missionaries at the end of the sixth century.

The strikingly original black Virgin of Meymac in Limousin, France—surprisingly alive in her wooden peasant shoes and gold oriental turban—also sits in this Byzantine frontal position (Plate 14). The look of steady compassion in the eyes of the mother in a number of Thrones, especially that of Marsat (Plate 13), in the French Auvergne, is similar to that in many Eastern icons, most notably the twelfth-century Vladimir Mother of God (Plate 16).

The most celebrated Thrones of Wisdom contained relics; sometimes a relic associated with Mary was kept in a church or shrine that also contained a Throne, attracting throngs of pilgrims. Chartres had Mary's tunic, Le Puy her slippers. In some cases a door was ingeniously carved in the hollow back or neck of the Virgin to keep the relics intact. The miraculous power of relics authorized artists to reproduce a type of statue very close to pagan idols, although there is no direct history or record of the making of the Thrones of Wisdom or of the origin of the style. The prototype of the first such statue at Clermont-Ferrand was lost when the statue was destroyed, but fortunately art historian Louis Bréhier found a tenth-century sketch in the Clermont-Ferrand municipal library that gives a clear idea of its appearance (Plate 12). The evidence suggests that these movable statues originated in the Mediterranean area, but spread north via trade routes following the Rhône from Marseilles, ultimately reaching as far as Germany and Sweden.[44] The large number of such Virgins in the Auvergne, such as the beautiful statues at Orcival and Marsat, appear to have come from the same atelier in Clermont-Ferrand.

The most frequent story of the origins of the black madonnas, however, is that they were found by chance in a natural setting: a bush, a cave, or a river. When people tried to take the statue to town to build a suitable chapel, it escaped and returned again and again to its original site until they gave up and built the chapel where they had found it. In the Pyrenees, in Puy de Dôme and elsewhere, these black madonnas seemed to be witnessing to the holiness of the natural site. Our Lady of Vassivière insisted on being returned to a mountain pass where she served as guardian of the route and protector of travelers. Other such statues associated Mary with the watery or dark chthonic origins of mother goddesses like Ceres and Cybele, who had been venerated in caverns. Notre Dame de Confession in St. Victor's in Marseilles and Notre Dame de Sous-Terre at Chartres were both venerated in crypts. The Marseilles madonna seems to have inherited the qualities of Epona, the Gallic divinity of the moon and wild nature, as well as those of Diana and even of the dark Hecate, who was worshiped at crossroads in Marseilles and never forgotten in Provence. Mary took on their power over death as well; the black Virgin of Arles was originally located in the Gallo-Roman necropolis of Alyscamps.

People did not want to think such statues were carved by human hands; they sensed that the great natural forces of life and death were present in them. Medieval historian Sophie Cassagnes-Brouquet says that many wanted to believe that these statues, as powerful and fruitful as nature, had been present in their village, hidden in water or soil, from time immemorial.[45] For ordinary people in small towns, these local madonnas, portable representations of the Incarnation, summed up their hope of intimate contact with the divine. At the same time they incorporated the elemental force of human life that their ancestors, since prehistoric times, had perceived in the Goddess.

Legends also say that the Virgin chose those who were to discover her. Frequently her first contact with an area was with cows or bulls; sometimes it was with shepherds, children, or humble souls on the edge of society, close to nature. Because bulls embodied vital energy, they played an essential role in symbolizing the fecundity of the Goddess. Followers of the cult of Cybele ritually bathed in the blood of bulls. Even today, in Seaulieu, a small town in Burgundy, the statue of a bull sits in the center of a small park near a statuette of Mary bearing grapes.

It is impossible to draw a neat line separating pagan reverence for life from Christian imagery: Ephrem had called the Eucharistic wine, the blood of Christ's sacrifice, "grape of Mary." Mystery is evoked, not contained, in the metaphors of liturgy. Among twelfth-century peasants, the bull was the biological complement of the Virgin; both were fecund. Although most churchmen did not share such beliefs, they were willing to commission statues of

the Virgin in Majesty, convinced that the Mother of God was capable of healing. Notre Dame de Bon Espoir at Dijon was
sculpted with heavy breasts and a somewhat pendulous stomach
to emphasize her fertility (Plate 17). When life was so short and
good medical care almost unavailable, such a statue was enormously popular as a source of hope and healing, especially in matters of childbirth and child care. It was not looked on as art, but as
a reminder of Mary's—and her son's—presence in the community. Accommodation to such needs by local bishops and priests
was not just a matter of realizing that such madonnas had enormous appeal and would bring fame and wealth to their shrines.
The merchants and butchers in town promoted the statues as essential to local well-being. No doubt such motives were behind
much of the competition to produce statues similar to those at
popular pilgrimage sites, and when black madonnas became the
biggest miracle-workers, earlier statues were repainted black.[46]

What was more important, however, was that the Thrones of
Wisdom could take on earlier pagan functions and nevertheless
be seen as suitable for Christian devotion. These statues represented the central mystery of the Incarnation, God become human, in a comprehensible yet still mysterious symbol. Mary had
long been called the Throne (or Seat) of Wisdom in the prayer of
the church.[47] Church authorities could invoke the Song of Songs
as justification for her blackness:

> I am as dark—but lovely,
>   O daughters of Jerusalem—
> As the tents of Kedar,
>   as the curtains of Salma.
> Do not stare at me because I am swarthy,
>   because the sun has burned me. (Song of Songs 1:5–6)

These statues embodied the essential meaning of God's choice
in the Annunciation and in Mary's Magnificat. For André Malraux, Notre Dame de Bon Espoir at Dijon expressed the tran-

scendence of humility. Although Mary's arms were missing and the figure of her son had disappeared, the statue combined a vulnerable face with a still invulnerable body, the emotionally moving in a beautifully elaborated form. "Through that simple face, inconceivable to the Byzantines, almost like that of a village idiot visited by the eternal," Malraux says, "God calls out to humanity sorrow by sorrow."[48]

Why so many Thrones of Wisdom are black poses mysterious and seemingly unanswerable problems. Art historian Ilene Forsyth says that they were not intended to be black; they became so over time because of fire, smoke, or other natural causes. Yet in viewing the Virgin of Marsat or Notre Dame de Bonne Délivrance in Neuilly, Paris, it is striking to see the contrast between the black skin of the mother's face and hands and her extremely bright clothes. Mere accident, it seems, would have blackened everything.

Some recent anthropological research indicates that while many of these madonnas were made black by accident, perhaps thirty of the statues—all in regions once occupied by Roman legions—may have always been black. These include those at Montserrat, Marseilles, Chartres, and at Enna in Sicily. Sometimes it is not certain if a statue was originally a goddess or Mary. In Enna, a statue of Demeter and Kore was used in church at the Nativity to represent Mary and Jesus until the nineteenth century, when Pius IX became aware of it and had the statue moved. Statues of Demeter and Isis were black because they were associated with the fertility of the dark earth, recalling the appearance of Isis at night in the beautiful vision of Apuleius. Such findings suggest that the black madonnas were Christian borrowings from earlier pagan forms that retained the power of their models.[49]

But this cannot be the whole answer; many Byzantine and Russian icons were blackened by fire and time, and people accept their blackness as part of their holiness. In fact, similar legends about finding them occur in the East and in Russia, where no

Roman troops could have brought them.[50] The Kazan Mother of God was found in the sixteenth century after a young girl dreamed of Mary and was commanded in the dream to tell both secular and ecclesiastical powers where the icon was buried.

In the West, whether or not the statues were black by accident or by origin, it is clear that white statues were often deliberately painted black because people preferred them that way. For example, when the Black Virgin of Einsiedeln in Switzerland was moved to Austria in 1798 to escape Napoleon, it was first restored to its original whiteness; public outrage caused it to be repainted black. The feeling that icons of Mary should be black may reflect the common European memory of prehistoric millennia in which blackness stood for the life-giving, regenerative energy of the goddess, while whiteness stood for death,[51] meanings that are just the opposite of those the colors held in the Middle Ages.

PILGRIMAGES AND MIRACLE STORIES

In the twelfth century, legends and miracles that had been associated with Mary earlier in other locations now began to cluster around the shrines that contained her statues. Each locality had its own special days and rites, but sometimes such enterprises were populist and cooperative. Bishops of large city cathedrals might take their relics on the road in the hope of obtaining cures and securing funds necessary for the building or repair of churches.[52] All this was possible because the cult of the Virgin, unlike that of most saints, was both local and universal. Miracles could be attributed to Mary everywhere precisely because her power was so well established that it did not need to be reinforced. Legends and stories or miracles attributed to Mary from much earlier Syrian or Coptic sources—like the apocryphal stories of her conception, her childhood in the temple, and the Transitus legend—were well known throughout Christendom.

Early Coptic miracle stories, which were read in churches in Cairo by the end of the twelfth century, show similarities to those that appear in Western Europe, while preserving local differences. People from all classes of society in these Coptic stories received Mary's mercy. She provided cures from blindness and leprosy, arranged marriages, regained stolen property, punished thieves, and even delivered souls from hell. On one occasion she moved a monastery full of monks to a new site beside a flowing stream. She healed an aged Jew who had broken his back and meted out justice to a dishonest bishop. These Coptic stories reveal more about the attitude of their tellers than they do about Mary. One mentions her mercy to Abbas, bishop of Rome, who cut off the hand with which he had been distributing communion because "he smelt the odour of a certain woman as she was embracing his hands, and the unclean desire of the flesh entered into his heart and he burned with the flame of lust." Later, he passed a picture of the Virgin Mary and wept, asking for mercy; she graciously created a new hand for him and attached it.

An unhappy characteristic of these Coptic stories, also present in European miracles, is their delight in vengeance against the enemies of local devotees. One, for example, tells of three Arabs threatened at sea by a terrible storm. Two pray to Mary and one to Allah. The third Arab lashes out at the other two for their unfaithfulness, whereupon he is swept overboard, while the two who pray to Mary are saved: "Thine enemy, O my Lady at every time and season, shall become the food of the crocodile and of the crusher of bones."[53] Obviously, the story reflects the anti-Muslim prejudice of those who recorded it.

Anti-Semitism, which we have met already in the apocryphal Book of James, forms a thread in many other Near Eastern legends as well. One such story, about a Jewish boy, made its way to France and was included in Gregory of Tours's sixth-century collection of such miracles. This boy, the son of a Jewish glass-maker, often went to church with the Christian children, and one day he took Holy Communion. When his father heard of it, he was so furious that he threw his son into a fiery oven. All the town came running when they heard the cries of the mother, and they were startled to see the boy lying in the flames as if he were on a featherbed. The miracle was attributed to Mary, because the boy told them that the lady whose image he had seen in church had covered him with her mantle. The townspeople thereupon threw the father into the oven, and the boy and his mother converted to Christianity. Undercurrents of anti-Semitism were thus preserved as part of popular tradition and would later be fanned into destructive flames.

The vast majority of European miracles, however, show the Virgin's generous response to anyone who asks for her protection. Records at Rocamadour reveal her help to the deserving poor and the undeserving rich. Peasants, servants, and cowherds received cures, but noble knights and their ladies were also rewarded. Sometimes Mary won a knight's battle for him; at other times, she rescued a pet falcon or saved boys from drowning. As one collector of such tales, William of Malmesbury, said of them, "They are helpful in kindling simple souls to the love of the Lord."[54] Perhaps "The Juggler of Our Lady" is the loveliest and most popular of such tales: a humble juggler performs before Mary's statue as the only way he knows of honoring her, and is rewarded by her living presence.

But Mary did not stop at helping the innocent. One legend reports that she even stood in for a nun who had run off with her lover, so that the nun was never missed at the convent. Mary outwitted the law, saving even murderers and thieves who called on her. But she never promised material rewards, and in all cases she assured her clients of pardon and salvation only when they repented. As Henry Adams says, "The people loved Mary because she trampled on conventions; not merely because she could do it, but because she liked to do what shocked every well-regulated authority. Her pity had no limit."[55] Only the Queen of Heaven had such freedom in this feudal society. It is not surprising, therefore, that the crusaders who brought back the game of chess from Syria changed the rules in one significant way. As played in the East, the King was followed by a Minister. The crusaders changed the piece to give it more freedom, making it the most arbitrary and formidable champion on the board, and they called it the Queen or the Virgin.

For a brief moment, then, the figure of Mary served to hold many ideological, cultural, and economic forces in delicate balance. The twelfth century produced the most imposing yet approachable images of the Virgin ever created. These madonnas are never sentimental; even beneath the cross Mary bears her grief without tears. They speak to the mind through symbols that demand interpretation; in cathedrals as well as in small-town churches, they were available to all. The mother in the Thrones and the Queen of Heaven in the stained glass of Chartres share an essential humanity, suggesting that all things natural are alive with the sacred. Created at the peak of the medieval period, they show how Mary functioned as the center of a coherent and inclusive divine creation.

REFORM, COUNTER-REFORM, AND CONQUEST:
The Virgin Divided

O Blessed Virgin, Mother of God, you were nothing and all despised, yet God in His grace regarded you and worked such great things in you. You were worthy of none of them, but the rich and abundant grace of God was upon you, far above any merit of yours.

—MARTIN LUTHER[1]

> If you meet the Virgin
> Coming down the road,
> Ask her into your house
> She bears the word of God.

—JOHN OF THE CROSS[2]

Our Lady of Guadalupe has been a sign in which each epoch and each Mexican has read his destiny.

—OCTAVIO PAZ[3]

W ESTERN CHRISTIANITY DIVIDED IN TWO IN THE SIX-
teenth century. Each side was hostile to the other politically and
militarily, and each had an identity often invested in separate
nations as well as in separate Protestant and Catholic churches.
Focusing on this development today through a Marian lens, I
believe that despite the tragedy of Christians fighting each other
for so long, this acrimonious schism has ultimately served to
create a dynamic for reform throughout Christianity worldwide. Although Marian devotion was not a central cause of the
break, Mary was often the most visible image of much that angered Reformers: veneration of the saints at the expense of close
reading of the Scriptures, and a general tendency to substitute
rituals, images, and pilgrimages for interior accord with the divine. Mary was a mirror that reflected both the causes and consequences of the Reformation, revealing and for many years
exaggerating the divisions between Protestants and Catholics.
The process can be seen clearly in the art and devotion that preceded the split.

LATE MEDIEVAL DEVOTIONALISM

For the first thousand years of Christianity, interest had focused
on the risen Lord. In twelfth-century monasticism, Bernard began to shift the focus to Christ's humanity, advising the faithful
to cultivate his love through images: "The soul at prayer should

185

have before it a sacred image of the God-man, in his birth or infancy or as he was teaching, or dying, or rising, or ascending." Anselm had already shown the purpose of such imagining: to become an actor in the drama, which then became a model for one's conduct in daily life. "Why, O my soul," he asked, "were you not there to be pierced by a sword of bitter sorrow when you could not bear the piercing of the side of your Savior with a lance? Why could you not bear to see the nails violate the hands and feet of your creator?" Anselm then turned to Mary: "What can I say about the fountains that flowed from your most pure eyes when you saw your only Son before you, bound, beaten, and hurt."[4]

In late medieval Christendom, this tendency to humanize Jesus intensified. A visual, emotional piety was greatly stimulated by the new mendicant, or begging, orders of Dominicans and Franciscans; their preaching spread the life of prayer, which earlier had been practiced chiefly in monasteries, to wider groups of laypeople. Mary was at the center of these new devotional practices because she, best of all, could introduce believers to the human Jesus.

Interest in the realistic details of Jesus' birth and death grew stronger in the late Middle Ages. St. Francis of Assisi (d. 1226) had been converted from his earlier hedonism when he prayed before a crucifix. His joyous life of total poverty—embracing lepers with the same spontaneity with which he sang of Brother Sun, Sister Moon, and Brother Wolf—was a powerful example. Francis brought the Nativity scene to life for ordinary people by instituting the use of the crib and living animals at the Christmas midnight mass. Two years before he died, he received the stigmata, the five wounds of Christ's passion, on his own hands, feet, and side.

The Franciscan sensibility is at the center of St. Bonaventure's late thirteenth-century retelling of the Gospels, *The Tree of Life*, which advises the reader to enter its scenes imaginatively. The widely read *Meditations on the Life of Christ*, written around 1300 by an unknown Franciscan friar, provides further insight into the new piety. In the retelling of the Magi's visit, for example, Mary feels uncomfortable accepting their rich gifts of gold, frankincense, and myrrh. Like Francis, she gives these costly things to the poor, among whom she and her child wish to remain.

Describing the Nativity, the author of the *Meditations* stops to suggest that readers should pick up the child, kiss him, and, if possible, help the mother. They are not only meant to share in the life of Christ imaginatively and emotionally, but also to carry such sharing into daily life. The many small art objects inspired by such piety served a similar function; they were meant to assist active, imaginative prayer in the home and even on the road. Small sculptures, folding paintings, and Books of Hours (illuminated prayer books) allowed the nobility and many well-to-do townspeople to pray the Office at home, just as monks and nuns did in their cloisters.

The Virgin was crucial to this interaction of art and devotion. In Dante's early fourteenth-century *Divine Comedy*, the prayer to the Virgin at the conclusion of the *Paradiso* reveals her central place among late medieval believers:

> "Virgin mother, daughter of your Son,
> more humble and sublime than any creature,
> fixed goal decreed from all eternity,
>   you are the one who gave to human nature
> so much nobility that its Creator
> did not disdain His being made its creature."[5]

Giotto covered the walls of the Arena Chapel at Padua with scenes from the life of Jesus and Mary drawn from the apocryphal Book of James, by now well known in Latin translations; these included Anne and Joachim kissing—and Anne conceiving—at the golden gate outside the city, and the child Mary ascending the steps of the temple. Giotto's early fourteenth-century frescoes are a visual reworking, in accordance with new conventions, of the stories popular in the first few centuries of Christianity. The sacred characters have become ordinary citizens with whom all could identify.⁶ Gabriel now kneels before Mary, because that is the way the Annunciation is described in the *Meditations*. God's choice and action in the conception of the child is given special emphasis: many paintings of the Annunciation show the Father gazing directly down at Mary. In new Nativity scenes, Mary kneels as a sign of adoration before the baby, thus instructing those who pray to assume the same attitude. She is the intermediary between past and present, God and believer; her feminine presence represents the whole church.⁷

Along with the Nativity, the Passion and Crucifixion were the most prominent themes of late medieval art. Sienese painters of the fourteenth and fifteenth centuries treat Calvary in terms of the *Meditations*, heightening the emotional tension by having the crowd separate Mary from Jesus. Death, suffering, and judgment were credible concerns in a Europe that had gone through the devastating destruction of the Black Plague and was under repeated siege by the Ottoman Turks, who captured Constantinople in 1453. Such agony perhaps found its ultimate depiction in the new image of the naked Jesus, wounded and crowned with thorns, called the Ecce Homo, and in the figure of Mary holding her dead son stretched out on her own body, the Pietà. Introduced in the early fourteenth century as sculpture, the Pietà appeared in small statues individuals could own as well as in large ones for display in public areas. It long maintained its appeal outside of formal church settings, and became a standard scene in painting in the next century. The great altarpiece Grünewald created at Isenheim between 1505 and 1516 (now in the museum at Colmar in Alsace) links painterly technique with deep human feeling as Mary Magdalene and Mary the mother of Jesus weep and faint under the cross, something they never did in twelfth-century art (Plate 19).

To museum-goers today, the flowing blood and signs of torture in some of these works may seem morbid. But joy and love were the predominant themes of saints like Francis and of the English anchoress Julian of Norwich (1342–c.1413), who also derived her understanding of God's love and mercy from a vision of Christ's suffering on the cross. Julian described the Crucifixion in gory detail during what everyone thought would be her final hours. Reflecting on the meaning of her visions years later, however, she produced the most consoling of Christian mantras: "All shall be well, and all shall be well, and all manner of thing shall be well."[8] Ordinary women could relate to Mary in the Pietà because they, too, tended the sick and the dead (Plate 18). At a time when communion was received infrequently, Mary's reception of the crucified body of Christ reminded women that they were participating spiritually in the Eucharist through their day-to-day work.[9]

Widespread acceptance of the new sensibility created by interaction between images and devotion can be seen in a lovely story about Mary as Mother of Mercy that developed in the thirteenth century. Icons of Mary and her protective veil had emerged earlier in Byzantium; when returning crusaders brought back tales of a relic of Mary's mantle, a new image of Mary reached the West. In it she spread her cloak over kings, nobles, monks, nuns, and ordinary men and women alike, suggesting that the mercy of God sheltered the whole human community. The message was one of equality for all repentant sinners, and encouraged the belief that the protective force emanating from the Virgin's cloak was sustained, in part, by the prayers of the faithful. It was their spiritual insurance policy. Some Dominican nuns in Strasbourg developed an exercise of communal prayer in which, when one nun died, they began a new series of prayers to ask the Mother of Mercy to spread her cloak spiritually over the next sister to die. They settled on ninety thousand Hail Marys as the equivalent of the cloak's cost. The order of service declares: "This is the cloak of the worthy Mother of God for the first sister who shall come to die. May Mary protect her beneath her maternal cloak from all her enemies when her life ends."[10]

The rosary became a very popular devotion in the fourteenth and fifteenth centuries because it, too, encouraged imaginative prayer. It was used as a substitute for the recitation of the Divine Office by lay monks and laypeople who could not read. Saying the rosary was an inexpensive way to recall scenes from the life of Jesus and Mary, for it combined repetition of well-known prayers with meditation on fifteen selected mysteries of faith. In the late Middle Ages the final, nonbiblical words of the Hail Mary were added: "Holy Mary, Mother of God, pray for us now and at the hour of our death, Amen." The "beads" of the rosary may originally have been simple knots on rope; later they were pebbles, berries, or whatever could be threaded. Five decades, or groups of ten beads, for Hail Marys, each preceded by the Our Father and followed by "Glory be to the Father," made up one set of "mysteries." Praying the entire rosary consisted of saying the beads three times, covering all fifteen of the Joyful, Sorrowful, and Glorious mysteries.

The Dominican order did most to popularize the rosary and eventually to put it into the form we have today. As an addition to biblical and liturgical worship the rosary is exemplary, but its emphasis is clearly Marian; it does not dwell on the teaching or mission of the adult Jesus. All five Joyful mysteries concentrate on Jesus' conception and childhood, the Sorrowful mysteries on his Passion and death, and the last two Glorious mysteries on Mary's Assumption and Coronation as Queen of Heaven. Near the end of his life, Fra Angelico painted all fifteen mysteries.[11] The use of the rosary was similar to that of devotional art: to help the one praying to think and act as Mary did.

Just as earlier centuries had developed legends that gave Mary parents and a childhood, in the fifteenth century she was portrayed in paintings and statues as part of a female kinship network in which Jesus' grandmother St. Anne was often the central figure. Devotion to Anne, in fact, rivaled that to her daughter in the fifteenth century, when glorification of the family and the ideals of order and respect accompanied the rise of the middle class. People said quick prayers to the grandmother of the Savior, such as, "Stand by me, O mother of the worthy mother of God" or "Help me, Anne, with your threesome." The thirteenth-century Golden Legend had popularized the apocryphal tale of Anne's three marriages, each producing a daughter named Mary. The other two Marys, along with Mary Magdalene, were the holy women who visited Christ's tomb. This made Anne the legendary grandmother of James the Major, John the Evangelist, James the Minor, St. Jude, St. Simon, and Joseph the Just, inspiring a number of artists to produce kinship scenes that offered a female alternative to the male genealogies of Jesse, father of David, in earlier church windows.

Another popular and related scene in the fifteenth century was that of St. Anne with the Virgin and Child; many statuary groups of this type remain in France, Germany, and Holland. Leonardo's painting at the Louvre is another example of this genre. The Holy Family with St. Joseph became very popular, too, in fifteenth-century painting. In a Nativity scene (c.1400) that was part of a portable altarpiece owned by Philip the Bold, Duke of Burgundy, Joseph is shown cutting up his stockings to make clothes for the still-naked baby; he is the very model of a nurturing father.

Good poetry as well as painting emerged from the Franciscan emphasis on the humanity of Jesus and Mary. The Stabat Mater, perhaps the most moving of all medieval Latin hymns, and one I sang in church when I was young, was composed in the late thirteenth century. It begins:

> At the cross her station keeping,
> stood the mournful mother weeping,
> close to Jesus to the last.

Interest in the Mother of Sorrows was evident in numerous paintings and carvings of the Crucifixion, deposition, and burial of Christ. In these the weeping mother stands beneath the cross, her heart pierced with suffering. The author of the *Meditations* instructed his readers to see our Lady and Mary Magdalene and "Feel for them, for they are in great affliction."[12] In a poem of Jacopone da Todi (to whom the Stabat Mater is often mistakenly ascribed), Jesus responds primarily to Mary:

> Mother, why have you come?
> Your agony and tears crush Me;
> To see you suffer so will be my death.[13]

The faithful obviously identified with the mother's suffering as much as with the son's. Poignant texts for English music from the thirteenth to fifteenth centuries tell the story of the Passion from Mary's point of view.[14] In art, too, as Margaret Miles points out, "Christ's passion is narrated through the perspective of the Virgin and becomes the Virgin's passion."[15] The author of the *Meditations* says that "She hung with her son on the cross and wished to die with him rather than live any longer."[16] Perhaps the most unusual artwork I saw embodying this identification was a double-sided stone crucifix from the fifteenth century in the cloister of the cathedral at Vaison-la-Romaine in Provence; on one side Jesus is shown nailed to the cross, while on the other, Mary, holding her child (now decapitated), is herself crucified. She does not appear to be nailed to the cross—she is simply affixed to it—but such a depiction might well startle those who thought the artist was making Mary the equivalent of her divine son. The American Catholic widow with whom I visited the cloister simply said, "Yes. She certainly suffered as much as he did, though in a different way."

Such imagery would, however, be shocking to those concerned to make the Bible, rather than images and devotions, central to Christian life. After all, many of the homilies of the late Middle

Ages that emphasize Mary have little theological or scriptural basis. Most of the clergy at that time were poorly educated, and before the invention of printing it was not easy to find bibles. Under the circumstances, it is hardly surprising that thirteenth-century admiration of Mary often seems excessive. Richard of St. Laurent's praise of her received wide and respectful attention because until 1952 it was believed to be the work of the learned Dominican Albert the Great. It includes these memorable lines: "Our mother who art in heaven, give us our daily bread" and "Mary so loved the world, that is, sinners, that she gave her only-begotten Son for the salvation of the world." Applying to Mary what belonged to God, Richard justified his words by his ingenious argument that Mary the Mother was more merciful than Christ or the Father. He even stated that "in the sacrament of her Son we also eat and drink her flesh and blood."[17] Richard's devotion was so intense that he devoted an entire book to Mary's beauty (six pages to the spiritual, forty to the physical), advocating the veneration of each part of her body with genuflections and the recitation of Hail Marys.

Only somewhat more sober was the Franciscan Bernardine of Siena (d. 1444), the most beloved preacher of his day, who praised Mary as a kind of spiritual seductress:

> O the unthinkable power of the Virgin Mother! One Hebrew woman invaded the house of the eternal King; one girl, I do not know by what caresses, pledges or violence, seduced, deceived and, if I may say so, wounded and enraptured the divine heart and ensnared the Wisdom of God.[18]

Another Franciscan, Bernardine of Busti, offered a series of miracles from Mary's childhood: she did not cry like other children; she knew rhetoric, logic, physics, and all other branches of knowledge without having to study them. "She is the mistress of the world," he concluded, "because if a son dies without issue his mother succeeds him. . . . No grace or virtue comes to man that is not dispensed by Mary."[19] Such preaching may well have reached many hearts in a culture that venerated motherhood so deeply, but one of the foremost twentieth-century Mariologists, René Laurentin, rendered a needed judgment on such opinions: "A purification was necessary."[20]

ERASMUS AND THE PROTESTANT REFORMATION

By the sixteenth century, some influential Christians agreed that claims for Mary had become extreme. Chief among them was the respected humanist Erasmus of Rotterdam, who had been educated by the Brethren of the Common Life in a simple piety that showed its sincerity through action. In his early years Erasmus himself composed prayers in Mary's honor and even produced a liturgy for the Virgin of Loreto, honoring the miracle that Mary is said to have performed in having angels rescue her house in Nazareth from the oncoming infidels. The angels, so the story goes, flew through the air with the house, moving it several times before finding a hospitable site in Loreto, Italy, where it has rested ever since.[21]

After Erasmus sharpened his prodigious intellect with a classical education and deepened his understanding of the Greek Bible and the Fathers, he came to a more critical view of such legends. He had also visited the shrine of Our Lady of Walsingham in England, two hundred years older than Loreto. What he observed so offended his sense of what was due to God that he composed several dialogues mocking popular devotional practices at the shrine, and circulated them in his *Colloquies*, or conversations.

In one of the early colloquies, "The Shipwreck," a character who has returned from pilgrimages at Compostella and Walsingham is asked why all threatened sailors sing the Salve Regina and pray to Mary as "Star of the Sea, Queen of Heaven, Mistress of the World, and Port of Salvation."[22] Erasmus knew that the eighth-century English historian Bede had reproduced an earlier misreading of Jerome's suggestion that Mary was a "stilla," or drop of the ocean. That scribal error had made Mary "Stella Maris," or star of the sea, long before Bernard's sermons. Erasmus has his character offer a succinct explanation of this mistake that was too tart to please the devout and too flippant to satisfy Reformers: "Formerly Venus was protectress of sailors, because she was believed to have been born of the sea. Since she gave up guarding them, the Virgin Mother had succeeded this mother who was not a virgin."

Like his friend Thomas More, Erasmus aimed to instruct and to purify the faith, but he alienated many believers with his satiric portrait of devotions at Walsingham, the most popular pilgrimage site in Britain. The traditional date of the founding of this replica of the Virgin's house was 1091; it had been constructed according to the specifications of Richeldis de Faverches, a pious woman who had three visions in which Mary led her to her home in Nazareth, gave her the exact measurements of the house, and commanded her to make a duplicate at Walsingham. Many royal and noble benefactors left money to the Holy House, but in his colloquy "A Pilgrimage for Religion's Sake," Erasmus exposed the venality of those making money from the shrine and mocked the credulity of those who accepted the authenticity of the relics, in particular the drops of the Virgin's milk. There was so much of "the heavenly milk of the Blessed Virgin" left on earth, he commented, "it's scarcely credible a woman with only one child could have so much, even if the child had drunk none of it."[23] Erasmus obviously had sound reasons for criticizing such practices when they replaced liturgical worship and everyday charity, but his intellectual elitism may have prevented his appreciating the community-building value of pilgrimages, which, despite inevitable abuses, were genuine expressions of popular piety.[24]

The irony in Erasmus's colloquy on pilgrimages reveals a more serious side when a character cites a letter supposedly written by Mary to Zwingli, the Swiss Reformer. In it, Mary thanks Zwingli for persuading people not to invoke the saints, confessing she has been exhausted by all their petitions:

> a merchant, off for Spain to make a fortune, commits to me the chastity of his mistress. And a nun who has thrown off her veil and is preparing to run away entrusts me with her reputation for virtue—which she herself intends to sell. . . . A gambler cries, "Help me blessed saint; I'll share my winnings with you!" And if they lose at dice, they abuse me outrageously and curse me, because I wouldn't favor their wickedness. . . . If I refuse anything, they protest at once, "Then you're no mother of mercy."

Mary tells Zwingli he has been successful in reducing such petitions: "Formerly I was hailed as Queen of Heaven, mistress of the world; now I hear scarcely an Ave Maria even from the few." But Mary appeals to Zwingli to think again about what he is doing:

> However defenseless, you shall not eject [me] unless at the same time you eject my Son whom I hold in my arms. From him I will not be parted. Either you expel him along with me, or you leave us both here, unless you prefer to have a church without Christ.

The attentive reader today can appreciate that Erasmus was criticizing external devotion and the abuse of relics, not the veneration of Mary. Luther or Zwingli might have made the same complaint: people pile up images to the Virgin "and think she'll help them because at eventide they chant her a hymn they do not understand," while "to Christ they do not turn." But Erasmus's satire was too sophisticated for men embroiled in bitter controversy. A number of Catholics wanted to burn the *Colloquies* for their Lutheran errors, while Luther denounced their author as an atheistic mocker of religion. Catholics found Erasmus subversive; Protestants considered him evasive.

Erasmus was close to the Protestant Reformers, however, on central biblical questions. More important than his *Colloquies* was his work in editing the Fathers and publishing the Greek New Testament with a new Latin translation in 1516, six years before Luther published his German translation of the Bible. Both Erasmus and Luther were word men, in this era when the invention of printing revolutionized the dissemination of learning through language. Painting and sculpture would no longer be the people's bibles; they could now read the text itself. Comparing Jerome's Latin edition of the Bible with the Greek, Erasmus and Luther discovered mistakes in the Vulgate which are central to understanding Mary's role. The angel's greeting to her at the Annunciation was not to one "full of grace" but to one "full of favor," a more accurate translation of the word *kecharitomene* in Luke 1:28. Both scholars found that, in the Magnificat, Mary refers to herself as "lowly," not "humble," more a class than a character description. Such emended translations are acknowledged as accurate by Catholic and Protestant scholars today, but in the sixteenth century forces working against Christian reconciliation and scholarly consensus drove Catholics and Protestants apart despite the agreement between Erasmus and Luther.

MARTIN LUTHER UNDERWENT A DEVELOPMENT IN FAITH similar to that of Erasmus. He came from a pious family of miners, of whom Anne was the patron saint. Fearing Christ as a judge, the young Luther invoked Mary and Anne to help him decide on his vocation to become an Augustinian monk: "We held Christ to be our angry judge, and Mary our mercy-seat, in whom alone was all our trust and refuge."[25] Luther was so fierce in his attempts to be perfect at this time that John Staupitz, the vicar general of the German Augustinians, advised him to concern himself more with the love of Christ, and told him to study the Scriptures. There the words of Paul in Romans hit him with the force of new revelation: everything depended on faith in God's grace—works do not earn us salvation. This overwhelming insight transformed his belief and his life. He determined that all must hear the word of God as it comes through the Scriptures. Thereafter, this linguistic genius would use his talents as exegete, translator, and preacher to spread that word.

Although Mary was not central to Luther's concerns, like the early Fathers he had to deal with her because of her relationship to Christ. His emphasis, however, led to greater changes in his followers' attitudes to Mary than he himself demanded or envisioned. The progression of his own thought can be charted with remarkable clarity by observing the differences between two of his writings on Mary—the first an analysis of the Magnificat, the second a sermon he delivered nine years later.

His fifty-seven-page exegesis of Mary's Magnificat was written in 1521, when Luther was uncertain where his movement was going. It reflects his own preoccupation as much as his scriptural knowledge. Mary, he insisted, sang this prayer out of her own experience, but "she sang it not for herself but for us all, to sing it after her."[26] She tells us about God, not herself, he says, when she insists she came of despised and lowly parents, yet God lifted her up. She is telling us that God preferred her, no more than a servant to her neighbors, over any princess.

Again and again, Luther stresses Mary's representative quality. She does not want to be esteemed; "she thrusts this from her and would have us honor God in her and come through her to a good confidence in His grace." Of those who believe that "there is found in her nothing to be despised, but only great and lofty things," he asks: "what are they doing but contrasting us with her instead of her with God?" Up to this point Luther's scriptural exegesis is strikingly similar to that of the majority of bishops at the Second Vatican Council in the 1960s who believed, as John XXIII said, that "the Madonna is not pleased when she is put above her Son."

But then come hints of something different. The greatest honor that we can give God, Luther goes on to say, is that which comes from deep within the heart, "not merely in saying the words, bending the knee, bowing the head, doffing the hat, making images, or building churches; for this even the wicked can do." Suddenly he becomes passionate as he explains which words are from the heart: "not nicely chosen or prescribed" words—like so many prayers developed over centuries in Catholic usage—but those that "flow forth in such a way that the spirit comes seething with them, and the words live and have hands and feet, in fact, the whole body and life with all its members strives and strains for utterance—that is indeed a worship of God in spirit and truth, and such words are all fire, light and life."

The implications of this intense affirmation of inspired words were further revealed in a sermon Luther delivered nine years later at Christmas in 1530. In his commentary on the Magnificat he had called Mary God-Bearer—as he did throughout his life—accepting her perpetual virginity as well: she was the fruit of the promise to Abraham that his seed was blessed and would multiply. But he also emphasized her role as a simple housewife and hence an example of God's exercise of mercy: "it is better to take away too much from her than from the grace of God. Indeed, we cannot take away too much from her."

Luther's message now takes up this undercurrent of conflict, like a zero-sum game in which the more Mary loses, the more Christ wins. There is no doubt, Luther observes, that Christ is the Virgin's son, but does this mean that "we may make an idol of her"? No, for "the text does not sound forth the honor of the mother. . . . We dare not put our faith in the mother but only in the fact that the child was born."[27] Here Jesus begins to be separated not only from his mother but from the rest of creation. Luther insists that we are to see "nothing but the child which is born . . . that all created things should be as nothing compared with this child, that we should see nothing, be it harps, gold,

goods, honor, power, and the like, which we would prefer before
their message."

And then he strikes his main note: our honor is greater than
that of Mary who mothered Jesus' body. "Christians, boast in
your heart: 'I hear the Word that sounds from heaven and says:
this child who is born of the Virgin is not only his mother's son. I
have more than the mother's estate. He is more mine than
Mary's, for he was born for me, for the angel said, 'To you is
born the Savior.' " And if this is true, he continues, "I have no
angry God and I must know and feel that there is nothing but
laughter and joy in the heart of the Father." The power of God's
grace in liberating Luther from fear and scrupulosity is palpable
in these ringing lines. The sermon goes on to suggest many other
implications of this belief in faith alone. "Our papists," he says,
want to "retain the mass, the invocation of saints. . . . This is as
much as to say I do not believe in the Savior and Lord whom
Mary bore; and yet they sing the words of the angel, hold their
triple masses and play their organs. They speak the words with
their tongues but their heart has another savior. And the same is
true in the monasteries. . . . The text says that he is the Savior.
And if this is true, then let everything else go."

Luther explicitly rejected the influence of St. Francis of Assisi,
though Francis had emphasized the very lowliness in Mary that
Luther accepted. Franciscan poverty had led to art that depicted
the peasant Mary with bare feet, nursing her child. But Francis
drew a different conclusion; he asked people for involvement not
only with Christ but, because of Him, with "everything else."
Luther's point was that God alone deserved such attention; he
did not want a merger of subjective feeling with Mary or with the
humble earth that Francis had celebrated.

Other Protestant Reformers like Calvin and Zwingli held
views similar to Luther's. Calvin believed in Mary's perpetual
virginity but rejected any need for her intercession: "It is quite
absurd to teach that we are to seek anything from her which she

receives otherwise than we do ourselves." Her blessedness is due not to her being mother but to her "rebirth into newness of life by the Spirit of Christ." Calvin, like Augustine, saw her as the disciple Luke portrayed, but added a sterner note; before "the majesty and glory of God, all creaturely being and action has almost no importance whatsoever."[28] The effect of Calvin's teaching was that in Geneva all the festivals of Mary were eventually suppressed. Zwingli honored Mary's lowliness and virginity as well as her fortitude under the cross, but, like Luther, he rejected any veneration of her as a saint. English Reformers such as Hugh Latimer took a similar approach. Latimer sounds much like the early Fathers when he blames Mary for losing her twelve-year-old son in the temple and suggests that she showed personal ambition at the wedding in Cana.

Renaissance scholar Walter Ong sees an unconscious connection between the Reformers' resentment of authority and their "desire to write off Our Lady." In his opinion, a curious anomaly marks their new freedom. In the twelfth century, St. Bernard had emphasized Mary's choice, her consent to God's will as central to human salvation. In the sixteenth century, Luther put all the emphasis on God's choice of Mary. Ong does not believe that the problems of the Protestant Reformers were primarily with church authoritanianism but rather with the "mitigated, mediated authority, the symbol of which must be feminine, the initial experience of which each human being ordinarily knows in relation to a mother."[29] Luther's position ruled out "the still unimpeachable vision of the old earth-cults and of the Scriptures themselves, which see in woman the very opposite of abstraction." Protestants called the pope "the Scarlet Woman of the Apocalypse"—hardly an attack on his authoritarianism. They were, says Ong, casting out the mother and strengthening the father. By his diminution of Mary, Luther perhaps unconsciously denied the feminine dimension of the sacred and eliminated the one symbol that had for many embodied it.

Such effects, of course, were not the thrust of the Reformers' aims, nor did they undercut their positive achievements. Making the Bible available in fresh language, they made Jesus and Mary seem like contemporary people. The Reformation also brought lasting improvements to church and society by rehabilitating marriage and expanding education to all, including women. Paradoxically, if the Reformation took power away from Mary's image, it put more power into the hands of ordinary women, reversing the decisions of fourth-century Fathers. Luther insisted on the goodness of married life for most people. In "The Estate of Marriage" (1522), he argued against the preference for virginity that had long marked the church, saying that there were no class distinctions among the baptized. In fact, his own marriage to Catherine von Bora helped him see marriage and family as the preferred school of faith: "For it is nothing to wear a hood, fast, or undertake other hard works of that sort in comparison with those troubles which family life brings, and the saints [i.e., the patriarchs] bore them and lived in patience."[30]

Calvin, too, celebrated the goodness of marriage; celibacy was a rare vocation, not to be maintained if the man could not sustain it. He rejected on principle a required vow of celibacy, saying it was, rather, a grace given for practical reasons. He thought it absurd to call marriage a sacrament and at the same time consider sex unclean. Although the Reformers in general did not see marriage as a sacrament, they effected many legal changes that benefited both men and women, including the right, though rare, to divorce and remarry. Probably their most significant change in attitude to marriage, affirmed in the Westminster Confession of Faith in 1646–1647, was the recognition that the mutual love of spouses was as important a goal as procreation.

Protestantism also provided a theological basis for equality of responsibility between clergy and laypeople, including women, closing much of the gulf between them that still marked Catholicism. The laity found greater meaning in their everyday occupa-

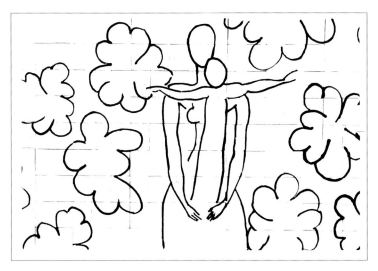

Plate 1. Henri Matisse created this bare outline of the Virgin and Child for the wall of the Rosary Chapel in Vence, France. The child's arms are raised so that his body becomes a cross, recalling the traditional premonition of sorrow in many earlier Nativity paintings. When light and shadow enter through stained glass windows on the opposite wall, this Everywoman Madonna surrounded by clouds seems to hold her son in the heavens. (Ch. 1, Epilog).

Plate 2. Mary and Elizabeth huddle together in kinship in this Romanesque bas-relief version of the Visitation scene on the tympanum of the chapel of St. Gabriel near Arles, France. In a partly defaced scene on the left, Gabriel tells Mary she is to bear a child. Here the two cousins stare in awe at the revelation of this mysterious event, and their amazement awakens similar feelings in the viewer. (Ch. 2).

Plate 3. In this catacomb fresco from the early fourth century, Mary looks much like a Roman matron holding her child in her arms, but the symbols on either side proclaim her identity. Her hands are raised in the Orans, or praying, position common to ritual gesture at the time. (Ch. 4)

Plate 4. Abraham cradles the just to his bosom in this charming sculptured capital from Alspach (c. 1149), now in the Musée d' Unterlinden in Colmar (Alsace), France. In his paternal solicitude, Abraham resembles the Mother of God, who protects believers with her veil in Eastern icons, and the European Mother of Mercy, who shelters all petitioners under her mantle. (cf. Chs. 2,6).

Plate 5. This *Mater Misericordia* (Mother of Mercy) is a painting by the Provencal artist Jean Miralhet (c. 1442). The image became widely popular in Europe in the late Middle Ages and many versions are extant, though they were later curtailed by the artistic literalism of the reforming Council of Trent. The international character of Miralhet's painting can be seen in the rich Flemish detail of Mary's dress and jeweled fastener, and the Sienese sweetness of her expression. Her facial features and elegant gesture mark her as French. When viewed together, the image of Abraham in illustration and the one of Mary here underscore the comparison between their roles in salvation history. As discussed from a biblical perspective in Ch. 2.

Plate 6. Mary's connection with the Eucharist is strikingly evident in her presence on one side of this sixth- or early seventh-century silver chalice from Northern Syria. Her figure, with arms upraised in the familiar Orans position, decorates one side of this communion cup. (Ch. 4).

Plate 7. The young mother holds her son as she rides sidesaddle on a donkey on the Flight into Egypt. In this detail from a capital sculptured by Gislebertus for the Cathedral of Autun, France, in the twelfth century, Joseph leads them to safety, just out of sight on the right. Like the ox and ass at the Nativity, the donkey was a recurring figure in art portraying Jesus and Mary. Simple animals became symbols of the humble, anti-imperial power of this new king. (Chs. 3, 4, 5).

Ἡ ΚΟΙΜΗCΙC ΤῆC ΘΕΟΤΟΚΥ

Plate 8. The Dormition of the *Theotokos* (Mother of God) is presented in traditional design and colors by Basil Lepouras, a twentieth-century Athenian iconographer. Mary lies on her bier surrounded by the apostles as described in the fifth-century story of her Transitus, or passing, to the next life. Christ holds a tiny depiction of her soul as his mother once held him as a baby. (cf. Ch. 4).

Plate 9. The birth of Mary, depicted here in a fourteenth-century painting by Ambrogio Lorenzetti from the Duomo in Siena, reflects the continuing popular interest in details of Mary's life down to the Renaissance. Unlike her son's birth in a cave or stable, Mary's is usually shown in well-appointed rooms with servants assisting her mother Anne. (Ch. 4).

Plate 10. This encaustic icon of the Mother of God enthroned (from the Monastery of St. Catherine in the Sinai desert) is one of the earliest surviving examples of a new image of Mary to emerge after she was proclaimed Mother of God at the Council of Ephesus (431). Here she sits with her son on her lap, protected by two warrior saints; her central significance is emphasized by the light streaming from the hand of God above her head. (Ch. 4)

Plate 11. The Virgin and Child enthroned with angels at the corners is one of the intricately ornamented illuminations in the eighth-century Book of Kells, a manuscript of the Gospels now preserved in the Library of Trinity College, Dublin. Its bright colors and interwoven designs are Irish variants on the ancient pose of the Mother of God enthroned. (Ch. 5)

Plate 12. This design of the original tenth-century Virgin in Majesty in the Cathedral at Clermont-Ferrand was discovered accidentally in the city's municipal library. Since the statue had disappeared long before, the drawing provides valuable evidence of the link between ancient icons of the Mother of God enthroned and the new portable reliquary statues designed for popular veneration. (Ch. 5)

Plate 13. The beautiful black Madonna of Marsat seems to look soberly past the viewer to rest her eyes on the sorrow of the world as she holds her son in her large hands. This wooden Romanesque Throne of Wisdom from the twelfth or thirteenth century still sits in the small village church of Marsat (Auvergne), France. Our Lady of Marsat is credited with saving the nearby city of Riom from plague in 1621. Originally painted in polychrome, the statue darkened over the years. When it was restored in 1830, her face and hands were intentionally painted black, while her robe was done in brilliant scarlet and gold. (Ch. 5)

Plate 14. Despite her wooden shoes, Our Lady of Meymac (Corrèze), France, is strangely exotic in her golden oriental turban. As in all the Romanesque Virgins in Majesty, she and her son look alike; even the curious intensity of her gaze is mirrored in her son's. This resemblance affirms the mysterious nature of the incarnation in visual form, a reminder that the flesh of the son comes entirely from the mother. (Ch. 5)

Plate 15. The twelfth-century stained glass Madonna from the Cathedral of Chartres (Notre Dame de la Belle-Verrière) translates the compassionate, protective Mother of God proclaimed at Ephesus into a powerful, similarly compassionate Queen-Mother in medieval France. (Ch. 5)

Plate 16. The celebrated icon of Our Lady of Vladimir is perhaps the most beautiful of all the icons of Tenderness, a pose in which the baby lifts his face to his mother's cheek and her head inclines over his. The profound sorrow in her eyes is similar to that in many Western Thrones of Wisdom. It was probably painted in Constantinople, c. 1130; it has been moved many times since, residing in Moscow since the mid-fifteenth century. Its fate was thought to be connected to the destiny of the Russian people. (Ch. 5)

Plate 17. The hands, feet, and child of Our Lady of Good Hope at Dijon (third quarter of the twelfth century) disappeared in the French Revolution. But her heavy breasts and pendulous stomach still reveal the maternal source of her power in the Middle Ages, when she was seen as a symbol of fecundity and healing. André Malraux saw in this statue "the transcendence of humility." (Ch. 5)

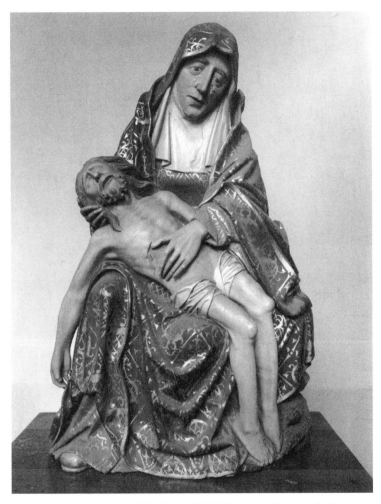

Plate 18. The sculptured Pietà, in which Mary cradles her dead son on her lap, is one of several late medieval scenes emphasizing the suffering of Christ. This fourteenth-century Leuven Pietà from the Low Countries would have had both sacramental and practical meaning for its viewers. Mary's reception of her son was almost a visual experience of communion —a woman taking the body of the crucified Christ. At the same time, it was a reminder that daily work for others, particularly care of the sick and dead, was also care of Christ. (Ch. 6)

Plate 19. In this detail of the famous Isenheim retable painted in the early sixteenth century by Matthias Gruenewald, now at Colmar (Alsace), France,
Mary, John, and Mary Magdalene are shown on Calvary beneath Christ dying on the cross. The painting embodies the new realism and heightened
emotional tone that entered devotional art in the fourteenth century. Faint-
ing, Mary falls into John's arms, while Mary Magdalene, head thrown back,
reveals the violence of her feelings signified through her disordered fingers.
Between them the women provided a range of emotional reactions believers
were meant to share. (Ch. 6)

Plate 20. This Education of the Virgin from the early seventeenth century shows the girl Mary and her mother Anne in an intimate family setting that reflected the growing importance of middle-class families in Europe and the new role of the mother as educator. The painter, Georges de La Tour—from Lorraine, France—uses simplified colors and the light emanating from a single candle to heighten the tender patience of the mother's face and the girl's serious response to her lessons. (Ch. 6)

Plate 21. This typical fifteenth-century Virgin of the Apocalypse (stained glass, German) reveals the similarity between such European images and those of the Mexican Guadalupe. The use of the moon below and the rays of the sun surrounding the woman in Rev. 12:1 had become standard themes in the portrayal of Mary as the Immaculate Conception. Hence the Spaniards—who also venerated black Madonnas at home—could recognize the dark Mexican Virgin of Guadalupe as their own. (Ch. 6)

Plate 22. The image of Our Lady of Guadalupe as she appears today in Mexico City on the tilma of Juan Diego, the christianized Indian to whom she is said to have appeared in 1531. Her green eyes are cast down, her hair is black, and her skin olive. Her humility and coloring, along with the stars and gold rays of the sun, the turquoise color of her mantle, and the moon on which she stands—all signs of Aztec divinity—convinced the native Mexicans that the Mother of God had chosen to be a *mestiza*, one of them, not their conquerors. (Ch. 6)

Plate 23. The tender young mother in Raphael's Sistine Madonna (early sixteenth century) has long been beloved in the Catholic world. In the nineteenth century, it also began to appeal strongly to Protestant women. Harriet Beecher Stowe admired this work for its historic accuracy in representing Mary as believably Jewish, as well as for its revelation of the resemblance and sympathy between mother and child. But above all, she saw in Raphael's Madonna the suggestion of noble self-sacrifice she felt was essential to the ideal woman. (Ch. 7)

Plate 24. Piero della Francesca's Madonna Del Parto, the pregnant Madonna (1460-65), is a fresco in the cemetery chapel in Monterchi, Italy. Angels pull aside the flaps of the tent that shelter her to reveal eleven rows of goatskin pelts inside; these pelts recall the eleven curtains of goat hair God recommended to Moses for his tabernacle. This serious young woman announces her pregnancy by gesturing to her unbuttoned dress, while both tent and angels declare her to be the new ark, the tabernacle of the living God. (Ch. 8)

Plate 25. In this contemporary icon, Mother of the Disappeared, artist Robert Lentz presents a new Mater Dolorosa, one influenced by the recent experience of mothers in Latin America whose children were abducted and killed. She wears their white kerchief while she holds in her hands her son's crown of thorns. The white handprint smeared across the side of the icon is the signature of the El Salvador death squads. (Ch. 8).

MADRE DE LOS DESAPARECIDOS

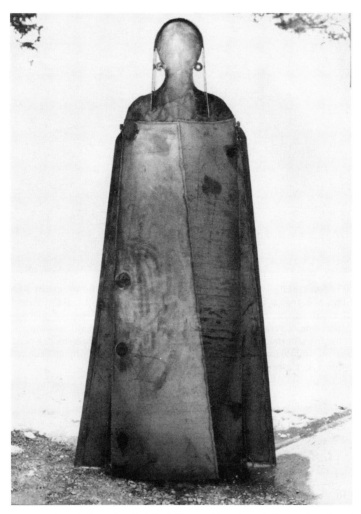

Plates 26 and 27. The Original Face: Closed and Open. Medieval wooden statues of the Vierge Ouvrante inspired this contemporary metal sculpture by Frederick Franck. In the medieval version, flaps over the Virgin's stomach open to reveal the Trinity within. Here the flaps open to reveal the ultimate human face, the face of Christ or "Original Face." In this bold, seven-foot sculpture, Franck links the Buddhist idea of the original face that each human has before conception with the Immaculate Conception, understood as a sign of revelation about all human beings. (Ch. 9)

Plate 28. In this design by Yaroslava Mills for the Nativity window in the Church of St. Demetrius in Weston, Ontario, Canada, Mary rests on a crimson mattress in the center of a dark cave, which represents the world without the light of Christ. The Christmas star shines its light directly on the baby beside her, swaddled in a stone manger that also symbolizes his tomb. The traditional figures of angels, shepherds, St. Joseph, a midwife, and the Magi surround them in the upper part of the window, while below, ordinary people celebrate Ukrainian Christmas rituals familiar to the artist from her own heritage. (Ch. 9)

Plate 29. In this design for a stained glass window of the Resurrection, Yaroslava Mills presents the story of Christ's descent into hell in the way Kievan Russian icons do. Surrounded by the prophets who foretold his coming, Christ shatters the fetters and locks of hell, releasing Adam and Eve from the effects of death and sin. The lower part of the window portrays Ukrainian folk traditions: decorating Easter eggs and blessing Easter baskets, again pairing activities at home with those of the community before the church. (Church of St. Demetrius, Weston, Ontario, Canada) (Ch. 9)

Plate 30. In the icons of John Giuliani, the human face of the sacred is revealed in the features of the indigenous people of the United States. The message bearer in this Lakota Annunciation painting is a red-winged falcon, regarded as a communicator of sacred power by Native Americans. The girl Mary, wearing a Siouan dress-cape, welcomes the holy greeting with open arms and appropriate astonishment. (Ch. 9)

Plate 31. A distinguishing feature of the Hopi Mother
and Child by John Giuliani is the fragile positioning of
their hands, which express the prophetic pain of human love and separation. Theirs is a common destiny:
the return of the gift received. Mary wears a traditional Hopi mantle and a multilayered bead necklace.
Her ceremonial mocassins rubbed with kaolin take on
the appearance of an old adobe wall. The black and
white plaid shawl over the child's shoulders is particular to Hopi children, as is the richly embroidered shirt
detailed with Hopi designs and symbols. (Ch. 9)

Plate 32. The figure of Crow Mother has become painter Meinrad Craighead's Southwestern Madonna, the spirit of her New Mexican home. "As her eye gives birth to me, my eyes bring out my images," Craighead explains. The jagged lines on the rug and the dark triangular face of "Crow Mother: Her Eyes, Her Eggs" recall the symbolic language associated with the old European Mother Goddess. Here she sits clasping eggs in her bony hands, a symbol of fertility and regeneration. Images of Mary preceded and mediated Craighead's imaginative visions of God the Mother. (Ch. 9)

tions when they were taught that all Christians had vocations. The Reformers insisted on the priesthood of all believers and thus created new opportunities for women as well as men. Most important, they not only made the Bible available in the vernacular, the language all could understand, but made sure that it was widely circulated, studied, and preached.

Every Protestant housewife now had a sense of religious vocation, because she was expected to teach her children. Previously, no public education had existed for girls. In 1524 Luther successfully pressed the civil authorities for schools that would include both sexes. Calvin, who had been deeply influenced by the humanists, was even more dedicated to the education of women. After the official beginning of the Reformation in Geneva in 1536, both boys and girls were required to attend school. Those who could not pay were to be sponsored by the city, which would instruct and feed them at its own expense.

Though the roles of nun and abbess were largely lost to women in the Reformation, new responsibilities as pastors' wives and sometimes as preachers and writers replaced them. Nevertheless, there remained distinct limits on what women could do in mainstream Protestantism, for the rule of the father in families replaced the rule of the clergy. All the Reformers assumed that wives were subject to their husbands; in his commentary on Genesis, Luther used the Augustinian argument that man's dominance was the result of the Fall. The man "rules the home and the state, wages wars, defends his possessions, tills the soil, builds, plants," and in general holds sway over creation. The woman, on the other hand, "is like a nail driven into the wall," and "should stay at home to look after the affairs of the household."[31] In "The Estate of Marriage," Luther spoke of mothers as apostles, priests, and bishops to their children, but stressed that "women's bishoprick was the nursery and the home."

Some women ventured out of the house at their peril. When Katharina Zell, wife of a leading Strassburg Reformer, was

insulted and denounced by the bishop after her husband's ex-
communication, she defended clerical marriage in public:

> You remind me that the Apostle Paul told women to be silent in
> church. I would remind you of the word of this same apostle that
> in Christ there is no longer male nor female and of the prophecy
> of Joel: "I will pour forth my spirit upon all flesh and your sons
> and your *daughters* will prophesy." I do not pretend to be John the
> Baptist rebuking the Pharisees. I do not claim to be Nathan up-
> braiding David. I aspire only to be Balaam's ass, castigating his
> master.

Despite her learning and humility, Katharina Zell's later funeral
address for her husband led to allegations that she aspired to be
"Doctor Katrina." Her interpretation of the Our Father compared God to a "mother who had known the pangs of birth and
the joy of giving suck," and she observed that "since through his
son we are born again we may call him grandfather too."[32]

She was by no means the only woman spurred on by the idea
of a common priesthood and love of the Bible to carve out a career in preaching and teaching outside of the home. But such efforts were made at great cost, and were by no means encouraged
by most male reformers. Nevertheless, there is no question that
Protestantism brought about positive changes for women. Historian Gerda Lerner judges that, "viewed from the vantage point of
intellectual and religious history, the Reformation was a decisive
turning point for women and very positively affected their ability
to come to feminist consciousness."[33]

A MORE AMBIGUOUS LEGACY OF THE REFORMATION WAS THE
fury unleashed against images associated with the medieval
church, particularly those of Mary. In their emphasis on greater
individual response to Scripture without priestly intermediaries,
the Reformers tapped popular resentments against earlier abuses

of authority. Though Marian feasts were retained in the Book of Common Prayer in England, they existed in name only. All the Marian shrines, including Walsingham, were destroyed. Motives for this destruction were mixed: the shrines had been the sites of great abuse, but the desire to acquire their wealth prompted the attacks. Little by little the titles Mary held were transferred to Henry VIII's daughter, the Virgin Queen, Elizabeth. Mary as Queen of Heaven became a symbol of foreign powers now that English royalty had broken with the pope. By 1645 the House of Commons was prepared to order that "all such pictures as have the representation of the Virgin Mary upon them shall be forthwith burned." The destructive process continued until the Restoration of the monarchy in 1660, and the same mind-set was exported to New England.

Norway, Denmark, Sweden, and England broke with Rome as a result of the Reformation, while populations in Germany and France divided themselves into Protestant and Catholic camps that waged bloody warfare against one another. Religious tolerance seemed like an absence of conviction, and martyrs increased in number on both sides. In England, Germany, and parts of Switzerland, public anger at vestiges of the older Catholic tradition vented itself in the wholesale destruction of medieval paintings, statues, and carvings. Since Mary had been closely associated with royalty in both France and England, the struggles to substitute parliamentary government for the rule of kings in those countries offered another reason to eliminate her image. Luther had not called for the removal of images from the churches, and the other Reformation leaders were probably surprised at this furious public iconoclasm. They may not have been aware of the powerful political implications of their egalitarian theological opinions. But the Reformers had regularly insisted that visual images in churches distracted congregations from hearing the Word, and their alert followers realized that such figures, often wearing crowns, also reinforced social hierarchies.

What the leaders of the Reformation had seen as academic, theological disputes, middle- and working-class people felt as personal oppression.

In France, the fury of the Protestant Huguenots was aimed particularly at the black madonnas, considered evidence of "Gothic superstition"; at least twenty-five were destroyed in the sixteenth century, particularly in the north and in Alsace. During the wars of religion, the Black Virgin of Lyons disappeared, and two in Orléans were burned in a public place, one of them the Lady of Miracles to whom Joan of Arc had prayed before the siege of the city in 1429. This statue was attacked with special fury as "the Egyptian"—an epithet used for several other black madonnas that revealed the strains of nativism and nationalism often intertwined with religious polemic.

Altars were stripped in Germany and Switzerland. Bare communion tables meant that celebrants faced the congregation directly; no screens or ornaments should block access to the word of God. Soon Protestant churches were structures with bare white walls and a prominent pulpit, befitting the primacy of the word and the equality of attentive hearers. The barriers that separated the wealthy from the general public were removed, as were the distracting devotions carried on at the side altars of medieval churches. The bells, incense, and vestments that disgusted Luther disappeared; liturgical chant and ritual were abolished in the name of reform.

These changes continued into our own day. I loved the spare beauty of the Protestant churches I visited as a child. Their aesthetic was close to the Cistercian simplicity of St. Bernard, who found it hard to tolerate the elaborate carving and rich color of Cluny. In the emerging strong nations of the sixteenth century, Protestants and Catholics would divide these poles of taste—one side stressing primarily the verbal and musical (with Bach's masses and chorales as its greatest expression), the other side producing a luxuriant visual art, evident in baroque painting and architecture.[34]

These divergent tendencies of the Protestant and Catholic imaginations were further nourished by differences in the standard biblical texts each adopted. Striving for evangelical purity, newly translated Protestant bibles placed a number of books composed in Hellenistic times into a separate, apocryphal section, or eliminated them altogether—Tobias, Judith, Esther, Susanna, Ecclesiasticus, and the Wisdom of Solomon, for example. These were precisely the texts that had been the source of much visual art and liturgical prayer among Catholics. A verse from Ecclesiasticus linking Mary with Holy Wisdom was preserved in the Saturday Office of the Blessed Virgin by Catholics until the Second Vatican Council in the 1960s, further exaggerating the split: "Before all ages, in the beginning, he created me, and through all ages I shall not cease to be" (Eccl. 24:9).

CATHOLIC COUNTER-REFORM

Despite the formal separation of Roman Catholic and Protestant churches and their differing aesthetics, sixteenth-century Catholicism also carried out its own, long-delayed impulse to reform. Greater emphasis was placed on preaching, on eliminating physical barriers between priest and people in the churches, and on placing the faithful nearer the altar in new churches. Nevertheless, though the Council of Trent (1545–1563) condemned the apocryphal legends and the matrilineal imagery associated with the kinship of St. Anne, it indirectly encouraged visual imagery of Mary's mother. Trent's emphasis on teaching the catechism at home placed new responsibilities on Catholic mothers, who found a model in the figure of St. Anne teaching Mary and Jesus. The theme of Mary as learner is powerfully developed at this time; in most Annunciation scenes Gabriel now finds Mary reading rather than spinning or weaving.

Unfortunately, the struggle with Protestantism fostered a defensive attitude in Catholicism, evident in its scriptural scholarship for the next four hundred years. The art of the Counter-Reformation triumphantly celebrated all the dogmas attacked by the Protestants. A fresco by Domenichino in the church of San Gennaro in Naples depicts the triumph of the Virgin over the Reformation; the lower part shows a young hero treading on Luther and Calvin alongside a woman praying the rosary. In heaven above, the Virgin portrayed as the Immaculate Conception accepts the woman's prayer.

Since the Lutherans denounced the rosary, Pope Pius V officially recognized it. He also instituted the feast of the Rosary, attributing the naval victory over the Turks at Lepanto (October 7, 1571) to the rosaries recited that day. The rosary would be taken up by the Jesuits, especially by Peter Canisius (d. 1597), who saw in the renewal of Marian devotion the best way to repair the damages of the Reformation.

Defensiveness caused by the Reformation encouraged a break with medieval art. In France, Emile Mâle observes, "the Reformation put an end to the long tradition of legend, poetry, and dream by forcing the Catholic church to watch over all aspects of its thought and to turn strongly in upon itself."[35] Catholics became suspicious of their long tradition of mystery plays, which had grown up out of the liturgy but had accumulated many local legends and stories. In 1548 the parliament in Paris forbade the confraternities to perform any of these plays.

Catholic humanists, steeped in Renaissance learning, could be as obtuse as Protestant reformers when it came to respecting older traditions, especially those that sprang from popular sources. For example, Guillaume Briçonnet, the humanist bishop of Meaux and friend of King Francis I, admired the new painting of the Renaissance. He had the Romanesque statue of the Black

Virgin in the church of St.-Germain-des-Prés in Paris destroyed as an embarrassing remnant of medieval superstition.

Rome also announced it would keep a close watch on new works of art. In its last session, the Council of Trent decreed:

> The Holy Council forbids any image to be exhibited in churches which represents false doctrines and might be the occasion of grave error to the uneducated; it earnestly desires that all lasciviousness be avoided and that images not be adorned with seductive charms. In order to assure respect for these decisions, the Holy Council forbids exhibiting in any place, even in churches not subject to visits by the Ordinary [the local bishop], any unusual image unless it has been approved by the bishop.[36]

In other words, since Protestants had declared war on images, enlightened Catholics (like Bishop Briçonnet) did not want to hand them weapons. In the name of reform, therefore, the Council of Trent tried to put an end to artistic freedom and playfulness with religious subjects. Several late sixteenth-century books spelled out the artistic rules implied by Trent; the most important of these was by Jean Molanus from Louvain. With no sense of symbolism and no grasp of typological meanings, he proscribed the Golden Legend and any other stories not found in Scripture. Recommending the absolute elimination of legendary scenes of the Virgin's life, he criticized popular Franciscan spirituality for showing her in "undignified" poses such as the Pietà.

Nevertheless, the Council of Trent had in principle reaffirmed the value of images themselves, "because the honor which is showed them is referred to their prototypes which they represent, so that by means of the images which we kiss and before which we uncover the head and prostrate ourselves, we adore Christ and venerate the saints whose likeness they bear." The Counter-Reformation soon developed its own characteristic art, employing anti-Protestant themes and seizing every opportunity to engage the feelings and senses of worshipers. The result was a more literal rendition of heavenly themes. Marina Warner describes the baroque decoration of the Gesù, the Jesuit church in Rome, with its hosts of cherubim and seraphim on the ceiling, "kicking and beating and pressing against one another in the chaos of a thriving paradise."[37] To be experienced as it was intended, suggests Margaret Miles, the worshiper at the Gesù must be there with a crowd during the liturgy, for only then is it possible to overcome the power with which the visual images dominate a single visitor. The presence of many worshipers attending to the words at a Sunday mass combines with the images to evoke the intended sense of lively communion between heaven and earth.

On the whole, the seventeenth century produced just those Catholic representations of Mary that Reformers would have deplored. Her Assumption into heaven was stressed in the work of Spanish artists like Velázquez and Murillo. The latter's painting of the Immaculate Conception in the Prado in Madrid is Counter-Reformation art at its most flagrant, presenting Mary as a beautiful young girl gazing upward at a heaven that bathes her in an unearthly light, while angels bear lilies and a cornsheaf, emblems of her virginal fruitfulness. The Council of Trent tended to foster pictures of a younger Mary alone, without Anne and Joachim, which served to detach her from their sexuality. Murillo was merely the best-known practitioner of this subject, which provided visual support for popular belief in the Immaculate Conception.

However, two great painters portrayed Mary in a new, natural style. Georges de La Tour (d. 1652) produced several paintings (two of the Nativity, and a series on the education of Mary as a young girl) using natural symbols to express the tenderness and sanctity possible in intimate family relationships (Plate 20). His figures of Mary, Anne, and the shepherds emerge from darkness in simplified reds and blues, the light from candles illuminating them and symbolizing their holiness. The *Death of the Virgin* (early 1600s) by Caravaggio, who had influenced de La Tour, had represented a new approach to the expression of Mary's saintliness in its dramatic relationships between light and figures, its symbolic use of simple materials such as drapery, wood, and ropes. The Carmelite fathers who had commissioned it for the altar of their church in Rome rejected it; they wanted the more conventional Queen of Heaven with angels, clouds, and haloes. Yet the absence of supernatural phenomena focuses the meaning in both these artists' pictures on internal events. There are no external trappings; that is why we still find them so powerful today. At the time, however, a veritable orgy of crowns appeared on other statues and paintings of Mary; sometimes they were added to much older works that had been painted without them—a sacrifice of art to Catholic triumphalism.

The Counter-Reformation was at its most intense in Spain, then at the height of its worldly power. The Spanish Pope Alexander VI, a great champion of Mary and the rosary, presumed to divide the whole unknown New World between the crowns of Portugal and Spain. In 1492, the same year in which Ferdinand and Isabella sponsored the voyage of Columbus to America, these "most Catholic monarchs" conquered Granada, the last bastion of Arab power in the Spanish peninsula, and forced Jews who had been living peaceably in Spain for generations either to leave or to become *conversos*.

Ferdinand and Isabella also instituted a state-controlled Inquisition to spy on converts from Judaism and Islam, and later on Protestants; it was complete with a spy network and the means to torture those who were not considered sincere in the faith. Even Teresa of Avila was suspected by Inquisitors, and Ignatius Loyola and John of the Cross were imprisoned; holy men and women like these represented the reforming wave of Spanish Catholicism. Devotion to Mary figured in their personal stories as well as in the larger background of the Counter-Reformation Spain that shaped them. Ignatius, Teresa, and John all accepted Mary's central role in the Incarnation and felt united with her through the traditional Catholic doctrine of the communion of saints.

Ignatius (d. 1556), founder of the Jesuits, made no sharp break in his devotion with the theology and imagery of the Middle Ages. Wounded on the battlefield of Pamplona while fighting the French, he underwent a long discipline during a retreat at Manresa that deepened his understanding of the spiritual life. In an incident he reports in his *Autobiography*, he mocks his own early blindness of soul, which was divided between stories of knight errancy and the true service of Christ. Starting out on a pilgrimage, the young *cabellero* found himself traveling beside a Moor who began to challenge Mary's perpetual virginity, explaining why it was impossible. Ignatius's counterargument did not convince his companion, and later, when they parted, Ignatius was worried that he had not sufficiently defended the honor of Our Lady. He was sorely tempted to follow the man and defend her with his dagger, but, Ignatius tells us, his mule chose not to follow the Moor. After a long night of prayerful vigil at the shrine of Our Lady of Montserrat, the ex-soldier left both his dagger and his sword on the altar, aware that totally different weapons were necessary for his new service.

Studying first at Barcelona and then at Alcalá in Spain, Ignatius was suspected of false mysticism, tried, and imprisoned by the Inquisition. After escaping to the freedom of Paris to continue his studies, on August 15, 1534, the feast of the Assumption, he and a group of nine Catholic students climbed Montmartre to make their vows of poverty and chastity in the chapel of St.-Denis, declaring their intention to become missionaries overseas. This was the beginning of the Society of Jesus, which took into account the criticisms of the Reformers against the older religious orders. The Jesuits demanded longer periods of preparation for the priesthood, avoided excessive asceticism, did not seek to distinguish their members by special clothing, and dedicated themselves to humanistic teaching and the preparation of priests. The founding principle of the order was very close to the fourth rule Erasmus presented as the guide to a Christian life: Christ is the only goal and all else should be subordinated to it.

Luther might have uttered the same principle. In retrospect, Ignatius's aims were surprisingly compatible with those of the Reformation leader, says Jill Raitt, a distinguished historian of Christianity. This is clearest, she believes, in the *Spiritual Exercises*, which Ignatius wrote as a handbook for Christians wanting to be closer followers of Christ. Its purpose was to help them grow in virtue, but even more important, to learn to discern spirits and to follow the guidance of the Holy Spirit. In this aim of centering their lives in Christ, Raitt points out, Roman Catholics and Lutherans had the same focus. They differed in attitudes to authority and spirituality. Luther advocated passivity under grace and active asceticism in the service of one's neighbor. Ignatius saw both service to neighbor and prayer as means of serving God, and insisted on the need to be active, not passive, in the acquisition of virtue and in the beginning stages of the spiritual life.

The *Spiritual Exercises* of Ignatius have had profound effects on the Catholic imagination. He absorbed the earlier tradition that used visual imagery to stimulate prayer and passed it on to later generations. Mary's place is central in God's plan and she stands for all human beings. In the meditation on the Incarnation in the thirty-day Ignatian retreat, for example, the retreatant is asked to visualize three scenes: first, Mary's consent to the angel that will make her the mother of God; second, a representative group of human beings, all caught up in sin; and finally, God in heaven looking compassionately down on humanity, awaiting the redemptive birth Mary's consent makes possible. The theology is centered on the age-old doctrine of the communion of saints, but the techniques for interior visualization to develop a personal connection with divine action are psychologically modern.

The same combination of medieval sacramental theology and

shrewd psychological insight characterized the great Carmelite mystic, reformer, and spiritual director Teresa of Ávila (d. 1582). Born to a large, well-to-do family (with one grandfather a Jewish convert), she wrote that, as children, she and her brothers and sisters wanted to be martyrs and hermits. When at age twelve she lost her mother, Teresa stood before an image of Our Lady, weeping and begging her to be her mother now. "Whenever I have turned to the supreme Virgin," she wrote later, "I have always been conscious of her aid, and in the end she brought me back to myself."[38]

At twenty-one Teresa entered the Carmelite order in her native town of Castile against her father's wishes. She managed to gain his acceptance of her religious vocation, but only slowly did she learn to resist the attractions of the social world she enjoyed even within the convent. It took her many years to discover her true calling to a life of quiet prayer and habitual union with God. An almost fatal illness which incapacitated her for some time facilitated her turn to this vocation. Her experience as a mystic inspired Bernini's famous statue of Teresa in the ecstasy she described in such sensuous terms in her autobiography. The Inquisitors naturally kept a constant eye on her, since they saw interior inspiration as a threat to the external rule of authority and to public worship.

At the age of forty, Teresa realized that she was being asked to found and reform convents for women. Despite her preference for the contemplative life, she took on the enormous correspondence, constant travel, and other responsibilities this active vocation required. Her social contacts were vast, stretching from peasants and merchants to King Phillip II, who supported her reforms. At at time when convents were often more like social clubs for unmarriageable daughters, she undertook a complete reform of the Carmelite Order, with results that have endured to the present. From all accounts she enjoyed the little human encounters and negotiations of life and maintained a wonderful sense of humor. Complaining to God of her trials, she reports Him as responding: "Teresa, that's how I treat my friends." "That's why you have so few," she replied candidly. Even those who had to carry "la Madre" over difficult terrain to reach her far-flung convents used to enjoy being with her for the sake of the delightful conversations.

In a world dominated by males, Teresa had a remarkable sense of her own worth and that of women in general. She was eager to educate her novices in prayer, but understood well the importance of humor and encouragement. Inspiration and visions were unnecessary, she insisted, deprecating her own gifts; what mattered was the practice of charity in daily life. Rooting herself and her nuns firmly in daily chores and relationships, she shared with them everything she knew from her own experience about growth in the spiritual life. She cleverly fended off Inquisitorial suspicion by saying there was no need to bother the "learned men." Poor, weak women could only learn from the simple spiritual food another woman could provide.

Teresa could not get her male spiritual directors to understand her approach to prayer; for twenty years she suffered so much from uncomprehending priests that she wondered how she could endure it. Finally, she was able to influence the younger Carmelite, John of the Cross (d. 1591), to reform the male branch; he became her supporter and the confessor of her order for five years. He was her mentor in mysticism while she tutored him in practical ways to achieve reform. The short poem by John at the beginning of this chapter, composed one Christmas, is a window on his devotion. The context is one in which the Virgin is heavy with child, making her way without shelter; those who receive her into their hearts also receive the reality of the Incarnation.

In Teresa of Ávila, Counter-Reformation Spain produced a deeply Catholic spirituality that was surprisingly congenial to Luther's theology. Teresa believed in the primacy of interior devotion to God, parallel to the great Reformer's emphasis on "God alone." Her best-known work on the spiritual life, *The Interior Castle*, speaks of the need for active human cooperation with grace in the first three dwelling places, but stresses the passivity of the four higher places where God directs the more mystical stages. Like Luther, Teresa insisted that the humanity of Christ always accompanies the soul, purifying it with his divinity; she emphasized both the interplay between doctrine and experience and the primacy of the interior life. Unlike Luther, however, her rootedness in the earlier medieval framework made her feel—like Ignatius and John of the Cross—the need for active use of the senses and the imagination, as well as the importance of intercessors, in her attempt to follow Christ. In her traditionally sacramental view, the Incarnation continues to connect Christ not only to believers, living and dead, but to all creation. It is his presence, rather than his death, that is central, and Mary's humanity confirms that truth:

> I believe I've explained that it is fitting for souls, however spiritual, to take care not to flee from corporeal things to the extent of thinking that even the most sacred humanity causes harm. Some quote what the Lord said to His disciples, that it was fitting that he go. I can't bear this. I would wager he didn't say it to His most blessed Mother, because she was firm in the faith; she knew He was God and man, and even though she loved him more than they did, she did so with such perfection that His presence was a help rather than a hindrance.[39]

Teresa's prayer of quiet was more psychologically introspective than Luther's, providing insight into the way in which receptive attentiveness to God serves to enlighten and strengthen the individual and at the same time make her feel connected to a benevolent universe. Luther's emphases were necessary theological corrections that brought about greater lay participation, including that by women, in teaching and active ministry which followed from hearing the word of God. Yet they did not provide as much psychological insight for individuals as Teresa's guidelines to prayer, based on her own, different experience. Her attitude before God, however, was one that matched Luther's in its sense of awe, praise, and receptivity. It is God who does all, she emphasized; he "remakes me."

If Teresa had been able to share her insights into prayer with Luther, he might have understood that it was not different conceptions of God's grace that divided them, but method, style, and different ideas about human nature. But the historical reality is that these great souls served the same God in a divided Christianity, reforming their churches in different styles. No one in those years could hear a voice of moderation like that of priest-poet John Donne, who insisted in a 1624 sermon that "They hurt religion as much, that ascribe too little to the Blessed Virgin, as they who ascribe too much." Ignatius, Teresa, and John of the Cross, it should be noted, never ascribed too much to Mary. There was nothing excessive in their devotions; they were simply expressed in aesthetic and cultural forms that seemed at the time incompatible with Protestant belief and worship.

There was no schism in Eastern Orthodoxy. Mother and child are seen enthroned in much the same way then as in the sixth and seventh centuries. The many poses of Mary standing as guide, pointing to her son who rests on her left arm (the *Hodigitria*), are almost exactly the same in sixteenth-century Smolensk as in ninth-century Byzantium.

Unfortunately, the European schism between Roman Catholicism and Protestantism further separated nation-states that were already developing in opposition to one another. When European countries spread their control to Africa, the Americas, and Asia, they divided colonial peoples as well. New spiritual inspiration would come, however, from the lives and legends of the people, even though their culture was crushed and transformed

by European missionary expansionism. As so often in the past,
this new inspiration is most visible in what happened to Mary,
this time as she traveled overseas to the New World.

MEXICO: LA CONQUISTADORA
OR GUADALUPE?

At the height of its power, Spain would try to transport the in-
grown, militant Catholicism of the Iberian peninsula as part of its
conquest of the indigenous populations of South and Central
America. But something extraordinary happened on the conquis-
tadors' trail of death and despoliation. In the midst of a massive
export of European power and technology across the ocean, Mary
became a sign of hope to the conquered.

In the beginning, she seemed to mean victory for the Spaniards
and death for those whom they—seeking trade routes to the
East—had mistakenly called Indians. Under Mary's military protection, the sixteenth-century conquest of Mexico was launched
in the same spirit as earlier attempts to eradicate the Muslims.
Spanish reports claimed that Mary cast dust in the Indians' eyes
during crucial battles. Having won a great victory at Tabasco in
1519 on March 25 (the feast of the Annunciation), the Spaniards
gave the town the new name of Santa Maria de la Victoria. Cortés,
landing on Cozumel in March 1519, installed a typical image of
the Immaculate Conception in place of the cult image of the
Mayan moon goddess. Portrayed as the woman in the Apocalypse,
Mary stands on a crescent moon. The Franciscans had persuaded
Cortés that he had been chosen by God to set up a new apostolic
church in uncorrupted Mexico. After the battle of Tabasco, the
indigenous chiefs, who felt they had witnessed the death of their
world, received instruction in the faith before a statue of Mary and
her child.

Under the new Spanish government, women were routinely

raped, and the native inhabitants were reduced to virtual slavery. Many men committed suicide; many women deliberately avoided giving birth. Because of disease and overwork, the population declined from seventy million or more to ten million in the fifty years after the Conquest. Ironically, some of the missionaries were men who had been influenced by Erasmus and had hoped to bring an enlightened Christianity to the New World. In this painful first encounter between two radically different cultures, however, they knew of no way to relieve the natives' despair.

As a result of the Conquest, the Aztecs were in danger of losing their entire symbolic system. It would be Our Lady of Guadalupe, not the missionaries, who changed the situation. According to the legend, Mary appeared to Juan Diego, a poor Indian, on December 9, 1531, a mere ten years after the Conquest, though it would take decades for the meaning of that appearance to reach the wider community.

The reason that Mary's apparition was so meaningful to the Aztecs was that she could be seen as one of their goddesses returned, now showing her favorable, nurturing side. The Aztec mother goddesses had terrible aspects, but during the Conquest the indigenous population had seen a dark side of Mary as well, when she seemed to demand human sacrifice. The earliest account of her appearance to Juan Diego was in the Aztec language of Nahuatl recorded by Antonio Valeriano, an Indian who had studied with the Jesuits.[40]

According to this testimony, a "little Indian woman" first appeared to Juan Diego in a village near Mexico City, as he walked at daybreak at the foot of the small hill called Tepeyac. First he heard many birds singing in concert from the top of the hill. Then he noticed a white, shining cloud, and around it a beautiful rainbow of colors coming from a bright light in the middle of the cloud. He heard a woman call his name, telling him to come closer. She spoke in his native Nahuatl tongue and told him that she wanted a church built on this hill where, she said, "I will hear your weeping and prayers to give you consolation and relief. I will show my loving favor and the compassion I have for the natives and for those who love and seek me."[41]

The lady told him she was "the ever-Virgin Mary, Mother of the true God by whom all live," but she used the Aztec name Tonantzin, or Mother of the Gods. She requested him to go to the bishop to ask that the church be built; he went, but was ignored. She insisted he go again, and again he was refused, till he begged her to send someone else, "someone noble and illustrious, worthy of respect, who will compel belief." He was just "a poor country person, a lowly man of the people." But the lady insisted, telling him kindly that the work "was fitting" for him. "Tell him [the bishop] I say so!" On December 12, Juan Diego found Castilian roses blooming on the cold, barren hill of Tepeyac; he gathered them into his *tilma*, a cloak of coarse fabric, and hurried toward the city. On the way he again met the lady, who rearranged the roses and told him not to open the cloak to anyone but the bishop. When he did, the bishop fell to his knees, for on the *tilma* was printed the image of Our Lady of Guadalupe, just as Juan Diego had described her (Plate 22). The cloak hangs now in the basilica in Mexico City that bears her name. That this name was understood to be "Guadalupe" may have been the result of a coincidence: Juan's Nahuatl name for Mary, Tlecuauhtlacupeuh (roughly, St. Mary who appeared on the rocky summit), sounded very much like "Guadalupe" in Spanish.

The impact of Mary's appearance as Guadalupe was tremendous: the indigenous people became convinced that the Virgin did not have the same attitude to them as their white oppressors. In one minor incident in the legend, the lady appeared to Juan's sick uncle and cured him, referring to herself as "Mary who drives away those who eat us."[42] The Indians began to believe that Mary had come with the Spaniards in order to be with them on their own soil. She appeared as one of them, the *morenita*, or little dark one, as they came to call her. Guadalupe made it possible for the indigenous population to accept the religion of the conquerors, since the Mary so significant to the Spaniards helped them gain back their self-respect. The church was built on Tepeyac, although some churchmen long suspected that the Indians had simply translated their ancient deities into this feminine form.

No attempt to explain Mary's encounter with Juan Diego has been very successful. Efforts have been made to interpret the stars on the lady's robe as astrological evidence of her dual manifestation as Great Mother and the Woman of Revelation, and even to analyze the paint on the *tilma*, but all efforts have been inconclusive. Rays of the sun, the Aztec symbol of God, emanated from the lady's robe; accordingly, her innermost being was understood to be divine.[43] In any case, the Indians came to understand Mary's image as part of their own symbolic system as well as that of Christianity and celebrated her in dance and song. The chief response of the Indians to the image of Guadalupe was joy, reflected in a song recorded in the sixteenth century which contains the following verses.

> I took delight in all the many-colored flowers, so sweet-smelling,
> that, startled and magnificent, were scattering,
> with petals half-opened, in your presence, O Mother,
>   Our Holy Mary.

> Your spirit, O Holy Mary, is alive in the picture. We men
>   praised her,
> taking after the Great Book, and danced the perfect dance.
> And you, Bishop, our father, preached there by the shore
>   of the lake.

> O! I would live securely here.[44]

Our Lady of Guadalupe united not only the Spanish and the Nahuatl languages but also the Nahuatl and Spanish understandings of God. From this time on, the indigenous people became active Christians; Mary gave them the strength to endure their continuing oppression. Father Virgil Elizondo, a contemporary leader in the effort to acculturate Mexican spirituality in the United States, says that belief in Our Lady of Guadalupe as a compassionate mother was passed on to him through this tradition: "When no one else understood, she understood."[45]

Some social scientists have interpreted Guadalupe as a case in which the church co-opted the uneducated, superstitious indigenous population, and have argued that Our Lady of Guadalupe functioned in a macho culture to keep women down.[46] But Latina theologian Jeanette Rodriguez views the situation very differently; Mexican-American women told her that for them the symbol was not a model of servility and suffering, but one of liberation and empowerment.[47] Guadalupe was ultimately a complex and mysterious event, whose effects are still unfolding.

The historical irony is that "the little dark one" was also accepted by the Spanish. Clearly, there were elements in the image that resonated in their memory. The style of the painting is Spanish, and except for the "star-skirt" of the goddess, her robes might well be associated with the famous statue of Guadalupe in Spain, whose mantle was covered with golden stars. Even more striking was the fact that the original statue from Estremadura, the province in west-central Spain where Cortés was born, was black, and had received her name from the river near which she was found. This wooden madonna, which had been the center of a cult of great importance to Spanish royalty ever since King Alfonso XI of Castile defeated the Moors at Río Salado in 1340, was obviously related to medieval legends about the discovery of images of Mary by shepherds, cowherds, and farmers.

Miguel Sanchez's 1648 Spanish translation and interpretation of the Diego story, linking Guadalupe both to biblical imagery and to the promise of new birth in the Mexican nation, provided a way to make sense of a community that was neither Spanish nor

Indian, but Mexican. Sanchez called attention to the tradition of Spanish apocalypticism that the Mexican image invoked. The woman framed by the sun's rays and standing on a crescent moon is a faithful if stereotypical representation of the Immaculate Conception as she appeared in much of Catholic Europe (Plate 21). It was like the one Cortés had brought. For Sanchez, its appearance was a sign that the conquest had been ordained by God precisely in order that this "most divine image" could appear there. Tepeyac was the new Mt. Zion; Mexico was the Promised Land, and the new world of Christ was replacing the old world of Adam.

The appearance of Mary to Juan Diego gradually extended her significance to the nation as a whole and to all of Latin America. The great Mexican poet Sor Juana de la Cruz (d. 1695) celebrated Mary in major liturgical compositions and religious poems as scholar, musician, knight in armor, and orator, incorporating the voices of slaves, Indians, and Spaniards in Mary's praise. The priest-revolutionist Hidalgo hoisted the image of Our Lady of Guadalupe on a spear at the head of his army in the fight for Mexican independence, and Simon Bolívar, the visionary of a united South America, carried the Virgin's image on his banners in difficult battles.[48]

Inevitably, the ruling class invoked the Virgin for its own cause. During the insurgency of 1810, for example, the Spanish viceroy in Mexico put a marshal's baton into the hands of the statue of the Virgin of Los Remedios, who represented an alternative understanding of Mary, and made her spiritual commander of the Spanish forces. In our day, Guadalupe has been showered with an embarrassing excess of ecclesiastical approval in an attempt to control her interpretation. At the World Marian Congress in July 1959, she was hailed as Empress of the Americas. But Ursuline sister Michelle Guerin, who worked as a missionary in Mexico for eighteen years, says that the real devotion

to Our Lady of Guadalupe takes place before her shrines in ordinary homes all over the country: "Hers is the matriarchal mystique that guides the psyche of the Mexican."[49]

Guadalupe is just one of many images of Mary that became
symbols of divine compassion for the conquered in the New
World. The patron saint of Brazil is Our Lady of the Immaculate
Conception, whose chief image was found, blackened by the
water, in the Paraíba River. Brazilian slaves believed that this
Virgin "disapproved of slavery and identified with them through
her blackness."[50] As Marian images appeared throughout Latin
America, elements of the Mother Goddess common to all these
indigenous people merged with the Christianity of their conquerors just as they had in medieval Europe. In each country
where Mary became patroness, her own name and story became
identified with the hopes of the people.

THE CONTRASTING MARYS OF THE NINETEENTH CENTURY

"I am the Immaculate Conception."
—Bernadette's report of the Lady's words
at Lourdes, 1858

I say that we are wound
With mercy round and round
As if with air: the same
Is Mary, more by name.
She, wild web, wondrous robe,
Mantles the guilty globe,
Since God has let dispense
Her prayers his providence . . .
—GERARD MANLEY HOPKINS[1]

Mary's image has helped all realize that women are in themselves possessors of and possessed by immortal souls.
—MARGARET FULLER[2]

If the image of Mary contributed to the division of Christianity during the years of the Reformation, by the nineteenth century that division had hardened. Both Catholics and Protestants lacked balance in their approach to Mary, largely because of their mutual isolation. For European Catholics this was a Marian century, the high point of enthusiasm for apparitions at Lourdes and elsewhere, and of attempts to maximize Mary's role in God's plan of salvation. Predictably, such developments only confirmed Protestants in their distrust of Marian piety as nonbiblical and near-idolatrous. But minority voices in this same century suggested other roles for Mary. John Cardinal Newman, a convert from Anglicanism and probably the most clear-sighted Catholic thinker of the century, developed a sober conception of Mary's place in the church that was both restrained and attentive to the traditions of early Christianity. Perhaps just as significantly, a growing number of Protestant women in England and the United States, though not attracted by Catholic Marian dogma, recognized the absence of a strong feminine presence in Protestant life and devotion and turned to Mary as a compelling and unifying symbol. The details of these developments create a fascinating mosaic in which Mary continued to elude easy definition and to demonstrate her appeal to the spiritual needs of the most diverse groups.

CATHOLIC EUROPE: DEVOTIONS,
APPARITIONS, AND DOGMAS

Nineteenth-century Catholics felt defensive; the papacy saw its power and the dogmas such power helped to preserve threatened by tides of change. Democracy, science, and the protests of workers in an increasingly industrialized society—often championed by those who questioned traditional Christian assumptions— were easily perceived as hostile influences. Pope Pius IX encouraged devotion to Mary as the church's best defense against these threats. Of course, nineteenth-century Marian theology was not new. It had arisen in the claustrophobic atmosphere of seventeenth-century Catholicism, when theologians in Spain, France, and Italy highlighted the very claims about Mary that had disturbed Protestants, biblicists, and humanists at the time of the Reformation.

The Capuchin Lawrence of Brindisi (d. 1619) is a good representative of such thinking. He wrote a Mariale praising Mary more as bride of Christ than as mother, calling her similar to Christ in "nature, grace, virtue, dignity, and glory." Following a fifteenth-century Franciscan theme, his sermon on the Annunciation suggested that God had fallen in love with Mary: "Great is the might and power a beautiful woman has over a man who is in love with her . . . she causes him to rave and causes the lover to go out of his mind . . . the Virgin could do this with God himself."[3]

The seventeenth century had been a period of devastation in Europe, with the Thirty Years' War largely powered by religious division. In France, Jansenism combined its instinct for reform with an exaggerated pessimism about human nature. In contrast, most Catholic theologians appealed to a private, emotional spirituality, asking believers to see their own sufferings as insignificant in the light of those of Jesus and Mary. Pierre de Bérulle

(d. 1629), for example, a highly respected cardinal diplomat and founder of the French Oratory, asserted that Mary gave greater life to Jesus than Jesus gave to her. He talked about the life of Jesus in Mary's womb, stressing the nearness of their two hearts before he was born. Mary was in "perpetual ravishment" in this condition, he claimed, and understood perfectly the mystery of the Incarnation. Since Mary already shared her son's future as victim, her heart as well as his was pierced.

Jean-Jacques Olier (d. 1657), founder of the famous seminary of St. Sulpice, took up this theme, insisting that Jesus was "but one heart, one soul, one life with Mary." He, too, wrote of the time Jesus spent in her womb as the most important of his life, and consequently the most important mystery the church should ponder. Olier saw the relation of the Father with the Virgin as a real marriage—in which, however, Mary was completely passive. Since he felt that anything to do with real childbirth was unclean, he did not speak of Mary as having a child, but rather a perfect man. In Olier's interpretation of the Crucifixion, Christ, abandoned by the Father, turned to his tender mother, whose sufferings caused him more pain than his own. At that moment, he ceded to her the right to dispense all his treasures: "He wills what she wills."[4]

Devotion to the suffering hearts of Jesus and Mary and the need for sacrifice and reparation for sins were also encouraged by the growing number of religious orders of men and women. Such piety increased greatly in the 1670s after the appearance of the bleeding and suffering Christ to Margaret Mary Alacoque, a sister in the Order of the Visitation at Paray-le-Monial in France. Devotion to the Sacred Heart, already practiced in convents and monasteries, became widely popular.

Jean Eudes (d. 1680) was another French Catholic theologian who supported devotion to the hearts of Jesus and Mary. He drew up a formal contract of marriage between himself and Mary: "I accept and recognize you as my sovereign . . . by your goodness treat me as the subject of your authority."[5] Eudes suggested that Mary should be considered the bride of every priest.

Even more extreme was the "slavery" to Mary advocated by St. Louis-Marie Grignion de Montfort (d. 1716), author of *True Devotion to the Blessed Virgin*. Such slavery, of course, was metaphoric, intended to dramatize complete surrender to God's will; *True Devotion*'s "Totus tuus" ("I am all yours") provided Pope John Paul II with the motto for his coat of arms. De Montfort claimed that the way to salvation was complete obedience to Mary: we cannot dare approach Christ on our own. At communion we should tell Christ to ignore us and pay attention only to Mary acting on our behalf.

St. Alphonsus Liguori's *The Glories of Mary* gave further support to such dependence on Mary. The most popular modern book of Marian devotion, it took Counter-Reformation distortion for granted: "all graces that God gives to men pass through the hands of Mary." Hilda Graef observes that Liguori (d. 1787) presents Mary as the wise wife of an angry God-husband who, without her, might at any time do something he would later regret. Since Mary is made the source of all mercy in heaven, Jesus seems almost an adjunct beside her and her role tends to replace that of the Holy Spirit: "Mary has only to speak and the Son executes all."[6]

Such excesses led to a reaction during the French Revolution that was both political and religious. Many images of Mary were seen either as superstitious or as reminders of aristocratic privilege, and accordingly were destroyed. Celebrated black virgins that had escaped the ravages of earlier times were now burned or hacked to pieces, among them those in the crypts of Mont-St.-Michel and Chartres. Mary seemed to stand in diametrical opposition to Marianne, the allegorical figure who personified the French Republic: "Virgin of Liberty, deliver us from King and Popes! Virgin of Equality, deliver us from aristocrats." Shamelessly parodying the Ave Maria, revolutionaries sang, "Hail Marianne, full of strength, the People are with thee, Blessed is the fruit of thy womb, the Republic."

After the defeat of Napoleon, efforts were made to restore the older order. Most Catholics tended to see demands for democracy as threatening the traditional alliance between throne and altar; such an atmosphere, however, can only partly account for a widespread turn to Mary among ordinary laypeople. In 1824, the influential German Catholic poet Brentano brought out *The Life of the Virgin Mary* by Catherine Emmerich, an Augustinian nun from Westphalia. The book described revelations "in pictures," especially from Our Lady, which Emmerich and her publisher both thought of as meditations, similar to the representations of artists. Emmerich presented an ideal of self-immolation and redemptive suffering that reflected her own experience and resonated with that of the wider church. She endured the stigmata—the five wounds of Jesus on the cross—and offered her physical sufferings, which were serious, as a sacrifice for what she saw as threats to the church. The fears of many Catholics are reflected in the belief that she was able to detect in advance plots on the life of the pope.[7] "I saw the Holy Father surrounded by traitors . . . the destroyers attacking the Church of Peter, Mary standing with her mantle over it, and the enemies of God put to flight."[8]

In 1830 Catherine Labouré, the daughter of a French peasant, had a vision that reaffirmed a long-held popular belief in Mary's Immaculate Conception. On the eve of the feast of St. Vincent de Paul, this twenty-four-year-old postulant of the Sisters of Charity deliberately swallowed a small piece of the saint's linen surplice before going to sleep in her convent on the rue du Bac in Paris. Later that night, according to her account, a child whom she took to be an angel told her to go to the chapel. She dressed hastily, walking through the dark corridors to a brilliantly illuminated but empty chapel. Suddenly she heard the rustle of silk and

saw Mary sitting in a chair by the altar. Catherine rushed to her
and put her hands on Mary's knees. Among other things, Mary
told her that "Misfortunes will come crashing down on France.
The throne will be toppled." A few days later Charles X abdi-
cated in favor of his grandson, and revolutionaries sacked the
palaces of bishops throughout France.

In November, Catherine reports, Mary appeared again, wearing a white silk robe, her head covered with a white veil that fell
to her feet, which rested on a globe. Her hands were lifted up,
holding a golden ball with a cross on top. On each of her fingers
she had three rings, which emitted brilliant rays of light. The
rays were, Mary said, the graces she gave to all who asked
for them. A green serpent with yellow specks lay stretched out
nearby.

Suddenly an oval frame formed around the vision, and inside
was written in golden letters: "O Mary, conceived without sin,
pray for us who have recourse to thee." The golden ball disappeared, but the Virgin's arms remained outstretched, the rays of
light still visible. When Mary turned around, Catherine saw a
large letter *M* surmounted by a cross; two hearts were below, one
circled with thorns, the other pierced by a sword. A voice instructed the young nun to have a medal struck according to this
pattern. She told her confessor, who received the approval of the
archbishop of Paris to commence making the medals, though her
connection with the vision was not revealed until after her death.
Mary told Catherine that she would not see her again, but would
hear her voice in prayers.[9]

Mass production of the Miraculous Medal began; within seven
years, ten million copies were circulated worldwide, and cures and
conversions began to be reported. Soldiers, nurses, and missionaries brought the medal to Africa, the Crimea, and the Far East. Its
circulation went over the billion mark in Catherine's own lifetime.
Such widespread response surely made it easier to work for the

doctrinal definition of the Immaculate Conception, which came in 1854.

Two more apparitions occurred in France, one before and one after the definition; they marked a qualitative change in the importance of Marian visions and their significance to church life: the first at La Salette, near Grenoble, in 1846, and the most famous of all, at Lourdes, in 1858. At La Salette two children, Maximin Giraud, eleven, and Mélanie Calvat, fourteen, were tending cattle near a spring when they saw a bright light, from which a woman emerged. Speaking gently in French, and then, when they did not understand her, in their local dialect, she told the children she was tired of holding back her son's anger. Only old women went to mass any longer, and cart drivers used her son's name when swearing. "If my people will not submit," she said, "I shall be forced to let go the arm of my son; it is so heavy and oppressive that I can no longer restrain it." The woman went on to predict a famine if people did not pray and mend their ways; if they repented, however, the stones would turn into wheat and potatoes. Before disappearing she implored them: "Make this known to my people."[10] The two children were not especially pious and did not at first suspect that Mary was the weeping woman they had encountered, but the warning of famine and impending disasters touched a deep chord in the community.

Anthropologists Victor and Edith Turner see La Salette as the first intervention of the Virgin in a modern economic crisis, one that would become the pattern for her spiritual manifestations in industrialized society. They explain that post-Napoleonic France was "a peculiarly appropriate soil for the seeds of Marian devotion." Exhaustion after the failure of the Emperor's campaigns combined with "the growth of industrialism and bureaucracy, the emergence of a proletariat . . . the overt failure of rationalism and the Goddess of Reason made people anxious, longing for a collective salvation."[11] Mary's importance also grew because modern life tended to undermine the power of local saints as guarantors of water or grain, just as Christ and the saints had undermined the seasonal gods centuries before.

Marian apparitions, the Turners emphasize, point to the hidden, nonhierarchical domain of the church and stress the power of the weak, the community, "the rare and the unprecedented, as against the regular, ordained, and normative."[12] In addition, the message at La Salette resonated with lower-middle-class concerns. It was not an appeal, as in earlier times, to build a church on the spot; Mary was asking humanity to "Repent, pray, and be saved," a message understood to be relevant to world events, especially if people did not heed her warning. Reports of the local curate indicate that attendance at mass improved after the apparition at La Salette, as did the behavior of local males. Hilda Graef points out that Mary's admonitions were an echo of contemporary local sermons that dwelled on the sins of poor people, not their lack of charity or social injustice. Nevertheless, the apparition was a communal manifestation of belief in God and the church, and a powerful affirmation of Mary's—as a sign of God's—caring presence among them.

At first neither the priests nor the police—who had extra work handling the crowds—believed the apparition at La Salette to be legitimate. But slowly, despite scathing editorials and the sarcasm of the educated clergy, acceptance grew among a wide public. On the fifth anniversary of the apparition, the local bishop approved official devotions at the site. In fact, the church does not make it easy for apparitions to gain such approval; officials are initially prudent and skeptical, demanding that considerable testimony be gathered. According to the rule Pope Benedict XIV had provided in the eighteenth century, formal approval can only be given by the local bishop. Even then, it is never asserted as a fact that Mary has appeared, only that devotion is not prohibited and not contrary to faith: "One can refuse assent to these revelations providing that one does this with the modesty that comes from having good reasons and without the intention of being divisive."[13]

The important question of who controls the meaning of such apparitions also surfaced at La Salette. Anthropologist Sandra Zimdars-Swartz is particularly helpful in explaining the process by which public meaning developed out of what was at first a private experience. The two seers of La Salette, she says, were pressured throughout their lives by journalists and ecclesiastics to reveal additional messages they had unwisely hinted that Mary had given them. Eventually the children were persuaded to send written versions of these "secrets" to the pope, who did not release their contents. When Mélanie published her account independently much later, it included strong criticism of the clergy for lax and immoral conduct. She insisted that Mary predicted even worse catastrophes than her own first report indicated—not only famine but disease, earthquake, perhaps the end of the world. La Salette was the first modern apparition to feature "secrets" and to take on the doomsday tone typical of such events in times of crisis.

Meanwhile Pius IX, who thought of himself as something of a reformer, with hopes for progress and democracy, ascended to the papacy in 1846. But the revolutions that broke out across Europe in 1848, in which one of his own key ministers was assassinated, made him adopt a very different policy. He had always had deep personal devotion to Mary, attributing the remission of his childhood epilepsy to her intercession; now he called on her as champion of Catholicism against the unbridled confidence in reason that he saw emerging from the Enlightenment.

Determined to bring Marian devotion to the broadest possible public, the pope revived interest in de Montfort's *True Devotion* and Liguori's *Glories of Mary*, and he consulted a group of theologians as to whether or not he should declare the Immaculate Conception a dogma of the church—that is, one that has been divinely revealed and must be believed. Mary's preservation from the guilt of Original Sin had long been held by the faithful and celebrated liturgically on December 8, but in the past such theologians as Aquinas, Bonaventure, Bernard, and Anselm had all opposed the doctrine. Some had reservations that reflected the Augustinian view that, because of Original Sin, every conception by sexual means was sinful, including that by Mary's parents. Others raised the theological point that if she were born without sin, Mary would have had no need of a redeemer. The group assembled by Pius IX, however, responded favorably to the idea of a doctrinal statement, 17 to 3. The pope then consulted the bishops, and nine tenths were positive. Meanwhile, the dynamics of Italian nationalism seemed to offer direct challenges to papal power. In November 1854, two thirds of the religious congregations in Italy were dissolved, and Massini and Garibaldi were gathering troops for an attack on Rome. Perhaps partly in response, on December 8, after a magnificent procession to St. Peter's, Pius read the constitution *Ineffabilis Deus* with tears streaming down his cheeks:

> the doctrine which holds that the blessed Virgin Mary, at the first instant of her Conception, by a singular privilege and grace of the omnipotent God, in consideration of the merits of Jesus Christ, the Savior of mankind, was preserved free from all stain of original sin, has been revealed by God, and is to be firmly and constantly believed by all the faithful.[14]

The definition acknowledged Mary's need for a redeemer and avoided discussion of Anne and Joachim's part in their daughter's conception, thereby skirting points that had given difficulty to earlier theologians. That it delighted royalists and militarists can be seen in the actions of Napoleon III, who sent a picture of the Immaculate Conception as a standard for his fleet in the Black Sea during the Crimean War.

Ineffabilis Deus not only stunned Protestants, it also startled the Eastern Orthodox, who feared that it denied Mary's humanity and separated her from the rest of creation. In the view of the late Orthodox theologian John Meyendorff, only Jesus Christ "benefited from an Immaculate Conception in her [Mary's] womb."[15] Even Anglicans, who could see some justification for the belief itself, were outraged by the articulation of such a precise dogma and such an assertion of power by the pope. A number of Catholic observers today see a connection between the pope's declaration and his concern for political inviolability in the Italian context. "In broader terms," historian Ann Taves points out, "it expressed the papacy's need to defend its authority to define truth in the modern world by linking itself as the mother and teacher of all churches with Mary as the mother and teacher of the faithful."[16] But as always seems the case with Mary, there are other interpretations. According to English Dominican Herbert McCabe, the definition was "the fruit of popular Christian devotion that stubbornly asserted itself against the most determined opposition of theologians, saints and bishops." It was "a victory for the affective over neat rational systems; it was a liberation of the human spirit; it was a very Franciscan thing."[17]

The momentum of Marian doctrine continued into the twentieth century and the reign of Pius XII, who proclaimed the second and related dogma of the bodily Assumption of Mary into heaven. Ever since the definition of the Immaculate Conception, petitions had poured in to Rome for the second definition. St. Bernard had had difficulties with the idea of an Immaculate Conception, but none with the Assumption, on which he had frequently preached. Mary's purity from sin at birth made it "fitting" that she should not decay in the tomb like the rest of humankind before the final resurrection, but should join her son as soon as she died, or—in some traditions—fell asleep.

There were many arguments for the Assumption, though none of them were biblical or apostolic. One was based on the fact that no one had ever located Mary's burial place or tomb. Hints of her possible Assumption went back to the early centuries of the church, and the belief had been incorporated into the liturgical calendar, as well as in legends and art, since the fifth century. It was this tradition of popular belief reflected in centuries of prayer and story on which Pius XII based his decree.

Even when such a doctrinal decree is issued, however, only the statement of it, and not the reasons given, is held to be incontrovertibly true. The decrees on both the Immaculate Conception and the Assumption were minimalist in their wording. The definition of the latter dogma is deliberately vague about Mary's death, saying only that "when her earthly life was finished" she was "taken up body and soul into the glories of heaven." When the Assumption was pronounced dogma, the Orthodox were not disturbed, for they had long held the belief that her body was glorified after death, seeing in her "the goal and perfection of all creation."[18] But they were upset by the claim of papal authority. Protestants were more shaken, judging that both the content of the decree and the manner in which it had been declared were a setback to the cause of Christian unity. Although the Assumption seemed an enigma and even a scandal to contemporaries accustomed to thinking in secular and scientific terms, most Roman Catholics accepted the dogma as a mystery and also as a hopeful sign that, as Pius said, "the exalted destiny of both our soul and body should be clear to all men." The response of psychologist Carl Jung was surprisingly similar; he welcomed the definition as necessary and significant, indeed, as "the prototype of man's bodily resurrection."[19]

Looking back from today's vantage point, the proclamation in 1950 of the doctrine of the Assumption seems to have been the climax of what was largely a nineteenth-century Catholic obsession with Mary. During those years there were reports of hundreds of other Marian appearances, from Italy and Spain to Bohemia and Poland. These apparitions seemed almost a cry of the heart from the poor women and children who were their recipients; as civil society grew increasingly hostile to evidence for the supernatural, such accounts of Mary's presence were far more compelling to most believers than church decrees. And no manifestation of Mary so caught the public imagination as did the apparitions in 1858 at Lourdes, a small town in the foothills of the Pyrenees.

Lourdes represents the first serial public appearances of the Virgin in history—again to a poor child, but without the dire prophecies of La Salette. That Our Lady of Lourdes is known primarily as a healer and that the shrine itself is the most popular pilgrimage site in the world may well be due to the good judgment, the silence, and probably the holiness of Bernadette Soubirous. As Victor and Edith Turner suggest, "Something of Bernadette has tinctured the social milieu—a cheerful simplicity, a great depth of communion."[20]

Mary's appearances were a mixed blessing to this fourteen-year-old daughter of an extremely poor family that lived in a foul-smelling hovel. On February 11, 1858, in a grotto at Massabielle, near Lourdes, Bernadette heard a rustling noise in the bushes and saw the image of a girl close to her own age and small in size. The girl wore white with a blue sash and carried a rosary. In her first reports, Bernadette referred to her as *aquerò*, a dialect term that means roughly "her" or "that one." She agreed to Aquerò's wish that she come back every day for two weeks with her friends to pray the rosary.

The first people in whom Bernadette confided told her that her experience was an illusion. Her mother did not believe in it, and later became furious with Bernadette for wasting time on visitors who trampled the garden and whose gifts her daughter refused. But others responded to the story and began to accompany the young seer on her visits to the grotto. When Aquerò asked Bernadette to have a chapel built there, the girl reluctantly went with her aunts to the local rectory to convey the message.

The curate was highly skeptical, even hostile, and suggested that Bernadette ask her mysterious visitor for a sign—to make a rosebush bloom in winter.

No rosebush bloomed that February, but crowds began to accompany Bernadette to the grotto where she prayed and sometimes went into a trance. On February 25, a number of people saw her scratch the mud and splash her face with the muddy water she uncovered. Aquerò had asked her to drink and wash in what was until then an invisible spring. From prehistoric times springs have been associated with holy places, and much has been made, too, of the spring at which the Virgin had appeared at La Salette. This incident in the grotto was the beginning of the enormous popularity of Lourdes water, which has continued to be plentiful, though it is now shipped all over the world. I still have an old rosary of my aunt's certifying that the clear plastic bubble on the back of the crucifix contains genuine water from the grotto at Lourdes.

Prompted by the local curate, Bernadette finally asked the apparition who she was. Aquerò identified herself on the feast of the Annunciation, March 25. Smiling, she extended her arms in the well-known pose of the Miraculous Medal and replied, "I am the Immaculate Conception," seeming to confirm the papal pronouncement four years earlier. But of course Bernadette's motive was not to lend support to dogmatic decrees; she sought only to be faithful to her experience. She, too, had been given a secret, but Mary had told her to reveal it to no one. When the bishop's commission asked her if she would tell her secret to the pope, she is said to have replied, "The Pope is someone." When the commission persisted, asserting that "the Pope has the authority of Jesus Christ," she replied, "The Pope has authority on earth. The Blessed Virgin is in heaven," and refused to speak further on the subject.

Despite harassment, ridicule, and constant interviews, Bernadette survived with dignity as a Sister of Charity at Nevers until her death in 1879. A story that a French friend told me, however, suggests Bernadette's human loneliness. As a young girl in the late 1860s, my friend's grandmother lived near Bernadette's convent at Nevers. She used to see the nuns walking two by two—except for one who was always alone at the rear. When she asked a sister one day why that was, the nun replied: "Oh, that's the crazy one from Lourdes who thinks she saw the Blessed Virgin! She doesn't even speak proper French. None of the other nuns want to walk with her."

When I was young, I read Franz Werfel's *Song of Bernadette* and loved the movie with Jennifer Jones. I identified with a glamorized Bernadette then as part of my own defensive Catholic identity, scorning the skeptical doctors who could not accept the cures of the crippled as miracles. Since then I have come to a more ambivalent yet still affirmative attitude. Helped by the insights of contemporary observers, I now see Lourdes as a far more complicated phenomenon; neither simple credulity nor skepticism can account for it. The Turners, for example, interpret the Lady's desire "for people to come here in procession" as a reaffirmation of the wider community of the church, a lay expression leading to spiritual renewal. Sandra Zimdars-Swartz was moved to pursue her serious study of apparitions by observing just such renewal among pilgrims at the shrine, whether or not they were cured physically. In her memoir, *Virgin Time*, Patricia Hampl records the same surprising power of communal faith to transcend the highly commercial atmosphere of the town.

In the nineteenth century, Lourdes and the other Marian apparitions succeeded in rallying most of Catholic Europe behind Pius IX, despite evidence of the latter's increasing alienation from the wider world.[21] Another alleged appearance, in July 1876 at Marpingen in the Catholic Saarland, is a striking example of how a different community supported what at first seemed a dubious occurrence. Three young girls reported that they saw a woman in white carrying a child in a wild meadow. Afterward they said they saw her in many other places. The clergy were not disposed to accept their claims and journalists made disparaging remarks about the town's backward, superstitious beliefs. But the reaction of the Bismarck regime was so arrogant—Saarland was then part of Prussia—that the town backed the girls. Although there is evidence that the girls' families helped shape their story to make it more acceptable to church authorities,[22] when the government ordered in soldiers, and even sent the young visionaries and the parish priest to jail, Marpingen rallied behind the persecuted seers. Many tourists, even some aristocrats, began to visit the town, and soon there was talk of "the German Lourdes." Historian David Blackbourn believes that the events of Marpingen help illuminate the significance of all such apparitions. He points out that the economic crisis in the Saar was severe at the time, and Catholics in Prussia were feeling the effects of Bismarck's Kulturkampf, during which many priests were jailed and Catholic institutions closed. In these circumstances, the alleged Marian apparitions at Marpingen helped foster a sense of Catholic identity; for Blackbourn, the community's unified support of the apparitions was a form of passive political resistance to a repressive regime.

The same pattern of complex forces is visible in the next famous series of apparitions, which occurred at Fatima in Portugal from 1915 to 1917. In the hostile atmosphere of another secular state, three young shepherds, Lucia dos Santos and her younger cousins, claimed to have a series of visitations from the Virgin. These appearances were similar to those at Lourdes in their serial and public nature, but more like those at La Salette in their political aspects and doomsday predictions, as well as in the publicity surrounding their secrets. Fatima is unique among approved apparitions in the public experience of "signs" that seemed to confirm its authenticity.

Eight-year-old Lucia was praying the rosary on a hillside with some friends when she saw something in the air above the trees, like a statue made of snow, suffused with the light of the sun. In the next vision, an angel of peace told Lucia and her cousins that the hearts of Jesus and Mary were attentive to their prayers. The children claimed that on one occasion the angel gave them the Eucharist from a chalice suspended in the air. Lucia was the seventh child of a family whose father was a drunkard and a gambler. In many ways the little girl had been the star performer of her family, boasting an unusual memory and the ability to entertain other children with stories. When her brother was drafted in 1917, her mother sent her in place of her brother to herd the sheep. At a time when bread riots were breaking out in Lisbon, Lucia and her cousins, Jacinta and Francisco, experienced six appearances of the "beautiful lady."

The religious meaning that this lively and imaginative girl found in these events enabled her to survive in very adverse circumstances. Her mother called her a liar and beat her; representatives of the local church tricked and threatened her, insisting that they would find out whether or not "the devil" was responsible for her visions. The mayor tried to frighten Lucia so that she would reveal the secret the lady had told her, but the terrified girl stood her ground, even though her parents took no steps to protect her. At one point all three children were placed in jail and told they would be thrown alive into a boiling cauldron if they did not tell what the lady had said to them. Nevertheless, they revealed nothing.

The stakes were high for the community, because these apparitions occurred just after the Republican government of Portugal had passed strongly anticlerical laws, seized church property, and renamed Christmas "the day of the family." Although people were wary about what the government would tolerate, others, too, began claiming to have seen the vision. At the Virgin's last public appearance, on October 13, 1917, thousands of people gathered at the Cova da Iria reported seeing the sun dance and tremble. Growing belief in the authenticity of the apparitions probably represented an unconscious groundswell of support for a threatened church. It came too late for Jacinta and Francisco, who died in the flu epidemic of 1918–1919. Lucia entered the convent in 1925, and on October 13, 1930, the anniversary of the great sign, the bishop of Leiria recognized Our Lady of Fatima as worthy of assent.

Cast in the mold of nineteenth-century apparitions, Fatima was not well known outside of Portugal until Lucia's notes on a hitherto unmentioned aspect of the Virgin's revelations were published in 1941. In response to requests from her bishop, Lucia wrote four different memoirs from 1935 to 1941 in which the nature of Mary's messages changed considerably. In the third, Lucia finally gave an account of part of the secret she said the Virgin had confided at Fatima: she predicted a world catastrophe during the reign of Pius XI if people did not cease offending God. (In fact, World War II broke out in 1939, the last year of his reign.) Lucia also claimed that in an appearance in 1929, the Virgin had made an addition to her earlier warning, saying that "The moment has come in which God asks the Holy Father in union with all the bishops of the world to make the consecration of Russia to my Immaculate Heart, promising to save it by this means." The publication of the memoirs coincided with the widespread fear of communism in a world already at war, and to a growing number of believers the Virgin's prophecies in 1917 and 1929 seemed to explain twentieth-century world events. In the postwar years, Fatima literature swamped the Catholic press, and Our Lady of Fatima was seen as a bulwark against communism. The last part of the secret Mary gave to Lucia was never revealed publicly, but there was much speculation as to its content.

Modern apparitions like those at Lourdes and Fatima have occurred largely in the same natural sites in which medieval statues of black madonnas seem to have been found—in caves, in trees, or near springs. Popular religion seems to crave tangible evidence of mystery, whether in relics or apparitions. Such continuity of tradition in a rural community suggests an affirmation of its own experience in the face of insufficient response from the official church. Zimdars-Swartz believes that such conflict frequently surfaces "between the church's need for a single, unified order and the human need for expressions of physical well-being that often crystallize around an apparition." The latter are creative communal expressions, the art and authority of those who lack both.[23]

There are no exact formulas by which to translate the meaning of apparitions; to pretend to explain them fully is to deny that anything supernatural occurred. They are, inevitably, as open to exploitation as to holiness. But time and examination of their fruits can help in assessing their basic soundness as part of Christian tradition. It is often hard for a bishop or for the institutional church to prohibit devotion arising from such events, once the process of communal crystallization has begun. On the whole, the church has responded to the phenomenon of apparitions with great caution. A relative handful received approval in this period, starting with those to Catherine Labouré, that at La Salette (1846) and those at Lourdes (1858) and Pontmain (1870) in France, Fatima (1917) in Portugal, and Beauraing (1932) and Banneux (1933) in Belgium. But other apparitions have received enough unofficial approval to thrive.

Sandra Zimdars-Swartz reminds us that "Marian events are not simple events with self-evident meaning." The entire process of coming to an understanding accepted both by the seers and by the community reflects interaction and wider human concerns. The apparitions begin to make sense only when it is possible to read the stories of seers in the light of other information about them, the people around them, and the general environment. On the whole, Zimdars-Swartz observes, "This context has been one of suffering, suffering with which the subjects, through their special experiences, have begun to come to terms."[24] But it is also one in which joy in the certainty of divine presence among them takes center stage. Belief in apparitions fills a deep popular need that cultural historian John Shinners believes the church can at best only channel, not control: "What theologians ignore, ordinary people will provide: Lourdes and Fatimas and even Medjugorjes [a series of apparitions beginning in the former Yugoslavia in 1981] will probably always be with us."[25]

ONE OTHER POINT ABOUT THE MARIAN DEVOTIONS AND apparitions of the nineteenth and twentieth centuries deserves to be underlined: women are at their center. The Turners suggest that the revival of pilgrimages to Marian shrines, including Walsingham in England and the sites of the black madonnas in France, perhaps represents a resurgent female principle defying "male" iconoclasm.[26] Blackbourn traces a sense of economic vulnerability, loneliness, and ill health among the predominantly female viewers of apparitions. Their visions seem to have been a resource for them, as they had always been for women who lacked power and office. Widespread acceptance of the apparitions by the community and the authorities played a significant part in feminizing the church in the nineteenth century.

The question arises: did such feminization foster spiritual and human growth in real women? The answer depended, of course, on the integrity and maturity of the respondent. The pious, sentimental images of the nineteenth century surrounded the real Thérèse Martin, known today as Thérèse of Lisieux (1873–1897), but they were transformed by her intelligence and her hunger for a deep spirituality that was always united to the love of others. Thérèse lived and advocated a "little way" to God through the trials and challenges of ordinary life. She had lost her beloved mother when she was four, a year after she had determined to "refuse nothing of what God asked of me." Her mother's death was a bitter blow; Thérèse seemed unable to overcome her tears, headaches, insomnia, and nervous weakness—

partly brought on by the regular departure of one beloved older sister after another for the convent. When Thérèse was ten, "finding no help on earth," she prayed earnestly one day before a statue of the Virgin. This statue—through which the Virgin had twice talked to her pious mother, Thérèse confides—smiled on her. From that moment she was completely cured and exhibited a healthy normalcy until her untimely death from tuberculosis at twenty-four. She always believed that Mary was responsible for her recovery.

Thérèse's "little way" led her, through correspondence and in her mind, far beyond the walls of the convent she entered when she was fifteen. She was drawn into ever deeper mental participation in the sin and suffering of the world that her sister Carmelites could not grasp. In the excruciating pain of the last days of her tuberculosis, Thérèse told them she felt nothing but doubt and darkness, but it did not matter—joy lay deep underneath. The sisters offered reassurances of how happy she would be in heaven; she told them she wanted to spend her heaven helping others on earth. In one of Thérèse's last conversations she showed how much she had grown in the spiritual life, and how much she had learned about Mary:

> How I would have loved to be a priest in order to preach about the Blessed Virgin! . . . I'd first make people understand how little is known by us about her life. We shouldn't say unlikely things or things we don't know anything about! . . . They show her to us as unapproachable, but they should present her as imitable, bringing out her virtues, saying that she lived by faith just like ourselves, giving proofs of this from the Gospel.[27]

For Catholic women who were not as strong and self-confident as Thérèse, the devotions around the Immaculate Conception provided hope and comfort in otherwise difficult lives. Feminist theologian Els Maeckelberghe recently reexamined the effects of images of the Immaculate Conception on women in nineteenth-century Belgium.[28] She discovered that the roles assigned to women were extremely confining. Though home and marriage were the only prescribed options, many women were forced to work in factories, where the death rate among young girls was actually higher than that among men. Those who married were under the legal rule of their husbands and were worn down by constant childbearing. The image of the Immaculate Conception, a woman in harmony with God and creation, was very popular among these women, Maeckelberghe found. Her head circled in stars, standing on the crescent moon, Mary offered a feminine ideal, the possibility of a better world, and the chance of being heard by someone while still in this world.

ENGLAND AND THE UNITED STATES: CONVERGING NEEDS FOR MARY

If nineteenth-century European Catholics turned to Mary as a refuge from the modern world, John Henry Newman turned to her as a stimulus and guide to thinking through the relation of the church to that world. At a time when scientific progress was eroding the faith of many English Victorians, Newman's intellectual doubts about Anglicanism led him to join the old Roman church. He took a different direction than the pope, however, because he was always convinced that religion, science, and freedom of thought were compatible. He did not fear Darwinism, which convinced many that the scientific and religious interpretations of creation could not be reconciled. Perhaps partly because he was a poet, he found evolution inherent in the images Jesus used—for instance, the small mustard seed that grew into the large tree of the church. Newman shared many of the questions and uncertainties of his English contemporaries, but the very habits of thought that made him an outstanding theologian of high Anglicanism at Oxford eventually led him to the Catholic church and to a modern interpretation of Mary's role as its model.

Ordained an Anglican priest in 1825, Newman became a vicar at the Oxford University parish where his sermons attracted others like John Keble and E. B. Pusey. The group around him became known as the Oxford Movement, and its activities sparked a spiritual renewal in the Anglican church. In reviving patristic studies, they came to an appreciation of Mary as *Theotokos* or God-Bearer, a theme that had been largely absent in the English church since the Reformation. In 1833 Keble composed a widely publicized hymn, "Ave Maria," which included the lines "Blessed Maid, lily of Eden's fragrant shade . . . whose name all but adoring love may claim"[29]—thereby distinguishing, as Catholics did, between the high praise due to Mary and the adoration due to God. Though Newman was uncomfortable with such sentimental piety, his historical studies slowly began to convince him that Mary played a central role in church tradition. Forced to struggle against his instinctive dislike of the emotionalism surrounding Marian devotions, he eventually came to understand that church teaching develops over time as it gains a fuller understanding of the tradition it inherits. This was the theory he advanced in his *Essay on the Development of Church Doctrine*.

In the texts of the early Fathers he found the thinking about Mary that we have revisited, particularly the Eve-Mary parallels of Justin Martyr, Irenaeus, and Tertullian. As proof of Mary's early importance to the church, Newman cited her image in the catacombs as an Orante, the representative praying figure with hands upraised, which he then related to Scripture. In his last sermon at Oriel College, on the Feast of the Purification in 1843, he chose as his text: "And Mary kept all these things and pondered them in her heart." Avoiding sentimental imagery, Newman seemed able to perceive the human Mary's reliance on observation and judgment, as well as her ability to live with ambivalence. She became for him the model of each person's need to reflect on the presence of God within, to face doubts and still be faithful, always trying to reconcile faith and experience without forcing them together. To Newman, Mary represented the necessary attitude to faith "not only . . . of the unlearned, but also of the Doctors of the Church, who have to investigate, and weigh, and define, as well as to profess the Gospel."[30] It is not surprising that he chose her as his patron saint when he received Confirmation as a Catholic in November 1845, a few weeks after he officially entered the church, or that he named the first house he and his fellow converts lived in Maryvale. Much later, asked to found a university in Dublin, the inspiration for his classic work on education, *The Idea of a University*, he chose Mary Seat of Wisdom as the model for the freedom of inquiry that should accompany the study of divine and natural reality.

He also began to integrate his thinking about doctrine with the attitude Christians should have toward Mary. Five years before the Immaculate Conception was proclaimed as dogma by Pius IX, Newman presented his own reasons for belief in the doctrine. In an 1849 sermon, "The Glories of Mary for the Sake of Her Son," he insisted that it was a misunderstanding to see the Immaculate Conception as attributing to Mary qualities found only in God.[31] Only God enters our inner being. But Mary is the *Theotokos*, the mother of Jesus, and therefore a model of humanity before the Fall. Just as Eve and Adam were created sinless, so, too, was Mary, who by her free consent would cooperate with God; she was a "daughter of Eve unfallen," yet still one of us. Newman treats Mary as a symbol of the church, as Ambrose and Augustine did, but he also explains that she modeled the church's ability to be patient, to let meaning emerge gradually:

> She raised herself aloft silently, and has grown into her place in the Church by a tranquil influence as a natural process. She was as some fair tree, stretching forth her fruitful branches and her fragrant leaves, and overshadowing the territory of the saints.[32]

She was always willing to waive her claims and wait when dispute arose about her until now, he went on prophetically: "in this very day, should God so will . . . she will be hailed as immaculate in her conception."

Newman's old companions from Oxford were more dismayed than he at what Pusey called "that vast system as to the blessed Virgin" set up by Rome. In 1865 Pusey expressed these doubts in a long letter to Keble published as the *Eirenicon*. In his book-length reply, *Letter to Pusey*, Newman revealed his mature thinking about Mary, compatible with Scripture and sense: "I will say plainly that I had rather believe (which is impossible) that there is no God at all, than that Mary is greater than God." He went on to describe his views of her role, based on the teaching of the Fathers. "I do not wish to say more than they suggest to me, and will not say less." Devotion has increased and changed over the centuries, he said, but added: "I do not allow that the doctrine concerning her has undergone a growth, for I believe that it has been in substance one and the same from the beginning."[33] He went on to trace what he saw as the developing meaning of that unbroken tradition, citing the Eve-Mary parallels, the extension to Mary of Scriptural images—particularly that of the Woman clothed with the sun in the Apocalypse—and finally the title *Theotokos*. He insisted that it had taken time for "these ideas of her sanctity and dignity" to penetrate "the mind of Christendom." The idea of her intercessory prayer followed and has persisted in history:

> She is the great exemplar of prayer in a generation which emphatically denies the power of prayer in toto, which determines that fatal laws govern the universe, that there cannot be any direct communication between earth and heaven, that God cannot visit his own earth, and that man cannot influence his own providence.[34]

Although he had written a friend during the deliberations of the Vatican Council to say "You are going too fast at Rome," Newman believed that time would sort out the meaning of infallibility in the church just as it had eventually defeated Arianism. He looked to the future for what he saw blocked in the present. Something of the patience and staying power he observed in Mary seems to have penetrated his own being. A sign that he was not mistaken came to him late in life when Leo XIII replaced Pius IX as pope and made the seventy-eight-year-old Newman a cardinal (1879). His views were gradually accepted by Catholic theologians, who ratified them in the Second Vatican Council in the 1960s, following his lead in seeing Mary as the human companion and model for all believers, best understood within an overall understanding of the church.

THE POETRY OF GERARD MANLEY HOPKINS (1844–1889) was an unavoidable stopping-place in my search for Mary. Hopkins shared Newman's view of Mary, though he came to it not by way of study of the Fathers, but through a passionate appreciation of nature and language. As a young man he kept journals that record in words and drawings his keen observations of wind, waves, birds, flowers, trees, and architecture. Like the Romantic poets, Hopkins sought transcendent meaning in nature, but his commitment to nature's preservation was intensely personal. Seeing an ash tree purposelessly slashed by an axe, he felt the wound himself, for he looked on every natural manifestation as the "good news" of God. To Hopkins, that news included "both lightning and love," "winter and warm." He suffered a long winter when his family was alienated by his conversion from Anglicanism to Catholicism; in an ardor of self-sacrifice when he entered the Jesuits, he burned his poetry.

Uninterested in theological distinctions, Hopkins responded

to the Christ he encountered in the world as well as in sacrament, liturgy, and meditation. This can be seen in the poetry he began to write again seven years after he joined the Jesuits, probably influenced both by the *Spiritual Exercises* of Ignatius and by the thinking of Duns Scotus, the fourteenth-century Oxford divine, who seemed to corroborate his theory of "inscape," the vital life that lay beneath the sensible surface of experience and word.

In 1876 Hopkins finished "The Wreck of the *Deutschland*," in which his mature poetic power first emerged. He wrote it to commemorate the deaths of five German Franciscan nuns aboard an ocean liner wrecked in a snowstorm off the coast of Kent. They had left Bismarck's Germany because the government's Kulturkampf against Catholics prevented them from working there; the nuns had hoped to teach and nurse in Missouri. Hopkins was deeply moved by newspaper reports of the cry one nun made before she died: "O Christ, Christ, come quickly." In his poem, this nun becomes another Mary, giving birth once again to Christ the Word as the ship goes down on the vigil of the feast of the Immaculate Conception.

> What was the feast followed the night
>   Thou hadst glory of this nun?—
> Feast of the one woman without stain.
> For so conceived, so to conceive thee is done;
>   But here was heart-throe, birth of a brain,
> Word, that heard and kept thee and uttered thee outright.[35]

Hopkins identified with the nun who tried to conceive Jesus in words on the deck of the sinking ship. But was it happiness or fear that moved her to that cry? To the poet, the nun's words revealed acceptance of the suffering and death necessary for the ultimate vision of God. Hopkins had always understood Mary's

attitude at the Annunciation as the model for such human response—one of free choice and commitment.

It is this possibility of incarnating Christ afresh, the traditional
implication of Mary's role as God-Bearer, that Hopkins celebrated in several of his lyrics about her. Among these is the well-
known "May Magnificat" in which the joyous natural emergence
of spring, "Flesh and fleece, fur and feather,/Grass and green-
world all together," is especially fitting for the month dedicated
to her. Marina Warner praises these lines as standing for "all that
is best and happiest in the cult of the Virgin," but goes on to say
that they represent the absorption of a fertility role by the Virgin,
a "late but successful attempt to draw the teeth of secular and
originally pagan rites by incorporating them into Catholic worship." She even suggests it was part of a Jesuit plot to "transform
the Queen of the May into the Virgin Mary."[36] But pagan absorption into the Marian tradition, though plentiful, had begun centuries earlier. The connection between Mary's giving flesh to
Jesus, growth in nature, and the celebration of the Eucharist was
already present in sixth-century chalices and in Ephrem's fourth-
century verses in which Mary said: "I clasp the wheat-sheaf of
life/that provides bread for the hungry."

Hopkins did not expect miracles or need apparitions but he
believed that the inevitable suffering of the soul must issue in a
word of response. At the same time, he could not employ the
standard, pietistic images or diction of European Catholic devotion; instead, in "The Blessed Virgin Mary compared to the Air
we Breathe," he draws on what critic Helen Vendler calls his
"characteristic personal intensities," which tended rather to be
psychological, physiological and visual.[37]

This delicate lyric makes use of common sense, scientific observations, and natural symbols from the world Hopkins saw as
primary revelation, to evoke Mary's presence: "Wild air, world-
mothering air,/Nestling me everywhere." He may have had
the Immaculate Conception in mind, for he addresses "Mary

Immaculate,/Merely a woman, yet/Whose presence, power is/Great as no goddess's." The poem shows how a believer might accept the dogma as part of the mystery of divine being present within the purity of natural things:[38]

> I say that we are wound
> With mercy round and round
> As if with air: the same
> Is Mary, more by name.

Hopkins summarizes the Incarnation in simple terms, pointing to its physical yet mysterious and continuing reality in the liturgical year, and in the life of nature that it inhabits:

> Of her flesh he took flesh:
> He does take fresh and fresh,
> Though much the mystery how,
> Not flesh but spirit now
> And makes, O marvellous!
> New Nazareths in us . . .

In one section he invites the reader to an outdoor experiment:

> . . . Nay do but stand
> Where you can lift your hand
> Skywards: rich, rich it laps
> Round the four fingergaps.
> Yet such a sapphire-shot,
> Charged, steepèd sky will not
> Stain light.

Mary does not block or stain the light of God but rather lets it through so we can see it. Employing a more modern idiom, Hopkins makes the same point Hildegard of Bingen did when comparing Mary to a gem. Honor to Mary does not lessen honor to God. Her function is rather to make God more visible to human nature by rendering him human, as medieval artists did by giving Mary's son her flesh and features:

> Through her we may see him
> Made sweeter, not made dim,
> And her hand leaves his light
> Sifted to suit our sight.

Hopkins is writing a poem, not making theological distinctions, but he is careful to credit God for whatever power of prayer Mary has:

> She, wild web, wondrous robe,
> Mantles the guilty globe,
> Since God has let dispense
> Her prayers his providence.

Drawing on the tradition as he found it, one in which Mary had long stood as a visible sign of the work of the Spirit, Hopkins reimagined Mary in a way that showed her at home in a unified, scientifically conceived universe.

STARTING FROM DIFFERENT ASSUMPTIONS, THE BROADLY Protestant culture of England and the United States in the nineteenth century tended to idealize women while still denying them equality or a public voice. In part because Mary seemed so much like the Victorian ideal, especially because of her maternity, she began to receive a curiously positive reception among some distinguished Protestant writers. Hawthorne's attitude is instructive. When Hester Prynne stands on the scaffold before a Puritan assembly in *The Scarlet Letter*, the narrator says: "had there been a Papist among the crowd of Puritans, he might have seen in this beautiful woman, so picturesque in her attire and mien, and with the infant at her bosom, an object to remind him of the image of Divine maternity."

Part of this cultural idealization of maternity, however, was a tendency to polarize women into good or bad, describing repentant prostitutes as "Magdalens" and even naming charitable houses designed to care for them after the saint. There were some forty thousand prostitutes and four thousand brothels in London at mid-century, the peak of this idealization of the maternal, stay-at-home woman. Trying to help them, rescue workers were encouraged by the example of "one sacred Mary sitting at the foot of the Divine, with the Magdalen's soiled hand in hers, and the publicans and sinners bidden to her pure companionship."[39]

A number of educated Victorian women, however, could not accept either the idealized maternal model of woman or the good-bad dichotomy thrust upon them. The poet Christina Rossetti, a devout Anglican, turned to Mary instead as a model of her own celibate state. Rossetti found the single life much more compatible with spiritual growth than marriage because "the wife must approach God indirectly through her husband." At the same time she exhibited a typical Anglican attitude in criticizing overemphasis on Mary as "the cardinal error of Roman Catholicism. . . . Lily we might call her, but Christ alone is right."[40]

Her acceptance of the traditional interpretation of Genesis— with Eve as the fallen temptress—made Rossetti believe in the greater weakness of women and accept their lower place in society. But she was an ambitious poet and a deeply religious person who turned to a trinity of women—Eve, Mary, and Mary Magdalene—to strengthen her own identity and devotion. Her greatest sympathy went to Mary Magdalene as the model of a repentant sinner, though she never considered Magdalene a sexual sinner, as tradition mistakenly had done. She thought of her instead as one who struggled to place love above all other concerns. It was Magdalene—transformed by the love of Christ—whom she saw as the beloved in the Song of Songs.

Rossetti was also drawn to Eve, whom she found a more maternal figure than Mary. In her devotional commentary on the Apocalypse, she turned to all three women as positive possibilities of the feminine. The sign of the woman clothed with the sun assured her that all Eve's daughters "will be made equal with men and angels . . . from the lowest place she has gone up higher."[41]

Charlotte Brontë was even less constricted by orthodox categories in her revisioning of Eve. Breaking with traditional definitions, the bold heroine of her novel *Shirley* describes Eve as a living, liberating symbol of the divine in feminine form. Refusing one day to go to church, where she knows all too well what she will hear, Shirley stays outside with Nature, which is "praying for a fair night for mariners at sea; for lambs on moors, and unfledged birds in woods. . . . she is like what Eve was when she and Adam stood alone on earth."[42]

Shirley's friend observes that this is certainly not what Milton's Eve was like. No, replies Shirley, challenging the literary establishment as well as the church; Milton could describe Satan, sin, and angels, but not the first woman. All he could see was his cook! Eve was heaven-born: "I will stay out here with my mother Eve, in these days called Nature. I love her—undying, mighty being. Heaven may have faded from her brow when she fell in paradise; but all that is glorious on earth shines there still."

A growing number of educated women in nineteenth-century England were reassessing supposedly Christian values that supported a social system that idealized motherhood and at the same time victimized women. They were aware of the distortions in social arrangements and the limitations on their own development caused by a patriarchal understanding of God. In America, meanwhile, Elizabeth Cady Stanton, initiator of *The Woman's Bible*, would raise a central question in her 1885 essay "Has Christianity Benefitted Women?" She suggested that the Catholic church had at least "in its holy sisterhoods" and its "worship of the Virgin Mary, mother of Jesus . . . preserved some recognition of the feminine element in its religion; but from Protestantism it is wholly eliminated."[43]

It was in this context that a number of Anglo-American women writers began to explore Marian symbols more closely. They were not interested in converting to Catholicism like Newman and Hopkins, but they envisioned a Marian presence as a necessary feminine addition to public and sacred space, one that would improve women's sense of self, confirm the nobility of women and motherhood, and mediate the divine compassion they felt was missing in social relationships.

In addition, educated nineteenth-century Protestants began to take art seriously. A heavy proportion of the art they encountered from previous centuries was drenched in Catholic and Marian imagery. In the 1850s Anna Jameson awakened the interest of many English and American women to Marian symbolism through her popular guidebooks to continental art. She found the contemplative virtues of Catholic art a nurturing antidote to the brutal industrial world. Though Ruskin believed her insufficiently schooled in painterly technique to be considered a serious critic, Jameson supported herself and her family with stories and reproductions of the art she encountered on her European travels, first as a governess, later as a writer visiting churches, chapels, and museums. It was the content of this art that attracted Jameson and her readers, especially the symbolic meaning of angels and saints, and the legends that surrounded the figure of Mary.

Jameson's *Legends of the Madonna* (1852) focused on Mary's multiple roles, including her absorption of the powers of earlier goddesses.[44] Jameson did a good job retelling the ancient stories that had grown up around Mary's life, from the charming grain miracle and the tale of the Holy Family meeting the two thieves on the Flight into Egypt, to variants on the purported eyewitness accounts of Mary's death. She showed how important such stories were to the history of Marian art through detailed descriptions of actual paintings and statues. Jameson's taste reflected that of the period in its focus on ancient and Renaissance art and its neglect of the great medieval works. She did not like the "lifeless" Byzantine and medieval madonnas, despite their "nobility," because of their "static" quality, and she found the old Greek icons "dark" and "ugly." To be fair, the icons Jameson saw probably were dark. It is only in our time that centuries of paint and dirt have been removed from many of the earliest and most beautiful icons.

Jameson's interest in Mary was not primarily aesthetic, however; it was Mary's nobility as a woman that interested her. Jameson found in the Gospel of Luke a true portrait of "the most perfect moral type of the intellectual, tender, simple and heroic woman that was ever placed before us for our edification and example" (xl). This standard of moral beauty guided her as she looked at hundreds of madonnas, which she organized under "devotional" and "historical" poses, describing their appearance and location in detail. Thus, she contrasted Raphael, who created his many Virgins from an ideal in his mind, with Andrea del Sarto, who used to "feature his handsome but vulgar wife in every Madonna he painted" (xxxii). Jameson frankly admitted that she had seen her ideal woman only once in all her travels, in Raphael's Sistine Madonna in Dresden (Plate 23), which was "a revelation":

> There she stands—the transfigured woman, at once completely human and completely divine, an abstraction of power, purity, and love, poised on the empurpled air, and requiring no other support; looking out, with her melancholy, loving mouth, her slightly dilated, sibylline eyes, quite through the universe, to the end and consummation of all things; sad, as if she beheld afar off the visionary sword that was to reach her heart through HIM, now resting as enthroned on that heart; yet already exalted through the homage of the redeemed generations who were to salute her as Blessed [xlii].

Though Jameson was a confirmed believer in Protestantism and progress, she wrote that "Religion, which now speaks to us through words, then [in earlier, Catholic eras] spoke to people through visible forms universally accepted." She tried to give her audience the key to those images, describing the poses of Queen of Heaven, Mother of Mercy, Mother of Tenderness, Mother of Sorrows, finding in Mary the necessary bridge to a deeper understanding of women's greatness.

In her day, Jameson was considered a wild feminist; in fact, she protested only the double moral standards of the time. Marriage was "the holiest of all human institutions," but she felt that its burdens lay unfairly on one sex. For her as for many Victorians, domestic life was the "sacred province" of women. She considered that "Mary employed in needlework, while her cradled Infant slumbers at her side, is a beautiful subject" for a work of art. She did not object to the exclusion of women from public life because she believed that motherhood and its duties fully occupied them. Yet she was convinced that change in society must come, and that it might be furthered by recovering a feminine ideal that Catholicism had preserved. In Mary, Jameson saw women's heroism and tenderness, which the new industrial world did not properly acknowledge.

> In the perpetual iteration of that beautiful image of THE WOMAN highly blessed—there, where others saw only pictures or statues, I have seen this great hope standing like a spirit beside the visible form: in the fervent worship once universally given to that gracious presence, I have beheld an acknowledgement of a higher as well as a gentler power than that of the strong hand and the might that makes the right [xix].

In the 1860s Jameson's enthusiasm found a widening circle of sympathy. *The London Review* declared that her work had awakened artistic interest in Mary in "the most Protestant of English minds." Margaret Oliphant wrote a novel, *Madonna Mary* (1867), in which Mary was presented with renewed respect. Frances Power Cobbe, an acclaimed writer and social reformer, was struck by the power of the Madonna during her travels in

Italy (1864). It would be a mistake, she said, to think this devotion is something controlled by priests or limited to the self-interest or infantilism of worshipers. What Catholics are drawn to in their madonna is "Goodness, mildness, pity—in a word, motherly tenderness. She is the representative of all the feminine virtues and perfections." Protestants should ask themselves whether, "in abjuring Mariolatry, they have not also abjured something with which their creed can ill dispense." The Catholic church has discovered "that Love, motherly tenderness and pity, is a divine and holy thing, worthy of adoration. . . . The heart of humanity longs to rest itself on the compassion of its Creator. Catholics reveal this truth in the myth of the Virgin's Coronation."[45]

Across the Atlantic, the American reformer and women's advocate Margaret Fuller struck a similar note. In an essay on Christmas, she voiced her regret that works of art and legends concerning Mary had not been more reverenced in Protestantism: "In casting aside the shell, have we retained the kernel?" She saw devotion to Mary as potentially beneficial to women's social position, since "Man looks upon Woman, in this relation, always as he should. . . . Frivolity, base appetite, contempt are exorcised, and Man and Woman appear again in unprofaned connection as brother and sister, children and servants of one Divine love, and pilgrims to a common aim."[46]

Harriet Beecher Stowe, the wife and daughter of Calvinist ministers, also longed for visual art that affirmed the power and goodness of woman. Inspired by the work of Anna Jameson, she used the money earned from her book *Uncle Tom's Cabin* to take a long and adventurous trip to Europe, partly as a socially concerned Christian and partly as an "art-pilgrim." She did not see much of the earlier—and most authentic—Marian art, however, and dismissed most of what she did see: "There is more pathos and beauty in those few words of the Scripture, 'Now there stood by the cross of Jesus his mother,' than in all these galleries put together."[47]

There was one portrait of Mary, however, that she loved—the same Sistine Madonna that Jameson preferred. Her viewing of it was dramatic. At first she was disappointed by its faded color. Then she expressed annoyance at others in the picture; she found Pope Sixtus II—after whom the painting was named—"a very homely old man" and St. Barbara "like a theatrical actress." But the standing figure of the Madonna and child met her standard of spiritual beauty. She appreciated "its historic accuracy in representing the dark-eyed Jewish maiden" and loved "the mysterious resemblance and sympathy between the face of the mother and the divine child." Identifying deeply with the subject of the painting, Stowe observed "a conflict of emotion in that mother's face, and shadowed mysteriously in the child's," of which she queried,

> Was it fear? was it sorrow? . . . was it a presage of the hour when a sword should pierce through her own soul? Yet, with this, was there not a solemn triumph in the thought that she alone, of all women, had been called to that baptism of anguish?"[48]

Like Jameson, Stowe was emotionally drawn to Raphael's Madonna because it seemed to capture the noble self-sacrifice essential to the ideal woman. "This picture . . . has formed a deeper part of my inner consciousness than any I have yet seen," she reported, for it also depicts the "idea of sorrow in heaven—sorrow, for the lost, in the heart of God himself—which forms the most sacred mystery of Christianity."[49]

Most European madonnas, Stowe believed, did not embody this ideal, but seemed trite, enervated through mechanical imitation. After calling for a new American Protestant art, closer to nature, she tried to create a New England madonna in her novel *The Minister's Wooing*. Her heroine, Mary Scudder, grows

through marital suffering and motherhood into an intercessor
for others. Like Stowe herself, who scandalized her Hartford
neighbors by hanging an image of the Madonna on her bedroom
wall, Mary Scudder often gazed at a madonna by Leonardo da
Vinci as "a constant vague inspiration." Finally, the heroine
"passed into that appointed shrine to woman, more holy than
cloister, more saintly and pure than church or altar—a Christian
home. Priestess, wife, and mother, there she ministers daily in
holy works of household peace."[50] The book's message might almost be seen as an American Protestant version of Thérèse's
"little way."

IF HIGH MARIAN ART CONFIRMED THE NOBILITY OF WOMEN'S
experience to the educated Harriet Beecher Stowe, an old devotional statue of questionable artistic value from an Italian village
near Naples served a similar purpose in restoring confidence to
the immigrant Italians of New York's East Harlem a few decades
later. American Catholicism was an immigrant phenomenon; its
religious practices imitated those popular in Europe—the rosary,
and devotion to the Immaculate Conception and the Sacred
Hearts of Jesus and Mary. When southern Italians began to arrive
in America in the 1880s, the Irish-American leaders of the arch-
diocese of New York were shocked at what they considered
the superstitious and pagan ways of this new community, particularly their yearly festival in honor of Our Lady of Mount
Carmel. Sociologist Robert Orsi explains why: "The fusion of
sacred and profane, of the serious and the apparently trivial,
troubled observers of the *festa*, who were offended by the noise
and food and emotion in the presence of the sacred."[51] Carrying
the statue of the Madonna del Carmine, who had crossed the
ocean like her people from her village home in Polla, the new immigrants would walk barefoot on the hot July streets to honor the
vows they had made to her and would pin dollars to her robe in

thanksgiving for her favors. Even on the mean streets of this new urban world she was ready to bless them, reminding them of home and of who they were. To upwardly mobile, middle-class Irish-Americans, now at home in a Yankee land, however, she was an embarrassment.

The *festa* was a celebration of popular religion, expressing the values of a hard-pressed community that did not think religion consisted as much in going to church as in going to baptisms, weddings, funerals, and celebrations. As in the processions honoring the Black Virgin in the Middle Ages, priests and parishioners had somewhat different experiences of the festival, which was planned and run by the people. To the priests of the Church of Our Lady of Mount Carmel, the eating, dancing, and merrymaking were incidental. To the people, these activities were central to the festival's religious meaning. Eating was the sacrament of the home, and home and family were at the core of the immigrants' religious commitment.

By insisting on a personal relationship with a compassionate heavenly figure who could share their most intimate sorrows and hopes, the Italians of East Harlem were implicitly acknowledging the inadequacy of an all-male God. Women in particular seemed to doubt that such a God could understand their needs and hopes, and so they turned to another figure whose life was one of suffering for her child—a story that resonated deeply with the economy of Italian-American family life. The popular Mariology in Italian Harlem was quite different from official versions, but consistent with a long European tradition: the women in the community believed that Mary had suffered the pains of childbirth, that she had menstruated, and that she worried constantly about her child. They felt that she could understand and help them because she had shared their most private experiences; she was as powerful—and as powerless—as they were. Similar attitudes pervaded Italian-American life in most communities. A friend told me about her Italian-born mother, who had endured the death of her son. "She would sit in her armchair and nod her head over and over, saying, '*Madonna capisce, Madonna capisce*'— only the Madonna understands. It kept her going."

At the same time that Marian devotion offered Italian immigrant women this consolation, it also reaffirmed those aspects of the culture that oppressed them. It dignified women, but insisted on constricting their role; their individuality had to be sacrificed to the family. Orsi concedes that "Women found the Madonna's azure cloak, so ceremoniously draped over their shoulders, a heavy one." Through their prayers to Mary, they tried to transform their suffering into sacrifice and so redeem it. The experience and taste of these immigrant women were very different from those of Harriet Beecher Stowe—she could never have called Mary "Mamma" as they did—but was their feeling for the Madonna del Carmine really so different from hers for the suffering Madonna painted by Raphael? Perhaps for both, their lives "became the way of faith, their suffering, the nexus with divine suffering, and through that, the way to the hope of redemption."[52]

IN RETROSPECT, WHAT IS MOST EXTRAORDINARY ABOUT THE role of Mary in the nineteenth century is that she again succeeded in crossing lines of faith, class, and society. Although her extraordinary apparitions at Lourdes and elsewhere, along with the emphasis on the Immaculate Conception, at first seemed to confirm her as an exclusively Catholic symbol, her image also appealed powerfully to a wide range of Victorian women who saw in her not merely the ideal woman but hints of the feminine divine. Much of this identification of different viewers and agendas with Mary was possible because the age itself venerated motherhood. It was not Mary's motherhood, however, but her place as first among seekers in a developing faith community that Newman found significant, while Hopkins saw her as a symbol reconciling all nature with the divine.

These nineteenth-century responses also bore the seeds of historical demands whose reverberations are far from complete. Ideas of progress and equality that had been the source of nationalistic wars and labor agitation now began to suggest the need for equality between men and women. Nowhere was that connection more forcibly made than in Sojourner Truth's outburst from the floor at the Women's Rights Convention in 1851: "That little man in black there, he says women can't have as much rights as men 'cause Christ wasn't a woman. Where did your Christ come from? . . . From God and a woman! Man had nothing to do with Him."[53] This striking and positive connection of the role of Mary with the condition of women prepared the way for our own century's critique of the paternalistic exploitation of her image. Again one has the feeling that the mother of Jesus is already at the next turn of the road, waiting patiently for us to catch up.

CHAPTER EIGHT

THE LIBERATION
OF MARY

"The best image of Mary I ever saw was on a friend's refrigerator. Mary was sitting at the kitchen table laughing, while St. Joseph was standing beside her, burping the baby."

—MAVIS ALEXANDER

I now find Mary a taproot that reaches to the center of the earth and a root system that stretches around the globe.

—CHINA GALLAND, *Longing for Darkness*[1]

IT'S BEEN A LONG JOURNEY SINCE WE LEFT THE BARE BUT striking outline of Mary's story in the Gospels. We've revisited many interpretations of her meaning and looked at a variety of portraits that the human imagination has made of her in the intervening years. But where and how is she present today? Is her story only a beautiful but possibly irrelevant memory of the past, or is she still someone whom contemporary women and men can invoke with confidence?

What is startling, in a supposedly post-Christian time, is the persistence of old devotions to Mary. On a weekday afternoon in July 1994, when I visited the chapel in Paris where Catherine Labouré saw Mary in 1830, the crowd was so big I could scarcely squeeze inside. The nuns of Catherine's order were doing a brisk business in miraculous medals outside on the pavement of the rue du Bac. Similarly, men and women are visiting Lourdes in greater numbers than ever to pray for healing, hope, and renewal, and Our Lady of Guadalupe has become a vital force in North as well as South America. Perhaps the worldwide sense of insecurity has encouraged a renewal of the nineteenth-century Catholic impulse to turn to Mary. The papacy once again has championed Marian devotion. Pope John Paul II even credited his survival from an assassin's bullet to the protection of Our Lady of Fatima and has visited a number of apparition sites.

At Medjugorje in Bosnia pilgrims flock to a new apparition site much like Fatima, where since 1981 Mary has been delivering to young seers her perennial request for men and women to repent,

271

pray, and lead good lives. As before, such pleas seem more real to those who hear them at her shrines than back home in church. Father Michel de Roton, rector of the sanctuary at Lourdes, makes the point shrewdly: "People find religious life too monotonous and want something more intense, more festive, more emotional. Perhaps the form our religion has taken today does not respond to their needs." Those who make pilgrimages to places identified with Mary are touched emotionally; their behavior seems to change. A young woman I know well who went to Medjugorje told me that it was the extraordinary kindness of the pilgrims to one another, the help and attention given to the ill and the lame, that warmed her faith there. She and her husband responded by taking a refugee family from the area into their home. Another woman told me she was strengthened spiritually by the palpable force of prayers in every language she heard at Medjugorje. Other testimonies, such as that of a woman who wrote that her silver rosary was changed to gold at the apparition site, seem hard to credit. One priest friend who has a strong devotion to Mary himself told me he was put off by well-to-do Catholics who go on such pilgrimages but don't relate Mary's message to the pressing human needs in their own towns. However mixed the motives, large numbers of people, by no means only Catholics, still look to Mary as their most credible intercessor with God. When I visited the medieval shrine at Le Puy in 1994, the last petition in the visitor's book before the small statue of the Throne of Wisdom read, "Mary, please preserve peace in the Middle East."

After revisiting older interpretations and images of Mary as they developed in different contexts, I believe that many of them are in use for reasons that are still valid. But as Newman observed, Marian thinking must be repeatedly translated into contemporary forms if it is to continue to be meaningful. What is not so evident in the public media is the serious reconsideration of Mary that is going on among many men and women, both specialists and thoughtful ordinary believers, who are making such translations today. Extensive study of the place of Mary in the Bible, church tradition, and personal spirituality is being carried out across and outside of religious lines, often with increased sympathy for the beliefs and practices of popular religion. The process is leading to the construction of a more adequate symbol of Mary, one that is true to the Bible and church tradition, that fosters reverence rather than contempt for Jews, and that does not praise Mary by denigrating other women. In this chapter I present a sampling of significant elements of this new portrait. It is instructive to observe how frequently experiential and scholarly attention focuses on the same theme: Mary as a representative human being, a model of human development at its best.

WOMEN IN PARTICULAR HAVE BEEN LOOKING MORE CLOSELY at their own experience and discovering that the mother of Jesus can be a force to empower them today. Even the idea of Mary as simple housewife, so uncongenial to me as a young mother, still provides strength to some American women: being a housewife is "emotionally draining work and physically tiring," admitted one woman. "It's hard to remember that it's service, physical, very direct service to human beings. Thinking of Mary and how she would have been doing these exact same things helps very much."[2] When I asked an old friend from the West Indies what was the best image of Mary she had seen, Mavis told me of a picture on a friend's refrigerator of Mary sitting at the kitchen table laughing while Joseph stood beside her, burping the baby. Mavis comes from a very large family in a culture where such a reversal of roles would have been unthinkable until quite recently.

Something is clearly going on in the interchange between Mary and women today that works in two directions: empowering women and at the same time changing their idea of her. Mary Gordon claims that it is the "impulse to reexamine and to understand in a deeper way the history of women, female genius, female work, often anonymous, hidden, uncredited, to look for the values that are not simply male values dressed for success, that is leading women back to Mary."[3]

Mary's own power was suggested by the verse from the second-century Odes of Solomon that spoke of her bringing forth her child "like a strong man with desire." As we have seen, however, for most women at that time, "being male" meant undervaluing their bodies and their experience, bowing to social and ecclesial control of their life choices, and losing their public voices. As women overcome such social restrictions, they are better able to rediscover Mary's strength and gain a deeper sense of human solidarity with her.

The Marian teaching that had a negative effect on women's development was part of a worldwide pattern in which male experience and power were accepted as human norms. Such assumptions, of course, are by no means Christian, nor are they inherent in traditional Marian liturgy, art, and devotion. As God-Bearer, Mother of Mercy, and Queen of Heaven, Mary has been the carrier of the feminine divine in Western culture. As we have seen, nineteenth-century women like Anna Jameson and Margaret Fuller came to realize that her absence from Protestant life tended to limit women's development, just as a distorted Marian piety restricted Catholic psychological and spiritual maturity. Carolyn, an Episcopal priest, summed up the sad results in a letter to me, observing that Mary has been "very much a victim of patriarchy, raped by the church's preoccupation with the female organs, but also abandoned by much—even most—Protestant Christianity."

Carolyn is right: the early Fathers were obsessed with the gynecological details of the Virgin Birth, believing they were crucial in order to establish orthodox teaching regarding Christ's humanity. Most Christians, however, showed a surer sense of faith's priorities, singing their praise of Mary as God-Bearer. From the liturgical hymns of Ephrem in the fourth century, which reflect even earlier devotion in Eastern Christianity, to the antiphons and art of the medieval West, Mary was seen as rooted in created reality, a sign of human access to the Creator.

I experienced the continuing power of such Marian imagery when I went to a concert with Nancy, a Presbyterian minister who is a spiritual counselor at a Manhattan West Side church. That night, the Anonymous 4, the a cappella women's group that has helped send medieval liturgical music to the top of the classical charts, sang antiphons that accompanied Mary's feasts. After the early morning hymn for the feast of the Assumption ("Like the glow of dawn she rises to heaven's heights; like the sun Mary shines, like the loveliest moon")[4] came the processional hymn, "*O genitrix aeterni*," with all its cosmological implications:

> O bearer of the eternal word, virgin Mary,
> what voice, what human tongue can praise you well enough?
>
> You new star of the sea, window to the lofty heavens,
> ladder from earth to heaven, from the lowest to the highest.
>
> You conceived eternity, you gave birth to your parent;
> the maker came from what he made, the creator from the
> creature.[5]

Stunned, Nancy turned to me and asked, "Why have I never heard this before? It's so healing!" She told me it was the first time she had ever felt the feminine power of God flow over her like a wave, reaching to the core of her belief. This was the symbol that was missing, she said, in the work she was doing to reconcile religion and ecology.

The power that Nancy and I experienced at the concert helps explain the attitude of Kathleen Norris, poet and author of *Dakota: A Spiritual Geography*. As a Methodist child, Norris envied her Catholic friends their Mary—the rosary, the images and statues in their rooms. As an adult, she told me she is discovering Mary for herself, slowly and deeply. "I love the wise, patient strength of the Black Madonna. . . . More and more, Mary has become an image of *home* for me. She is the 'house of God,' where they always have to take you in."

A longer personal testimony to women's need for such a feminine symbol has been given by another writer, Sue Monk Kidd. Kidd recounts a slow recovery from Mary's absence in her Baptist childhood.[6] Her first hint of the need for Mary was an unusual experience when she was twelve, staying overnight at the home of a Catholic friend. In the guest room she saw a porcelain statue of Mary standing on a crescent moon. The figure called forth "an inexplicable rush of feeling," which today Kidd attributes to the pull of the Eternal Feminine. In her religious upbringing, she says, it was easy to forget that Jesus had a mother. She instinctively knelt down and whispered the only words that seemed adequate: "Hail Mary, full of grace, the Lord is with thee."

Significantly, Kidd makes a connection between the power of Mary and the real-life powerlessness of women:

> I was taught that in both church and home men held authority over women. My task was to submit. I tried, both as a good daughter of the church and later as a young wife. At times I felt like a coat rack upon which the church hung its projections of what a good Christian woman should be. I bent and folded my soul, trying to adapt to the patriarchy, but inside I kept asking, who am I that I cannot choose and initiate without masculine permission?

She mentions a sketch she once saw of a madonna with no hands. A woman who can't "hand-le" anything is not whole; Kidd insists that this had been the Baptist Mary of her early education.

Later she came to understand the ancient definition of the Virgin as "one unto herself," balanced and contained, whole. "If we had allowed Mary to be a symbol pointing to God, our Mother, if we had let her be a metaphor for Sophia-Wisdom, a feminine personification of the Holy Spirit, perhaps we might have been less inclined to create a purely masculine God."

Kidd recalls a dream she had in her early thirties that captures the significance of her recovery through Mary. Riding in a speeding train past some shacks in the South, she sees through the window a weeping black woman on a run-down porch. She calls out to the other passengers to look, but they turn away. The deep loneliness in the eyes of the tearful woman suddenly merges with Kidd's own religious quest: "This black woman in the quarantined slum is Mary, the mother of Jesus. I beat on the train window and call to her, 'I will come back for you.' " When Kidd awoke, she knew she had found Mary in her own soul. She began to say the rosary, the beads becoming way stations of return back to the unknown house. As she herself became whole, she saw Mary differently, as a "complete feminine image . . . not just as pure, heavenly Virgin, but as the powerful, dark earth mother and Black Madonna," an image that "affirmed the joyous song God sings through my body and creation."

This Protestant woman's journey—one that caused her to deepen her spirituality but not to change her church affiliation—is very similar to those of Catholic women who received a one-sided picture of Mary as a negative model of passivity and selflessness. When I asked Vivian, a magazine editor, what Mary meant in her life, she replied with unexpected tartness that Mary meant nothing to her. I was afraid I had rubbed a sore spot. She called me the next day to apologize: "I was wrong," she said, "Mary had everything to do with me. That ideal woman promoted in convent school didn't allow us to grow up. The Annunciation was interpreted to mean, 'Don't question things, just accept them.' It took me years of therapy, but now when I read the Bible, I see that Mary was questioning and thinking all the time."

Vivian, too, had a dream, one that marked the beginning of her painful awakening. She was in Maryland. Suddenly she saw a beautiful field of blackberries, her favorite fruit, and she ran inside to get a basket to gather some. But one after another, her children came and asked her for containers, and soon there were none left in which she could put her own berries. When she woke up, she thought, "Right! I was in Mary's land—living the totally selfless life. And it felt *all wrong.*"

Strength is the key attribute that Adele, an artist and woman religious in her sixties, believes Mary must have possessed: "She didn't know what was coming; her whole life was one of mystery." It was the women's movement, not the church, that helped Adele see Mary more accurately: "Most of the earlier devotional stuff emphasized sheer weakness," she says: "It's too easy to fall into that saccharine trap."

Both Vivian and Adele are stating a strange paradox. In the simplest terms, the Mary we meet in Scripture had the spiritual courage to say yes without any kind of social support. That "yes" meant accepting a mysterious new life, enduring great suffering and humiliation, and taking a public role as witness for a cause the authorities considered unlawful. Yet Mary has been turned into a model of passive obedience and artificial goodness that has often served to keep women from exercising their freedom and developing their strength. That is why so many Catholic women today remain inoculated against her appeal, fearing that Mary's "virtues" are dangerous for their human growth.

Nevertheless, I keep encountering other Catholic women who have managed to liberate Mary from the false associations with which she has been surrounded. Denise, a mother of teenage boys who works as a patient advocate in a large city hospital, sums up their attitude:

For a long time I was angry that Mary was presented as almost featureless, ghostlike, invisible, asexual, obedient—everything I was trying not to be. Now I just ignore what I can't connect with, her perennial youth and perfection, her role as passive victim, empty vessel. To me she is open, adventurous, willing to risk and tolerate uncertainty, able to weather great suffering graciously. I love the idea of her rushing to tell Elizabeth the good news. We should look to Mary as a symbol of what is best in our female beings, our human selves; we are all life-bearers.

Denise's words are reaffirmed in those of Sr. Margaret Dorgan, a Carmelite nun, who included this address to Mary in her response to my questionnaire:

I ponder you "blessed among women," and I, a woman, experience your blessedness reaching me—but not like a ray of light from a far-off star descending on worthless earth. Your warmth penetrates me because you had a woman's heart and could sing when beauty held you, or weep at rejection.

You have never been a celestial empress to me or a Renaissance madonna, but a country woman brushing back hair from a perspiring forehead. As I grow older, you become more sister than mother. I sit beside you, a childless widow, and remember with you loved ones who have crossed over the limits of time and are now invisible presences beckoning to everlasting reunion. When I ponder with you my own dying, you lead me into the deep inward silence where your Son speaks words of eternal life and I sing your song of joy in God, my savior.

I also remember how a Hispanic-American woman connected her revisioning of Mary with a woman's sense of self-understanding and self-reliance. At a hearing called by the American Catholic bishops in 1976, she explained why she was passing around a statue of a pregnant Mary that she had made in ceramics class:

I have always wanted to see a statue like this because I can identify with a Blessed Mother more than a Blessed Virgin because I am a married woman. This is the Blessed Mother pregnant, expecting the Baby Jesus. . . . I had a poor image of myself as a mother and as being married because so much emphasis was put just on the Blessed Virgin, something so far out of my reach I could never be like her.

I could not identify with celibate clergy or nuns, either. It was hard for me to live a Christian life when I could find no examples like me. But how can there be a universal church if the root of the tree that is to give fruit is not a priority within the church?

Younger Latina women seem more self-confident. Carmen Badillo, a divorced mother of five who works as a parish consultant in the diocese of San Antonio, calls Mary a real influence on her life. "She's a super lady. All that she had to deal with—the rejection she exposed herself to, I mean she was gutsy." Carmen sees Mary's appearance at Guadalupe as her way of sending a message to the church that it didn't understand. "Build my temple" didn't mean "Build a basilica," but "Be concerned about these people that you're doing these things to."[7] Bernice Cortez adds further insight into how many Latina women see Guadalupe as a woman challenging the system:

She appears to an Indian who is ignorant and poor and says, "I want a temple in this place," and she already knew what the bishop was going to say, so she says, "but I want you to insist." She knew where the power was, and she was role-playing with him about how it was going to go.[8]

Some Asian Christian women, too, have been recovering a Mary who strengthens them. Korean theologian Chung Hyun Kyung has made a composite analysis of recent statements about Mary by her Protestant and Catholic women colleagues.[9] Interestingly, these theologians echo the less formal criticisms of ordinary believers we have just encountered. On the one hand,

Protestantism's repudiation of Mariology is seen as "avoidance of responsibility to address women's place in realistic terms"; the exaltation of Mary in Catholic tradition, on the other hand, has too often made her an inhuman exception, teaching "fear and degradation of birthing and female sexuality." Some connect the way Mary was turned into a complete "yes-woman" with the conditioning of Asian women to blame themselves for the violence used against them. In a world of widespread abuse of women, these critics can no longer look on Mary primarily in biological terms; they stress the relationships she chose that drew her out of her private safety. "I can feel her fear," an Indian woman theologian admits, but Mary refuses to be victimized. "Deeply rooted in the heritage and wisdom of the strong women of Israel," she takes a risky road. Kyung says that Mary strengthens women to tell the truth; her unbreakable spirit is their model. Mary formed her son; she was his model of compassionate justice when he placed humanity above the law, healing the blind and the sick, eating with public sinners.

VIRGIN AND MOTHER

Against this background, we can appreciate the significance of the Asian Christian women's insistence that "virgin" is a symbol of Mary's autonomy, not of her sexual celibacy. Mary's meaning is distorted, says Kyung, when her life is summarized in terms of her sexual relationships; what needs to be emphasized is how she matured to wholeness, opening more and more to others. Kyung does not repudiate traditional doctrine, but argues that its effect in real life has tended to make women resigned victims with few options.[10] The issue connects with deeply felt attitudes of women in general, who were traditionally offered only two extremes—to be "pure" women or whores; no one seemed to question men's restrictions on the former or their exploitation of the latter. A centrist Catholic theologian like Elizabeth Johnson expresses what many women feel: "The image of her [Mary's] virginity has functioned to impede the integration of women's sexuality into the goal of wholeness."[11]

More and more, believing women have been coming to their own conclusions about the meaning of Mary's virginity as a necessary part of their rediscovery of her. Many are undisturbed by the possibility of irregularities in the conception of Jesus. For some, these "irregularities" bring her down to earth. Jane Schaberg's suggestion that Mary might have been raped, while understandably shocking to many, has helped abused women see the possibility of a new, affirming relationship with the mother of Jesus. The Reverend Johnny Ray Youngblood, pastor of a largely African-American parish in Brooklyn, New York, doesn't preach about the Virgin Birth but focuses on Mary as a single mother, helping both men and women in his congregation to develop an immediate relationship with her. One older Catholic woman I know, a pillar of her parish and a member of a key committee in her diocese, doesn't blink at the thought that Mary may have had an illegitimate child. "I see her as courageous," she says, "obedient to God, a woman willing to accept social misunderstanding and raise her child." The Episcopal woman priest I quoted earlier confided: "I regard the physical details of much churchly discussion about Mary—the preservation of her hymen, etc.—as perverse and false. But I have no problem with the idea that she might have been a rape victim; she was certainly not asexual."

Modern women, whether believers or agnostics, completely reject the sharp rebuke of Tertullian: "The curse pronounced on your sex weighs still on the world. Guilty, you must bear its hardships." They see sex and their bodies as part of a good creation. This widespread revalorization of matter and the flesh, rooted in human experience and scientific understanding, helps to make all people participants in the ongoing struggle toward wholeness and harmony. It also corrects the still-prevalent assumption that the holy is completely separate from everything else, existing in isolation, perhaps in church. A key part of the message conveyed by Mary's "yes" is that the physical and the material are both to be incorporated in more loving relationships.

The many different women who have been reconsidering these questions in connection with Mary seem to echo one another in their understanding of her virginity as autonomy. It's as if women have "taken back" physical facts that were used in the past to diminish them and have turned these facts on their heads. Instead of allowing male authority to assign significance to their experience, they assign meaning to it themselves. We should remember that in the Mediterranean world from which Mary and the church arose, virginity symbolized the independence and self-direction of the great goddesses, not their abstinence from sex. It was their *freedom* that made them virgins: no one owned them. In Scripture, Mary is never portrayed as under the control of any man: "The image of Mary as a virgin," Elizabeth Johnson reminds us, "has significance as the image of a woman from whose personal center power wells up, a woman who symbolizes the independence of the identity of women."[12]

One of Flannery O'Connor's stories gives me insight into the positive meaning virginity can have for a woman who feels the pull of a dedicated life, whether or not she marries. "A Temple of the Holy Ghost," which has suggestive autobiographical implications, places a contemporary reconception of women's autonomy into the dawning consciousness of its central character, a talented, independent-minded Catholic girl on the verge of puberty. Biblical scholar Raymond Brown speaks of the intact flesh of the Virgin as a "fragile oasis of freedom." That is what her own flesh, which at first seemed problematic, becomes for this stubborn girl, who can't fit into her girl cousins' world of painted toenails and anxiety to please the local farm boys. The cousins giggle when reporting that the nuns at the convent school they attend told them that each girl should consider herself "a temple of the

Holy Ghost." In contrast, the twelve-year-old girl finds the phrase appropriate. Dimly aware of the development of her adolescent body, she overhears her cousins whisper about what a hermaphrodite said at the county fair: "He made me thisaway." The message is important to her: if the freak can accept himself, O'Connor implies, the girl can accept her body. She really *is* a temple of the Holy Ghost. He made her "thisaway."

The girl determines to be kinder to her mother after this revelation: "Hep me not to be so mean." The significance of her self-acceptance becomes even more apparent when, after attending Benediction at the convent, she links the Christ in the host with the Creator revealed in the bloodred setting sun. As for O'Connor herself, despite the lupus she contracted in her early twenties, and her isolated, unmarried life in her mother's home until she died at thirty-nine, she showed a rare capacity to see her female self as whole.

Evidence that the contemporary understanding of Mary's virginity functions positively for women in different cultures comes from many sources. It is visible, for example, in a video showing a group of Poor Clare nuns, of Lilongwe, Malawi, as they dance and sing before the black statue of Our Lady of Africa. As African Christianity comes of age, such women can choose the celibate life and still play significant roles in their communities. This would have been far more difficult in the past, when they would have been pressured to enter into arranged marriages as a result of family and tribal decisions.

In good African fashion, these Poor Clares have transformed a village dance into their morning prayer, just as the wider community shares their liturgy, singing, and dancing. In their prayer-dance, the sisters bow to the statue of Mary, clothed in blue like themselves. One raises and lowers a large mortar and pestle, while the others sift in pantomime, mimicking typical local occupations. They wave their hands and sway:

> Before the sun comes up,
> We, your children of Africa
> Want to praise you joyfully, Mary.
> You are black but beautiful . . .
> We love you more than the
> drum music of the evenings.[13]

Their movements grow faster and faster, the singing louder, and finally they ululate—making an extraordinary high wailing sound with their tongues that signifies great excitement. All approach the statue of Mary with deep reverence, clap hands, and bow three times.

Such joyful, communal living as unmarried women is a new and liberating choice for some African women. Most, of course, would not choose to be celibate nuns, but a Nigerian novel like Buchi Emecheta's ironically titled *The Joys of Motherhood* shows how difficult it has been for African women to find equality in marital relationships. The book's theme connects with the lives of women wherever motherhood is seen as the all-consuming function of women, who must for its sake deny their own identities.

It is inevitable, therefore, that Mary's motherhood, too, is being redefined by women today. In *The Second Sex*, Simone de Beauvoir offered a harsh judgment on the Christian tradition that exalted Mary's motherhood as passive and submissive in her comment on the Nativity: "For the first time in human history the mother kneels before her son; she freely accepts her inferiority."[14] Because of the long history in which Mary's acceptance of her role in the Incarnation was appropriated by a dominantly male culture, de Beauvoir's remark was understandable. But Christian women today do not see the same pose as female inferiority to the male, but rather as the creative submission of a fully liberated human being to the will of God.

Was Mary different from all other women because she had no blood flow, no pain in childbirth, no sex? Very few contemporary women think so. Elizabeth Johnson told me that in her college religion classes, adult Catholic women students say they feel sorry that Mary could not enjoy sexual relations with a good man. Unquestionably the prevailing culture makes it difficult to see the traditional vow of dedicated chastity in positive terms, but in any case the Bible does not place Mary in such a life. At a prayer meeting Johnson attended in Capetown, South Africa, she noticed that the Catholic women insisted on dropping "mother inviolate" and "mother undefiled" from the official liturgy because they considered the implications of such invocations insulting. Not only did they have more positive attitudes to sex and mothering; they also did not want to permit such arbitrary barriers between themselves and Mary.

FINDING NEW MEANING IN MARY'S VIRGINITY AND MOTHER-hood has also caused a number of men to see women differently. Priest-sociologist Andrew Greeley, for example, now insists that "The high tradition of Mariology is compatible with a theory of the role of women which emphasizes the freedom, independence, strength, passion and responsibility of maternity." He sharply criticizes the kind of feminine passivity that Mary was mistakenly considered to represent: "The quiet, docile, retiring, passive, fragile role of women that was so dear to both the Victorians and the Nazis, as well as to some of the fertility cultists who seemed to believe that the number of children one had was a measure of how well one had discharged maternal functions and responsibilities."[15]

Reexamining the meaning of Mary's virginity is crucial in order to understand healthy male development, according to the English Benedictine Dom Sebastian Moore, who has long wrestled with the question. In a recent reflection on the Virgin

Birth, Moore interprets Mary's virginal motherhood as a liberating model for men as well as for women. In so doing he hopes to offer a constructive challenge to the church, which "spearheaded the earlier, and now unraveling phase of patriarchy . . . to play a creative role in the next phase."[16]

Moore sees Western men as stuck in a state of arrested development, trying to break away from their memories of emotional domination by mothers through their social subjugation of women. His judgment seconds the findings of one of the best-known long-term psychological research projects dealing with successful American men, the Grant study. Although the chief interest of that research was to determine what made men successful, George Vaillant's summary of the study's conclusions included the surprising fact that "the more successful the man, the more he feared women—not as individuals but as mythic beings." Psychiatrist Robert Stoller partially explained this complex phenomenon by saying that "Masculinity as we observe it in boys and men does not exist without the component of continuous push away from the mother, both literally in the first years of life and psychologically in the development of character structure that forces the inner mother down and out of awareness."[17]

At first, says Dom Sebastian Moore, the Virgin Birth appears to support just such distancing. It seems to give revelatory support for a pattern in which a mother's perceived domination of a son produces a relationship of reverse domination:

> All through Christianity, the image of the Mother and the Son has been pulled into the overpowering magnetic field of the culture and reshaped according to its pattern of domination and reversal, the Mother dominating the Son as Mother, the Son dominating the Mother as Lord.[18]

Moore's analysis is supported by German theologian Maria Kassel. Depth psychology, she says, shows that as long as men pay honor to the Great Mother but are unconscious of their own fear of women, "the fear of the masculine ego for the feminine is seen as something negative in women themselves, and then it is imagined to be right to keep them down."[19]

Kassel believes, however, that "Virginity in the archetype 'Mary' can . . . be grasped as a challenge for both sexes to develop their own specific form of psychological independence." Similarly, Moore goes on to say that when we look more closely at the meaning of Mary's virginity, it changes dramatically. The Virgin Mother is a woman subject to God alone. She does not have to dominate her son, and the son acknowledges her as partner, revealing an equal, spousal relationship as the goal of Christian revelation. Moore sees Mary as the new New Eve who corrects— on behalf of Eve and of all women—the inequality of their relations with men.

Such a Mary helps men see women in a more positive light, as Margaret Fuller wrote a century ago: "Man looks upon Woman in this relation always as he should . . . in unprofaned connection as brother and sister, children and servants of one Divine love, pilgrims of a common aim." Kassel, similarly, finds that from the viewpoint of depth psychology, Mary's virginity promotes a liberating equality between the sexes: "It is precisely the archetype of Mary, the Virgin Mother, that can make us aware of the goal of becoming human: the whole human being who grows together out of the contradictions of feminine and masculine, unconscious and conscious, earthly and divine."[20] All these possibilities are inherent in the mysterious story of the Virgin Birth, and in much of the early liturgy and medieval art depicting Mary as spouse of Christ. Despite the overarching difference between divine and human in the relationship between God and Mary, such spousal equality on the human level is implied subliminally in many of the sculpted and painted madonnas with child, and even more in the Triumphs of Mary as Queen of Heaven, bride of her son, that flourished in the Middle Ages.

Moore was challenged by the "natural" explanation of the Virgin Birth in Stephen Mitchell's *The Gospel According to Jesus*, where Mary is presented as an unwed mother. At first Moore found this interpretation deeply upsetting because it was so persuasive; he couldn't sleep the night after he read it. A voice in his head kept repeating, "She's nothing but a whore; the church has made her into the Madonna and it's all a huge fake." But after a deep sleep the following night, he suddenly felt at peace. In this experience, he realized, God was telling him that our petty social categories mean nothing; concepts like "legitimate" and "illegitimate" do not exist in God's mind. Why couldn't God's son be begotten out of wedlock in order to tell us who we really are—God's own sons and daughters? Such an interpretation could help break the cycle of domination and submission in human relationships for the first time: "We need to restore the mystery in all its starkness," he concludes. "The Word is made flesh. The flesh is the Mother's. The Mother is willing. That says it all."

Such speculations about Mary's virginity and motherhood, we should remember, all respect the underlying claim of the Gospels. Her child is God's, and whatever Mary's physical or marital relationships, her creative faithfulness was her true glory. These converging reflections by ordinary people and scholars draw on Mary's example to argue that gender is not the essential component in serving or imaging God.

It is hard to understand, therefore, in a church of which Mary is the chief representative, why women cannot function as priests. As I write, there remains extraordinary resistance at the Vatican even to discussing the possibility. On May 30, 1994, Pope John Paul II issued an apostolic letter affirming the Roman Catholic ban on women priests as "closed to debate" and "definitively held by all the church's faithful." John Paul II's resistance on this issue seems to rest firmly on his conception of Mary. Even in his extraordinary letter to women of June 29, 1995, in which he apologized for any sexism in the church, John Paul II referred to Mary as the highest expression of "the feminine genius," with its "special" gifts. Yet in the long history of Marian veneration, she has been understood by the wider church community to be a human, not merely a feminine model. Perhaps the pope's tendency to see women as separate and distinct beings from men prevents his seeing Mary in this way. Yet from the earliest Christian era she has been understood to be both passionately committed to justice and intimately related to the Eucharist; much later she became a symbol of the church's development in understanding its own tradition. A new conversation about the possibility of women priests might well focus on Mary herself and should include biblical scholars, theologians, and the witness of ordinary people.

Already, increasing numbers of Catholic theologians and church leaders see no serious obstacle to women priests. I remember hearing Dom Helder Camara, at the time archbishop of Recife, Brazil, respond to a question about such a possibility. "I am not a theologian," he replied, smiling. "But if God chose a woman to be mother of his son, I see no reason women cannot be priests." Thérèse of Lisieux wanted to be a priest in order to engage in missionary work. It seems time to honor the saint's wish by making it possible for other women to answer such a call.

IN RECENT DECADES, MARY HAS ALSO BECOME A SIGNIFICANT ecumenical force, reaching out to those Christian traditions that once saw her as a divisive figure. In the 1980s, for example, the women's movement influenced the Swedish Lutheran church to restore Marian songs, absent since the Reformation, to their official prayer books. Because Swedish young people had suffered no history of warped Marian interpretations, they accepted these songs readily, refusing to surrender Mary to the rift caused by Reformation and Counter-Reformation.

On a more formal theological level, John Macquarrie, Anglican professor of divinity at Oxford, has explained that he has few problems with the content of the Marian dogmas that shocked the Anglican church when they were first proclaimed.[21] The Second Vatican Council's decision to relate doctrines about Mary to teaching about the church helped him see that the Immaculate Conception and the Assumption are not biological or literal, but are related to the overall pattern of meaning in Scripture and tradition. For him, the two Marian dogmas illuminate and fulfill the more central doctrines of the Incarnation and the Resurrection, offering hope to all Christians. He sees the Immaculate Conception as teaching that we can all lead good lives in right relationship to God, and the Assumption as affirming that we are to be lifted up to be with God again—not literally or spatially, but into a different mode of being. Macquarrie believes that if Roman Catholicism would reexamine the relation of papal authority to tradition and accept the development of dogma along the evolutionary lines Newman envisaged, most barriers between the churches could be overcome.

Mary will not be central for everyone in efforts toward unity, of course; she is still a barrier for many, even to ecumenically minded Protestants. John W. Dixon, Jr., a retired Methodist professor of religion who has written with great insight on the madonnas of Michelangelo, says that he has "never gotten over the Protestant mistrust of the whole idea of Mary in devotional life. Jesus is the intermediary and the idea of an intercessor between Christians and Jesus still makes me uncomfortable." And some Catholic feminists give primary attention to women who appear as more active disciples than Mary. Rosemary Ruether, for instance, concedes: "though I have explored a liberation Mariology drawing on the Magnificat, I have been more interested in the other Marys of the New Testament: Mary of Magdala and Mary of Bethany." This is hardly cause for alarm: the Mary I have been getting to know is not competitive. Several women told me that they admired her most because of her ability to let things happen and to work with others; as one woman observed, "She was not a controller."

MARY AND EVE AGAIN

Inevitably, a central subject for those rethinking the role of Mary has been her relationship with Eve, which forces them to come to grips with the very roots of Marian tradition. Some believe the whole concept of the New Eve is anachronistic and should be dropped.[22] Others are reinterpreting Eve herself. In the responses to a national questionnaire I sent out just after Vatican II, there was already considerable evidence of a distinct shift among American Catholics away from the stereotypical idea of Eve as temptress. I had asked how they felt about the statement of Belgium's Cardinal Suenens—one of the liberal leaders at Vatican II—that a woman must choose to be Eve or Mary: "Either she ennobles and raises man up to her presence . . . or she drags him down with her in her own fall." The vast majority of married laymen and all the laywomen among my fifteen hundred respondents disagreed, for reasons much like those of this married woman convert:[23]

> I have always found it difficult to venerate Mary (whom I have equated since earliest childhood with repression and joylessness) and felt drawn to Eve, who has always symbolized affection, spontaneity, unselfconsciousness, delight in nature, and a noncritical regard for people.

A young wife from Milwaukee argued that Eve and Mary were not opposites, but complemented each other:

> Taking Eve as a mental construct, and a beautiful one at that, I feel that women can choose to be Eve, as they do when marrying and assuming the responsibility of creating a new race. . . . We

will become new Eves as Mary is. The understanding of Eve is incomplete without Mary and Mary's role is best understood in relation to Eve.

Thoughtful individual believers are even more convinced today that the bad girl–good girl dichotomy behind the old Eve-Mary thinking has done enough harm. The best recent reassessment I have seen is one by Barbara Grizzuti Harrison, who calls Eve "my sister" because "without the genetically transmitted knowledge of good and evil that Eve's act of radical curiosity sowed in our marrow, we should not desire to know and to love God, we should have no need of him. We should have no need of one another."[24]

Scholarship and biblical criticism support such personal revision, partly spurred on by the increasing number of women entering the field of religious studies. Ancient Near Eastern scholar Tikva Frymer-Kensky offers evidence for understanding Eve as one who transformed human culture; for her, Eve "takes on the qualities of the ancient Sumerian goddesses who transformed raw into cooked, grass into baskets, babies into social beings."[25] Even when Mary lived, says Frymer-Kensky, Eve might have been seen in some Jewish circles more as Prometheus, bringer of fire to humankind, than as Pandora, who brought the world all its troubles.

Religious scholar Carol Meyers confirms such a reading. She calls Eve the Israelite Everywoman of the pre-monarchic period in which the story was composed—when the need for hard work and for children gave women rough gender parity with men. She insists there was no Fall in the Hebrew story; the sense of a departure from Paradise was meant to help people deal with nature and existence as they experienced it, to see it as God's will.[26] In both the Jewish view and current Christian revisioning, the image of Eve as mother of life replaces that of the cliché seductress still prevalent in popular versions of the Adam and Eve story.[27]

This positive understanding of Eve has been further strengthened by the widespread acceptance of Phyllis Trible's groundbreaking rereading of Genesis.[28] Trible asks us to look closely at the verses of chapters two and three, emphasizing that in the Hebrew original they do not say what almost everyone thinks they do. In presenting a second, or Yahwist, account of Creation, the text does not concern itself with sexuality, nor does it make Eve inferior to Adam. Attention to the form of the story shows that the creation of Eve is a culmination rather than an afterthought. Eve came last because no other creature was good enough to be Adam's *'ezer*, a "helper who is a counterpart," equal but different. "To call woman 'Adam's rib,' " Trible insists, "is to misread the text." It is Yahweh alone who creates: the Hebrew speaks of God's building the rib of Adam into a woman, just as God breathed into the dirt to produce Adam.

In Trible's reading, the man "is not dominant when the snake appears; he is not aggressive; he is not a decision-maker." Nor does Eve tempt him. She talks to the serpent, explaining their situation; she reflects on his arguments, and then decides to eat the fruit. Adam is passive; "his one act is belly-oriented," says Trible. He follows his wife without question or comment, but afterward he blames God and Eve: "The woman whom you put here with me—she gave me fruit from the tree, so I ate it." Eve explains that "The serpent tricked me into it, so I ate it."

Trible finds these character portrayals extraordinary in a culture dominated by men. She points out that God does not curse either Eve or Adam, but only the serpent, accepting Eve's explanation. God does, however, judge them responsible. When He tells Eve that her husband shall rule over her, He is not issuing his mandate; what He is describing is the perversion of the ideal He had wanted in His good creation:

Rather than legitimating the patriarchal culture from which it comes, the myth places that culture under judgment. And thus it functions to liberate, not to enslave. . . . The Yahwist narrative tells us who we are (creatures of equality and mutuality); it tells us who we have become (creatures of oppression), and so it opens possibilities for change, for a return to our true liberation under God.[29]

If this is the Eve of contemporary biblical scholarship, and Mary is now the sister of all believers, the prototypical human, then the relationship between Eve and Mary is more continuous than oppositional. We should no longer blame Eve for the loss of a mythical Eden, nor look down on sex, the flesh, and human possibility. Seeing the continuity between Eve, Mary, and ourselves, we might instead see our own responsibility for building the peaceable world their Creator desired.

THE HUMAN GOD-BEARER

Because we are better able to understand the meaning of biblical revelation in a holistic context today, we can see Mary as the woman who connected matter and spirit in life as well as in the history of Christian art and devotion. Even for those who cannot accept Catholic doctrinal claims regarding Mary, therefore, she can be meaningful in her role as human God-Bearer, a reminder that all of us are meant to bear the Spirit. That was the unexpected conclusion to which China Galland was led at the end of her remarkable odyssey in search of human wholeness, recounted in *Longing for Darkness: Tara and the Black Madonna.*[30]

Like many Catholic women, Galland had become alienated from her religion because she believed that it meant surrendering vital life-choices to priests who had little knowledge of family reality. She thought she had buried her spiritual life as well, but out of deep personal need she began to search again. At church services, however, the language of "His," "Father," and "man" made her feel "smaller and smaller," she writes, "as though something in the room is suffocating me." The idea of Mary was a consolation, but "she is so remote! Impossibly good, inhumanly pure, I cannot reach her. . . . I ache for the comfort of the Blessed Mother, but her perfection and purity leave me in despair."

Galland had to take an indirect path to the mother she sought because the Mary she knew was too perfect and controlled. She was attracted to the goddess Tara, who took a vow to be enlightened only in a woman's body and became a Tibetan Buddhist female principle: darkness as emptiness, God as woman, divine mother. At the same time she decided to pursue Tara, Galland heard Gilles Quispel, a religious historian who was influential in bringing the Nag Hammadi texts to Europe, call the Black Madonna the only living symbol left in Christianity. He related her to the early Christian Gnostic tradition in which the Mother was also called "Wisdom," "the Holy Spirit," "Earth," and even "Lord." To Quispel, the Black Madonna recalled the powerful feminine voice that reverberates in some of the Nag Hammadi texts and in such earlier Syriac Christian texts as the Odes of Solomon, which was lost to the West, where Christian liturgy developed outside of the traditions in which the Holy Spirit was feminine.

Galland journeyed to India and Nepal in search of Tara. But oddly, she also began dreaming that Mary and Jesus were *with* Tara and Buddha. At a temple of Shiva, Galland saw the peaceful Kali, an image that surprised her. It reminded her of the Black Madonna at Einsiedeln, Switzerland, and she wondered if it might be related both to Tara and to her own longing for darkness as spiritual wholeness. When the Dalai Lama told her that seeking to know more of Mary as well as Tara was "a good direction," Galland decided to go to Europe.

She visited Einsiedeln, and hearing the monks sing the Salve Regina that had been chanted in their chapel for hundreds of years, she began to realize that there might be "a way back to the place that had been lost." But first she needed to pray before other black madonnas. Galland went on the popular yearly pilgrimage to the shrine of Our Lady of Czestochowa, Poland, with its famous dark painting. She found the icon a mysterious presence. Since she visited it before the fall of communism, she saw that the compassionate face of Mary functioned as a communal symbol of hope for a people whose life was otherwise brutal.[31] The experience convinced her that "The Black Madonna presents us not with an issue of sex or gender, but of life, life with all its teeming diversity of people, our different colors, our fullness."

The impact of Galland's visits to Marian shrines followed her back to the United States. When she visited her original home in the Rio Grande valley to see a black madonna in San Juan, Texas, her search again produced unexpected connections. "I had come to see the Madonna de los Lagos, *morenita*, the little dark one, but I was being shown something else. . . . It was as though the Madonna had led me there," as if Mary were revealing her presence among migrant workers and refugees from El Salvador with their stories of torture and murder. At first she felt uncomfortable with the activist direction in which the Madonna seemed to be taking her. Staying overnight in a house run by women religious in San Antonio, however, she saw a poster of Robert Lentz's icon of the Mother of the Disappeared, depicting a brown-skinned Mary overlaid with the white handprint that death squads used to mark their victims (Plate 25). Galland felt an immediate connection between the image and the stories she had just heard of family massacres: "This was the madonna I had come to see; this was what I had been led to by the Madonna de los Lagos. Everything I had not understood began to fit. There's a point at which the spiritual and the political intersect."

Lentz's image made her critical of the many representations that make Mary a passive sufferer. This Mary was anything but passive; she was "a woman rising up against authority, a woman strong and fearless . . . a Mary that we need now, a fierce Mary . . . a protectress who does not allow her children to be hunted, tortured, murdered, and devoured." For Galland, the Madonna was "like a meteorite falling out of the sky." She writes: "I didn't see that following Tara would take me back through Mary, would knock me off a solitary path into the heat and controversy of community." Galland understands another reason why so many madonnas are black or brown: "Mary is dark from entering lives on fire."

Galland's search for personal spiritual wholeness was transformed through her repeated meetings with Mary into a new awareness of the communal connections as well as the spiritual depths in the Christian tradition. Such a convergence of personal search with political involvement while encountering Mary is echoed in the testimony of two Brazilian liberation theologians, Ivone Gebara and Maria Clara Bingemer. "In her pregnant virginity," they write, "Mary is what humankind is called to be from the creation: temple and dwelling place, open and available, with all possibilities latent."[32] They stress that the Immaculate Conception is interpreted differently in the world of power than in one of individual existential need. Men and women in poor countries believe that Mary is free of sin, but they also see her as a symbol of a re-created people, a sign of hope that energizes them to work for the Kingdom of God on earth. For Gebara and Bingemer, "Mary's Assumption restores and reintegrates women's bodiliness into the very mystery of God." It is not a statement about Mary herself, or just about women; it is about the bodily, personal transfiguration of humanity, of whom Mary is the prototype. Their interpretation is supported by anthropologists Victor and Edith Turner, who insist that Mary has always represented collective humanity; "She incites awe not because of any divinity, but because she is 'one of us.' "[33]

This positive sense of Mary empowering ordinary people is widespread in the homes and churches of Latin and Central Americans who have migrated to the United States. Statues of Mary, including some from Caribbean and Cuban cults, usually with African roots, are venerated in cities throughout the United States. The many small offerings (*milagros*) pinned to these statues are testimony to Mary's help in crisis situations: they offer powerful evidence of the continuing phenomenon of Mary's care for repeated waves of new immigrants.[34]

Among the Virgins venerated, however, none seem so empowering as Guadalupe. Jeanette Rodriguez, who grew up in an Ecuadorean household in New York, discovered this with surprise when she started to work with Mexican-American women. These women were strengthened by their devotion to Guadalupe, unlike the women she remembered in her mother's generation who approached the traditional Mother of Sorrows with total resignation. Many of the Mexican-American women she met did not go to church often but had daily conversations with Our Lady of Guadalupe: "Just touching the frame of where she's at," one of them told her, "I feel that strength comes to me that keeps saying, 'Yolanda, you can do it, don't worry. I will always be here.' "[35]

There are times, of course, when the Mother of Sorrows may be the only image that matches the experience of human tragedy. The awareness of Mary standing under the cross calls people to extend their concern beyond their biological families, just as her dying son asked his mother to do in accepting John as her son. An old friend shared with me her recovery of Mary as a human model after years of alienation following the senseless death of her daughter. A lifelong Catholic, she had always assumed, like Thérèse of Lisieux, that she was the apple of God's eye:

> With marriage we continued to feel protected. We faced challenges—collected scars—but all was well enough. Until the sudden, violent reversal of fortune; the automobile accident death of our son-in-law, followed in three short months by our doctor-daughter's death caused by a DWI driver. Suddenly we were vulnerable, abandoned. If this could happen to me, anything—everything—could happen.

I had great faith in God when things were right, but lost it in crisis. Isn't it supposed to be the other way around? Go to God in crisis; forget when things go right? After a short time, I returned to weekday masses, but it was not the same, no sense of relationship or reference point.

Until one summer day, when I experienced a shock of recognition, a connection in violent death. I saw a poster for an art exhibit—a painting of Mary with the crucified Christ—and felt immediate identification. It was only a first step. Still groveling, crawling back, searching for the tranquility that belief gives. Three more years feeling abandoned, or was it abandoning on my part? Only then happening upon Augustine's Pauline pronouncement that faith is not of ourselves or given according to merit but a given requiring belief. "To believe is to think with assent." This advent, thinking about the annunciation to Mary, I realized that if ever anyone's power of belief and assent was tested, hers was. And so is mine. Only now can I appreciate what Thomas Merton called the imposed "asceticism of tribulation."

As the bearer of God's compassion Mary reminds us that we are not alone in our suffering, that it was not caused by an angry or inattentive God, nor does it mean the end of hope. Today such personal understandings of Mary leading us to an understanding of God are being amplified and clarified by a revival of interest in Sophia theology. Early Christian communities shared a sense of Jesus as related to God's Wisdom, or Hagia Sophia, to whom the great cathedral in Constantinople was dedicated. Both John and Paul associated Jesus with the figure in Proverbs and the Wisdom of Solomon who personified the gracious presence of Yahweh in female form.[36] Just as much as Jesus was Son of Man, even Son of God, he was Sophia's son, Wisdom personified. As we have seen, the idea of Wisdom gradually became associated with Mary in liturgical readings, and in the hymns and antiphons of the

Divine Office. In the medieval Thrones of Wisdom, she was presented literally as the seat of her son, understood as Wisdom. In Eastern Christianity, Mary was portrayed as a created image of Wisdom; the tenth-century apse mosaic of Mary-Sophia still dominates the cathedral at Kiev, expressing the central be-lief of Orthodox theology that all humanity can reflect the image of God. The communal and cosmic dimensions of the mystery of the Incarnation were preserved in this tradition through Mary. In Western Christianity, however, her role as mother, presented as holding back the anger of the Father—and sometimes even of the Son—tended to diminish her representative quality as God's image. Rediscovering her as a vulnerable human being through our own day-to-day experience, contemporary biblical interpretation, and the recovery of the Wisdom tradition, we can more easily see that Mary points to a different kind of God than one who relies on authority or force. As Gebara and Bingemer say, she is "the human permeated with the divine who helps us see who *God* is: the tireless Creator always working for the poor, the Spirit freeing and giving birth to new creation."[37]

Both in the past and in the experience of many women today, Mary has become the feminine face of God. She brings greater hope to me, however, because she is preeminently human, pointing to a compassionate divinity, teaching us how to make room for God everywhere in our lives. Standing under the cross, our companion in life's passages, she reminds us of how we have circumscribed that God—made God too angry, vengeful, omnipotent, and self-contained to be concerned with us. Mary's suffering reminds us of an aspect of divinity we have suppressed, God's vulnerability. Her God is not a father who demands reparation from his own children, but one who loves the world enough to accept even the disgraceful death that inevitably accompanies this solidarity.

The recovery of Mary's human vulnerability has made her a credible image of this compassionate God's involvement with all reality. Sally Fitzgerald, editor and biographer of Flannery O'Connor, says that the sense of the absolute reality of Mary's suffering increases her own faith and sense of *real* reality. "I guess Mary used to seem too good really to suffer." Sue Kidd echoes this understanding of Mary as revealing the holy in everyday life. In birthing Christ, she tells us, Mary "portrayed the marriage of matter and spirit. In her we are called to birth the divine life, the transcendent which is neither male nor female, but simply is. But we do so on a pile of stable straw, earthed in creatureliness."[38]

Do you notice the crossovers, the echos from earlier parts of the book, the patterns that have been repeating themselves in this chapter? A black madonna appears in the dream of a white Baptist woman. The mother who doesn't dominate reveals to a Benedictine monk that the true meaning of the Virgin Birth is the need to grow toward sexual equality and mutuality. A Catholic woman seeking to escape the burdensome inferiority that accompanied Mary's image is turned toward a compassionate, communally oriented Mary by Eastern holy men and women. A spiritually mature woman crushed by the violent destruction of her daughter feels the seeds of new life awaken through a chance encounter with an image of Mary standing beneath the cross. Rethinking the reality and the meaning of Mary's presence appears to be leading many to recognize the image of Divine Wisdom in this woman who lived two thousand years ago and is still a model both for men and women.

Perhaps I sense these connections because I have been deliberately searching for Mary, and friends who have heard me talk of my search have been ready to tell me their stories and share their dreams. But these dreams are not idle; their revisioning of Mary is tied up with action as well. Angered by the lack of support in the church for women ministering to other women in prisons, for example, a small group of professional women in Chicago set up Mary's Pence in 1985 to solicit funds for that purpose. It happened spontaneously at a prayer service in the apartment of Patty Crowley, distinguished first copresident of the Catholic Family Movement, who has been spending her retirement years working in shelters for abused and needy women. A small sum compared to the annual worldwide Peter's Pence collection that is taken up to support Vatican initiatives, it has nevertheless enabled Dominican Sister Maureen Gallagher to coordinate a movement that has now funded over two hundred women involved in grassroots projects to help other women.

Devotion to Mary today, then, seems to lead both to spiritual wholeness and to a sense of solidarity with all reality. Encountering Mary pulls people beyond their customary enclaves, challenging them to feel their relationship with others as well as with God. Such an evolution cannot be speeded up by force. As Newman said, Mary's influence grows slowly. That it will spread or be successful is far from inevitable. It is as unlikely a basis for hope as was Mary's pregnancy.

In fact, the pregnant madonna may well be the symbol that best suggests the present meaning of the Mary I have begun to find, the human person permeated with the divine. Piero della Francesca's *Madonna del Parto* still captures our human hopes and possibilities in its representation of this central image (Plate 24). I have found that many other people resonate to this great painting, which stands in a small cemetery chapel near the town of Monterchi, Italy, where the artist's mother was born. Poet Jorie Graham has written a poem about it,

celebrating its representation of all human life as potentially
God-bearing.

> It is this girl
>   by Piero
> della Francesca, unbuttoning
> her blue dress,
> her mantle of weather,
> to go into
>
> labor. Come, we can go in.
>   It is before
> the birth of God. No-one
> has risen yet to the museums, to the assembly
> line—bodies
>
> and winds—to the open air
>   market. This is
> what the living do: go in.
>   It's a long way.
> And the dress keeps opening from eternity
>
> to privacy, quickening.
>   Inside, at the heart
> is tragedy, the present moment
>   forever stillborn,
> but going in, each breath is a button
> coming undone, something terribly
>   nimble-fingered
> finding all of the stops.[39]

Piero deliberately placed Mary in a tent held open on either side
by angels, recalling both the Ark of the Covenant and the tabernacle holding the Eucharist. He painted pomegranates on the
tent as well, ancient symbols of fertility. Does not this pregnant
Mary remind us that her God represents the hope of new life? Is
hers not the strength of imaginative, wholehearted cooperation,
not control? It allows for the intrusion of spirit and the contribu-

tions of others. Rather than being alone of all her sex, she is the most representative of women in her combination of self-respect and the ability to work for significant human ends.

One thing is certain, however; Mary would not try to run the world. As a number of women pointed out to me, Mary has a style quite different from that of presidents and CEOs. She doesn't seem comfortable trying to control events or push people around; her strength consists in accepting reality and responding to it thoughtfully and compassionately. Her power is based on relationship to nature and to others, something like the power that medieval people felt in her when they wanted her to shelter them under her mantle.

But Mary is not a goddess, for goddesses were not human. I can understand how women might benefit from a goddess, and why many do. There is so much overpowering and unacknowledged maleness in our learned experience of God that the encounter with a feminine creator, even the very idea of it, can be a source of personal strength. But I would have just as many problems with an exclusively female God as I have with a male one—when either sex takes over the mystery as total image, it is bound to be a distortion. Neither sex can adequately represent the God of reality; what is needed is a developing communal tradition that sees both sexes as images of the divine. If Sebastian Moore and Maria Kassel are right in their reinterpretation of the Virgin Birth, a goddess might help women—but if she replaces other images of the divine, she could also reinforce men's fear of women, promoting male immaturity and resentment. Seeing Mary only as a stand-in for God—as cultural history has sometimes cast her—is as bad as limiting her to the role of inimitable virgin-mother.

No, Mary is essentially human, and because she is representative, her Immaculate Conception, Virgin Birth, and Assumption say hopeful things about our human nature which have not yet been fully explored. I believe these doctrines are potentially true about all of us, even if no one knows exactly what they mean. Mary Gordon's summary of what we hope they mean is a good one:

> In the end, the devotion to Mary is the objective correlative of all the primitive desires that lead human beings to the life of faith. She embodies our desire to be fully human yet to transcend death. The hatred of women is the legacy of death; in Mary, Mother and Queen, we see, enfleshed in a human form that touches our most ancient longings, the promise of salvation, of deliverance, through flesh, from the burdens of flesh.[40]

It is clear to me now that the woman in the Gospels stands for our need to be as open to new influences as we are faithful to tradition. Mary calls those who hear her to a deepening of the self that reveals its connection with a reality that is constantly in creation. As God-Bearer, she reveals that God both comforts and challenges us to new creation at all times. Her very capacity to be translated into images of every culture shows that she is what Ephrem called her—the daughter of humanity. A strong woman whose example helps us break through any identity that defines us only as separate individuals, who helps us see that we are related to one another.

CHAPTER NINE

ICON OF HUMAN POSSIBILITY

I think . . . it is through poetry, through painting, sculpture, music, through those human works that are magnificently innocent of the terrible strain of sexual hatred by virtue of the labor, craft, and genius of their great creators, that one finds the surest way back to the Mother of God.

—MARY GORDON[1]

If Christ is a lion, as he is in traditional iconography, why wouldn't the Virgin Mary be a lioness? Christ lies in her lap in the form of a cub. Anyway it seems to me more accurate about motherhood than the old bloodless milk-and-water Virgins of art history. My Virgin Mary is fierce, alert to danger, wild. She stares levelly out at the viewer with her yellow lion's eyes. A gnawed bone lies at her feet.

—the narrator, in MARGARET ATWOOD's *Cat's Eye*[2]

ICON OF HUMAN POSSIBILITY

JUST AS MEN AND WOMEN HAVE BEEN FINDING NEW MEAN-
ing in old ideas about Mary, so have ancient Marian images come
alive for them with fresh implications. Many of these images, of
course, are perennially significant both as devotional objects and
as art. The mother holding her dead son finds a response among
all those who suffer the loss of loved ones. Rumanian sculptor
Marcel Guguiano, whose abstract Pietà stands in a Washington,
D.C., courtyard, considers the Pietà "a spiritual gesture from all
time for all time." The Virgin as student is another image that
has special resonance in the present, for it harmonizes Luke's
questioning, pondering heroine with contemporary women's passion for education. Equally significant are statues of a strong, vital
Anne with Mary at her knee, a sign to women of their inclusion
in the plan of salvation.[3]

But Mary, like her son, is a presence among us who cannot be
fully captured in any single view. She is a complex figure, both a
vulnerable sharer of the human condition and a signal of hope, of
what we can become at our best at different stages of our lives. In
scenes of the Nativity and the Crucifixion Mary embodies the
greatest joy and the greatest suffering that life offers. She is the
wise human figure who reveals the presence of the sacred in all
creation, as well as the absorbing passion of the divine for the human. The combination evokes memories of the great cosmological epithets of praise from the sixth-century Akathistos hymn.
Many contemporary viewers also see Mary as a prophet because

of the reversal of power, the thirst for justice shown to be God's, in the words of her Magnificat: "The hungry he has filled with good things; the rich he has sent away empty."

Old images, however, like old concepts, constantly need reinterpretation. It may be especially hard for lifelong Catholics to see what Mary signifies, since our eyes are apt to be dulled by habit; taking the mystery of her role for granted, we may notice only surface details. Storytellers, poets, and painters who translate their deeper perceptions into verbal and visual forms can startle us into looking again. My own vision has certainly been sharpened by sometimes chance encounters with the work of contemporary artists. The insights I have gained from them may encourage others to make their own discoveries.

WRITERS

Let us look first at a small group of poets and novelists whose work shows Mary's ability to reflect personal, local, and universal themes, just as she did in medieval shrines and nineteenth-century apparitions. As these writers revisit traditional images, however, they incorporate them into an understanding of our world in surprising ways. One presents the experience of those who see apparitions in a psychologically credible way. Another places a traditional scene against a background of contemporary horror. Others show Mary in their homes, speaking their language. None allow creedal differences to keep them from approaching her.

THE DIVISION OF MATTER AND SPIRIT, DIVINE AND HUMAN, that Mary overcomes as God-Bearer is expressed in a Caribbean setting in Nobel Prize–winner Derek Walcott's poem "For the Altar-Piece of the Roseau Valley Church, St. Lucia." Walcott, who grew up on St. Lucia, has written a tribute both to the native painter of the mural and to the life of the island re-created in it. In the painting, that life circles around a huge, Caribbean Mother-Mary:

> The chapel, as the pivot of this valley,
> round which whatever is rooted loosely turns
> men, women, ditches, the revolving fields
> of bananas, the secondary roads,
> draws all to it, to the altar
> and the massive altar-piece;
> like a dull mirror, life
> repeated there,
> the common life outside
> and the other life it holds. . . .

Walcott re-creates the island life that is reflected in the stunning altarpiece: the workers, lovers, and dancers circling around mother and child are penetrated by the same spirit, so that

> After five thousand novenas
> and the idea of the Virgin
> coming and going like a little lamp,
>
> after all that,
> your faith like a canoe at evening coming in,
> like a relative who is tired of America, . . .
>
> . . . one might see,
> if one were there, and not there,
> looking in at the windows
>
> the real faces of angels.[4]

MARY HERSELF IS AS FAMILIAR AS A RETURNING RELATIVE to South African poet Dennis Brutus, who was imprisoned and long-exiled for his antiapartheid views. When he courteously

apologizes to her for his inattention one Christmas Day, he seems
to speak for most of us who celebrate Christmas:

> Being the mother of God
> you need not overly concern
> yourself with such a churlish child
> —indeed might well dispense
> with such a bad-mannered son:
>
> So I must beg you to excuse
> any inattention and neglect of you
> in the midst of what is really your event
> and hope that you will accept my anxious thought
> and planning for the joy of others
> as something which is really yours.[5]

REFLECTING IN A MORE SOMBER MOOD, THE BELGIAN-BORN
American poet Catherine de Vinck rethinks the meaning of the
Magi's gifts in terms of the terrible events of recent history, their
bitterness intermixed with the gifts today's Christians offer to the
mother and her son:

> What do we bring to your feast
>   we of the faithless tribe, shepherds,
>   dubious kings, dwellers of nervous cities. . . .
>
>   GOLD FRANKINCENSE MYRRH
> Here
>
>   at your feet
>
>   the ashes of Auschwitz
> prayer shawls of old men, jewels
> carved from the bones of Israel.[6]

MARY'S SORROW AND JOY TAKE ON CONTEMPORARY EMO-
tional and social dimensions in these poems; her story seems to
make immediate human connections with any mood or culture.
The biblical Mary is right at home in a cycle of short poems by
Lucille Clifton, who has her speak a simplified Rastafarian language, based on that of the Jamaican religious sect. It seemed appropriate to Clifton to use this language because the Christianity
of Mary's time was also that of a small, nonconformist sect,
looked down upon by the majority. Clifton starts with the astrologer's prediction at Mary's birth: "this one old men will follow calling Mother Mother/. . . at a certain time when she hear
something it will burn her ear." Clifton shows Mary's mother,
Anna, afraid for her daughter, dreaming that "she washed in
light, whole world bowed to its knees." Anna wants to fight that
dream. But Mary, too, has a dream, of winged women in "light
beyond sun and words." In the poem "how he is coming then,"
her son is born on the straw, "like a loaf a poor baker sets in the
haystack to cool." At the end of her life, Mary looks back and
wonders: "Could i have fought these things?" She is alone, her
son is gone, she is surrounded by old men calling her Mother, as
the astrologer predicted. But her concern is not for herself; it is
for other, younger women who follow her:

> . . . i one old woman
> always i seem to worrying now for
> another young girl asleep
> in the plain evening.
> what song around her ear?
> what star still choosing?[7]

This Mary of Clifton's speaks convincingly in the voice of one
contemporary black subculture, while she simultaneously echoes
the universal concerns of the mother of Christ.

•   •   •

CANADIAN POET AND NOVELIST MARGARET ATWOOD pro-
vides another traditional yet highly original Mary in *Cat's Eye*, a
novel about a girl who almost met her death in a frozen ravine,
but was rescued by a dark lady with sorrowful eyes who floated
down to save her. A few days earlier, the unhappy girl had by
chance picked up a Catholic holy card: Our Lady was wearing a
long blue robe, light rays came out of the halo behind her crown,
and she smiled sadly. No wonder, for her red, satin-pincushion
heart was pierced with what looked like seven swords. The
girl had never seen such a picture before, because in the Protestant Sunday school she attended Mary had no crown, no visible
heart, and was never by herself. Nevertheless, she was familiar
to her: "I know what the picture is; it's the Virgin Mary." In the
novel as in life, even bad art can penetrate the receptive, seeking soul.

The desperate girl knelt and spoke a wordless prayer to Mary.
"But she knows already; she knows how unhappy I am." Before
she slept, the child had a vision of Mary's face, then her fiery
heart, surrounded by luminous blackness. The very next day she
was rescued from the ravine, lifted up half-frozen by a woman in
a dark cloak. The semiconscious girl glimpsed her heart inside
the cloak, and experienced happiness for the first time in
months. "You can go home now; it will be all right," the woman
told her.

After this, the girl's life changed for the better. But was the apparition real? Or was it merely the product of her overheated
imagination? Later, as an adult artist, she keeps looking for the
Mary she believes she has seen but cannot find in the churches
she visits: "The statues were of no one I recognized. They were
dolls dressed up, insipid in blue and white, pious and lifeless."
One day, however, in a village church in Mexico, she sees her
again. At first she doesn't recognize her because she is dressed in
black and her head is bowed and shadowed:

Around her feet were the stubs of candles, and all over her black dress were pinned what I thought at first were stars, but which were instead little brass or tin arms, legs, hands, sheep, donkeys, chickens and hearts. She was the Virgin of Lost Things, the one who restored them to their owners. She was the only one of these wood or marble or plaster Virgins who had ever seemed at all real to me. There could be some point in praying to her, kneeling down, lighting a candle.[8]

Atwood has it both ways. Although she never says that the apparition is "real" in the journalistic sense, the vision not only effects the child's rescue, it marks the beginning of her trust in herself, which develops into human understanding and artistic expression. What is remarkable is the psychological acuity with which Atwood explores the mind of a visionary. Her rendering of this fictional experience makes more understandable the consciousness of other, almost "lost," young women—like Bernadette, or Lucia—whose real lives were similarly transformed. Her vision reinforces Harriet Beecher Stowe's discovery in Mary of the "sorrow, for the lost, in the heart of God himself—which forms the most sacred mystery of Christianity." Even more surprising, Atwood's imagined Mother of Lost Things bears a striking resemblance to the Mary in St. Anselm's twelfth-century prayer: "O most blessed, all that turns away from you, and that you oppose, must needs be lost, and equally, it is not possible that whatever turns to you and you regard with favor should perish." Rendering this psychic experience without reducing its complexity, Atwood is faithful to a long tradition in which the Mother of Sorrows fulfills the human need for divine compassion. The statue of Our Lady of Mt. Carmel, which served the same need in late nineteenth-century Italian Harlem for those who were looked down on by "respectable" society, was also covered with testimonies of gratitude for her help.

Atwood's artist-narrator is later moved to create a startling, contemporary Mary:

> I paint her in blue, with the usual white veil, but with the head of a lioness. Christ lies in her lap in the form of a cub. . . . My Virgin Mary is fierce, alert to danger, wild. She stares levelly out at the viewer with her yellow lion's eyes. A gnawed bone lies at her feet.
>
> I paint the Virgin Mary descending to the earth, which is covered with snow and slush. She is wearing a winter coat over her blue robe, and has a purse slung over her shoulder. She's carrying two brown paper bags full of groceries. Several things have fallen from the bags: an egg, an onion, an apple. She looks tired.
>
> *Our Lady of Perpetual Help*, I call her.[9]

Atwood's symbol connects with the desires of the many women who have said they need a strong Mary, yet one they can relate to. Here she is: a lion who is also sister, cousin, old woman, one who can help a young girl as well as cook a meal. Someone who gets tired while she carries out all those miraculous rescues that are necessary in daily life. Recognized at last as worthy of the lions of the mother goddess Cybele or of King Solomon, this is the mother of Christ the lion, someone who says we are all to be bearers of the Spirit.

VISUAL ARTISTS

Since the church has largely forsaken its role as a patron of art, it is unusual to find contemporary artists choosing Mary as a subject. Nevertheless a surprising number have been drawn to her. The Marian library at Dayton University has some four thousand slides of twentieth-century madonnas, including the works of a number of Americans who have had the insight and the technique to fashion adequate and illuminating symbols of the mother of Jesus. Those artists I have had the good fortune to interview and whose views I share here have begun to relate Mary both to modern cosmology and to human need. They offer fresh approaches to Mary's significance for men, women, and the earth, often pointing to connections I never imagined. Their insights may have something to teach professional theologians; they certainly challenge believers as well as agnostics to think about Mary's story as if for the first time. Two of the painters in this section make new sense of the Immaculate Conception and the Assumption by relating spiritual insight to contemporary scientific understanding. As these artists probe the deep connection Mary makes between self, earth, humanity, and the divine, they seem to echo earlier themes in new combinations.

Yaroslava Mills

I start with my visit to an artist who lives near me in West Nyack, New York, and practices the centuries-old art of icon making. Faithfulness to a tradition she loves, not originality, marks Yara's lifelong dedication to icons. But that does not mean she is closed to influences that add new emotional and social dimensions to her art. Her work reflects personal passion as well as skill, and she stretches the form whenever she sees a good reason and finds at least some precedent.

Clearly, Eastern Christian icons continue to offer Yara a powerful channel through which to pass on what she believes is most important. She is intent that everyone who sees one of her icons will feel a sense of joy in its presence. "I want it to help them by its beauty. Not prettiness, but a deep beauty that reaches the emotions. Making an icon is so organic, the making of a whole thing, done the way it has been done for centuries. It points to a reality beyond human understanding."

Yara meets regularly with a group of novice icon painters. If they want to add new subjects or make changes in old poses, she discusses with them the reasons not to, then gives them support as they follow their own inspiration. One Catholic woman wanted to make an icon of St. Peter and his wife; she herself is married to a priest and wished to encourage and strengthen other such couples. The icon group reread the New Testament, trying to imagine what St. Peter's wife would look like, deciding—after some discussion—that she should have a halo.[10]

It is Mary to whom Yara is drawn most—especially to the icon of tenderness, because, she explains, "I understand it. Being a mother has not been easy, but it has been the most significant thing in my life." Her husband died when her son was only two, and she raised the child alone. "Of course, when my grown-up son comes home again, after a week we revert to old roles. But then I didn't understand my own mother until after she was dead. That is when my understanding of Mary deepened, too. It takes such a long time to realize what you know. For me, mother-hood is the best experience."

The majority of her icons of Mary recapitulate that feeling about motherhood found in the tenderness pose, in which the baby leans his cheek against his mother's, and her head inclines over his. Mary's head and shoulders are covered by the tradi-tional mantle of red-violet—a mixture of earthly and heavenly colors, Yara explains—adorned with three stars that indicate her physical, psychic, and spiritual virginity. At the top of one icon, Yara has painted in a Ukrainian shawl given to her by her mother. The gesture reveals her filial relationship to an extended family that is both physical and spiritual. As I look more carefully at her recent paintings, including one of Mary below the cross, I realize how much variety there is among them despite their for-mality. In each, however, Mary is both gentle and sober, her dark eyes looking just beyond ours, filled with awareness of the sorrow that surrounds present joy. It is the same expression one finds on

Romanesque Thrones of Wisdom or on the twelfth-century Vladimir Mother of God. As Yara explains, "Whenever I paint Mary, I think: what if my son were to die on a cross? Then I remember how hard it was for women in those early times, especially her."

Love of icons came almost naturally to this daughter of a Ukrainian shop owner on the Lower East Side of Manhattan. Her mother was deeply religious, with the fierce devotion of a peasant, but her father was not. And it was he who had to decide whether she could go to Cooper Union to study art when she was accepted there. He finally agreed, but only if she would work in his store to support herself. She did so for many years, teaching the art of Ukrainian Easter-egg painting there as well.

At Cooper Union she met other artists interested in icons, friends of Thomas Merton. To fulfill her thesis requirement, she carved a blessing prayer: a large, handsome plaque with elegant lettering asking the Lord to bless the dwelling where it rested. The school wanted to buy her plaque, but her father bid for it and won. All the rest of her life, if Yara did a piece she liked so well she didn't want to sell it, her father bought it. It was his way of telling her she was good, something he never said in words. Although he insisted that she work hard for her money, when he died he left her all the works she loved.

Through the years, whatever else she did—teaching, marrying, bringing up her son—she persevered in the desire to learn more about icon painting. As a young woman she saved all her money to buy icons, still relatively inexpensive after World War II, on the trips she took to Europe to view the great art of the past. She kept seeking a teacher who knew the rules of icon painting. Finally, in the eighties, she found Vladislav Andreyev, who taught her the techniques she shares with the novice icon painters who work with her now. "There is so much to learn, and none of it from a book. You must learn from a master. Learning to paint icons is different from other painting," she insists. "Its rules carry over from the technical to the conduct and attitude of the painter's life, and they have been traditional for over a thousand years."

One of Yara's most public achievements was the creation of three stained-glass windows for the Byzantine Ukrainian Catholic church of St. Demetrius in Weston, Ontario: the Nativity, the Resurrection, and Sophia. The upper halves of these windows follow the themes and perspectives of traditional icons; the lower halves are filled with joyous details taken from her Ukrainian folk heritage. In the Nativity scene, for example, shepherds, Magi, and angels all approach Mary, who reclines on a crimson mattress in the center. Her child lies swaddled in a stone manger nearby, while the Nativity star shines its light into the dark cave. At center left, Joseph successfully resists the temptation of the devil, while at the right a midwife bathes the baby. Below left, a family celebrates the Ukrainian Christmas Eve Holy Supper, while on the right the people assemble for the feast of Jordan's Great Blessing of the Waters—the women's babushkas and the gold onion domes in the background indicating their Ukrainian origin (Plate 28).

At only one point did Yara feel constrained by the traditionalism of the art she reveres. In the iconography of the Resurrection, one of the windows she was asked to make, Christ reaches down his hand to release those in Purgatory. Yara observed that he usually holds out his hand to Adam, raising him up, but does not touch Eve, whose hands are completely covered in red cloth. When I told her that I had seen icons in which Christ lifted both Eve and Adam, his hands touching theirs, she said that this was not true in her tradition. What was more upsetting was that she was told this was connected with Eve's uncleanness. "Isn't it time we changed that?" she asked, when she was about to make her Resurrection window. "Couldn't I uncover her hands, too?" The answer was no, and she did the windows as her sponsors wished. In all other respects, her Resurrection window is a joyous affirmation of popular faith. In the upper half, Christ lifts Adam and the prophets surround him; below, the crowd in Ukrainian costumes assembles outside the church for the blessing of baskets filled with paska, their traditional Easter bread (Plate 29).

Despite the inner conflict caused by her sense that it would be right to uncover Eve's hands, Yara doesn't believe she can change tradition by herself; change must be a communal development. When I saw her last, she was hoping that her idea for a new chapel she has been asked to decorate at the health center of the church of St. Demetrius would be accepted. She wanted the major theme to be the Mother of God in Paradise. The idea is somewhat unusual, but she found an old icon that she has adapted and hopes to paint as a fresco on the front of the chapel's curved inner ceiling. It depicts Mary sitting on a red pillow above a simple chair between the archangels Gabriel and Michael, a sign that the setting is heaven. "Many of the people who go there to pray will be from the nursing home," she explained. "They are facing imminent death. What greater symbol of joy could they find than the Mother of God—her hands raised in protection over them? It would be a sign that death can be positive." When I called a few weeks later, she was brimming with joy because "we have all come to accord" on the plan; she was already starting work for the chapel.

In red pants and sweatshirt, Yara herself seems a living icon, her dark brown eyes flecked with light, her curly white hair an incongruous halo framing a childlike face. Humble about her work, she is faithful and joyous in the way I imagine Mary was, keeping alive the tradition she has inherited, asking fresh questions about its components, urging others to work creatively in response to their own visions.

Frederick Franck

To see how Mary's meaning can be illuminated by a contemporary artist who does not claim to be a Christian, I interviewed

Frederick Franck, whose drawings, paintings, and sculptures are part of the permanent collections of many museums, including the Whitney and the Museum of Modern Art in New York and the National Museum in Tokyo. I was familiar with some of his handwritten books, such as *The Zen of Seeing* and *My Days with Albert Schweitzer*, and knew that he had completed several unusual sculptures of Mary. Visiting Frederick and his wife, Claske, now in their alert eighties, at their home in Warwick, New York, is a sensory awakening. You announce your arrival by banging a black gong that makes a surprisingly soft sound. A metal spiral hangs from a tree, its center a red bull's-eye. Everywhere there are little signs, painted, etched, or carved by Franck that catch you up short. The feeling is partly *Alice in Wonderland* and partly *Grimm's Fairy Tales*. A statue of a fish four feet long with human faces on either side swivels on a metal pole about shoulder-height; it is Franck's Cosmic Fish, his symbol for the connectedness of life in the universe. Across the river that runs by the side of the house is the John XXIII chapel he and Claske reinvented from an old water mill—a place of meditation for those who chance by, and one where professional musicians love to play, giving free concerts in the summer. Celebrations of life and peace take place almost impromptu here because, combined with its riverside setting and the sculptures nearby among the trees, the chapel offers an invitation to the sacred that is never oppressive.

Claske and Frederick usher me into the house; she offers some old-fashioned cookies she has flavored with real ginger, then turns her attention to practical matters that continue to pile up even when visitors come. Frederick is about to participate in a New York symposium on sacred art, and the following month he will be knighted by Queen Beatrix in the Netherlands, where he was born. He sits in a rocking chair, reflecting on the most recent madonna he has created: a tall steel version of the medieval *Vierge Ouvrante* that he calls *The Original Face*.

In the medieval original, wooden flaps over the Virgin's stomach open to reveal Father, Son, and Holy Spirit. In Franck's seven-foot sculpture, her long black robes open to reveal a round face—the Original Face, he explains. "It is the human face, or 'The Face of Faces' (Nicholas of Cusa) that is the Face of Christ" (Plates 26 and 27).

The idea was inspired by Beatrice Bruteau, director of the Philosopher's Exchange and a creative interpreter of Eastern and Western spirituality. She links the Buddhist concept of the Original Face to the description of Mary as the Immaculate Conception, which she understands as "a sign of revelation of the truth about all of us. Our spiritual task is to discover the point in ourselves where we are the Immaculate Conception."[11] Franck takes care to mention the Zen koan that inspired Bruteau to make the connection: "Show me your original face, the one you had before your parents were born." His elfin grin accompanies a disclaimer: "I'm not a theologian, thank the Lord, but I see a connection here with the statement Jesus made: 'Before Abraham was, I am.' Christ is the Original Face, the Absolute Human, and this is what all of us are called to be.

"Now let me tell you what I understand that to mean in terms of human evolution. Do you know about the research on the triune brain by Dr. Paul MacLean of the National Health Institute?"[12] I tell him I've heard of it, but would appreciate a brief summary. "Every human brain," he explains, "contains three levels of development: the reptilian and the mammalian brain that survive in us, and the prefrontal cortex—the most recent outcropping that enables us to have insight into our own life processes. Out of this introspection comes our capacity to identify with the life process in other beings.

"From empathy to compassion is a small step; MacLean's work seems to me to be a definition in contemporary biological terms of what it means to be human: empathetic, compassionate, a creature who uses foresight. I translated that understanding into the idea of the Original Face as Immaculate Conception. Although the possibility of such empathy and compassion is born in all of us, it is a very recent and vulnerable capacity. If not stimulated at certain stages of the child's development, the capacity for empathic growth becomes recessive. It can only mature after puberty—which, I think, casts light on how cruel children can be. And it can justify a pessimistic prognosis for many of our city youth whose openness may have been blocked by TV violence."

This seems a long, winding road to an understanding of the Immaculate Conception, but it is obvious that Franck has been storing up these observations for years and sees the goal quite clearly. "Christ has and shows the Original Face," he continues. "In Him the reptilian and mammalian automatisms are totally under the control of his prefrontal capacity. Not separated from them, they're integrated into a specifically human whole. It is a total flowering of the absolute human. Is he divine or not? I cannot say. I'm not a theologian; I don't call myself a Christian. I don't even like the *word* 'Christian'; it's become a religious-social category that's been hand in glove with monarchical and later corporate power. But 'Christic,' that's a good word for a spiritual orientation. Christ says, "Who sees me has seen the Father." The Buddha says, "Who sees me has seen the Dharma." I cannot help but see the analogy: Christ is the light of the world, Buddha is the eye of the world. I'm just an artist who plays with these things, turns them around, but I often find that theology is the essence of word-idolatry."

Finally, Franck speaks of his own need to create images in order to explore these connections, and of finding Mary the obvious image with which to work. "The time has come," he states, "in which we must take the freedom to play reverently and freely with religious concepts—to extract some relevant sense from these things that have been abstracted to death. I was driven to do what I didn't think I intended—to make religious sculpture.

It stems from a religious attitude toward existence as such. For me, Mary is the person who can accept and contain the Original Face, her son's and her own. That is why she is the Immaculate Conception. Yes, I see her as a modern *Vierge Ouvrante*. When she opens her cloak, she reveals the Original Face inside. Her own face is blank because she is potentially every woman, every man."

Franck's conviction that Mary is the inevitable focus of any art attempting to capture mature compassion in human form has deep roots in his remembered past. "Though I was not a member of a Christian community, I grew up in Maastricht, Holland, just on the Belgian border, where Mary's presence was everywhere, and I picked up Catholic symbolism by osmosis. Our town had a miraculous madonna, about whom many tales were told. She stood in a Romanesque church which had been built over an earlier temple to Jupiter. In times of crisis, the statue is said to have walked in deep prayer to the cathedral—past my grandmother's house—pleading for divine aid. Later they found mud on the statue's feet. The town suffered through many crises: famines, plagues, and wars; through them all, Mary was the embodiment of mercy, like those huge madonnas who spread their cloaks to protect all sorts of people."

Like many other seekers today, Franck credits more than Christian inspiration for his choice of Mary as subject. "My other, wooden, madonna is a mixture of Eastern and Western manifestations of infinite mercy," he confides. "Let me tell you about the directly Eastern inspiration for that sculpture. In a temple in Kyoto, Japan, I saw in the middle of an altar one hundred yards long a huge statue of the goddess Kwannon, or Kwan Yin, the embodiment of infinite mercy. She had forty hands, each with a slightly different compassionate gesture. She was flanked by one thousand life-size Kwannons, fourteenth-century statues that stand for the multiple endowments of mercy. This waterfall of mercy on the altar before me merged with my memories of Mary in my Kwannon Madonna."

When the cookies are all eaten, we walk outside to see both sculptures: the seven-foot-tall metal Original Face, and the Kwannon Madonna in the sculpture garden across the street, carved on the inside of a broad tree trunk. Mary's head is at the top; below are the faces of countless men and women of all ages and conditions. The carving is a contemporary Mother of Mercy, no longer sheltering only the people of European Christendom, but sharing the existence of a universal family.

John Giuliani

After seeing a number of reproductions of his icons of Mary with Native American features—the spirit-bird hovering over her in a Lakota Annunciation, Mary standing on the crescent moon in a Sioux Assumption—I decided to pay a visit to artist-priest John Giuliani. A slim, energetic man in blue jeans, he welcomed me warmly. "I'm not into comfort; the furniture's all from thrift shops." I have been to this beautiful spot in the northwestern Connecticut countryside to attend mass, which Giuliani celebrates in a barn-church for a small, deeply involved liturgical community. Entering his simple living space, cluttered with icons, statues, and carvings of saints, I see that Mary is prominent among them. "They are my family," he explains. "Seriously, I consult with them every day."

When I ask him why he paints Mary so often, he places his hands behind his head and takes a while to respond. "I can't answer that conceptually." The expressive arms come down to his sides and he sighs. "I have to go back to the beginning. It was not unimportant that my birth was in my mother's bed, and that she nursed me at her breast till I was two. My mother was a kind of earth goddess. She grew up in Italy with her mother and grandmother, close to the earth, cooking, crocheting, growing and using herbs, practicing the healing sciences that primitive peoples are gifted with.

"She brought them all to Greenwich. She was an incredible nurturer. More often than not when I was growing up, she would have strangers at the table. She'd bring them in from the shop— my father was a shoemaker—or just from the street. She was my first and last teacher in terms of the liturgy. For her, with her great gift of sharing, it was table-making.

"When I was a kid, I went to church at St. Mary's and lit candles in front of the statue of Mary. I loved to see them burn down. I'd keep staring at the statue, expecting a sign. It was a real presence to me, and it meant mother. For a long time Mary simply meant mother and the experience of mothering: generosity, nurturing resources, affirmation. My mother never made us feel the slightest bit of fear, of her or of God. If we really wanted to do something, she'd tell us it was all right. Both she and my father taught us how to make choices and how to spend money. The only caution my father gave us was, 'Just don't disgrace your family's name.' So Mary meant all that went into the making of a family, especially one centered around a table.

"Then as I grew older, Mary also became something more. It came to me on the feast of the Assumption shortly after I entered the seminary in 1950. I had been an art student at Pratt, but I got caught up in reading Merton, then Augustine, and felt a call to a different kind of life. Pope Pius XII had just pronounced the dogma of the Assumption and so many people were critical, but not Carl Jung. He applauded; at last, he said, the feminine in God is recognized. Five years later, in 1955, Salvador Dali painted the Assumption. I saw the painting in a gallery, a seven-foot panel, and I believe it helped me see something he saw—the connection between the dogma and the atomic bomb we had exploded at Hiroshima. Dali painted his wife as the Virgin; the head and neck were realistic, but the middle was disintegrated—like atomic particles—then the feet were natural again. Dali interpreted the

Assumption in the light of atomic destruction. We'd been so bound up in creedal definitions we couldn't see it clearly, but the psychologist and the artist could! There was the salvation of every atomic particle suggested in our mother Mary, Gaia, Holy Mother. It took me a long time to understand the relationship of doctrine to the meaning of Dali's painting; I was only able to speak of it on the feast of the Assumption in 1993. The new sciences—especially astrophysics—helped me to make the connections.

"Religious language is essentially poetic and symbolic; anything literal kills its meaning and limits our understanding of it. More and more, I sense Mary as the feminine principle in all things and related to all. There seems to be some flaw in human nature that blocks revelation. The most important thing is for us to *see* again. Our liturgy can't be liturgy if it isn't in touch with all the elements of creation, resting on the organic. That's the way we are; every river in the world flows in our system. We need to know about that connectedness, to recover what is in us. That is the basis of any sacrament. Mary is the recognition of what I know and an invitation to look more deeply and fully at everything else."

"Is there any connection between that insight and the reason you paint Mary so often with Native American features and clothing?" I asked him, and he nodded and leaned forward.

"I began thinking—it was only a few years before the five-hundredth anniversary of Columbus's arrival in 1992—about how wrong it had been to transplant European spirituality to this land without acknowledging the spiritual presence that was already here. I felt a personal need to do some kind of reparation. And at just that time I began to live in solitude. I took up my paintbrushes that I had put aside when I entered the seminary—after thirty-seven years—and it all just poured out and hasn't stopped. It began as a feeling for the first inhabitants of my country, where I am a transplant. Everything I had felt, all the old pictures I had seen and studied, fed this attempt to do homage to Native Americans.

"I felt icons were the proper form, but I had to do away with the Byzantine formality. And I had to do research among the tribes to see the differences in their features and ways. I have now made four trips West and I keep learning. Mary was the most natural figure for such icons for all the reasons I mentioned before (Plates 30 and 31). She helped me recognize the familiar in Native American spirituality, their relation to creatures, the land, their beautiful prayers:

> How could I cut this grass
> Do I dare cut the hair of my mother?

Like them, she feels the profound relationship between everything. It gave me great joy to wrap her in all the tribal robes. And in the Cheyenne madonna, I found that I had painted my mother's face. She could have been a Native American; she was a soul being, filled with the wisdom of the earth. Such beings have a celebratory appearance. They say to us, *look!* These are the apparitions of Mary—we don't have to go to Medjugorje—each place, each person is a revelation."[13]

Meinrad Craighead

Reality is just as inspiring to artist Meinrad Craighead, whose books of remarkable paintings are accompanied by stories that tell of their origin:

> God the Mother came to me when I was a child and, as children will do, I kept her a secret. We hid together inside the structures of institutional Catholicism. Through half a lifetime of Catholic liturgies, during years of Catholic education, from first grade through college, in my professional work in Catholic education, for fourteen years in a Catholic monastery, we lived at my inmost center.[14]

Mary has been the mediator between Craighead's early intuitions and her mature vision of God the Mother, which she began to distinguish in childhood. She told me about the power of holy cards on her childish imagination—similar to the one that fascinated Atwood's fictional heroine. As an adult, Craighead feels the older pull of the earth, breaking open and deepening her earlier, more conventional visions.

"Probably many children in Catholic schools, like me, collected holy cards, which the nuns awarded for achievements—like a perfect spelling test or a good history report. I still have some of them, poked into my old prayer books and missals. My favorites were pictures of our Blessed Lady.

"Now I can look back and think 'but of course,' understanding that the Great Mother powerfully inhabited my soul and my imagination from my earliest years. I knew, of course, that these holy cards represented Mary the Mother of God. But some of the images carried a different message—they reinforced my understanding of God as my Mother. My favorite (I no longer have it) was a holy card of the Immaculate Heart of Mary (all grays and light, no color). A huge heart glowed in her breast, dramatically illuminating the palms of her hands, which she held on either side of her heart. This was *not* Mary—this was God my Mother. How does a child arrive at such insights? I do not know. Artists are shape-shifters and I have been seeing in this way since childhood.

"To jump from then to now: for some years the image of Crow Mother has been one of the central figures in my paintings (Plate 32). She has become my 'southwestern Madonna,' the Spirit of this place. (To the Hopi people she is the 'mother of all Spirits.') Perhaps I am now making holy cards! I do know that my images of the Divine Mother are given to me. They flow from a deep interior source and are most certainly related to those holy cards that were gifts from the nuns in the 1940s."

Craighead's instinctive attraction to a Mother God gives her a profound sense of stability and security:

> She was the sure ground I grew in, the groundsill of my spirituality. Yet we remained comfortably at home in the bosom of Holy Mother church. My Catholic heritage and environment have been like a beautiful river flowing over my subterranean foundation in God the Mother. The two movements are not in conflict; they simply water different layers in my soul.[15]

Meinrad Craighead's analysis of her own spiritual life reveals the powerful need for the feminine in God. The theological aspects of this theme have been dealt with masterfully in Elizabeth Johnson's *She Who Is*, which emphasizes that what has been left out of tradition needs to be added to it if we do not wish to distort the image of God. Many are able to experience the richness of such a recovery in Craighead's paintings. It is fascinating to hear her speak of Mary's mediating mission in that process: In "Throne," she described a visit to Einsiedeln Abbey in Switzerland. With other pilgrims she visited the shrine of the small Black Madonna there, enthroned on a crescent moon, her face a dark hole in the surrounding brightness of her satin cloak and the hundreds of candles before her. That night Craighead dreamed that she was in a remote hill village, walking on a path that led to a cave:

> I step inside the entrance, adjusting to the sudden darkness.
>
> Groping through a twisting tunnel I perceive an object ahead, a dark triangular bulk filling the innermost chamber. She sits immobile on a roughly hewn stone throne. Her body is darker than the close dim interior, darker than the stone throne. Between her arms on the arms of the stone throne, her lap spreads out, a receptive center, a protective oval. . . . I gaze into her bigness, her oldness, into the broad lap where all the darkness is focused.
>
> Suddenly a young girl appears at the side of the throne, crawls

familiarly into the lap of the Black Madonna and vanishes in her
embrace. Within the same movement I am drawn forward, understanding that I am this child. Discovering the Mother, I find myself already with her.[16]

Dreaming that she lay in Mary's lap led this artist to the missing
feminine dimension of the divine. It has also opened her eyes and
revolutionized her way of living. Outside her home in New
Mexico, she has erected a four-sided altar at which she prays each
morning before she goes to her studio, named for the all-seeing
eye of the Mother: "I paint within her eye and she watches me
. . . keeps an eye on me. As her eye gives birth to me, my eyes
bring out my images."[17]

But before Craighead prays, she lights the fire on the altar and
places herself in "a time when the world was not divided into animal and human, divine and nondivine."[18] She communes with
Brother Wolf, Father Coyote, Mother Bear, Grandmother
Mountain Lion, and Grandfather Eagle, as well as with Sisters
Mole, Toad, and Turtle. She consciously acknowledges her biological connection with wind, water, and animals; drawing on
these connections heightens the sacredness of every moment.
Meinrad Craighead's visionary journey beneath the surface of
traditional forms and symbols has led to a reweaving of her life
with a deepened sense of reverence for the Spirit. The familiar
holy card and the litany of praise take on fresh meaning in their
connection with the religion of traditional people, including her
own father's Chickasaw heritage. In her book *The Litany of the
Great River*, we experience her full response to this sense of
God's nourishing presence in all things:

> each animal is summoned, a revered messenger from the Great
> Spirit, a carrier of the sacred, a word from God about God. But it
> is not a word, it is a beak or a claw, a shell or a quill, feather or fur,
> a wing or a tail or a hoof which carries the divine message to us.
> Love them, they too are my soul.[19]

Once again Mary's lap has served to support new life and vision, pointing to the continuing implications of the Incarnation. Whether it is her son or a contemporary artist who sits there, the result is always further creation. Nor is it accidental that a black madonna facilitated Craighead's transformation. Many people who have been alienated by a pure, detached Virgin are finding meditation on black madonnas helpful in their attempts to integrate life's earthy and tragic aspects into their sense of self. A number of male Jungian commentators have remarked that a dark madonna enables them to relate better to real women and to the feminine in themselves. Craighead's story suggests that such a madonna can be equally instrumental in facilitating change in women. In the view of Jungian Fred Gustafson, black Marian symbols can transcend local boundaries and relate to Western spirituality because they represent an archetype that resists all attempts at idealization.[20]

I find echoes of the third-century *Questions of Bartholomew* in Meinrad Craighead's dream of the throne, with its awe before the womb that bore the divine. It also reminds me of Hildegard's vision of Mother Church as an immense womb. Craighead presents the emotional, existential reasoning for the validity of the mother metaphor for God without claiming that it describes the indescribable, or erases Jesus' familiar term for God, "Abba," or Father. Nevertheless, her Mother God leads us, just as Mary's Magnificat does, to the more vulnerable, compassionate nature of the divine that is present in maternal biblical imagery, as well as in other artistic and theological views of God.

Craighead has absorbed earlier ecclesiological imagery, as well as many of the attributes of pre-Christian worship of the Goddess, into a distinctive Christian spirituality. It is instructive to note that her faith has deepened as she has given new form to her experiential insights. She shares with many women a deep need for the feminine divine, which they do not find mediated in mainstream religion. Despite its hierarchical structure, the

Catholic church offers great latitude to individuals and groups to focus on different aspects of the divine reality in their private devotions, and to select those most helpful for their spiritual growth. Individual saints have chosen to concentrate on the Passion of Christ, his holy childhood, or Mary's sorrows. Using feminine images and metaphors for God can remind us how little we know about either God or human nature, and at the same time can encourage us to continue the struggle for equality in our relationships that Mary declared was God's desire.

In her work, Craighead contributes to the long growth in understanding of Mary's meaning that Newman described; she extends the implications of Incarnation. Her vision is a fruitful reintegration of authentic pagan spirituality into a developed Christian consciousness. She reaches back to primeval awareness of the divine feminine and reintegrates it within a humble, communal Christianity of which Mary is the chief representative.

CONTEMPORARY ARTISTS LIKE THOSE WE HAVE MET IN THIS chapter see Mary freshly. They challenge the rest of us to look more closely at traditional elements of faith we may take for granted or assume we understand. They ask us to see the connections between our faith and everyday life crises, pressing social problems, and even advanced scientific theories about human nature and the universe itself. To see, in other words, the possible eruption of the holy at any point in life, not simply in a different and higher sphere. Author Nancy Mairs, a seer whose eyes have been sharpened by her serious disability and her husband's terminal illness, sums up this attitude clearly: "God is here, and here, and here. Not an immutable entity detached from time, but a continual calling and coming into being. Not transcendence, that orgy of self-alienation beloved of the fathers, but immanence: God working out Godself in everything."[21]

To point to this holy reality has always been the function of icons. And it has been Mary's function in particular; it is her image that has shown us the relationship of all things open to the sacred, pointing to a unity deeper than any divisions of time, reason, or race. Such unity with respect for difference was implicit in the figure of the God-Bearer at Ephesus and in the medieval Mother of Mercy. The work and words of our contemporary artists help us to see those implications in earlier images of Mary.

But their work also asks us to open our eyes, to ask questions, to leap beyond conventional understanding. It reminds us that the unity that she promises between the sacred and the human is not yet accomplished. Mary's witness suggests that if we are ever to attain human solidarity, we ourselves may have to become artists of reality.

THE END OF OUR
JOURNEY

W^E HAVE COME TO THE END OF THE LONG TAPESTRY in which I have tried to weave the figure of Mary as I found her evolving in human awareness. I see her in a more unified way than when I began; she is the woman of Scripture who is also the quintessential human being, the one whom all generations have called blessed.

She is a genuine model to me now as she was not when I was young. As pregnant mother and as witness at the cross, she testifies to the joy, the pain, and the promise of all human life. She unites the power of what early centuries saw in her as "male" virtue with the more demanding human virtue of compassion. Above all, she reminds me of God's insistence that all creation and every human being, no matter how poor or powerless, is truly significant. How could that message be sent more pointedly than by the story of the son of God born in a stable to a poor woman? Yesterday, today, and tomorrow, the image of Mary calls on us to be strong and creative in our responses to the sacred potentialities of all life.

Understanding Mary this way, I feel I am joining a long community of doubters, believers, seekers, and petitioners who have been drawn to this real woman at the center of the mystery linking God to life on our planet. I know, however, that many people who revere her see her differently than I do. This is nothing new. In all the previous cultures we have visited, Mary's image was divided because people themselves were divided. They turned to her to support their own positions, whether they did so in the fourth, the sixteenth, or the nineteenth century.

I do not want to gloss over the fact that deep divisions about Mary's role still exist today. In addition to the inevitably different emphases of women and men, and of varied ethnic and national groups, there are political and social advocates on both right and left who construct very different images of Mary to support their positions. Both conservatives who decry modern immorality and liberals who believe in the essential goodness of creation invoke Mary as the bearer of their messages, but she herself is not contained by either. Nor is she nullified by those who think her irrelevant. She is both pious and adventurous, decorous and slightly scandalous. In Scripture and in history she has always been capable of bridging and transcending differences without denying them.

Because the divisions between us began when Mary was separated from Eve and contrasted with her, our reconciliation might well begin, as the Bible itself suggests, with a meeting between Eve and Mary. Isn't it time to see Mary stretching out her hand to Eve to lift her up, the two mothers of the living united at last? I have seen no such image. Yet it would remind us that we are all linked together in the chain of life in which spirit may erupt anywhere. Others have begun to imagine it. "In that heaven for which we yearn but which we cannot imagine," writes Barbara Grizzutti Harrison, "Eve is united by Mary, carried by flights of angels to Mother God/Father God. She has become Mary's twin in purity, her sister."[1]

In my imaginary icon, Eve and Mary are joined by Adam and Abraham, Sarah and Jesus. Streams of people are walking toward them on the pilgrimages that are their lives, reaching out their hands to the two women who demonstrate that our physical and spiritual destinies are united both within ourselves and over time. In this ever-growing chain, the sight of Mary would comfort those who suffer, who have been abandoned and humiliated, who are lonely or feel ignored. Ultimately, we are all included in this group, for even if we are spared the horrors of war, natural disasters, and human cruelty, each of us inevitably faces loss and death.

But despite the comfort that she offers, Mary would never let us rest in false security or promise to take care of our problems for us. She would lend us her strength, of course, just as she supported the terrified apostles after her son's crucifixion, but she would want us to understand that her "yes" at the Annunciation was also a summons to action. A Jewish mother, committed to justice, she would join Eve in asking us not only to repent and pray, but to get on with our unfinished business.

Another Jewish mother has helped me see the nature of that unfinished business. I heard about her when Tillie Olsen, author of *Tell Me a Riddle*, spoke of her own dying mother. A Jewish immigrant, Olsen's mother passionately rejected official religion, because in her native Russia it was part of her people's oppression. Just before her death, however, she dreamed that someone was knocking on her bedroom door. She smelled a marvelous smell, heard a neighing sound, and saw three wise men in gold, blue, and crimson robes that were embroidered as in her native village. "We've come to talk to you," the first one said. When she replied, "I'm not a believer," he assured her, "We don't want to talk about that. We want to talk about wisdom." "Come in," said the dying woman. Then she saw that they were really women, not men, peasant women as in the old country. They were worn out, but they had come, they said, to worship a universal human infant who was going to be crucified into divisions of sex, race, and class. In her dream, shortly before she died, Olsen's mother joined them in this worship.

The desired incarnation in this dream seems to me to be the same as that of the God Mary praised in her Magnificat. Her God clearly wants human cooperation in the seemingly endless task of building a peaceable world, in which the tears of children would finally be wiped away. And the dream of the dying mother casts Mary in her continuing role as symbol of new life.

Our shared search for Mary ends here. It has helped me understand that devotion to her does not require a choice between faith and critical inquiry. Instead, it asks for a difficult faithfulness to both, even when they appear to be contradictory and force us to live with ambivalence.

Since I have finished this book, I continue to make new discoveries about Mary. There is a mysterious power inherent in this woman who has remained significant through all the centuries when women themselves have had little power. I am convinced that Mary requires other searches besides my own; they should come from as many directions as do the angels, shepherds, and villagers who stream toward her in Eastern Christian icons of the Nativity. Attention to the woman portrayed in the Bible and to the prayers, music, and art that convey her symbolic significance seem able to evoke ever wider yet converging circles of meaning today.

In these explorations of Mary's symbolic meaning she is, as she has always been, first of all a comfort, a sign of continuity in the human quest for encounter with a compassionate God who cares about us and lives among us. But she also serves as a stimulus to creative thinking that reflects real changes in the human situation. No longer is Christianity a religion that assumes Judaism is merely a forerunner of itself, or that other religions are simply false and need to be defeated in debate; Christianity now listens to these religions as coseekers of the truth to which it points and believes it bears witness. No longer is our world one in which men can unconsciously assume a closer relation to that God than women, and Mary is the sign that this is right.

Today, we are also able to see Mary in all her symbolic representations as the real woman sketched so tellingly in the Gospels. There she is God-Bearer and disciple—human, not an idealized male fantasy. Later images portray her as a woman diverse in skin color and feature. She takes her place as one symbol among many in world religions. She has no need to dominate or displace others. Yet she can be meaningful in all cultures because she is a human being whom God and human creativity have repeatedly endowed with the attributes of holiness. She represents the hope of human unity in her own basic humanity, the acceptability of diversity in cultural expression.

At the end of his account of Jesus' infancy, Luke says, "His mother kept all these things in her heart." The blank, suggestive outline of Matisse's Everywoman-Mary at Vence is a contemporary appeal to continue to fill in her features as we come to understand what we have kept in our own hearts. New portraits of Mary will be made as long as women and men seek to know who they are and why they are here. Only with the whole truth that their experience represents will we be able to finish her portrait. Until then, both as woman and as symbol, Mary will remain as much of a challenge to us as she is a comfort.

NOTES

INTRODUCTION

Rediscovering Mary

1. Gerald L. Bruns tells this story in "Midrash and Allegory," *The Literary Guide to the Bible*, ed. Robert Alter and Frank Kermode (Cambridge: Harvard University Press, 1987), 628.

CHAPTER ONE

Why Search for Mary?

1. As quoted in Chung Hyun Kyung, *Struggle to Be the Sun Again: Introducing Asian Women's Theology* (Maryknoll, N.Y.: Orbis Books, 1990), 74.

2. Ivone Gebara and Maria Clara Bingemer, *Mary: Mother of God, Mother of the Poor*, trans. from Portuguese Phillip Berryman (Maryknoll, N.Y.: Orbis Books, 1987), 174.

3. Cf. Constitution on the Church, *Lumen Gentium, the Documents of Vatican II*, ed. Walter Abbott (New York: America, 1966), 85–95.

4. The results of my interviews and questionnaires on this and other subjects relating to the changing consciousness of Catholic women were published in my *Sex: Female; Religion: Catholic* (New York: Holt, Rinehart & Winston, 1968).

5. Henry Adams, "The Dynamo and the Virgin," in *The Education of Henry Adams* (New York: Time, Inc., 1964).

6. My reflections on the need to give and receive such "mothering" in the Church led to my *Mother Church: What the Experience of Women Is Teaching Her* (Mahwah, N.J.: Paulist Press, 1991).

7. Victor Turner and Edith Turner, *Image and Pilgrimage in Christian Culture* (New York: Columbia University Press, 1978), 143.

8. Marina Warner, *Alone of All Her Sex: The Myth and the Cult of the Virgin Mary* (New York: Vintage Books, 1983), 338–339.

9. Elisabeth Schüssler Fiorenza, "Feminist Spirituality, Christian Identity, and Catholic Vision," in *Womanspirit Rising*, ed. Carol P. Christ and Judith Plaskow (New York: Harper & Row, 1979), 136–148.

10. Mary Gordon, "Coming to Terms with Mary," *Commonweal* (January 15, 1982), 12.

11. Jaroslav Pelikan, "Exemplar of the Development of Christian Doctrine," in *Mary, Images of the Mother of Jesus in Jewish and Christian Perspective* (Philadelphia: Fortress Press, 1986), 80.

12. Ivone Gebara and Maria Clara Bingemer, "Mary," in *Mysterium Liberationis: Fundamental Concepts of Liberation Theology*, ed. Ignacio Ellacuria, S. J., and Jon Sobrino, S. J. (Maryknoll, N.Y.: Orbis Books, 1993 [reprint of 1990 ed.]), 483.

13. Ibid.

CHAPTER TWO

Miriam of Nazareth, Mary of the New Testament

1. Harriet Beecher Stowe, *Sunny Memories of Foreign Lands* (Boston: Phillips, Sampson, 1854), 2:350.

2. St. Thérèse of Lisieux, *Her Last Conversations,* trans. John Clarke, O.C.D. (Washington, D.C.: ICS Publications, 1977), 161.

3. Elisabeth Schüssler Fiorenza, *Jesus: Miriam's Child, Sophia's Prophet* (New York: Continuum, 1994), 187.

4. Raymond E. Brown, *The Virginal Conception and Bodily Resurrection of Jesus* (New York: Paulist Press, 1973), 17.

5. I am indebted to Raymond E. Brown, *The Birth of the Messiah: A Commentary on the Infancy Narratives of Matthew and Luke* (Garden City, N.Y.: Doubleday, 1977), and to Joseph A. Fitzmyer, ed. and

trans., *The Gospel According to Luke I–IX* (New York: Doubleday Anchor Bible, 1981), for much of this information.

6. Krister Stendahl, "Quis et Unde," in *Meanings: The Bible as Document and as Guide* (Philadelphia: Fortress Press, 1984), 76–77.

7. John P. Meier discusses this question in *A Marginal Jew: Rethinking the Historical Jesus*, vol. 1 (New York: Doubleday, 1991), 318–319.

8. Raymond E. Brown et al., *Mary in the New Testament* (Philadelphia: Fortress Press, 1978).

9. Meier, *Marginal Jew*, 230.

10. Jane Schaberg, *The Illegitimacy of Jesus: A Feminist Theological Interpretation of the Infancy Narratives* (San Francisco: Harper & Row, 1987).

11. Alice L. Laffey, "Images of Mary in the Christian Scripture," in *All Generations Shall Call Me Blessed*, ed. Francis A. Eigo, O.S.A. (Villanova, Pa.: Villanova University Press, 1993).

12. Laffey stresses the importance of establishing Mary's role as a prophet because it opens up to women roles, other than that of mother, to which Mary and they have been called and continue to answer in church and society.

13. Translation by Brown, *Birth of the Messiah*, 566–567.

14. Cf. Meier, *Marginal Jew*, 276.

15. Elisabeth Schüssler Fiorenza, *In Memory of Her: A Feminist Theological Reconstruction of Christian Origins* (New York: Crossroad, 1985), 327.

16. Ibid., 331.

17. Nancy Mairs, *Ordinary Time: Cycles in Marriage, Faith, and Renewal* (Boston: Beacon Press, 1993), 10.

18. Thomas Moore, "Annunciation," in *A Gathering of Angels: Cultural Reflections on Expanding Reality*, ed. Robert Sardello (Dallas, Tex.: Dallas Institute Publications, 1990).

19. Gary Pearle, "Listening to Angels," *Psychological Perspectives*, no. 28 (1993).

20. Rainer Maria Rilke, *The Life of the Virgin Mary*, trans. C. MacIntyre (Berkeley: University of California Press, 1947).

21. Scholem Asch, *Mary* (New York: G. P. Putnam & Sons, 1949), 415, 417.

22. Frances Queré, *Les femmes de l'Evangile* (Paris: Seuil, 1982), 131–135.

23. Rilke, *Life of the Virgin Mary*, 28.

24. China Galland, *Longing for Darkness: Tara and the Black Madonna* (New York: Penguin Books, 1991), 277.

25. Jaroslav Pelikan, *Jesus Through the Centuries: His Place in the History of Culture* (New Haven: Yale University Press, 1985), 20.

CHAPTER THREE

Stories and Struggles:
Mary's Transformation in the Greco-Roman Church

1. Wilhelm Schneemelcher, ed., *New Testament Apocrypha*, translation edited by Robert McLachlan Wilson, rev. ed., 2 vols. (Louisville, Ky.: Westminster/John Knox Press, 1991–1993), 1:429:3.

2. Ode 19, *The Odes of Solomon: The Syriac Texts*, trans. and ed. James Hamilton Charlesworth (Missoula, Mont.: Scholars Press, 1978), 82–83.

3. As quoted in Hilda Graef, *Mary: A History of Doctrine and Devotion*, 2 vols. in 1 (Westminster, Md.: Christian Classics, 1985), 1:38.

4. Carol L. Meyers, *Discovering Eve: Ancient Israelite Women in Context* (New York: Oxford University Press, 1988), 296.

5. See 1 Enoch and *The Book of Jubilees*—a midrashic Targum on Genesis.

6. For much of this information I am indebted to Bernard P. Prusak, "Woman: Seductive Siren and Source of Sin," in *Religion and Sexism: Images of Woman in the Jewish and Christian Traditions*, ed. R. Ruether and E. McLaughlin (New York: Simon & Schuster, 1974), 89–116.

7. From the *Paedagogus* 2, 12 as translated in "The Instructor," *A Treasury of Early Christianity*, ed. Anne Fremantle (New York: New American Library, 1953), 101.

8. Irenaeus as quoted in Prusak, "Woman," 100.

9. Irenaeus as quoted in Graef, *Mary*, 1:40.

10. Ibid. This can be linked with a view of the potential spiritual transformation suggested in a passage at the end of the apocryphal

Acts of Andrew, probably originating in the third century, in which the apostle, transformed by the dedication of Maximilla, sees "Eve repenting and in myself Adam being converted." Cf. Schneemelcher, *New Testament Apocrypha*, vol. 2, 130. Such a possibility allows women and men both to identify with Eve and to work with Mary to reestablish the harmony of God's creation, restoring conditions before the Fall as Mary does in this theology of Irenaeus.

11. Lucius Apuleius, *The Golden Ass*, trans. Robert Graves (New York: Pocket Books, 1954), 230.

12. As quoted in Graef, *Mary*, 1:43.

13. As quoted in Prusak, "Woman."

14. All page references here to the Protevangelium and the Infancy Story of Thomas are to Schneemelcher, *New Testament Apocrypha*, vol. 1, 421–453.

15. Rainer Maria Rilke, *The Life of the Virgin Mary*, trans. C. MacIntyre (Berkeley: University of California Press, 1947), 7.

16. Schneemelcher, *New Testament Apocrypha*, vol. 1, p. 460.

17. I have tried to piece together different reports of this event, which were written much later and depended on oral transmission. The outlines at least are quite similar.

18. Cf. Graef, *Mary*, 1:47. In the fourth century, Gregory of Nyssa recalled his grandmother's version—she had lived in the early Gregory's diocese. In the nineteenth century, Newman used the report by Gregory of Nyssa of this vision as part of his argument for the early presence of Mary as an intercessor in the church. Cf J. H. Newman, *The New Eve* (Oxford: Newman Bookshop, 1952).

19. As quoted in Graef, *Mary*, 1:45.

20. As quoted in Peter Brown, *The Body and Society: Men, Women and Sexual Renunciation in Early Christianity* (New York: Columbia University Press, 1988), 33.

21. Cf. ibid., 175.

22. Schneemelcher, *New Testament Apocrypha*, 2:618.

23. Ibid., I, 444.

24. Ibid., 445.

25. Ibid., 446–447.

26. See the translations in James M. Robinson, ed., *The Nag*

Hammadi Library (San Francisco: Harper & Row, 1988) or in Schneemelcher, *New Testament Apocrypha.*

27. Irenaeus in *Against Heresies* vol. 2, p. 2, as quoted in Rosemary R. Ruether, *Gaia and God: An Ecofeminist Theology of Earth Healing* (San Francisco: Harper San Francisco, 1992), 235.

28. Robinson, *Nag Hammadi*, 526.

29. Ibid., 527.

30. The same opposition occurs in a number of other Gnostic works, for instance, the Gospel of Thomas, Pistis Sophia, and the Gospel of the Egyptians.

31. Tertullian, "The Veiling of Virgins," ix ANF4:33. Quoted in Margaret Miles, *Carnal Knowing* (New York: Vintage Books, 1991), 205, n. 117.

32. Elaine Pagels, "God the Father, God the Mother," in *The Gnostic Gospels* (New York: Random House, 1979) gives detailed examples of such imagery. See also her ch. 2, "One God, One Bishop—the Politics of Monotheism," which reveals how women were involved in the struggle for ideas that was also a power struggle.

33. Robinson, *Nag Hammadi*, 129.

34. Ibid., 138.

35. Clement of Alexandria, "The Instructor," in Fremantle, *Treasury of Early Christianity*, 56. And see commentary by Rosemary Ruether in *Religion and Sexism*, 157–158.

36. "The Martyrdom of Saints Perpetua and Felicitas," in Fremantle, *Treasury of Early Christianity*, 186–196, 189.

37. Ibid., 190.

38. Ibid., 192.

39. Ibid., 197.

40. Stephen Davies in *The Revolt of the Widows: The Social World of the Apocryphal Acts* (Carbondale: University of Illinois Press, 1980) and Virginia Burrus in *Chastity as Autonymy: Women in the Stories of Apostolic Acts* (Lewiston, N.Y.: Edwin Mellen Press, 1987) propound such theories, but Wilhelm Schneemelcher, the editor of the Acts of the Apostles in the *New Testament Apocrypha*, disagrees with them, claiming that it is largely ideological American writers bringing their "ahistorical" assumptions to these texts who see them as a form of women's liberation. He insists such

scholars are biased against marriage and family as a way of life for women, and that the apostles are the center of the stories. But it is hard not to see Thecla as the heroine of her story, and Schneemelcher's attitude to marriage and family seems ahistorical to me. Marriage and the family were totally different institutions in the Greco-Roman era than in our own.

41. All Thecla quotes are from Schneemelcher, *New Testament Apocrypha*, 2:240–246.

42. Cf. "The Pilgrimage of Etheria," in Fremantle, *Treasury of Early Christianity*, 361–370. The journal can also be found in Elizabeth Clark, *Women in the Early Church* (Wilmington, Del.: M. Glazier, 1983). I came across an old chapel dedicated to St. Thecla, now used as a museum, in Séguret, a twelfth-century hillside village in northern Provence.

43. Cf. Schneemelcher, "The Gospel of Bartholomew," *New Testament Apocrypha* 1:539, and Felix Scheidweiler, "The Questions of Bartholomew," *New Testament Apocrypha* 1:539. All page references are to vol 1. of this text. The English translation of this work was pieced together from incomplete texts in different languages, all part of a Bartholomew tradition.

44. The Metropolitan Museum in New York has a sixth-century chalice from northern Syria which bears a carving of Jesus on one side and of Mary on the other, a striking realization of this ancient understanding of Mary's connection to the Eucharist (see Plate 6).

45. Raymond E. Brown, *The Churches the Apostles Left Behind* (New York: Paulist Press, 1984), 145.

CHAPTER FOUR

Triumph of the Church,
Emergence of the God-Bearer
(313–431 C.E.)

1. As quoted in Hilda Graef, *Mary: A History of Doctrine and Devotion* (London: Sheed & Ward; Westminster, Md.: Christian Classics, combined ed. 1985), Part 1, 52–53.

2. Ephrem of Syria in *The Harp of the Spirit*, trans. Sebastian Brock (London: Fellowship of St. Alban & Sergius, 1975), 62.

3. Eusebius, *Ecclesiastical History* (Baltimore: Penguin, 1966), 10:2, 1.

4. Ibid., 10:4, 67.

5. Historical theologian Margaret Miles has pieced together the evidence from art and written church history to describe how believers must have acted and felt inside them in "The Evidence of Our Eyes: Fourth-Century Roman Churches," in *Image as Insight: Visual Understanding in Western Christianity and Secular Culture* (Boston: Beacon Press, 1985).

6. As quoted in J. G. Davies, *The Early Christian Church: A History of Its First Five Centuries* (New York: Doubleday Anchor, 1967), 171.

7. From *De sacramentis* 1:2, 4, as quoted in Thomas F. Mathews, *The Clash of Gods: A Reinterpretation of Early Christian Art* (Princeton: Princeton University Press, 1993), 164.

8. Peter Brown's *The Cult of the Saints: Its Rise and Function in Latin Christianity* (Chicago: University of Chicago Press, 1981) describes the imaginative diplomacy involved in this complete turnaround from pagan practice. The bishops succeeded in wresting control of cemeteries from rich families. The church built and opened them as sanctuaries where rich and poor, men and women, could meet outside the usual social restraints.

9. See Mathews, *Clash of Gods*, for detailed examples of such reversals on fourth-century sarcophagi: the animals at the crib, the ass on which Jesus rides, the clothing and hairstyles of Jesus and the apostles. All participate in redefining the power of Christ.

10. See Jaroslav Pelikan's *Jesus Through the Centuries: His Place in the History of Culture* (New Haven: Yale University Press, 1985) for development of these images of Christ.

11. Cf. Mathews, *Clash of Gods*, for an informed analysis of the meaning and variety of Jesus imagery in the fourth- to sixth-century church.

12. Origen, *Contra Celsum*, 1:68.

13. As early as the third century in Dura-Europus small frescoes emphasize miracles: the paralytic carrying his bed, Jesus walking on water, David slaying Goliath.

14. Mathews, *Clash of Gods*, 138.

15. The Gospel of Luke (7:33–35) has Jesus present himself as a teacher of Wisdom (Sophia). Paul proclaimed the crucified Christ as "the power of God and the wisdom of God" (1 Corinthians 1:24), and John described the Logos, or Word, in the language of Sophia. See Elisabeth Schüssler Fiorenza, *In Memory of Her* (New York: Crossroad, 1985), 135–136, for a feminist discussion of Jesus-Sophia. The concept of Sophia was central to debates about trinitarian theology in the fourth century and provided precedents from the early church for calling Sophia an image of God.

16. Jerome, "On the Perpetual Virginity of Mary Against Helvidius," quoted in Hilda Graef, *Mary* (Westminster, Md.: Christian Classics, 1985), 1:90–91.

17. See "The Mother of Jesus in the New Testament" in *Mary in the Churches*, ed. Hans Küng and Jürgen Moltmann (New York: Seabury, 1983), 7. McKenzie says this type of reasoning was summed up in a saying attributed to Duns Scotus: "God could have done it, he should have done it, therefore he did it."

18. Graef, *Mary*, 1:50–51.

19. Ibid., 51.

20. Ambrose, "On Paradise," 4:24, in *Fathers of the Church*, 42, 301.

21. *De Gen. ad litt.* IX, v.9, as quoted in Peter Brown, *Augustine of Hippo: A Biography* (Berkeley: University of California Press, 1969), 62, 75.

22. *Ep.* 243, 10, as quoted in Brown, *Augustine*, 63.

23. *The Confessions of St. Augustine*, book 13, xxxii, trans. F. J. Sheed (New York: Sheed & Ward, 1943), 351.

24. On this connection, cf. Elizabeth A. Johnson, *She Who Is: The Mystery of God in Feminist Theological Discourse* (New York: Crossroad, 1992), 216. She cites the same quote from the *De Trinitate* on 99 and wonders how Augustine could be so profound on God and so inaccurate about women, 202.

25. Cf. Susan Haskins, *Mary Magdalene: Myth and Metaphor* (New York: Harcourt Brace, 1994) and Gerald O'Collins, S.J., and Daniel Kendall, S.J., "Mary Magdalen as Major Witness to Jesus' Resurrection," *Theological Studies* 48 (1987).

26. Miles, *Image as Insight*, 80. Miles analyzes at length the way

such representations of Eve, Mary, and Mary Magdalene acted as figures in a male discourse aimed at socializing and controlling women. For Mary and Mary Magdalene, cf. "The Virgin and Mary Magdalene," in *Image as Insight*, 75–82. For Eve and Mary, cf. "Adam and Eve: Before and After" and "The Female Body as Figure," in *Carnal Knowing* (New York: Vintage Books, 1991).

27. Ambrose, *De Virginibus* 2:2, 18, as quoted in Peter Brown, *The Body and Society* (New York: Columbia University Press, 1988), 343. I was delighted when I first heard Ambrosian chant, for, unlike Gregorian, it includes female voices. These chants were no doubt sung by the virgins and widows in the basilica of Milan.

28. As quoted in Miles, *Carnal Knowing*, 65.

29. Rosemary Ruether presents a balanced analysis of such attitudes in "Misogyny and Virginal Feminism in the Fathers of the Church," in *Religion and Sexism* (New York: Simon & Schuster, 1974).

30. Peter Brown tells the stories of these and other Christian women in "The Ascetic Life of Fourth-Century Women," in *Body and Society*.

31. Cited in both Ruether, *Religion and Sexism*, 170, and Miles, *Carnal Knowing*, 67.

32. Ruether, *Religion and Sexism*, 173.

33. Cited by Fiorenza, *In Memory of Her*, 308.

34. On the basis of the one letter of Paula's that survives in Jerome's correspondence, Peter Dronke (*Women Writers of the Middle Ages* [Cambridge and New York: Cambridge University Press, 1984]) says that her writing is not descriptive or personal like Perpetua's, but abstract and idealistic, suggesting that she accepted the view of the world and herself that Jerome created.

35. Both quotes are from *The Panarion of St. Epiphanius, Bishop of Salamis: Selected Passages*, trans. and ed. Phillip R. Amidon, S.J. (New York: Oxford University Press, 1990), 353. Alice Laffey believes that if there had been fewer such patriarchal assumptions at the time, church leaders might have seen that if Christ were King, Mary should be Queen or Queen Mother. Artists might have realized that Mary's riding a donkey was just as much a reversal of the meaning of power as Christ's doing so. Although it is suggested in legends, awareness on both counts does not surface in art until the twelfth century.

36. Graef, *Mary*, 1:51–52.

37. In the Greek tradition, *Theotokos* has remained one of the chief terms for Mary. In translation in the Latin-speaking West, however, "she who gives birth to God," was replaced by "mother of God."

38. As quoted in Graef, *Mary*, 1:79.

39. Code Theod. 26.1.2, quoted in Miles, *Image as Insight*, 60.

40. As quoted in Graef, *Mary*, 1:97.

41. *De mor. eccl. cath.* (1) xxx, 63, as quoted in Brown, *Augustine*, 225.

42. As quoted in Graef, *Mary*, 1:96.

43. Leonid Ouspensky and Vladimir Lossky, *The Meaning of Icons* (Crestwood, N.Y.: St. Vladimir's Seminary Press, 1983), 26, n. 3.

44. See Ruether in *Religion and Sexism*, 178.

45. Only in the last thirty-five years has most of the surviving work of Ephrem been translated into English from the original Syriac, a dialect of the Aramaic that Jesus spoke. I draw here on *Harp of the Spirit*, trans. Brock; *Hymns*, trans. and intro. Kathleen E. McVey (New York: Paulist Press, 1989); *Hymns on Paradise*, trans. Sebastian Brock (Crestwood, N.Y.: St. Vladimir's Seminary Press, 1990); and on Sebastian Brock, *The Luminous Eye: The Spiritual World Vision of St. Ephrem the Syrian*, 2d ed. (Kalamazoo, Mich.: Cistercian Pubns., 1992). Ephrem incorporates many themes from Jewish-Christian and Gnostic writings of the earliest Syrian Christianity, though he is firmly committed to Nicene orthodoxy. As his editor and translator, Sebastian Brock, has pointed out, Ephrem is the one great Asian-African father who is an heir of biblical Judaism, familiar with postbiblical midrashim (expositions of the texts) and Targums (translations of Hebrew biblical texts into Aramaic).

46. Ephrem of Syria, *Harp of the Spirit*, 36.

47. Brock, *Luminous Eye*, 45.

48. Ephrem's reasoning about images here is much the same as the argument in favor of icons that was affirmed at the Seventh Ecumenical Council, Nicaea II (787), which eventually succeeded in helping the Byzantine Church emerge from a period of iconoclasm.

49. Ephrem of Syria, *Hymns on Paradise*, 41.

50. Ibid., 46.

51. Brock, *Luminous Eye*, 91.

52. Ibid., 62.

53. Ephrem, *Hymns on Paradise*, 46.

54. Ibid., 47.

55. Graef, *Mary*, 1:59.

56. Ibid.

57. Ibid., 1:61.

58. Ibid., 1:60.

59. Ibid., 1:59, 61.

60. Ephrem, *Harp of the Spirit*, 67.

61. As quoted in Geoffrey Ashe, *The Virgin* (London: Routledge & Kegan Paul, 1976), 179.

62. J. H. Newman, *An Essay on the Development of Christian Doctrine* (New York: Doubleday Image Books, 1960), 153.

63. Mathews, *Clash of Gods*, 176. See also pp. 98–114, where he argues that the paintings on the apse at St. Pudenziana were of the bishop, not the emperor.

64. Cf. Pelikan, "The Cosmic Christ," in *Jesus Through the Centuries*, both for the image of the Cosmic Christ and the quote of Basil, 65.

65. Pamela Berger, *The Goddess Obscured: Transformation of the Grain Protectress from Goddess to Saint* (Boston: Beacon Press, 1986), 49.

66. As quoted in J. H. Newman, *The New Eve* (Oxford: Newman Bookshop, 1952), 36.

67. Cf. Graef, *Mary*, 1:134–135, and Marina Warner, *Alone of All Her Sex* (New York: Vintage Books, 1983), 82–96 for discussion of different versions of the story and Mary's more active role in Western versions.

68. See Kurt Weitzmann, *The Monastery of St. Catherine at Mount Sinai: The Icons*, photos by John Galey (Princeton: Princeton University Press, 1976), discussion of B.3 and Plate V.

69. See B.27 in Weitzmann, *Monastery of St. Catherine*.

70. As quoted in Graef, *Mary*, 2:132.

71. *The Service of the Akathist Hymn*, trans. from Greek by Holy Transfiguration Monastery (Boston, 1991).

CHAPTER FIVE

Mary, Her Son, and Their Extended Family:
Twelfth-Century Europe

1. Hildegard of Bingen, as quoted in Barbara Newman, *Sister of Wisdom: St. Hildegard's Theology of the Feminine* (Berkeley: University of California Press, 1987), 170.

2. Anselm of Canterbury, *The Prayers and Meditations of St. Anselm*, trans. Benedicta Ward (Baltimore: Penguin Books, 1973), 123.

3. See Eileen Power, *Medieval Women* (Cambridge and New York: Cambridge University Press, 1975), 20.

4. Emile Mâle, *Religious Art in France: The Thirteenth Century* (Princeton: Princeton University Press, 1984), v.

5. As quoted in Hilda Graef, *Mary* (Westminster, Md.: Christian Classics, 1985), 1:205.

6. Ibid., 1:207.

7. Program of Anonymous 4, "Guillaume Dufay and the Papal Choir (1428–1437)," Lawrence Rosenwald translator.

8. Anselm, *Prayers and Meditations*, 121–122.

9. Ibid., 123.

10. Ibid., 120–121.

11. Jacobus de Voragine, *The Golden Legend* (New York: Longmans, Green, 1941), 465.

12. Quoted in Mâle, *Religious Art in France: The Thirteenth Century*, 510.

13. Quoted in Henry Adams, *Mont-Saint-Michel and Chartres* (Princeton: Princeton University Press, 1933), 317–318.

14. Graef, *Mary*, 1:240.

15. Ibid., 1:237.

16. Ibid., 1:240n.

17. Anselm, *Prayers and Meditations*, 121.

18. *The Holy Qur'an*, trans. Maulana Muhammad Ali (Ahmadiyyah Anjuman Isha'at Islam Lahore, USA, 1991), 598.

19. J. M. Abd-el-Jalil, *Marie et l'Islam* (Paris: Beauchesne, 1950), 20, 25.

20. Caroline Bynum develops the twelfth-century spiritual focus on

the human Jesus and its use of maternal imagery in great detail in her *Jesus as Mother: Studies in the Spirituality of the High Middle Ages.* (Berkeley: University of California Press, 1982).

21. Friedrich Heer, *The Medieval World: Europe 1100–1350* (Cleveland, Ohio: World Publishing, 1962), 262.

22. Héloïse joined Abelard again only in death; their effigies are sculpted side by side on a common tomb in the Père Lachaise cemetery in Paris.

23. See Hildegard of Bingen, *Holistic Healing* (Collegeville, Minn.: Liturgical Press, 1994).

24. This quotation and other details of Elizabeth's life are largely from Anne L. Clark's *Elisabeth of Schönau* (Philadelphia: University of Pennsylvania Press, 1992).

25. Ibid., 21, and Newman, *Sister of Wisdom*, 36–37.

26. Cited in Bynum, *Jesus as Mother*, 11.

27. Newman, *Sister of Wisdom*, 6.

28. Hildegard was an unusually diverse genius. She founded two monasteries—getting her sisters away from male control at Rupertsberg. She preached throughout Germany on four extended tours and corresponded with people in all walks of life. She composed many songs for mass and the Divine Office at the monastery, wrote six major books on subjects ranging from visionary theology and ethics to science and herbology, and composed the first known morality play. We owe the nuns of Eibingen a debt of gratitude for preserving and translating her many manuscripts from Latin into German, making possible an international revival of interest in her works in recent years. If it had not been for them, the *Scivias* would surely have been lost, since the only manuscript vanished during the bombing of World War II. Fortunately, the nuns had spent seven years in the 1920s preparing a hand-copied facsimile of the work with all thirty-five of its painted miniatures; it is the sole source of the translations and reproductions we have. Her translator and biographer Barbara Newman believes that if Hildegard had been a male theologian, her *Scivias* would undoubtedly have been considered one of the most important medieval summas.

29. Hildegard of Bingen, *Scivias*, trans. Mother Columba Hart and Jane Bishop (Mahwah, N.J.: Paulist Press, 1990), 525.

30. In *Sister of Wisdom*, Newman develops these points as well as the complex interrelationships of Hildegard's feminine personifications within her overall imaginary universe in a sympathetic yet objective analysis of her writings as twelfth-century literature.

31. This play preceded other known morality plays by some two hundred years. Peter Dronke calls it the summit of twelfth-century dramatic achievement.

32. See Newman, *Sister of Wisdom*, 66.

33. Ibid., 250.

34. A reevaluation of Eve's guilt in comparison to Mary's gift to humanity that Christine de Pisan would repeat in 1405, in *The Book of the City of Ladies*, trans. Earl J. Richards (New York: Persea Books, 1982), 24.

35. As quoted in Newman, *Sister of Wisdom*, 189–190.

36. Rupert, Benedictine abbot of Deutz (d. c.1135), made the connection explicit. For quotation from Rupert, see Newman, *Sister of Wisdom*, 191.

37. Jaroslav Pelikan, *The Christian Tradition: A History of the Development of Doctrine*, vol. 3: *The Growth of Medieval Theology* (Chicago: University of Chicago Press, 1980), 160.

38. Eileen Power, *Medieval People* (New York: Barnes & Noble, 1963), 27–28.

39. Pamela Berger, *The Goddess Obscured* (Boston: Beacon Press, 1986), 136.

40. Perhaps my first awareness of these connections came in reading *My Antonia*, where Willa Cather evokes the sensibility of those close to a particular piece of earth and equates this love of one's own land with the classical paganism of Virgil. In Cather this love deepens and extends Christianity rather than conflicting with it.

41. Blaise was a fourth-century Armenian bishop whose name sounded like the French word for "grain." Grain was connected with his festivals in the Middle Ages, though he was considered a specialist in throat cure when I was growing up.

42. Power, *Medieval People*, 28–29.

43. Ephrem of Syria, Homily on the Nativity, in *The Harp of the Spirit*, trans. Sebastian Brock (London: Fellowship of St. Alban & St. Sergius, 1975), 68.

44. In his book on Black Virgins, *Nos Vierges Noires* (Paris, 1945), E. Saillens mapped their presence along this route in France in 1550 and in 1945.

45. Sophie Cassagnes-Brouquet, *Vierges Noires: Regard et fascination* (Rodez, France: Editions du Rouergue, 1990).

46. Marsat and Orcival are among those known to have been re-painted black as late as the nineteenth century. Orcival has been returned to her original polychrome, but Marsat's face and hands are still black, as are those of Notre Dame de Bonne Délivrance in Neuilly, Paris.

47. The statues in which she holds Christ on her knees are visible icons of Mary as Seat of Wisdom. This merger of theological, monastic, and popular meanings allowed both Bernard and illiterate peasants to visit her shrines, and Pope Urban II to preach the First Crusade from the crypt of Our Lady of the Port in the cathedral at Clermont-Ferrand. Eleanor of Aquitaine, her daughters, and Blanche of Castile were particularly devoted to the Virgins at Chartres, Le Puy, and Rocamadour. Henry II of England as well as his wife and daughter were frequent pilgrims at Rocamadour. The records at Rocamadour show that on May 2, 1244, Louis IX; his mother, Blanche of Castile; and three of his noble brothers visited there on foot in pilgrims' clothes as part of the grand pilgrimage to St. James at Compostela. The future St. Louis wanted to thank the Virgin for his recovery from malaria; he also hoped for a son, and this shrine was considered especially helpful for conception.

Even today, René Laurentin, the internationally known Marian priest-scholar, becomes eloquent in summing up the dense religious significance of the Thrones of Wisdom. Though she sits on a throne, he observes, she is herself the throne; like a monstrance displaying the consecrated host, she is the source and foundation of the uncreated Wisdom she holds out before her. The very position of her hands, he says, suggests the presentation of her son to the world. Where one hand is turned up and out (as at Rocamadour) it also includes the gesture of sacrifice. See *Vierges Romanes: Les Vierges Assises*, written with Raymond Oursel (Paris: Zodiaque, 1988), 106–109.

48. Cf. André Malraux, *Le Musée Imaginaire: Le Monde Chrétien*, vol. 3 (Paris, 1954), 55.

49. Cf. Stephen C. Cappannari and Leonard W. Moss, "Quest of the Black Madonna," in *Mother Worship: Theme and Variations*, ed. James J. Preston (Chapel Hill: University of North Carolina Press, 1982).

50. Many were believed to have been painted by St. Luke. Such authorship was frequently claimed for painted Byzantine, Russian, and Polish icons, like that of Czestochowa, but also for a number of the Western Virgins in Majesty, such as those at Montserrat, Rocamadour, and St. Victor in Marseilles.

51. Cf. the extensive findings of Marija Gimbutas demonstrating this different understanding of black and white in *The Language of the Goddess* (Thames & Hudson, Ltd., 1989).

52. The bishop of Laon sponsored such a tour to rebuild the cathedral of St. Mary, which had been destroyed by fire in 1112. For three months a group of canons and laymen from that church passed through northern France; at each stop the sick were encouraged to kiss the relics, pray, and make offerings. The local clergy and people brought relics to those unable to be present.

53. Cf. E. A. Wallis Budge, *Legends of Our Lady Mary the Perpetual Virgin and Her Mother Hanna* (Oxford, 1933).

54. Both Henry Adams, in ch. 13 of *Mont-Saint-Michel and Chartres*, and Benedicta Ward, in *Miracles and the Medieval Mind: Theory, Record, and Event, 1000 to 1215* (Philadelphia: University of Pennsylvania, Press, 1987), give extensive examples of European miracle stories.

55. Adams, *Mont-Saint-Michel and Chartres*, 264.

CHAPTER SIX

Reform, Counter-Reform, and Conquest:
The Virgin Divided

1. Martin Luther, Essay on the Magnificat, in *Works* (St. Louis, Mo.: Concordia Press, 1995 ff.), vol. 21, 322.

2. Poem XXI, "Of the Word of God," in *The Poems of St. John of the Cross*, trans. Kathleen Jones (Westminster, Md.: Christian Classics, 1993), 125.

3. Octavio Paz, as quoted in Jacque Lafaye, *Quetzalcóatl and Guadalupe: The Formation of Mexican National Consciousness, 1531–1813* (Chicago: University of Chicago Press, 1976), xix.

4. Both Bernard and Anselm are quoted in Ewert Cousins, "The Humanity and the Passion of Christ," in *Christian Spirituality*, vol. 2, *High Middle Ages and Reformation*, ed. Jill Raitt (New York: Crossroad, 1987), 377–378.

5. Canto XXXIII in *The Divine Comedy of Dante Alighieri: Paradiso*, trans. Allen Mandelbaum (New York: Bantam Books, 1984), 297 ff. The continuity of the theology with earlier belief is emphasized by the poet's placing this prayer on the lips of St. Bernard.

6. For an extended discussion of this interaction between fourteenth-century preaching and art, see Margaret R. Miles, "Women in Fourteenth-Century Tuscan Painting," in *Image as Insight* (Boston: Beacon Press, 1985).

7. This is particularly clear in some fourteenth- and fifteenth-century illuminations. The exhibit of Florentine painting at the Metropolitan Museum in 1994–1995 showed several scenes of the Pentecost and the Ascension that placed Mary at the head of the group of apostles and disciples, with the dove representing the Holy Spirit resting directly over her head.

8. See the *Book of Showings* of Julian of Norwich or her *Revelations of Divine Love* in any number of popular editions (e.g., Penguin, Paulist, and Doubleday) to read at greater length this wise writer's thinking about the Trinity in feminine imagery that combines realism, orthodoxy, and her characteristic optimism.

9. Art historian Joanna Ziegler has developed the probability of ordinary women's emotional response to such works of art (using the Beguines and describing these semireligious women as typical) in *Sculpture of Compassion: The Pietà and the Beguines in the Southern Low Countries c.1300–1600* (Brussels: Brepols Pubs., 1992).

10. As quoted in Eugène Honée, "Image and Imagination in the Medieval Culture of Prayer: A Historical Perspective," in Henk van Os, *The Art of Devotion in the Late Middle Ages in Europe: 1300–1500* (Princeton: Princeton University Press, 1994), 171–172.

11. Most of these paintings are now in the museum of San Marco in Florence.

12. *Meditations on the Life of Christ: An Illustrated Manuscript of the Fourteenth Century*, trans. Isa Ragusa and Rosalie B. Green (Princeton: Princeton University Press, 1977), 309.

13. Jacopone da Todi, *The Lauds*, trans. Serge Hughes (New York: Paulist Press, 1982), 280.

14. Anonymous 4's recording *The Lily and the Lamb* (harmonia mundi usa, 1995) is a collection of such English music.

15. Miles, *Image as Insight*, 79.

16. *Meditations*, 335.

17. Hilda Graef, *Mary* (Westminster, Md.: Christian Classics, 1985) 1:266, 268, 267.

18. Ibid., 1:317.

19. Ibid., 1:321.

20. Ibid., 1:322.

21. First recorded in the late fifteenth century, the story of the House of Loreto produced one of the most popular of all Marian pilgrimage sites, with its own celebrated black madonna.

22. All quotes from the two colloquies are from *Ten Colloquies of Erasmus*, trans. Craig R. Thompson (New York: Liberal Arts Press, 1957).

23. In a kindlier vein, Thomas More tells us he thought it very funny when he heard two old women argue over the relative merits of two madonnas, one exclaiming at last: "Of all Our Ladies, I love best Our Lady of Walsingham." John Shinners says that even today when pilgrims at Fatima are given Hail Marys as penance they

sometimes ask: to which Blessed Virgin should I pray? Cf. "Mary and the People: The Cult of Mary and Popular Belief," in *Mary, Woman of Nazareth*, ed. Doris Donnelly (New York: Paulist Press, 1989).

24. Cf. Victor Turner and Edith Turner, *Image and Pilgrimage in Christian Culture* (New York: Columbia University Press, 1978), 185.

25. Luther, *Works*, vol. 22, p. 377.

26. Luther, *Works*, vol. 21: quotes in this discussion are from pages 306, 323, 324, 326, 327, and 353.

27. "Sermon on the Afternoon of Christmas Day, 1530," in *Martin Luther's Basic Theological Writing*, ed. Timothy F. Lull (Minneapolis, Minn.: Fortress Press, 1989), 230, 232.

28. Graef, *Mary*, 2:12.

29. Walter Ong, "The Lady and the Issue," *Cross Currents* (spring 1952).

30. As quoted in Jane Dempsey Douglass, "Women and the Continental Reformation," in *Religion and Sexism*, ed. Rosemary Ruether (New York: Simon & Schuster, 1974), 294.

31. As quoted in ibid., 307.

32. Roland Bainton, *Women of the Reformation in Germany and Italy* (Minneapolis, Minn.: Augsburg, 1971), 66, 69.

33. Gerda Lerner, *The Creation of Feminist Consciousness: From the Middle Ages to Eighteen-Seventy* (New York: Oxford University Press, 1993), 94, 129–130.

34. Margaret Miles has an interesting discussion of the aesthetic results of this Reformation split in *Image as Insight*, 104–107.

35. Emile Mâle, *Religious Art in France: The Late Middle Ages* (Princeton: Princeton University Press, 1987), 440.

36. Ibid., 443.

37. Marina Warner, *Alone of All Her Sex* (New York: Vintage Books, 1983), 247.

38. Teresa of Ávila, *The Life of St. Teresa of Ávila by Herself*, trans. J. M. Cohen (London: Penguin, 1957).

39. Teresa of Ávila, *The Interior Castle* (New York: Paulist Press, 1978), 149.

40. The story became widely known when two Spanish translations

appeared, one by Miguel Sanchez (1648), the other by Luis Lazo de la Vega (1649).

41. As translated and quoted in Ivone Gebara and Maria Clara Bingemer, *Mary: Mother of God, Mother of the Poor*, trans. from Portuguese Phillip Berryman (Maryknoll, N.Y.: Orbis Books, 1987), 145.

42. As translated in Michelle Guerin, O.S.U., "Cosmic Mother of the Aztecs: Our Lady of Guadalupe," *Anima* XV, 2 (spring 1989): 117.

43. Virgil Elizondo, "Mary and the Poor: A Model of Evangelising Ecumenism," in *Mary in the Churches*, ed. Hans Küng and Jürgen Moltmann (New York: Seabury, 1983), 61.

44. Trans. by Miguel Ramos appearing in Patricia Harrington, "Mother of Death, Mother of Rebirth: The Mexican Virgin of Guadalupe," *JAAR* LVI, no.1: 34–35.

45. Virgil Elizondo, "Mary and the Evangelization in the Americas," in *Mary, Woman of Nazareth: Biblical and Theological Perspectives*, ed. Doris Donnelly (New York: Paulist Press, 1989), 147.

46. See Ena Campbell, "The Virgin of Guadalupe and the Female Self-Image: A Mexican Case History," in *Mother Worship: Theme and Variations*, ed. James J. Preston (Chapel Hill: Universtiy of North Carolina Press, 1982).

47. Jeannette Rodriguez, *Our Lady of Guadalupe: Faith and Empowerment among Mexican-American Women* (Austin: University of Texas Press, 1994), x.

48. Gebara and Bingemer, *Mary: Mother of God, Mother of the Poor*, 133.

49. Guerin, "Cosmic Mother," 121.

50. Gebara and Bingemer, *Mary: Mother of God, Mother of the Poor*, 493.

CHAPTER SEVEN

The Contrasting Marys of the Nineteenth Century

1. From "The Blessed Virgin compared to the Air we Breathe," in *The Poems of Gerard Manley Hopkins*, 4th ed., ed. W. H. Gardner and N. H. MacKenzie (London and New York: Oxford University Press, 1970), 94.

2. Margaret Fuller, *Woman in the Nineteenth Century* (1855 reprint, New York: Norton, 1971), 56.

3. As quoted in Hilda Graef, *Mary* (Westminster, Md.: Christian Classics, 1985), 2:28.

4. As quoted ibid., 2:36–39.

5. As quoted ibid, 2:41.

6. Ibid., 2:74.

7. *The Life of the Blessed Virgin Mary: From the Visions of Anne Catherine Emmerich* (London: Burns & Oates, 1954). Emmerich's *Life of Mary* was based on her visions and encompassed other times and places as well as her own. The book is a series of highly visual scenes. It presents Mary's attire and hairstyle at her wedding: her reddish gold hair was intertwined with pearls. It also describes in detail a house and tomb of the Virgin at Ephesus, which Catherine had never visited. Archaeologists later found ancient foundations and a small first-century house there as well as a tomb, which is now a tourist attraction.

8. As quoted in Nicholas Perry and Loreto Echeverria, *Under the Heel of Mary* (New York: Routledge, 1988), 79–80.

9. Most of the details of these appearances are reported in Joseph I. Dirvin, *St. Catherine Labouré of the Miraculous Medal* (New York: Farrar, Straus & Cudahy, 1958).

10. Sandra Zimdars-Swartz, *Encountering Mary: From La Salette to Medjugorje* (Princeton: Princeton University Press, 1991), 30–31.

11. Victor Turner and Edith Turner, *Image and Pilgrimage in Christian Culture* (New York: Columbia University Press, 1978), 212.

12. Ibid., 213.

13. Pope Benedict XIV, *De servorum Dei beatificatione*, as quoted in Zimdars-Swartz, *Encountering Mary*, 9. No later church pronouncement has replaced Benedict's, except to grant permission to write about unapproved apparitions.

14. As quoted in Graef, *Mary*, 2:81–82.

15. John Meyendorff, *The Orthodox Church: Its Past and Its Role in the World Today* (Crestwood, N.Y.: St. Vladimir's Seminary Press, 1981), 200.

16. Ann Taves, *Household of Faith: Roman Catholic Devotions in*

Mid-Nineteenth-Century America (Notre Dame, Ind.: University of Notre Dame Press, 1986), 109.

17. Herbert McCabe, "The Immaculate Conception," in *God Matters* (London: Geoffrey Chapman, 1987), 212.

18. Meyendorff, *Orthodox Church*, 200.

19. Carl Jung, "Answer to Job," in *The Portable Jung*, ed. Joseph Campbell (New York: Viking Press, 1971), 565.

20. Turner and Turner, *Image and Pilgrimage*, 230.

21. In 1864 Pius IX issued his *Syllabus of Errors*, in which he repudiated "progress, liberalism, and modern civilization." Hoping to compensate for loss of worldly power by monarchical control of the church, he called the First Vatican Council, which passed a decree (1870) declaring the pope infallible in matters of faith and morals.

22. David Blackbourn, *Marpingen: Apparitions of the Virgin Mary in Nineteenth-Century Germany* (New York: Alfred A. Knopf, 1994).

23. There are many examples of this tension between community need and permissible expression. In Ireland, for example, centuries of English repression have virtually eliminated the miraculous images that were so common at holy places in the Middle Ages. The simple white statues at Knock (where appearances of the Virgin were reported in 1879) show that repression. In their *Christian Pilgrimage in Modern Western Europe* (Chapel Hill: University of North Carolina Press, 1989), Mary Lee Nolan and Sidney Nolan say that such statues may be experienced as a "new form of holy thorn tree speaking from the sacred soil."

24. Zimdars-Swartz, *Encountering Mary*, 25.

25. John Shinners, Jr., "Mary and the People: The Cult of Mary and Popular Belief," in *Mary, Woman of Nazareth*, ed. Doris Donnelly (New York: Paulist Press, 1989), 181.

26. Turner and Turner, *Image and Pilgrimage*, 236.

27. Thérèse of Lisieux, *Her Last Conversations*, trans. John Clarke, O.C.D. (Washington, D.C.: ICS Pubns., 1977), 161.

28. Els Maeckelberghe, "Marian Iconography in Belgium," in *Desperately Seeking Mary: A Feminist Appropriation of a Traditional Religious Symbol* (Kampen, Netherlands: Kok Pharos, 1991).

29. As quoted in Graef, *Mary*, 2:106.

30. Ibid.

31. See J. H. Newman, *The New Eve* (Oxford: Newman Bookshop, 1952), 70–78, and Graef, *Mary*, 2:108–112.

32. Newman, *The New Eve*, 77–78.

33. Quotes from the letter to Pusey are from Graef, *Mary*, 2:108, 112.

34. In Graef, *Mary*, 2:113.

35. *The Poems of Gerard Manley Hopkins*, 61.

36. In fact, the Jesuits did not understand or support Hopkins's poetry. They rejected "The Wreck of the *Deutschland*" for their journal *The Month*; publication came only after his death. His loneliness in the order was a major part of his suffering in his last years, conveyed in several tragic sonnets he composed before his early death from tuberculosis.

37. Helen Vendler, "The Wreck of the *Deutschland*," in *The Authentic Cadence: Centennial Essays on Gerard Manley Hopkins*, ed. Anthony Mortimer (Fribourg, Switzerland: Fribourg University Press, 1992), 50.

38. Hopkins, "The Blessed Virgin compared to the Air we Breathe," in *The Poems of Gerard Manley Hopkins*, 93–97.

39. From *The Magdalen's Friend* (1862), 2:173, as quoted in Susan Haskins, *Mary Magdalen: Myth and Metaphor* (New York: Harcourt, Brace, 1994), 325.

40. As quoted in Diane D'Amico, "Eve, Mary and Mary Magdalene: Christina Rossetti's Feminine Triptych," in *The Achievement of Christina Rossetti*, ed. David A. Kent (Ithaca: Cornell University Press, 1987).

41. Ibid., 191.

42. From Charlotte Brontë, *Shirley*, chapter 18.

43. Elizabeth Cady Stanton, "Has Christianity Benefitted Women," *North American Review* 342 (1885):89–97.

44. Anna Brownell Murphy Jameson, *Legends of the Madonna: As Represented in the Fine Arts* (New York: Longmans, Green, 1890 ed.; reprint, Detroit, Mich.: Gale Research, 1972). All page references in parentheses are to this edition.

45. Frances Power Cobbe, "Madonna Immacolata," ch. 14 of *Italics* (London, 1864), 329–331.

46. Margaret Fuller, *Woman in the Nineteenth Century* (1855; reprint, New York: Norton, 1972), 305, 308–309.

47. Harriet Beecher Stowe, *Sunny Memories of Foreign Lands*, 2 vols. (Boston: Phillips, Sampson, 1854), 2:350.

48. Ibid., 2:342–343.

49. Ibid., 2:343. Further confirmation of Stowe's acceptance of the ideal of self-sacrifice in women is shown by the question the narrator raises in her novel *The Minister's Wooing*: "Is not the faithful Paula, with her beautiful face, prostrate in reverence before poor old, lean, haggard dying St. Jerome in the most splendid painting in the world [Domenichino's *Last Communion of St. Jerome*], an emblem and sign of woman's eternal power of self-sacrifice to what she deems noblest in man?" See *The Minister's Wooing* (1859; reprint, Ridgewood, N.Y.: Gregg Press, 1968), 104.

50. Stowe, *Minister's Wooing*, 321.

51. Robert Orsi makes this judgment on p. 231 of *The Madonna of 115th St.: Faith and Community in Italian Harlem, 1880–1950* (New Haven: Yale University Press, 1985), his sociological study of the interrelation of the Madonna and this community over several generations, which renders its life in dramatic human terms. In this study he evokes the sensory experience of the *festa* as a symbol of life and faith in Italian Harlem, providing an astute and sympathetic analysis of its religious and cultural meaning to the immigrant community. A few decades earlier, in Boston, the police—and later even settlement workers—had deplored the dissolute tendency of Irish immigrants to drink and dance, customs still uncommon in Puritan New England.

52. Ibid., 222.

53. As quoted in Gerda Lerner, *The Creation of Feminist Consciousness* (New York: Oxford University Press, 1993), 106.

CHAPTER EIGHT

The Liberation of Mary

1. China Galland, *Longing for Darkness: Tara and the Black Madonna* (New York: Penguin Books, 1991), 161.

2. Ruth Pakaluk, in Jane Redmont, *Generous Lives: American Catholic Women Today* (New York: William Morrow, 1992), 104.

3. Mary Gordon, "Coming to Terms with Mary," *Commonweal* (January 15, 1982).

4. Anonymous 4 program notes, "*Aurora velut fulgida,*" trans. Susan Hellauer.

5. Ibid., "*O genetrix aeterni,*" trans. Susan Hellauer.

6. Sue Monk Kidd, "A Protestant's Journey Back to Mary," *Anima* (Spring 1989). Quotes are from pp. 104–107.

7. Redmont, *Generous Lives*, 118–119.

8. Ibid., 103.

9. Chung Hyun Kyung, "Who Is Mary for Today's Asian Women?" in *Struggle to Be the Sun Again* (Maryknoll, N.Y.: Orbis Books, 1990), 74–94.

10. Els Maeckelberghe's study of popular preaching about the Immaculate Conception came to similar conclusions. See *Desperately Seeking Mary* (Kampen, Netherlands: Kok Pharos, 1991).

11. Elizabeth A. Johnson, "Marian Tradition and the Reality of Women," *Horizons*, vol. 12, no. 1 (1985):116–135.

12. Ibid., 133.

13. The dance of the Poor Clare sisters forms a part of Thomas A. Kane's hourlong video, *The Dancing Church* (Paulist Press), which records a number of powerful contemporary African liturgies.

14. Simone de Beauvoir, *The Second Sex* (New York: Alfred A. Knopf, 1953), 160.

15. Andrew M. Greeley, *The Mary Myth: On the Feminity of God* (New York: Seabury Press, 1977), 165–166.

16. Dom Sebastian Moore, "The Bedded Axle-Tree," talk given at the College Theology Society, June 1992.

17. George E. Vaillant, *Adaptation to Life: How the Best and the Brightest Came of Age* (Boston: Little Brown, 1978), reports on the methodology and findings of the Grant Study. Quotes are from pp. 298–299.

18. Moore, "Bedded Axle-Tree."

19. Maria Kassel, "Mary and the Human Psyche," in Hans Küng

and Jürgen Moltmann, *Mary in the Churches* (New York: Seabury, 1983). Quotations are from pp. 78 and 80.

20. Ibid., p. 80.

21. John Macquarrie, *Mary for All Christians* (Grand Rapids, Mich.: Eerdmans, 1990).

22. Norwegian theologian Kari Børrenson makes this proposal, saying the use of the New Eve helps to perpetuate ecclesial androcentrism. "Mary in Catholic Theology," in Küng and Moltmann, *Mary in the Churches.*

23. These quotations, and others related to the Eve-Mary split, are in my *Sex: Female; Religion: Catholic* (New York: Holt, Rinehart & Winston, 1968).

24. Barbara Grizzutti Harrison, "A Meditation on Eve," in *Out of the Garden: Women Writers on the Bible,* ed. Christina Büchmann and Celina Spiegel (New York: Fawcett Columbine, 1994), 1.

25. Tikva Frymer-Kinsky, *In the Wake of the Goddess: Women, Culture and the Biblical Transformation of Women* (New York: Free Press, 1992), 110.

26. Carol L. Meyers, *Discovering Eve* (New York: Oxford University Press, 1988), especially ch. 4, 75–79.

27. Eve is also an admirable figure in Ann Johnson's poetic recreation of Mary's life, *Miryam of Jerusalem: Teacher of the Disciples* (Notre Dame, Ind.: Ave Maria Press, 1991).

28. Phillis Trible in *God and the Rhetoric of Sexuality* (Philadelphia: Fortress Press, 1978) and in *Womanspirit Rising,* ed. Carol P. Christ and Judith Plasgow (San Francisco: Harper & Row, 1979), 74–83.

29. Trible in Christ and Plasgow, *Womanspirit Rising,* 81.

30. The quotes from China Galland's search are from *Longing for Darkness,* 14–15, 51, 157–158, 266, 273–275, 323.

31. An artist there told her that Mary's face in the painting was not "black" but "cosmic red"—a singularly evocative description.

32. Ivone Gebara and Maria Clara Bingemer, *Mary: Mother of God, Mother of the Poor* (Maryknoll, N.Y.: Orbis Books, 1987), 105–106.

33. Victor Turner and Edith Turner, *Image and Pilgrimage in Christian Culture* (New York: Columbia University Press, 1978), 154.

34. Information from Stephen C. Holler, "Exploring the Popular Religion of U.S. Hispanic-Latino Ethnic Groups," unpublished manuscript.

35. Jeanette Rodriguez, *Our Lady of Guadalupe* (Austin: University of Texas Press, 1994), 120.

36. The feminine figure of Wisdom can be seen in Michelangelo's Creation of Adam on the ceiling of the Sistine Chapel. As the Creator's right hand reaches out to Adam, his left encompasses the female Wisdom.

37. Gebara and Bingemer, *Mary: Mother of God, Mother of the Poor*, 174–175.

38. Sue Monk Kidd, "Protestant's Journey," 107.

39. Jorie Graham, "San Sepolcro," in *Erosion* (Princeton: Princeton University Press, 1983).

40. Mary Gordon, "Coming to Terms with Mary," *Commonweal*, (January 15, 1982): 11.

CHAPTER NINE

Icon of Human Possibility

1. Mary Gordon, "Coming to Terms with Mary," *Commonweal* (January 15, 1982): 14.

2. Margaret Atwood, *Cat's Eye* (New York: Bantam Books, 1989), 165.

3. For a description of the liberating emotional effect an encounter with such a statue of Anne holding Mary had on one contemporary feminist today, see Luce Irigaray, *je, tu, nous: Toward a Culture of Difference*, trans. A. Martin (London: Routledge, 1993), 25.

4. Derek Walcott, "For the Altar-Piece of the Roseau Valley Church, St. Lucia," in *Sea Grapes* (London: Faber & Faber, 1976).

5. Dennis Brutus, "Being the Mother of God," in *Seven South African Poets*, ed. Cosmo Pieterse (London: Heinemann, 1971).

6. From Catherine de Vinck, *IKON* (Ramsey, N.J.: Alleluia Press 1972), 5.

7. Lucille Clifton, *Two-Headed Woman* (Amherst: University of Massachusetts Press, 1980), Mary poems, 34–41.

8. Atwood, *Cat's Eye*, 212.

9. Ibid., 365.

10. Eileen McCabe gave Peter's wife a halo like her husband's. She wanted to make this icon to call attention to the fact that Peter was married, and that married priests were the rule until the eleventh century. They have always been accepted in Eastern Christianity, including the Catholic Uniate churches.

11. Beatrice Bruteau, "The Immaculate Conception: Our Original Face," *Cross Currents* (summer 1989):182.

12. Paul D. MacLean, chief of the laboratory of Brain Research at the National Institute of Health, has done thirty years of research into the structure and function of the human brain.

13. John Giuliani is now carving a Marian statue from a tree trunk for the church of St. Philip in Norwalk, Connecticut. It will be flanked by eight of his paintings depicting different mysteries of her life.

14. Meinrad Craighead, Introduction, *The Mother's Songs: Images of God the Mother* (New York: Paulist Press, 1986).

15. Ibid.

16. Craighead, "Throne," ibid, 43.

17. Meinrad Craighead, *Litany of the Great River* (Mahwah, N.J.: Paulist Press, 1991), 24.

18. Ibid., 28.

19. Ibid., 11.

20. Fred Gustafson, *The Black Madonna* (Boston: Sigo Press, 1990), xi.

21. Nancy Mairs, *Ordinary Time* (Boston: Beacon Press, 1993), 11.

EPILOGUE

The End of Our Journey

1. Barbara Grizzuti Harrison, "A Meditation on Eve," in *Out of the Garden: Women Writers on the Bible*, Christina Büchman and Celina Speigel (New York: Fawcett Columbine, 1994), p.1.

SELECTED BIBLIOGRAPHY

Here, as throughout the book, I use *The New American Bible: Catholic Study Edition*, ed. Donald Senior, et al. (New York: Oxford University Press, 1990) for all biblical quotations.

Abd-el-Jalil, J. M. *Marie et l'Islam.* Paris: Beauchesne, 1950.

Adams, Henry. *Mont-Saint-Michel and Chartres.* Princeton: Princeton University Press, 1933.

Anselm of Canterbury. *The Prayers and Meditations of St. Anselm.* Translated by Benedicta Ward. Baltimore: Penguin Books, 1973.

Apuleius, Lucius. *The Golden Ass of Apuleius.* Translated by Robert Graves. New York: Pocket Books, 1954.

Ashe, Geoffrey. *The Virgin.* London: Routledge & Kegan Paul, 1976.

Askew, Pamela. *Caravaggio's Death of the Virgin.* Princeton: Princeton University Press, 1990.

Bainton, Roland. *Women of the Reformation in Germany and Italy.* Minneapolis: Augsburg, 1971.

Berger, Pamela. *The Goddess Obscured: Transformation of the Grain Protectress from Goddess to Saint.* Boston: Beacon Press, 1986.

Bernard of Clairvaux and Amadeus of Lausanne. *Magnificat: Homilies in Praise of the Blessed Virgin Mary.* Translated by Marie-Bernard Said and Grace Perigo. Kalamazoo, Mich.: Cistercian Pubns., 1979.

Bible. *The New American Bible: Catholic Study Edition.* Edited by Donald Senior, Mary Ann Getty, Carroll Stuhlmueller, and John J. Collins. New York: Oxford University Press, 1990.

Blackbourn, David. *Marpingen: Apparitions of the Virgin Mary in Nineteenth-Century Germany.* New York: Alfred A. Knopf, 1994.

Brock, Sebastian. *The Luminous Eye: The Spiritual World Vision of St. Ephrem the Syrian.* 2d ed. Kalamazoo, Mich.: Cistercian Pubns., 1992.

Brown, Peter. *Augustine of Hippo: A Biography.* Berkeley: University of California Press, 1967.

————. *The Body and Society: Men, Women and Sexual Renunciation in Early Christianity.* New York: Columbia University Press, 1988.

————. *The Cult of the Saints: Its Rise and Function in Latin Christianity.* Chicago: University of Chicago Press, 1981.

Brown, Raymond E. *The Birth of the Messiah: A Commentary on the Infancy Narratives of Matthew and Luke.* Garden City, N.Y.: Doubleday, 1977.

————. *The Churches the Apostles Left Behind.* New York: Paulist Press, 1984.

————. *The Virginal Conception and Bodily Resurrection of Jesus.* New York: Paulist Press, 1973.

Brown, Raymond E., Karl Donfried, Joseph A. Fitzmyer, and John Reuman. *Mary in the New Testament.* Philadelphia: Fortress Press, 1978.

Budge, E. A. Wallis. *Miracles of Our Lady Mary.* Oxford: Oxford University Press, 1933.

Burrus, Virginia. *Chastity as Autonymy: Women in the Stories of Apostolic Acts.* Lewiston, N.Y.: Edwin Mellen Press, 1987.

Bynum, Caroline Walker. "And Woman His Humanity: Female Imagery in the Religious Writing of the Later Middle Ages." In *Gender and Religion: On the Complexity of Symbols,* edited by Caroline Bynum, Steven Harrell, and Paula Richman. Boston: Beacon Press, 1986.

————. *Jesus as Mother: Studies in the Spirituality of the High Middle Ages.* Berkeley: University of California Press, 1982.

Cappannari, Stephen C., and Leonard W. Moss. "Quest of the Black Madonna." In *Mother Worship: Theme and Variations,* edited by James J. Preston. Chapel Hill: University of North Carolina Press, 1982.

Carroll, Michael P. *The Cult of the Virgin Mary: Psychological Origins.* Princeton: Princeton University Press, 1986.

Cassagnes-Brouquet, Sophie. *Vierges Noires: Regard et fascination.* Rodez, France: Editions du Rouergue, 1990.

———. *Marie en Limousin.* Rodez, France: Editions du Rouergue, 1991.

Chadwick, Owen. *Newman.* New York: Oxford University Press, 1983.

Christian, William A., Jr. *Apparitions in Late Medieval and Renaissance Spain.* Princeton: Princeton University Press, 1981.

———. *Person and God in a Spanish Valley.* Princeton: Princeton University Press, 1989.

Clark, Anne L. *Elisabeth of Schönau: A Twelfth-Century Visionary.* Philadelphia: University of Pennsylvania Press, 1992.

Cobbe, Frances Power. "Madonna Immacolata," ch. 14 of *Italics.* London, 1864.

D'Amico, Diane. "Eve, Mary and Mary Magdalene: Christina Rossetti's Feminine Triptych." In *The Achievement of Christina Rossetti,* edited by David A. Kent. Ithaca: Cornell University Press, 1987.

Davies, J. G. *The Early Christian Church: A History of Its First Five Centuries.* New York: Doubleday, 1967.

Davies, Stephen L. *The Revolt of the Widows: The Social World of the Apocryphal Acts.* Carbondale: University of Illinois Press, 1980.

Dickens, A. G. *The Counter Reformation.* New York: Harcourt Brace & World, 1969.

Dillenberger, Jane. "Reflections on the Image of the Saint and Sinner in Christian Art." In *Women, Religion, and Social Change,* edited by Yvonne Yazbeck Haddad and Ellison Banks Findly. Albany: State University of New York Press, 1985.

Dirvin, Joseph I. *St. Catherine Labouré of the Miraculous Medal.* New York: Farrar, Straus & Cudahy, 1958.

Donnelly, Doris, ed. *Mary: Woman of Nazareth: Biblical and Theological Perspectives.* New York: Paulist Press, 1989.

Douglass, Jane Dempsey. "Women and the Continental Reformation." In *Religion and Sexism: Images of Women in the Jewish and Christian Traditions,* edited by Rosemary Ruether. New York: Simon & Schuster, 1974.

Dronke, Peter. *Poetic Individuality in the Middle Ages: New Departures in Poetry, 1000–1150.* Oxford: Clarendon Press, 1970.

————. *Women Writers of the Middle Ages: A Critical Study of Texts from Perpetua (d. 203) to Marguerite Porète (d. 1310).* Cambridge and New York: Cambridge University Press, 1984.

Elizondo, Virgil. "Mary and the Evangelization in the Americas." In *Mary, Woman of Nazareth: Biblical and Theological Perspectives,* edited by Doris Donnelly. New York: Paulist Press, 1989.

————. "Mary and the Poor: A Model of Evangelising Ecumenism." In *Mary in the Churches,* edited by Hans Küng and Jürgen Moltmann. New York: Seabury, 1983.

Emmerich, Catherine. *The Life of the Blessed Virgin Mary: From the Visions of Anne Catherine Emmerich.* London: Burns & Oates, 1954.

Ephrem of Syria. *The Harp of the Spirit.* Translated by Sebastian Brock. London: Fellowship of St. Alban & St. Sergius, 1975.

————. *Hymns.* Translated and introduced by Kathleen E. McVey. New York: Paulist Press, 1989.

————. *Hymns on Paradise.* Translated by Sebastian Brock. Crestwood, N.Y.: St. Vladimir's Seminary Press, 1990.

Epiphanius. *The Panarion of St. Epiphanius, Bishop of Salamis: Selected Passages.* Translated and edited by Phillip R. Amidon, S.J. New York: Oxford University Press, 1990.

Erasmus, Desiderius. *Ten Colloquies of Erasmus.* Translated by Craig R. Thompson. New York: Liberal Arts Press, 1957.

Eusebius. *Ecclesiastical History.* Baltimore: Penguin Books, 1965.

Fitzmyer, Joseph A., ed. and trans. *The Gospel According to Luke I–IX.* New York: Doubleday Anchor Bible, 1981.

Flusser, David, Jaroslav Pelikan, and Justin Lang. *Mary: Images of the Mother of Jesus in Jewish and Christian Perspectives.* Philadelphia: Fortress Press, 1986.

Forsyth, Ilene H. *The Throne of Wisdom: Wood Sculptures of the Madonna in Romanesque France.* Princeton: Princeton University Press, 1972.

Fremantle, Anne, ed. *A Treasury of Early Christianity.* New York: New American Library, 1953.

Frymer-Kensky, Tikva. *In the Wake of the Goddess: Women, Culture and the Biblical Transformation of Pagan Women.* New York: Free Press, 1992.

Fuller, Margaret. *Woman in the Nineteenth Century.* 1855 reprint; New York: Norton, 1971.

Galland, China. *Longing for Darkness: Tara and the Black Madonna.* New York: Viking Penguin, 1990.

Geagea, Nilo. *Mary of the Koran: A Meeting Point Between Christianity and Islam.* Translated and edited by Lawrence T. Fares. New York: Philosophical Library, 1984.

Gebara, Ivone, and Maria Clara Bingemer. *Mary: Mother of God, Mother of the Poor.* Translated from Portuguese by Phillip Berryman. Maryknoll, N.Y.: Orbis Books, 1987.

Gilley, Sheridan. "Victorian Feminism and Catholic Art: The Case of Mrs. Jameson." In *The Church and the Arts*, vol. 28, edited by Diana Wood. Oxford: Blackwell, 1992.

Gold, Penny Schine. *The Lady and the Virgin: Image, Attitude and Experience in Twelfth-Century France.* Chicago: University of Chicago Press, 1985.

Graef, Hilda. *Mary: A History of Doctrine and Devotion.* 2 vols. in 1. Westminster, Md.: Christian Classics, 1985.

Greeley, Andrew M. *The Mary Myth: On the Femininity of God.* New York: Seabury Press, 1977.

Guerin, Michelle, O.S.U. "Cosmic Mother of the Aztecs: Our Lady of Guadalupe." *Anima*, vol. 15, no. 2 (spring 1989).

Harrington, Patricia. "Mother of Death, Mother of Rebirth: The Mexican Virgin of Guadalupe." *JAAR* LVI–1.

Harvey, Susan Ashbrook. "Eve and Mary: Images of Woman." *The Modern Churchman*, vol. 24, no. 3 & 4 (autumn–winter 1981): 133–148.

Haskins, Susan. *Mary Magdalen: Myth and Metaphor.* New York: Harcourt Brace, 1994.

Heer, Friedrich. *The Medieval World: Europe 1100–1350.* Cleveland, Ohio: World Publishing, 1962.

Hildegard of Bingen. *Hildegard of Bingen: Mystical Writings.* Edited by Fiona Bowie and Oliver Davies, with new translations by Robert Carver. New York: Crossroad, 1992.

———. *Holistic Healing.* Collegeville, Minn.: Liturgical Press, 1994.

————. *Scivias*. Translated by Mother Columba Hart and Jane Bishop. Mahwah, N.J.: Paulist Press, 1990.

————. *Symphonia*. Translated and edited by Barbara Newman. Ithaca: Cornell University Press, 1988.

Hill, Patricia R. "Madonnas for a New World: Harriet Beecher Stowe's Iconography of Faith." In *Embodied Love: Sensuality and Relationship as Feminist Values*, edited by Paula M. Cooey, Sharon A. Farmer, and Mary Ellen Ross. San Francisco: Harper & Row, 1987.

Hopkins, Gerard Manley. *The Poems of Gerard Manley Hopkins*, 4th ed. Edited by W. H. Gardner and N. H. MacKenzie. London and New York: Oxford University Press, 1970.

Ignatius of Loyola. *The Autobiography of St. Ignatius Loyola*. Translated by Joseph F. O'Callaghan. Edited by John C. Olin. New York: Harper & Row, 1974.

————. *The Spiritual Exercises of St. Ignatius*. New York: Doubleday, 1954.

Jacobus de Voragine. *The Golden Legend*. New York: Longmans, Green, 1941.

Jameson, Anna Brownell Murphy. *Legends of the Madonna: As Represented in the Fine Arts*. New York: Longmans, Green, 1890 ed. Reprint, Detroit, Mich.: Gale Research, 1972.

John of the Cross. *The Poems of St. John of the Cross*. Translated by Kathleen Jones. Westminster, Md.: Christian Classics, 1993.

Johnson, Elizabeth A. "Marian Devotion in the Western Church." In *Christian Spirituality*. Vol. 2, *High Middle Ages and Reformation*, edited by Jill Raitt et al. New York: Crossroad, 1987.

————. "The Marian Tradition and the Reality of Women." *Horizons*, vol. 12, no. 1 (1985).

Kidd, Sue Monk. "A Protestant's Journey Back to Mary." *Anima* (spring 1989).

Kirk, Pamela. Unpublished ms. on Sor Juana de la Cruz.

Küng, Hans, and Jürgen Moltmann, eds. *Mary in the Churches*. New York: Seabury, 1983.

Laffey, Alice L. "Images of Mary in the Christian Scriptures." In *All Generations Shall Call Me Blessed*, edited by Francis A. Eigo, O.S.A. Villanova, Pa.: Villanova University Press, 1993.

Larson, Janet. "Protestant Hermeneutics and Heroines of the Reformation," ch. 2 of her forthcoming book on Victorian women's biblical and social interpretations.

Laurentin, René. *Marie Mère de Dieu*. Paris: Desclée, 1984.

Laurentin, René, and Raymond Oursel. *Vierges Romanes: Les Vierges Assises*. Paris: Zodiaque, 1988.

Luther, Martin. "The Magnificat." In *Works*. Vol. 21. St. Louis, Mo.: Concordia Press, 1955 ff.

————. "Sermon on the Afternoon of Christmas Day, 1530." In *Martin Luther's Basic Theological Writings*, edited by Timothy F. Lull. Minneapolis, Minn.: Fortress Press, 1989.

Macquarrie, John. *Mary for All Christians*. Grand Rapids, Mich.: Eerdmans, 1990.

Maeckelberghe, Els. *Desperately Seeking Mary: A Feminist Appropriation of a Traditional Religious Symbol*. Kampen, Netherlands: Kok Pharos, 1991.

Mâle, Emile. *The Early Churches of Rome*. London: Ernest Benn, 1960.

————. *Religious Art from the Twelfth to the Eighteenth Century*. New York: Noonday Press, 1958.

————. *Religious Art in France: The Late Middle Ages*. Princeton: Princeton University Press, 1987.

————. *Religious Art in France: The Thirteenth Century*. Princeton: Princeton University Press, 1984.

Mathews, Thomas F. *The Clash of Gods: A Reinterpretation of Early Christian Art*. Princeton: Princeton University Press, 1993.

Meditations on the Life of Christ: An Illustrated Manuscript of the Fourteenth Century. Translated by Isa Ragusa and Rosalie B. Green. Princeton: Princeton University Press, 1977.

Meier, John P. *A Marginal Jew: Rethinking the Historical Jesus*. Vol. 1. New York: Doubleday, 1991.

Meyers, Carol L. *Discovering Eve: Ancient Israelite Women in Context*. New York: Oxford University Press, 1988.

Miles, Margaret. *Image as Insight: Visual Understanding in Western Christianity and Secular Culture*. Boston: Beacon Press, 1985.

————. *Carnal Knowing. Female Nakedness and Religious Meaning in the Christian West*. New York: Vintage Books, 1991.

Newman, Barbara. *Sister of Wisdom: St. Hildegard's Theology of the Feminine.* Berkeley: University of California Press, 1987.

Newman, J. H. *An Essay on the Development of Christian Doctrine.* New York: Doubleday, 1960.

————. *The New Eve.* Oxford: Newman Bookshop, 1952.

Nolan, Mary Lee, and Sidney Nolan. *Christian Pilgrimage in Modern Western Europe.* Chapel Hill: University of North Carolina Press, 1989.

Olin, John C., and James D. Smart, eds. *Luther, Erasmus and the Reformation: A Catholic-Protestant Reappraisal.* Bronx, N.Y.: Fordham University Press, 1969.

Ong, Walter J. *Hopkins, the Self, and God.* Toronto: University of Toronto Press, 1986.

Orsi, Robert Anthony. *The Madonna of 115th St.: Faith and Community in Italian Harlem, 1880–1950.* New Haven: Yale University Press, 1985.

Ouspensky, Leonid, and Vladimir Lossky. *The Meaning of Icons.* Crestwood, N.Y.: St. Vladimir's Seminary Press, 1983.

The Oxford Dictionary of the Christian Church. Edited by F. L. Cross. London and New York: Oxford University Press, 1957.

Pagels, Elaine. *Adam, Eve and the Serpent.* New York: Random House, 1988.

————. *The Gnostic Gospels.* New York: Random House, 1979.

Pearle, Gary. "Listening for Angels." *Psychological Perspectives*, no. 28 (1993).

Pelikan, Jaroslav. *Jesus Through the Centuries: His Place in the History of Culture.* New Haven: Yale University Press, 1985.

Perry, Nicholas, and Loreto Echeverria. *Under the Heel of Mary.* New York: Routledge, 1988.

Pope, Barbara Corrado. "Immaculate and Powerful: The Marian Revival in the Nineteenth Century." In *Immaculate and Powerful: The Female in Sacred Image and Social Reality*, edited by Clarissa W. Atkinson, Constance H. Buchanan, and Margaret R. Miles. Boston: Beacon Press, 1985.

Power, Eileen. *Medieval Women.* Cambridge and New York: Cambridge University Press, 1975.

————. *Medieval People.* New York: Barnes & Noble, 1963.

Raitt, Jill, et al., eds. *Christian Spirituality*. Vol. 2, *High Middle Ages and Reformation*. New York: Crossroad, 1987.

Redmont, Jane. *Generous Lives: American Catholic Women Today*. New York: Morrow, 1992.

Rilke, Rainer Maria. *The Life of the Virgin Mary*. Translated by C. MacIntyre. Berkeley: University of California Press, 1947.

Robinson, James M., ed. *The Nag Hammadi Library*. Rev. ed. San Francisco: Harper & Row, 1988.

Rodriguez, Jeanette. *Our Lady of Guadalupe: Faith and Empowerment Among Mexican-American Women*. Austin: University of Texas Press, 1994.

Ruether, Rosemary R. *Gaia and God: An Ecofeminist Theology of Earth Healing*. San Francisco: Harper San Francisco, 1992.

———. *Religion and Sexism: Images of Woman in the Jewish and Christian Traditions*. New York: Simon & Schuster, 1974.

Schaberg, Jane. *The Illegitimacy of Jesus: A Feminist Theological Interpretation of the Infancy Narratives*. San Francisco: Harper & Row, 1987.

Schillebeeckx, Edward, and Catharina Halkes. *Mary: Yesterday, Today, Tomorrow*. New York: Crossroad, 1993.

Schneemelcher, Wilhelm, ed., *New Testament Apocrypha*. Translation edited by Robert McLachlan Wilson. Rev ed. 2 vols. Louisville, Ky.: Westminster/John Knox Press, 1991–1993.

Schüssler Fiorenza, Elisabeth, "Feminist Spirituality, Christian Identity, and Catholic Vision." In *Womanspirit Rising*, edited by Carol P. Christ and Judith Plaskow. San Francisco: Harper & Row, 1979.

———. *In Memory of Her: A Feminist Theological Reconstruction of Christian Origins*. New York: Crossroad, 1984.

———. *Jesus: Miriam's Child, Sophia's Prophet*. New York: Continuum, 1994.

The Service of the Akathist Hymn. Translated from Greek by Holy Transfiguration Monastery, Boston: 1991.

Shinners, John R., Jr. "Mary and the People: The Cult of Mary and Popular Belief." In *Mary, Woman of Nazareth*, edited by Doris Donnelly. New York: Paulist Press, 1989.

Stendahl, Krister. "Quis et Unde." In *Meanings: The Bible as Document and as Guide*. Philadelphia: Fortress Press, 1984.

Stowasser, Barbara. "The Chapter of Mary." In *Women in the Qur'an, Traditions, and Interpretation.* New York: Oxford University Press, 1994.

Stowe, Harriet Beecher. *The Minister's Wooing.* 1859. Reprint, Ridgewood, N.J.: Gregg Press, 1968.

———. *Sunny Memories of Foreign Lands.* 2 vols. Boston: Phillips, Sampson, 1854.

Taves, Ann. *The Household of Faith: Roman Catholic Devotions in Mid-Nineteenth-Century America.* Notre Dame, Ind.: University of Notre Dame Press, 1986.

Tentori, Tullio. "Madonna dell'Arco Naples." In *Mother Worship: Theme and Variations,* edited by James J. Preston. Chapel Hill: University of North Carolina Press, 1982.

Teresa of Ávila. *The Interior Castle.* New York: Paulist Press, 1979.

———. *The Life of St. Teresa of Ávila by Herself.* Translated by J. M. Cohen. London: Penguin Books, 1957.

Thérèse of Lisieux. *Story of a Soul.* Translated by John Clarke, O.C.D. Washington D.C.: ICS Pubns., 1976.

———. *Her Last Conversations.* Translated by John Clarke, O.C.D. Washington, D.C.: I.C.S. Pubns., 1977.

Trevor, Meriol. *Newman's Journey.* London: Collins, 1974.

Trible, Phyllis. "Eve and Adam: Genesis 2–3 Reread." In *Womanspirit Rising: a Feminist Reader in Religion,* edited by Carol P. Christ and Judith Plasgow. San Francisco: Harper & Row, 1979.

Turner, Victor, and Edith Turner. *Image and Pilgrimage in Christian Culture.* New York: Columbia University Press, 1978.

———. "Postindustrial Marian Pilgrimage." In *Mother Worship: Theme and Variations,* edited by James J. Preston. Chapel Hill: University of North Carolina Press, 1982.

van Os, Henk. *The Art of Devotion in the Late Middle Ages in Europe (1300–1500).* Princeton: Princeton University Press, 1994.

Vendler, Helen. "The Wreck of the *Deutschland.*" In *The Authentic Cadence: Centennial Essays on Gerard Manley Hopkins,* edited by Anthony Mortimer. Fribourg, Switzerland: Fribourg University Press, 1992.

Ward, Benedicta. *Miracles and the Medieval Mind: Theory, Record, and*

Event, 1000 to 1215. Philadelphia: University of Pennsylvania Press, 1982.

Warner, Marina. *Alone of All Her Sex: The Myth and the Cult of the Virgin Mary.* New York: Vintage Books, 1983.

Wright, David F. ed. *Chosen by God: Mary in Evangelical Perspective.* London: Marshall Pickering, 1989.

Ziegler, Joanna. *Sculpture of Compassion: The Pietà and the Bequines in the Southern Low Countries c.1300–1600.* Brepols Pubns., 1992.

Zimdars-Swartz, Sandra. *Encountering Mary: From La Salette to Medjugorje.* Princeton: Princeton University Press, 1991.

INDEX

PERMISSION ACKNOWLEDGMENTS

Grateful acknowledgment is made to the following for permission to reprint previously published material:

Bantam Books, a division of Bantam Doubleday Dell Publishing Group, Inc.: Six lines from *The Divine Comedy of Dante Alighieri: Paradiso* by Allen Mandelbaum. Translation copyright © 1984 by Allen Mandelbaum; excerpts from Margaret Atwood, *Cat's Eye*, copyright © 1988 O. W. Toad, Ltd.

The Regents of the University of California: An excerpt from Hildegard of Bingen in Barbara Newman, *Sister of Wisdom: St. Hildegard's Theology of the Feminine*, University of California Press, copyright © 1987 The Regents of the University of California; excerpts from Rainer Maria Rilke, *Life of the Virgin Mary*, trans./ed. C. F. MacIntyre, University of California Press, copyright © 1947 The Regents of the University of California.

Christian Classics: Poem by John of the Cross from *The Poems of St. John of the Cross*, trans. Kathleen Jones, with permission of the publisher Christian Classics, 200 E. Bethany Drive, Allen, Texas 75002, copyright © 1993 Kathleen Jones.

Christian Classics and Sheed & Ward: Lines from Hilda Graef, *Mary: A History of Doctrine and Devotion*, copyright © 1963, 1965 Hilda Graef.

Cistercian Publications: Four lines of Ephrem of Syria from Sebastian Brock, *The Luminous Eye: The Spiritual World Vision of St. Ephrem the Syrian.*

Commonweal magazine: Excerpts from Mary Gordon, "Coming to terms with Mary," *Commonweal*, January 15, 1982.

Curtis Brown Ltd.: "island mary" by Lucille Clifton, from *Two-headed woman* © 1980 by the University of Massachusetts Press.

Farrar, Straus & Giroux Inc. and Jonathan Cape Ltd.: Excerpts from Derek Walcott, "For the Altar-piece of the Roseau Valley Church, Saint Lucia" from *Sea Grapes*, copyright © 1970, 1971, 1973, 1975, 1976 by Derek Walcott.

Fellowship of St. Alban and St. Sergius, 1 Canterbury Rd., Oxford, England: Hymn of Ephrem of Syria from Sebastian Brock, *Harp of the Spirit*, 1975.

China Galland and Viking Penguin, a division of Penguin Books USA Inc.: Excerpts from *Longing for Darkness: Tara and the Black Madonna* by China Galland, Viking Penguin, 1991. Copyright © 1991 by China Galland.

Susan Hellauer: Lines from her translation of "Aurora velut fulgida" and "O genetrix aeterni," from Anonymous 4's program notes for *Guillaume Dufay and the Papal Choir (1428–1437)*.

Paulist Press: Eight lines from *Hildegard of Bingen* by Barbara Newman, copyright © 1990 by the Abbey of Regina Laudis: Benedictine Congregation Regina Laudis of the Strict Observance, Inc.

Penguin UK: Excerpts from *The Prayers and Meditations of St. Anselm*, Penguin Classics, 1973. Trans. by Benedicta Ward, copyright © 1973 Benedicta Ward.

Princeton University Press: "San Sepolcro" by Jorie Graham from *Erosion*, 1983. Copyright © 1983 by Princeton University Press.

Lawrence Rosenwald: The first six lines of his translation of "Alma Redemptoris Mater" from Anonymous 4's program notes for *Guillaume Dufay and the Papal Choir (1428–1437)*.

St. Vladimir's Seminary Press: Twelve lines of Ephrem the Syrian from *Hymns of Paradise*, trans. Sebastian Brock. Copyright © St. Vladimir's Seminary Press, 575 Scarsdale Road, Crestwood, NY 10707.

United States Catholic Conference: Scripture selections, which are taken from *The New American Bible*, copyright © 1991, 1986, 1970 by the ⁀nfraternity of Christian Doctrine, Washington, D.C. 20017. All reserved.

About the Author

SALLY CUNNEEN is the author of *Sex: Female; Religion: Catholic;
Mother Church: What the Experience of Women Is Teaching Her;*
and *A Contemporary Meditation on the Everyday God.* She is also
cofounder of the interreligious quarterly *Cross Currents.* She is
Professor Emeritus at Rockland Community College (SUNY).